Text Entry Systems:
Mobility, Accessibility, Universality

The Morgan Kaufmann Series in Interactive Technologies

Series Editors:

Stuart Card, PARC ■ Jonathan Grudin, Microsoft ■ Jakob Nielsen,
Nielsen Norman Group

Text Entry Systems:

Mobility, Accessibility,

Universality

Edited by

I. Scott MacKenzie
and
Kumiko Tanaka-Ishii

MORGAN KAUFMANN PUBLISHERS

AN IMPRINT OF ELSEVIER SCIENCE

AMSTERDAM   BOSTON   LONDON   NEW YORK
OXFORD   PARIS   SAN DIEGO   SAN FRANCISCO
SINGAPORE   SYDNEY   TOKYO

Publisher   Diane Cerra
Publishing Services Manager   George Morrison
Project Manager   Mónica González de Mendoza
Editorial Assistant   Asma Palmeiro
Editorial Intern   Marisa Crawford
Cover Design   Hannus Design
Composition   Charon Tec
Copyeditor   Valerie Koval
Proofreader   Charon Tec
Indexer   Charon Tec
Interior printer   Maple-Vail Book Manufacturing Group
Cover printer   Phoenix Color

Morgan Kaufmann Publishers is an imprint of Elsevier.
500 Sansome Street, Suite 400, San Francisco, CA 94111

This book is printed on acid-free paper.

Library of Congress Cataloging-in-Publication Data
MacKenzie, I. Scott, 1951-
    Text entry systems : mobility, accessibility, universality / I. Scott MacKenzie, Kumiko Tanaka-Ishii.
        p. cm.
    Includes bibliographical references and index.
    ISBN-13: 978-0-12-373591-1 (pbk. : alk. paper)
    ISBN-10: 0-12-373591-2 (pbk. : alk. paper) 1. Computers. 2. Electronic data processing—Data entry.
3. Human-computer interaction. 4. Natural language processing (Computer science) I. Tanaka-Ishii, Kumiko. II. Title.
    QA76.5M18747 2007
    004—dc22

                                                                                    2006037436

ISBN 13: 978-0-12-373591-1
ISBN 10: 0-12-373591-2

For information on all Morgan Kaufmann publications,
visit our Web site at www.mkp.com or www.books.elsevier.com

Printed in the United States of America
07 08 09 10 11   5 4 3 2 1

Working together to grow
libraries in developing countries

www.elsevier.com | www.bookaid.org | www.sabre.org

ELSEVIER   BOOK AID
             International   Sabre Foundation

Contents

Preface

Text entry has never been more important than today. In large measure, this is a follow on to the huge success of mobile computing and, in particular, text messaging on mobile phones and related devices. Yet, today's heightened interest is, arguably, within a second wave of text entry research. The first wave, so to speak, was in the 1970s and early 1980s in response to the new role of electronic computers in automating office tasks such as typing, word processing, document management, and so on. Modeling ten-finger touch typing, categorizing typing errors, task analysis, and comparing document editing strategies are some of the themes in this early research.

There was a lull in text entry research beginning around 1983, as marked by the arrival on the computing scene of the GUI (graphical user interface) and point-and-click interaction. For a time, researchers seemed to shift their attention to the challenges and opportunities in this new genre of direct manipulation interaction. Interest in text entry soon resurfaced. The early 1990s brought pen-based computing. Automatic handwriting recognition was the elixir for this new mode of interaction, or so it seemed. Unfortunately, the promise of pen-based computing did not meet the expectations of demanding users, and the market suffered for this. Yet products and interest continued. The most significant event in pen-based computing was the 1995 introduction of the *Palm Pilot* PDA with its popular *Graffiti* handwriting recognition system. However, it is the huge success of text messaging (aka SMS, for short message service) that most dramatically marks the second wave of interest in text entry. Juxtapose the observation that over one billion messages SMS messages are sent each day with the fact that the mobile phone keypad is the dominant input device for creating these messages, and it is no surprise that researchers are grappling with the problem of improving text entry techniques for mobile phones or other anticipated mobile products supporting similar services.

The introductory comments above ignore at least three other aspects of text entry – aspects that fall outside the scope of the two conjectured waves of interest. First, researchers in linguistics have long examined the nature of language and communication with a keen view to understanding and exploiting the inherent statistical properties of text. Word prediction, word completion, phrase completion, and other accelerating techniques have a long history of study that is only by coincidence related to mobile computing. Second, work in improving the quality of life for people with physical impairments involves today, as ever, the development of methods of efficient textual communication. Remember, what is efficient for an able-bodied person with full ten-finger dexterity may be untenable for someone capable of pressing just one button and doing so only once every few seconds. The third aspect is recognition that our world is diverse. While English may be the universal language for pilots traversing the globe in airplanes, such is not the case for the millions (billions!) of people using technology to communicate using text. A text message today is just as likely entered in Arabic or Punjabi as in English. We note, as well, that text entry is increasingly the domain of young and old alike.

Our goal in this book is to bring together researchers in text entry that span the mixed collection of interests noted above. Our themes are mobility, accessibility, and universality. The book is in four parts. We begin with an historical overview of text entry and follow with guidelines and frameworks for designing better entry systems, focusing on

- ✦ methodology – to develop and disseminate appropriate methods for validating research ideas;

- ✦ measurements – to more accurately and more thoroughly capture user behavior, in particular with respect to accuracy and error rate issues; and

- ✦ modeling – to exploit the statistical properties of language for better predictive interfaces.

The second part discusses devices and modalities. Each chapter summarizes the current state of the art for a basic technology. Then, ideas in applying the technology to text entry systems are summarized. Future possibilities are also elaborated as a basic technology becomes more advanced.

The third part examines entry systems in languages around the world, with each chapter revealing the unique characteristics of a language group. Based on this, the chapter provides the history of entry systems and problems solved so far in combination with current major entry designs. Each chapter also demonstrates how the study of a specific language leads to new ideas applicable to other languages.

The last part is concerned with text entry that is accessible to all. Each chapter summarizes the unique characteristics of a group of users and the problems they face for text entry, and shows how the study of a genre of people leads to new ideas and universal design.

This book is a small contribution on the theme of text entry. One large issue lies in the background of text entry systems – communication. As put by a seriously disabled person, "It is communication that keeps me living." In some measure this is a theme for us all. Communication today increasingly uses text entry. This book explores the opportunity to use technology to communicate in any language to anybody.

We wish to extend our deepest gratitude to a number of people who have helped in bringing this book to its present finished and published state. The book was conceived at a workshop on Efficient Text Entry in September 2005 in Dagstuhl Germany (http://drops. dagstuhl.de/portals/05382). We thank Karin Harbusch (University of Koblenz/Landau) who organized the workshop for her tireless effort in bringing together many of the top researchers in text entry, some of whom have authored chapters herein. Our initial proposal and subsequent draft chapters were enthusiastically and meticulously reviewed by Ravin Balakrishnan (University of Toronto), Poika Isokoski (University of Tampere), Roel Vertegaal (Queen's University), Ken Hinckley (Microsoft), and John San Giovanni (Microsoft). Many thanks, again. Working behind the scenes in editorial and production roles are many individuals who helped the process in critical yet often unsung ways. Those we worked directly with are Diane Cerra, Asma Palmeiro, Monica González de Mendoza, and Mani Prabakaran. Our journey has been both challenging and rewarding and the result is better because of you. Our sincerest thanks.

1 PART | Foundations

1 | Historical Overview of Consumer Text Entry Technologies

CHAPTER

Miika Silfverberg Nokia Research Center, Helsinki, Finland

1.1 INTRODUCTION

Text entry is much more than a feature in modern computers. Textual information and communication are essential parts of our lives. In fact, the wide variety of culture that we can see today is enabled by textual communication. The invention of writing accelerated cultural development, because individuals could store their ideas for later use and for use also by the following generations. Writing is the most specific and flexible way to store information. It has also allowed communication of information or emotions, even over long distances.

Writing systems have been around for several millennia. Writing, as we know it today, is believed to have been developed by the Sumerians in the late 4th millennium BC[1]. From those days, writing media have developed—through stone and clay, to papyrus and parchment, and even later to paper (around 100 AD; Meyer, 1995)—but for a long time writing was done by hand. Handwriting served the cultural needs of storing and communicating information and emotions very well for a long time. Even after the first text-production machine, the *printing press*, was modernized by Johannes Gutenberg in the 15th century, individual citizens still stuck to handwriting, because it met their needs adequately. Even the first "consumer text entry technology," the typewriter, which was invented in 1714, was taken into use only 160 years later, probably because there was not an actual need for such device before then.

Industrialization in the late 19th century changed the situation completely. The new order created a need to produce text in greater quantities. Since then, the amount of written information has increased continuously. The real information explosion, however, began even later, with the birth of the *Information Age* in the

---

[1] Simpler so-called "proto-writing" systems have existed even longer, probably from as early as the 8th millennium BC.

1980s. The final culmination of textual information is obviously the *Internet*. We are living in a world of text. Although the Internet is increasingly multimodal, the majority of the information within it is textual. The Internet provides an exceptionally powerful medium to share and communicate ideas and aspirations.

The Information Age has also created completely new types of devices. Personal computers started to gain ground in the 1980s and are now ubiquitous. More recently, *mobile computing* has emerged. Although most computing is still done using desktop computers, the vision of "a computer in every pocket" is slowly becoming a reality. One driving need is again communication. Mobility creates new impulses and needs for communication. While some communication remains to be handled through speech, text is better suited for *asynchronous communication*. The growth of text entry will continue, even at an accelerating pace. More and more of the text is being produced in less than ideal mobile settings, which creates new challenges for the creators of text entry systems.

In this chapter, we provide a historical overview of the developments of commercial text entry systems. Therefore, we will leave out many emerging methods that have not yet broken through in the market. Some of these are handled briefly at the end of this chapter, and many potential future technologies are covered in the later chapters of this book.

Our focus is on consumer devices, so professional systems that require long training (e.g., stenograms, Morse code) are left out. We will concentrate on devices for which text entry has an important role. We go through *four device categories* in rough chronological order: (1) typewriter, (2) personal computer, (3) mobile phone, and (4) handheld computers (smart phones and personal digital assistants (PDAs) are discussed together with handheld computers, since although they have different origins their interaction techniques and features clearly approach one another and the different terms are effectively synonyms nowadays).

Interaction techniques within the four device categories tend to be quite consistent, so it is often easy to name one or a few *dominant* text entry solutions for each device. However, as text entry is a very complex problem, even the dominant methods are hardly perfect. Therefore, for each device, numerous *alternative* text entry methods have been proposed. We go through each device category by presenting the dominant solutions first and then proceed to the proposed alternatives. However, due to space limitations, only the most salient solutions will be covered. This includes those solutions that have been particularly successful or novel.

1.2   TYPEWRITER, 1870s TO 1980s

The first commercially successful typewriter was the "Sholes–Glidden Type Writer" produced by E. Remington and Sons beginning in 1874[2]. Figure 1.1 shows this

---

[2] According to Yamada (1980) the first machine was manufactured in the previous year, but 1874 was the year when the Sholes–Glidden was first placed on the market.

FIGURE

1.1

Sholes–Glidden typewriter.

machine. Its keyboard has a striking similarity to the current computer keyboard layout. (We come back to this point later.) This typewriter was developed by Latham Sholes, Carlos Glidden, and Samuel W. Soule. The main inventor, Latham Sholes, was later referred to as the "father" of the typewriter, but the Sholes–Glidden machine was actually not the first commercially sold typewriter. The "Writing Ball" made by Malling Hansen had been on the market since 1870, although it met with little success. Sholes was not the first typewriter inventor, either. (Actually, he was the 52nd inventor of a typewriter!) The first typewriter is believed to have been invented by Henrik Mill as early as 1714! But most of these early keyboard inventions were not put into practice, or if they were, they were not commercially successful (Yamada, 1980).

One reason that made the Remington line of machines—starting from the first Sholes–Glidden version—a success, was that the time was simply right for a new text entry method. The late 19th century was an era of strong industrialization. Small companies were turning into large corporations, which created a need for improved communication. Also other inventions appeared at the same time, for example, the electric light, telegraph, and telephone. These inventions helped to fulfill the need for increased communication. The typewriter fit very well into the equation, and it is no surprise that the ability to create unambiguous documents with speed was well received in such a booming business environment. By the end of the 1880s the typewriter's monotonous click could be heard "in almost every well-regarded business establishment in the country [USA]" (*Penman's Art Journal*, 1887, according to Yamada, 1980).

Although the typewriter did very well in the business sector, its takeoff in the consumer market was much slower. Typewriters appeared in a culture with a strong tradition of handwritten communication. In the beginning, replying to a handwritten letter with a typewritten response could be considered an insult, because it could be interpreted as a "slander cast on the reader's ability to read longhand" (Yamada, 1980, p. 177). However, typewriters were also purchased by individual consumers. Exact numbers sold to consumers are unknown, but from the early 20th century the typewriter could be considered to have become also a consumer device[3].

During the 20th century typewriters evolved rapidly. Most improvements were mechanical and, later, electronic. Many of these improvements made typing more efficient and ergonomic. By the end of the typewriter era, in the 1980s, typewriters had acquired many features, making them almost like simple computers. Finally, with the success of personal computers in the 1980s, typewriters were phased out by computers due to their more advanced features and more versatile use.

1.2.1   The Dominant Text Entry Method for the Typewriter: The Qwerty Keyboard

As mentioned before, even the first successful typewriter had a keyboard very similar to that of current computers. The arrangement of the alphabetic keys was already following the present-day so-familiar Qwerty layout, with only minor differences. The Qwerty name comes from the first six letters of the top alphabetic key row. The layout was invented by Sholes. Contrary to common belief, the layout itself was never patented. Sholes and his colleagues have several patents, but they are mainly on the keyboard mechanisms (e.g., Sholes *et al.*, 1868). The Qwerty layout was later copied by Remington for the successors to the first Sholes–Glidden model, as well as by many other typewriter manufacturers.

The reasons Sholes came up with the Qwerty layout are quite far from the today's user-centric design principles. The character locations were chosen mainly to overcome the mechanical limitations of the early machines. As anyone who has used an old typewriter knows, the successively actuated levers got jammed easily with one another. Sholes arranged the typebars so that some frequent digrams in the English language were located far away from each other in the typebar arrangement. The mechanical problems of the early machines would soon be overcome, but the later improvements

---

[3] The number of typewriters sold to individual customers was, however, very small compared to the number of personal computers on today's consumer market.

on the layout were limited to a few letters only. The exact date of the first Qwerty layout identical to today's computer is not known, but it was at least "well before 1887" (Yamada, 1980). Thus, the alphabetic key layout has remained unchanged for over 100 years[4]! The position "monopoly" was finally sealed when the American Standards Institute adopted Qwerty as the standard in 1971.

1.2.2 Alternative Text Entry Methods for the Typewriter

Despite the nearly monopolized position that Qwerty—and its language-specific variations—enjoys nowadays, there have always been competitors, even in the beginning. From today's position of a single standardized layout, the early decades of typewriters seem like a jungle with wide variety of species, in which only a few could survive.

Index Typewriters

In the early decades of typewriters, many of the machines used a text entry method that competed with the keyboard. These so-called *index typewriters* had just a single key (Fig. 1.2). Letters were highlighted by, for example, turning a wheel and then selected with the selection key (Yamada, 1980).

FIGURE   "World 1" index typewriter.

1.2

---

4   Some language-specific variations have appeared, though, such as the French Azerty and the German Qwertzu. However, these layouts are very similar to Qwerty, with only a few changed letter positions.

Index typewriters were actually more successful than the keyboarded machines in the beginning, first because the typing method was very straightforward and easy to learn and second due to their simpler structure and lower price. Dozens of different models were produced from the late 19th century to the early 20th century. The Virtual Typewriter Museum gives a very good overview of these models (http://www.typewritermuseum.org/collection/indexi.html).

Ease of learning was probably the main success factor of the index machines, but for the expert users, the keyboarded machines were clearly faster. *Touch-typing* was developed in the 1880s, and during the early 20th century more and more schools started teaching this technique. The speed of touch-typing was so superior that the sales of index machines started to decline, and by 1930s they had disappeared completely.

Double Keyboards

While index typewriters provided a very different approach, there was also competition within the keyboard machines sector. One dispute was related to the input of upper- and lowercase letters. The original Sholes–Glidden from 1874 could actually enter only capital letters! Shifting of the platen was introduced only in the second generation: the Remington Model 2 typewriter in 1878.

However, the so-called *double keyboards* provided a very different solution (Fig. 1.3). In these machines there were two complete sets of alphabetic keys, one for the lowercase and another for the uppercase characters. The "Calligrapher 2" from 1882 was the first such machine, followed by several successful models during the following decades. As happened with the index keyboards, the growth of touch-typing in the early 20th century was again the turning point. Since double keyboards are not at all

FIGURE   "Smith Premier 4" double-keyboard typewriter.

1.3

optimal for touch-typing, their success gradually waned. By 1922 Smith Premier, the last maker of double keyboards, introduced their first shift-key machine, and the double keyboards disappeared from the market.

Optimized Key Arrangements

As mentioned above, the Qwerty layout was mainly designed to overcome mechanical limitations inherent in typewriters. Keyboard typing is a complex skill, and the physiology of our hands and fingers is not very well suited to such a complex task. This problem became even more acute when touch-typing was introduced. The Qwerty layout was not optimized for human capabilities and limitations, not even for simple 2–4 finger typing, but especially not for touch-typing. There was no chance that Qwerty could have been optimized for touch-typing, since this technique was invented about a decade later than the layout!

With this background, it is not a surprise that a lot of effort has been made to create so-called "ideal" layouts. These layouts, starting with James B. Hammond's layout for the Blickensderfer Portable in 1893, sought to optimize the hand–finger movements. This is accomplished by arranging frequently used letters on one keyboard row and minimizing the load for the weak fingers, such as the ring and little fingers. Several layouts were proposed after the Hammond, especially during the touch-typing success era in the early 20th century. Yamada (1980) gives a good summary of these layouts.

By far the most studied and successful optimized layout is the famous *Dvorak simplified keyboard* designed by August Dvorak and William L. Dealey in 1936 (Fig. 1.4). The Dvorak layout was inspired by extensive research on human motion, and it was designed to be easier to learn, more accurate, faster, and less fatiguing than the Qwerty. The Dvorak layout is also the only optimized keyboard layout that has been thoroughly tested in psychological experiments. Many of these studies have directly compared the Dvorak with the Qwerty layout. However, many of the studies have been criticized of their methods, and despite the decades of testing there is still no consensus about the superiority of the Dvorak layout. For example, the two major summaries of Dvorak's research either declare the Qwerty an "error" (Yamada, 1980) or pronounce the Dvorak's superiority a "fable" (Liebowitz & Margolis, 1990).

FIGURE

1.4

The Dvorak layout (Dvorak & Dealey, 1936).

Settling a decades-long dispute is obviously beyond the scope of this book, but considering the conflicting research, at least two things can be said with relatively high confidence. First, given enough training the Dvorak layout probably becomes somewhat faster than the Qwerty. Unfortunately, we cannot say how much faster exactly, but 10–20% could be a rough estimate based on the past studies. Second, we can say that achieving the faster speed will take a relatively long time. Fast typing is an extremely complex skill, comparable to playing a musical instrument, and for a person who already knows the Qwerty layout, even reaching the Qwerty speed with Dvorak (or any new layout) will take a considerable amount of time.

A Ph.D. thesis study by B.J. Lessley in 1978 (referred to in Yamada, 1980) gives us an estimate of these two points. In this study, 100 hours of retraining of operators to the Dvorak layout resulted in a learning curve in which the final Dvorak typing speed was 97.6% of the pre-retraining Qwerty speed. The asymptote of the learning curve indicated that the eventual Dvorak speed would become about 17% faster than Qwerty. (There was no control group for retraining to Qwerty, though.)

So, we can predict that Dvorak could indeed be somewhat faster than Qwerty. However, the Dvorak layout has never become a commercial success, although it still has a small but loyal user base. This layout switching problem could be a classical example of Carroll and Rosson's (1987) *Production Paradox,* in which people are willing to learn new things, especially if they are useful, but they also "need to get something done," so they often do not have extra time to spend on intensive training. People *want* to learn better keyboard layouts, since Qwerty is indisputably suboptimal, but they *cannot* learn them, because they do not have the 100+ hours required to adjust to the new layout. Perhaps if the gain in typing speed were clearly better than 10–20%, there would be more Dvorak users, but in the current standing, Qwerty seems to be "good enough" for the majority of users.

1.3   PERSONAL COMPUTER, 1980s TO PRESENT

As mentioned before, personal computers rapidly replaced typewriters thanks to their more advanced features. While typewriters were single-purpose devices, personal computers are multipurpose devices that can do everything that a typewriter can do and much more. So, as soon as computers became affordable, it was only natural that they should replace typewriters.

1.3.1   The Dominant Text Entry Method for the Computer: (Still) the Qwerty Keyboard

Although personal computers are clearly more advanced than typewriters in many respects, the text entry method was simply copied from the typewriter. This was a natural path, since, as mentioned previously, the late electronic typewriters had already evolved into simple computers. It is difficult even to draw a line marking when typewriters changed to computers. Therefore, lacking any clear discontinuity, the text entry method remained unchanged.

Since computer keyboards can be more easily replaced and changed than those in mechanical typewriters, one could expect to see more variation in the keyboard layout. However, the situation is rather to the contrary. The prevalence of Qwerty has been stunning. The variation in keyboards has been limited to the addition of some special keys (for, e.g., Internet browsing or computer games) or some ergonomical optimizations, such as the Microsoft Natural keyboard (Chap. 15). Perhaps another reason for the lack of variation, in addition to the Production Paradox mentioned above, could be an *infrastructural* reason. Computers can nowadays be found everywhere, and they are often used by multiple users. Therefore, it is hard to change the keyboard in only some of the computers, while other computers would continue to feature Qwerty layouts. This would lead to situations in which a single user would have to use and remember several layouts during one day. Since keyboarding is a highly overlearned task, like playing a musical instrument, the switching between different keyboard layouts could be very difficult. Continuing with the music analogy, there are a few multi-instrumentalists, but most musicians are fluent in only one instrument.

However, there are also other skills, in addition to the keyboarding skill, that are widely spread. Two of these are institutionalized to a level at which most people learn them early at their lives, and these two are *handwriting* and *speaking*. This leads us to two possible text entry techniques: *handwriting recognition* and *speech-to-text*. The former, although also possible for personal computers, is more common in handheld computers, so we handle handwriting recognition later in Section 1.5. Speech-to-text is handled next, wherein we also introduce a more special solution: chording keyboards. Handwriting recognition and speech-based input are also presented in more detail in Chaps. 6 and 8, respectively.

1.3.2   Alternative Text Entry Methods for the PC

Speech-to-Text

Since most users can speak appreciably faster than they can write, speech recognition has gained significant research interest. Speech recognition in general involves the computer recording the user's speech and interpreting what has been said. More specifically, speech-to-text or *dictation* refers to the transformation of speech to textual content (as opposed to, for example, system commands).

Commercial speech-to-text systems have been available since the early 1990s. The recognition rate has been the main challenge throughout their existence; to maintain accuracy, the early systems could support recognition of *isolated words* only. The current text-to-speech products (such as IBM ViaVoice or Dragon NaturallySpeaking) have evolved to the extent that they accept *continuous speech*. The error correction techniques have also improved drastically.

Error correction is indeed critical in speech-to-text, since much of the speed potential of dictation can be lost to the correction of errors. Although most people can speak clearly over 100 words per minute, several studies have found significantly lower overall text entry speeds. For example, in the Karat *et al.* (1999) study, the overall text transcription speed with text-to-speech remained at 14 words per minute, which was clearly slower than the traditional keyboard–mouse combination (about 33 words per minute).

The speech-to-text speed remains low, especially if users stick to correcting errors through speech. When speech recognition fails, respeaking is often not an effective strategy. Instead, the new research stresses the importance of *multimodal error correction* (e.g., Karat *et al.*, 2000; Suhm *et al.*, 2001), in which erroneously recognized words are corrected by some other input channel, such as keyboard and mouse or pen input. In a study that involved both inexperienced and experienced users (Karat *et al.*, 2000), it was found that while novice users tend to stick to unimodal error correction (respeaking), the experienced users could much more effectively utilize multimodal strategies and could clearly reach higher overall speeds, in the range of about 30 words per minute.

Although the text-to-speech products already include some multimodal error correction features, this will be a critical area in deciding the success or failure of text-to-speech, since highly accurate recognition is not realistic in the near future. In the words of Karat *et al.*, "error rates in the 1–5% range are the best anyone should hope for."

Even if speech-to-text is not yet the fastest technique, it has potential for situations in which hand use is limited (Chap. 8). It can also help users who have some physical impairment (Chap. 15). For example, many keyboard users suffer from cumulative trauma disorders, and speech-to-text could help these users, perhaps not completely replacing the keyboard, but as a supplementary method, allowing the user to recover from the extended keyboard use.

Chording Keyboards

Text-to-speech presented above seeks to replace or supplement the PC keyboard by utilizing a completely new channel, human speech. A very different approach is taken by *chording keyboards*, which keep the channel of a regular keyboard, i.e., the physical operation through hands and fingers, but take the keyboarding skill to a completely new level. The operation of chording keyboards is based on pressing several keys simultaneously. The operation resembles playing chords on a piano, and thus the name chording keyboard[5]. Chording keyboards have generally very few keys,

---

[5] The terms "chord keyboard" and "chorded keyboard" are also used.

making them potentially interesting for use in mobile devices. They can also be designed to minimize the hand and finger movements, allowing gains in text input speed. A downside is that the complex chording patterns can be difficult to learn and master.

The idea of chording keyboards is not new, and a similar approach was used in a telegraph by Wheatstone and Cooke as early as 1836. The most widespread chording keyboard, the *stenotype* machine used by court reporters, was invented in 1868 and is still in use today.

Chording keyboards have also been designed for use with consumer devices. Some of these are used with two hands and hold on a table and thus compete directly with the standard PC keyboard. To our knowledge, none of the two-hand chording keyboards have been successful, probably because they are quite difficult to learn. While even touch-typing is too tedious to learn for many users, the chording patterns are motorically even more demanding. They also pose a cognitive challenge to the user, since unlike regular single keys that can be labeled and searched visually, the chording patterns need to be memorized.

Another category of chording keyboards is used with one hand. These are often designed for mobile handheld usage, for example *wearable computers*. This is a stronger potential spot for chording keyboard adoption, since handheld chording keyboards are not just a replacement for the regular keyboard, but might enable text entry for new types of mobile devices.

The most well-known and most studied one-handed chording keyboard is the *Twiddler* (http://www.handykey.com/). The first version of the Twiddler was made in the late 1980s. Regular characters can be obtained with one-key or two-key combinations. There are also special shortcut chords for frequent words (e.g., "and," "to") and common word endings (e.g., "-ing," "-ed"). Twiddler is held in one hand, with a strap supporting the grip. The 12 main text entry keys are placed on the back side of the device, so the keys cannot be seen without turning the device around. While such usage obviously takes a while to learn, the benefit is in the natural arm and hand position. When using an external display (Twiddler has no internal display), the forearm can be held in a completely extended position. Since the device also fits almost completely inside the hand, typing can be done almost "invisibly." This may be a benefit for mobile and wearable devices, and Twiddler has become the most widely used wearable keyboard to date. Lyons *et al.* (2004) have proposed that Twiddler might also be ideal for use with mobile phones.

Lyons *et al.* (2004) tested Twiddler in a longitudinal learning study with inexperienced users. The typing obviously took a while to learn. The speed started at about 5 words per minute, and after about 6 hours of net practice (20 × 20-min sessions), about 25 words per minute speed was obtained on average.

So far chording keyboards have been adopted only by a few wearable-computer "geeks" and some special mobile professionals, but they might be more successful in the future if wearable computing becomes more commonplace.

1.4 MOBILE PHONES, 1990s TO PRESENT

The telephone was invented in the late 19th century. As with typewriters, there is no consensus on who was the original inventor, but Alexander Graham Bell's name is most often mentioned in this context. The early phones used manual switchboards, and later rotary dials, but the 12-key *number keypad* was introduced as early as the mid-20th century (see especially the legendary studies by R.L. Deininger in 1960).

In the 1980s, the first *mobile phones* appeared (also called *cellular phones*). In the beginning, mobile phones were used very much like landline telephones, that is, mainly for speaking. The user interface was also copied from the predecessor, and most phones use the 12-key keypad even today (Fig. 1.5). However, more recently, mobile phones have gained a myriad of new features. The most advanced models are becoming very similar to handheld computers. These models are discussed in greater detail and grouped with handheld computers in Section 1.5.

Most basic models, addressed here, still incorporate the 12-key keypad, and their use is still very voice-call oriented. However, text-based messaging has become another cornerstone of these devices. Mobile phones entered the era of text messaging when the *Short Message Service* (SMS) emerged in GSM phones in the early 1990s. Very soon, almost all GSM phones incorporated SMS messaging, and nowadays instant messaging, multimedia messaging, and even full-scale e-mail have also become used features of all mobile phones. The GSM Association (2006) estimates that "a worldwide total of 1 trillion" (1,000,000,000,000!) SMS text messages were

FIGURE The 12-key keypad on a mobile phone.

1.5

sent during the year 2005. In many markets, text messages have even outnumbered the amount of voice calls. This makes even the basic mobile phone an important text entry device. As such, mobile phones were the first widely successful *mobile* text entry devices. In the mobile context, the text entry systems are facing new challenges, since the users need (and want) to enter text in situations that are more restless and less controlled than the static office environment.

1.4.1 The Dominant Text Entry Methods for Mobile Phones: The 12-Key Keyboard

The 12-key keypad poses a special challenge for text entry, since most languages have at least 26 characters. This leads to an overloading, by which each key contains several characters. Special techniques need to be used to overcome this ambiguity. The two dominant techniques used in mobile phones, both of which can appear in the same device, are multitap and predictive methods.

In the *multitap* method, each key is pressed one or more times to specify which character is wanted. This method obviously increases the number of keystrokes and is therefore quite slow. Typing speed values around 10 words per minute are typical.

In *predictive*[6] methods, a dictionary in the phone's memory is typically used to find the matching words for the key sequence. The most well-known predictive method is probably the T9 by Tegic (www.t9.com; see also Chap. 15), but other similar methods exist as well. In T9, the user makes one key press for each character, and the key sequence for the whole word is matched with the phone's dictionary. If the prediction works well, text can be entered with only about one key press per character. However, the fluency of the typing depends a lot on the match between the user's vocabulary and the phone's dictionary. If the intended word is not in the dictionary, then the user must make an extra effort. Thus, it is not easy to give a single speed estimate for predictive methods. In optimal cases, when all words match with the dictionary, speeds of about 20 words per minute can be easily obtained. In the worst cases, the speed can fall lower than the multitap speed level.

It is obvious from the above that the current phone text entry methods are not very well suited to large-scale text entry. Therefore, several alternative solutions have been created. We present these in the next chapter.

The use of predictive methods is not limited to mobile phones. The study of predictive entry systems began in Japan in the 1960s (see Chap. 11). Although the English systems are limited to a phonetic base, various other predictive entry methods exist in East Asia, for example, the use of shape-based entry systems in Chinese

---

[6] The predictive methods discussed here are predictive only in the "narrow sense." See the discussion in Chap. 2.

(see Chap. 11). Predictive methods have also opened new possibilities for communication for the disabled (see Chap. 15).

1.4.2   Alternative Text Entry Methods for Mobile Phones

The 12-key mobile phone keypad is such a limiting feature for text entry that some advanced "smart phones," which are designed to support, for example, full-scale e-mail, have completely given up text entry with the 12-key keypad. (These phones might still have this keypad in some form, but it is not used for text entry.) We will discuss these smart phones in the handheld computer section below. Instead, we describe here alternative layouts that keep the numeric 12-key layout but introduce a new layout for the alphabetic characters.

One of the most studied alternative phone layouts is probably the *Fastap* layout (Levy, 2002), formerly known as OneTouch. See Fig. 1.6, left. Fastap has the standard 12 number keys, but character keys A–Z and some punctuation keys are interlaced between these. The character keys are organized in alphabetical order. The whole keyboard is quite small, containing over 40 keys in a space not much larger than a standard phone keypad. On the other hand, all the frequent letters in the English language are available through one key press. This makes the layout potentially quite fast. A study by Sirisena (2002) showed promising results. However, very few mobile phone models have adopted this layout to date (we discuss the slow adoption more below).

Another approach, used in some existing commercial devices (e.g., SonyEricsson M600 and BlackBerry 7100), is to retain the phone keypad number layout and overlap

FIGURE
1.6

Left: Fastap keyboard (www.digitwireless.com). Right: BlackBerry 7100v reduced Qwerty keyboard.

it with a *reduced Qwerty* keyboard. See Fig. 1.6, right. Reduced Qwerty, in this case, refers to the characters being ordered in a typical Qwerty fashion, but the number of keys has been cut down by placing two or more characters in each key. Similar to phone keypad input, multitap and predictive techniques can be used here also, to overcome the ambiguity. The SonyEricsson device uses a new strategy, in which each key can be *tilted* by pressing them down on the left or right side of the key to select one of the two characters. These layouts are interesting, but they are still relatively new, and so far no usability studies of any of the reduced Qwerty layouts have been published.

Both Fastap and the reduced Qwerty layouts are quite new and have not been widely adopted in mobile devices. This may perhaps change in the near future. The situation is reminiscent of the position of the Dvorak layout in the Qwerty-dominated computer world. A new layout can probably succeed only if it can overcome the Production Paradox. That is, the users will probably adopt a new layout only if it fulfills two needs. First, the layout needs to show a clear benefit to the user, e.g., in terms of improved efficiency or comfort of use. And, second, the layout needs to be quite easy to learn. The first point might be hard to estimate for the individual customer; it could perhaps be proven by research, but so far very few studies exist, and they have almost certainly not reached the individual customers. The second point, the ease of learning, might also be difficult to estimate. However, the reduced Qwerty layout might be in a better position in this respect, since the familiar Qwerty layout might make it easier to learn or at least might make it *appear* so.

In the future, mobile phones might become like PCs, with only one dominating text entry method, or we might see more variance. At the moment, the new layouts have existed for such a short time that it is too early to predict their future.

1.5   HANDHELD COMPUTERS

The idea of a powerful handheld computing devices has been around at least since 1968, when Alan Kay envisioned the *Dynabook* concept (Meyer, 1995). It was an idea of a small and light device that could be used to take notes and to interact wirelessly. Obviously, in the late 1960s, the technology was not mature enough to realize the Dynabook. However, its idea encouraged later concepts and prototypes. In 1987, Apple presented a prototype of the *Knowledge Navigator* concept, which in turn evolved to the first commercial handheld computer, the *Newton Message Pad* by Apple.

The first Newton was released in 1993, followed by several advanced devices during the next 5 years. A good summary of the Newton devices can be found in the Apple history site (http://apple-history.com).

The Newtons were highly advanced devices, with lots of visionary features, and they got a relatively small but very loyal base of users. On the downside, the devices were rather heavy, bulky, and expensive, and some of the technologies (e.g., the advanced handwriting recognition) were not yet very mature.

In 1996, a clearly smaller, simpler, and more affordable pen-operated device appeared: the Pilot organizer. Despite its technical inferiority to the Newton, the Pilot seemed to match the users' needs better. The sales of Pilot rose quickly, while Newton's sales declined. In February 1998, Apple officially discontinued the Newton and all related products. Pilot devices still exist and are sold under different names (Pilot, PalmPilot, Palm, HandSpring, etc.). Other operating systems (such as the Windows Pocket PC) and manufacturers have appeared, but all the devices today are still clearly just "simple pen-operated computers," and the advanced thinking found in the Newton has not (yet) reappeared.

Apart from these pen-operated devices, there was another category of devices that used a full Qwerty keyboard. The Psion organizers in particular were popular and advanced devices. They are no longer manufactured, but they have evolved into Symbian devices, such as the Nokia Communicators. Symbian is also used in smart phones, which nowadays cover such a wide range of features that they can also be classified as handheld computers.

1.5.1   Dominant Text Entry Methods for PDAs

Unlike for the previously presented devices, it is hard to name any single dominant text entry method for handheld computers. Instead, we present three methods: handwriting recognition, virtual keyboard, and physical mini-keyboard.

Handwriting Recognition

In *handwriting recognition* (HWR) the device interprets the user's handwritten characters or words into a format that the computer understands (e.g., Unicode text). The input device typically comprises a stylus and a touch-sensitive screen. There are many levels of HWR, starting from the recognition of simplified individual characters to the recognition of whole words and sentences of cursive handwriting (Chap. 6).

The HWR of Apple's Newton was very advanced. The first Newtons already accepted whole words and even the use of cursive writing. The Newton could also learn the user's writing style and had sophisticated features like the recognition of common shapes and symbols. However, the recognition accuracy was often not very good. Version 2.0 of the Newton operating system introduced a more simplified recognition of printed text, with better recognition accuracy. However, the suboptimal handwriting recognition was unquestionably among the reasons for the Newton's downfall.

In 1993, the same year that the first Apple Newton device was sold, Goldberg and Richardson from Xerox PARC published a paper about a very different approach: *Unistrokes* (Goldberg & Richardson, 1993). In many ways, Unistrokes are the complete opposite of the Newton. While the Newton tried to provide a completely "natural" method of handwritten text entry, and unfortunately failed, the Unistrokes

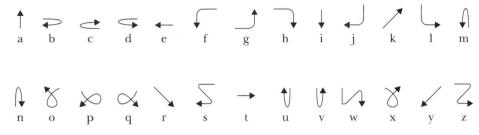

FIGURE

1.7

Unistrokes character set (Goldberg & Richardson, 1993).

technique completely distanced itself from natural usage. Instead of letting the user write freely, Unistrokes sought to optimize the recognition accuracy and text entry speed. Goldberg and Richardson wanted to design a character set that could be entered in an eyes-free manner (they even called their system "touch-typing with a stylus"). To meet these requirements a completely new, highly simplified character set was designed, in which each character could be drawn by a single stroke (thus the name Unistrokes). The downside of Unistrokes is that they require one to learn the character set (Fig. 1.7). Since some characters are quite far from their printed letter counterparts, this might slow down the adoption of the system. Goldberg and Richardson tested their system on users, but unfortunately they did not report the error rates (Goldberg & Richardson, 1993).

The learning problem was eased to some extent when the first Pilot organizer in 1996 introduced *Graffiti*. Graffiti is akin to Unistrokes in that most of its characters can be entered by single stroke, but the Graffiti characters are less "artificial" than the Unistrokes and much closer to printed letters. This naturalness was further developed in later versions of Graffiti and other similar systems, such as the one used in Windows-based Pocket PCs.

Graffiti got a lot of attention during the late 1990s, and it still has its advocates. However, other text entry methods, such as virtual keyboards and small mechanical (Qwerty) keyboards, have become increasingly popular in the recent handheld computers.

Handwriting recognizers are also available for all the main PC operating systems, such as the Tablet PC version of the Microsoft XP and the Inkwell for Mac OS X. The pen-operated PCs are still used mainly by, for example, graphical artists, and their use is driven much more by their drawing features than by text input.

The future of handwriting recognition is difficult to predict, but one scenario, not a very optimistic one, suggests that handwriting skills are starting to degenerate with the increased keyboard use. This trend will probably happen quite slowly though, and handwriting will probably not completely lose its significance, at least not during the next few generations.

Virtual Qwerty Keyboard

Even though the first Newton and Palm devices were clearly marketed and perceived as "handwriting devices," a backup method has been provided in every device: i.e., a *virtual keyboard*. To use the virtual keyboard, the user taps the "virtual keys" on a keyboard image (usually organized in the familiar Qwerty layout). The virtual keyboard serves as a backup method, but it is also used as the primary method by many users who do not want to learn the handwriting recognition or whose handwriting is not very clear.

Virtual keyboards are less prone to errors than handwriting recognition, but a few studies indicate that they might also be faster (e.g., MacKenzie *et al.*, 1994; Költringer & Grechenig, 2004; Luo & John, 2005). Another benefit of virtual keyboards is that they can be easily customized, for example using an optimized layout. We discuss the alternative virtual keyboards later.

Physical Mini-keyboards

As opposed to the virtual keyboard on screen, many recent handheld computers and smart phones also have a tiny mechanical keyboard. The most used layout is again the familiar Qwerty (Fig. 1.8).

While the full-sized PC keyboard is suitable for full 10-finger use, even for touchtyping, the use of the mobile mini-keyboards is mainly limited to two-finger typing. Most users hold the device in two hands and use the two thumbs for typing. Although such thumb typing is obviously clumsier than the full 10-finger typing, a recent study by Clarkson *et al.* (2005) showed that significant speeds can be obtained after very little practice. Even users with limited prior experience can type over 30 words per minute, and the average speed can exceed 60 words per minute (!) after a few hours

FIGURE   Qwerty keyboard of the Nokia 9500 Communicator.

1.8

of practice. This figure is clearly higher than the about 10–25 words per minute typical with other techniques, so physical mini-keyboards are a strong option for users who value efficiency.

However, the downside of these keyboards, as well as any finger-operated keyboard, is that they may create repetitive strain injuries with extensive use, especially since the thumbs are not as agile as, for example, the index fingers. At the moment, the mini-keyboards and extensive mobile text entry are relatively new phenomena, and so far no studies of ergonomical problems have emerged to our knowledge. However, we might see such problems in the future if the mini-keyboard and mobile o mail successes continue.

1.5.2   Alternative Text Entry Methods for Handheld Computers

Alternative Virtual Keyboards

Virtual keyboards are presented on the device screen and are therefore easy to change through software. Therefore, it is no surprise that alternative layouts have been proposed also for this category of keyboards. Since the virtual keys are pointed at with a stylus, the alternative layouts typically change the positions of the keys to minimize the time and effort needed for stylus movement. Sometimes also completely new keys are introduced. Since the Space character is very common, many alternative layouts provide more than one Space key.

Some proposed layouts are, for example, *Fitaly* (http://fitaly.com; tested by MacKenzie *et al.*, 1999), *OPTI* (MacKenzie & Zhang, 1999), *Metropolis* (Zhai *et al.*, 2000), and *ATOMIK* (Zhai *et al.*, 2002).

The use of alternative virtual keyboards is based on straightforward pen tapping with one hand. Therefore, their typing speed can be estimated by Fitts' law analysis (Fitts, 1954; see also MacKenzie, 1992). The results indicate that the alternative layouts could indeed increase text entry speed, even as much as about 50% (Zhai *et al.*, 2002)! It should be noted that speed is, however, not the only usability factor, and very few studies with actual users have been carried out.

The user studies by Smith and Zhai (2001) and MacKenzie and Zhang (1999) indicate that the initial typing speed is moderate (around 10–15 words per minute), and it takes about 4 hours net training time to surpass the typing speed of the Qwerty layout. This is a clearly shorter learning time than the over 100 hours found in the Dvorak vs Qwerty typewriter study (Yamada, 1980). However, to our knowledge, none of the alternative virtual keyboards have been very successful so far, although they have been available for several years. We do not know the reasons for this, but perhaps the Qwerty layout is again "good enough" for the users not to invest in the learning of a new layout.

Gesture-Based Input

An interesting direction for the future are gesture-based text entry methods. Since our focus is on commercial text entry, and none of the gesture-based methods have yet been successful, we will handle these only briefly.

Virtual keyboards require constant visual attention. Every character must be entered by hitting exactly within the boundaries of the virtual keys. This makes the use tedious, especially in mobile situations, in which the visual attention is often needed elsewhere. Gesture-based input methods have been created to overcome this problem. Instead of tapping on small keys, gestures are drawn on the screen. Unlike the handwritten characters, which can also be classified as gestures, the gesture-based methods discussed here do not utilize the letters in the alphabet, but are based on other metaphors, such as virtual keyboards or pie menus.

Some gesture-based text entry methods are *T-Cube* (Venolia & Neiberg, 1994), *QuikWriting* (Perlin, 1998), *Cirrin* (Mankoff & Abowd, 1998), *MDITIM* (Isokoski & Raisamo, 2000), and *EdgeWrite* (Wobbrock *et al.*, 2003, 2004).

A recent and interesting gesture-based input concept is *shape writing*. It has been developed through research by Zhai and his colleagues. The original version was called *Shark* (Zhai & Kristensson, 2003), and the later improved versions were *SHARK^2* (Kristensson & Zhai, 2004) and finally *ShapeWriter*. These methods have shown potential for high text-entry speed, although they have been tested in one informal trial only (Kristensson & Zhai, 2004). The average speed in this informal study was about 70 words per minute! The results need to be verified in more formal experiments using more subjects, but shape writing is a promising text entry concept for future mobile devices. ShapeWriter is handled in more detail in Chap. 7 of this book.

1.6   CONCLUSIONS

We have gone through four cornerstone devices in the text entry arena: typewriter, personal computer, mobile phone, and handheld computer. While text entry methods within each of these four devices are very consistent, the intradevice differences are very clear. While the typewriter and its successor, the personal computer, have been operated mainly through the keyboard, the newer devices use also different techniques. This suggests that despite the apparent conservatism within existing devices, the emergence of radically new device forms creates *discontinuity points* that give ground to new text methods.

The continuing trend of mobilization and device miniaturization will potentially create such discontinuity points. We are still in the early phases of the mobile device era, and while the clear majority of the current mobile devices can be classified as *handheld,* the future mobile use could be very different: *wearable, ubiquitous, implanted*— even some that have yet to be named or even conceived.

Although the Qwerty keyboard has served us well since 1874, we are better prepared for the future by studying new, radically different text entry methods for future device forms.

1.7 FURTHER READING

Due to space limitations, this chapter was able merely to scratch the surface of text entry history. Fortunately, good sources exist, both online and in printing. Meyer (1995) gives a thorough overview of pen computing technologies, including pen-based text entry. This paper also gives a summary of the early history of writing.

The history of typewriters and keyboards is pretty well documented. The history of typewriters is thoroughly analyzed by Yamada (1980). The Virtual Typewriter Museum gives a good overview of the early typewriters with lots of pictures and a nice time line (http://www.typewritermuseum.org/) Numerous alternative keyboards are listed in the Typing Injury FAQ site (http://www.tifaq.com/keyboards.html).

A more general history of human–computer interaction is given by Myers (1998).

REFERENCES

Carroll, J. M., & Rosson, M. B. (1987). *The paradox of the active user. Interfacing thought: Cognitive aspects of human–computer interaction* (pp.80–111). Cambridge, MA: MIT Press.

Clarkson, E., Clawson, J., Lyons, K., & Starner, T. (2005). An empirical study of typing rates on mini-QWERTY keyboards. *Proceedings of the CHI 2005 Conference on Human Factors in Computing Systems* (pp.1288–1291). New York: ACM Press.

Deininger, R. L. (1960). Human factors engineering studies of the design and use of pushbutton telephone sets. *Bell System Technical Journal, 39,* 995–1012.

Dvorak, A., & Dealey, D. L. (1936). Typewriter keyboard. U.S. Patent 2,040,248. U.S. Patent Office.

Fitts, P. M. (1954). The information capacity of the human motor system in controlling the amplitude of movement. *Journal of Experimental Psychology, 47,* 381–391.

Goldberg, D., & Richardson, C. (1993). Touch-typing with a stylus. *Proceedings of the INTERCHI '93 Conference on Human Factors in Computing Systems* (pp.80–87). New York: ACM Press.

GSM Association (2006). GSM world: *http://www.gsmworld.com/services/messaging.shtml*

Isokoski, P., & Raisamo, R. (2000). Device independent text input: A rationale and an example. *Proceedings of the Working Conference on Advanced Visual Interfaces* (pp.76–83). New York: ACM Press.

Karat, C.-M., Halverson, C., Karat, J., & Horn, D. (1999). Patterns of entry and correction in large vocabulary continuous speech recognition systems. *Proceedings of the Conference on Human Factors in Computing Systems—CHI* (pp.568–575). New York: ACM Press.

Karat, J., Horn, D., Halverson, C., & Karat, C.-M. (2000). Overcoming unusability: developing efficient strategies in speech recognition systems. *Extended Abstracts of the Conference on Human Factors in Computing Systems—CHI* (pp.141–142). New York: ACM Press.

Kristensson, P.-O., & Zhai S. (2004). SHARK: A large vocabulary shorthand writing system for pen-based computers. *Proceedings of the ACM Symposium on User Interface Software and Technology (UIST)* (pp.43–52). New York: ACM Press.

Költringer, T., & Grechenig, T. (2004). Comparing the immediate usability of Graffiti 2 and Virtual Keyboard. *Extended Abstracts on Human Factors in Computing Systems—CHI* (pp.1175–1178). New York: ACM Press.

Levy, D. (2002). The Fastap keypad and pervasive computing. *Proceedings of the Pervasive Conference* (pp.58–68). Heidelberg: Springer-Verlag.

Liebowitz, S. J., & Margolis, S. E. (1990). The fable of keys. *Journal of Law and Economics, 33,* 1–25.

Luo, L., & John, B. E. (2005). Predicting task execution time on handheld devices using the keystroke-level model. *Extended Abstracts on Human Factors in Computing Systems—CHI* (pp.1605–1608). New York: ACM Press.

Lyons, K., Starner, T., Plaisted, D., Fusia, J., Lyons, A., Drew, A., & Looney, E. W. (2004). Twiddler typing: One-handed chording text entry for mobile phones. *Proceedings of the ACM Conference on Human Factors in Computing Systems (CHI '04), 24–29 April 2004, Vienna* (pp.671–678). New York: ACM Press.

MacKenzie, I. S. (1992). Fitts' law as a research and design tool in human–computer interaction. *Human–Computer Interaction, 7,* 91–139.

MacKenzie, I. S., Nonnecke, R. B., Riddersma, S., McQueen, C., & Meltz, M. (1994). Alphanumeric entry on pen-based computers. *International Journal of Human–Computer Studies, 41,* 775–792.

MacKenzie, I. S., & Zhang, S. X. (1997). The immediate usability of Graffiti. *Proceedings of Graphics Interface 1997, 21–23 May 1997, Kelowna, BC* (pp.129–137). Toronto: Canadian Information Processing Society.

MacKenzie, I. S., & Zhang, S. X. (1999). The design and evaluation of a high-performance soft keyboard. *Proceedings of the ACM Conference on Human Factors in Computing Systems (CHI '99), 15–20 May 1999, Pittsburgh* (pp.25–31). New York: ACM Press.

MacKenzie, I. S., Zhang, S. X., & Soukoreff, W. (1999). Text entry using soft keyboards. *Behaviour and Information Technology, 18,* 235–244.

Mankoff, J., & Abowd, G. D. (1998). Cirrin: A word-level unistroke keyboard for pen input. *Proceedings of the UIST* (pp.213–214). New York: ACM Press.

Meyer, A. (1995). Pen computing: A technology overview and a vision. *ACM SIGCHI Bulletin, 27,* 46–90.

Myers, B. A. (1998). A brief history of human–computer interaction technology. *Interactions, 5,* 44–54.

Perlin, K. (1998). Quikwriting: Continuous stylus-based text entry. *Proceedings of the ACM Symposium on User Interface Software and Technology (UIST '98), 1–4 November 1998, San Francisco* (pp.215–216). New York: ACM Press.

Sholes, G. L., Glidden, C. & Soule, S. W. (1868). Improvement in type-writing machines. U.S. Patent 79,868. U.S. Patent Office.

Sirisena, A. (2002). *Mobile text entry.* Christchurch: University of Canterbury Department of Computer Science.

Smith, B. A., & Zhai, S. (2001). Optimised virtual keyboards with and without alphabetical ordering—A novice user study. *Proceedings of INTERACT 2001,* Tokyo, *Japan* (pp.92–99).

Suhm, B., Myers, B., & Waibel, A. (2001). Multimodal error correction for speech user interfaces. *ACM Transactions on Computer–Human Interaction, 8,* 60–98.

Venolia, D., & Neiberg, F. (1994). T-Cube: A fast, self-disclosing pen-based alphabet. *Proceedings of CHI '94 Conference on Human Factors in Computing Systems* (pp.265–270). New York: ACM Press.

Wobbrock, J. O., Myers, B. A., & Aung, H. H. (2004). Writing with a joystick: A comparison of date stamp, selection keyboard, and EdgeWrite. *Proceedings of the Conference on Graphics Interface (GI), London, Ontario* (pp.1–8).

Wobbrock, J. O., Myers, B. A., & Kembel, J. A. (2003). EdgeWrite: A stylus-based text entry method designed for high accuracy and stability of motion. *Proceedings of the ACM Symposium on User Interface Software and Technology (UIST '03), 2–5 November 2003, Vancouver, BC* (pp.61–70). New York: ACM Press.

Yamada, H. (1980). A historical study of typewriters and typing methods: From the position of planning Japanese parallels. *Journal of Information Processing, 2,* 175–202.

Zhai, S., Hunter, M., & Smith, B. A. (2000). The Metropolis keyboard—an exploration of quantitative techniques for virtual keyboard design. *Proceedings of the 13th Annual ACM Symposium on User Interface Software and Technology (UIST)* (pp.119–128). New York: ACM Press.

Zhai, S., Hunter, M., & Smith, B. A. (2002). Performance optimization of virtual keyboards. *Human–Computer Interaction, 17,* 229–269.

Zhai, S., & Kristensson, P.-O. (2003). Shorthand writing on stylus keyboard. *Proceedings of the ACM Conference on Human Factors in Computing Systems (CHI)* (pp.97–104). New York: ACM Press.

Language Models for Text Entry

Kumiko Tanaka-Ishii   University of Tokyo, Tokyo, Japan

2.1   INTRODUCTION

For many years, the design of text entry methods has reflected the statistics of language. For example, the Dvorak keyboard, proposed as an alternative to the standard Qwerty keyboard, was designed based on statistics concerning letter usage in the English language. Modeling the language better enables the construction of better entry systems.

In recent years, huge collections of electronic text have appeared and we have more opportunity to acquire language statistics. A body of text that is collected and organized under particular criteria is called a *corpus*. Gigabytes of newspaper corpora are now available, and international organizations, such as the Linguistic Data Consortium (http://www.ldc.upenn.edu/), provide various kinds of corpora. In addition to such manually collected text, terabytes of text are available on the Internet. This chapter presents statistical language models, created by using such data, which are useful for text entry.

Language models provide text entry systems with the power to *predict* unseen text likely to be generated by a user. The Dvorak keyboard is efficient, because it is designed based on an assumption that the user will use "e" more frequently than "y", which is a prediction that was based on existing examples of English text. The power of prediction enables people to create text in collaboration with machines; this was not previously possible, and in the past the creation of text was the user's exclusive responsibility. Based on the user's past text, and on huge amounts of general text greater than what an individual user could go through in a lifetime, an entry system can help the user be consistent and clarify vague recollections of expressions by predicting what the user might want to enter. Moreover, prediction enables text entry under difficult conditions. For example, a disabled user has an opportunity to generate more text, because text entry is enabled with fewer actions. Also, text entry on devices as small as watches is no longer a dream.

Of course, there is some controversy as to whether such computer-aided text generation is desirable. There are two objections. The first is that computers will always have a limited ability to predict since prediction is based on the use of past text to predict future text; as language evolves, future text will always include new phrases and forms of usage. However, recent search engines index almost all online human text, so nonindexed fragments will become scarce and this limitation of computer prediction will become less and less serious. The second objection is that people will gradually forget how to write text correctly. People who use word completion entry in English or kana-kanji conversion in Japanese already complain that they forget spellings and the details of logographs. However, this objection conversely illustrates how helpful entry systems have become. Indeed, looking at the history of text entry, a clear trend has been "from no prediction toward prediction." For example, in European languages, predictive methods[1] are gradually becoming prevalent. In Japan, where there was a vigorous debate in the 1970s and 1980s as to whether prediction should be adopted, most nonpredictive entry systems have died out.

Incorrect prediction can be a serious problem if there is no effective and easy way to correct the inaccuracy; on the other hand, if it is easy to fix a few mistakes that arise, some level of inaccuracy in prediction will be more tolerable for the user. Thus, one important path toward a better entry system is the creation of a system that can accurately predict the user's intended text. To this end, language models hold the key. In the following, we first model the action of text entry itself and then define what a language model is.

2.2   BASIC MODEL OF TEXT ENTRY

Many language processing tasks, such as speech recognition (Jelinek, 1997) and automatic translation (Manning & Schutze, 1999), are modeled by Shannon's noisy channel in the language engineering domain. The advantage of modeling in this way is that the tasks fit well within the model, and various information theoretic

---

[1] In text entry, the term "predictive" is used in two ways: (a) in a narrow sense, predicting forward for use in word prediction, word completion, phrase completion, etc., and (b) in a broad sense, predicting the user's intention. For example, Tegic's T9 is not predictive in the narrow sense, but it is predictive in the broad sense. The first interpretation distinguishes one-key with disambiguation (see Chap. 5) from word/phrase completion. The second interpretation is used by companies, in part because terms like "predictive" are more consumer-friendly than terms like "disambiguation." Both Tegic's T9 and Eatoni's Letterwise are marketed as predictive text entry. This is true, but only in the broad sense, i.e., upon receiving the key sequence "2273" on a mobile phone keypad, they predict that the user might intend "case" or "bare," but they do not anticipate or predict forward to other possibilities, such as "casement," "barefoot," "career," and "careful." In Chaps. 2, 4, 5, 10, 11, and 13, the authors adopt the term in the broader sense. Namely, references to a "predictive" method/technique/entry mean that the application suggests candidates to the user and the user selects from among them. When predicting forward is signified in these chapters, the term "completion" is used.

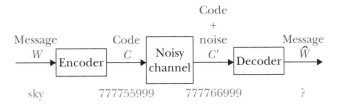

Shannon's noisy channel model and text entry.

tools are available to judge the task performance. The text entry task can also follow suit.

The text entry modeled by Shannon's noisy channel is illustrated in Fig. 2.1. A user who wants to enter a text W transforms it into a code sequence C with the *encoder*. For example, when the word "sky" is to be entered into a mobile phone using the multitap method, the code would correspond to "7-7-7-7-5-5-9-9-9." When code sequence C is actually entered, the user might make mistakes such as by mistyping or even in the transformation from W to C. Such mistakes can be considered as equivalent to a signal going through a noisy channel. In our example, the user might enter "7-7-7-7-6-6-9-9-9" instead of "7-7-7-7-5-5-9-9-9." We denote this actual entry as C'. When C' is provided to the text entry system as input, the *decoder* decrypts the entry and outputs its result $\hat{W}$ to the display.

Most text entry activity fits into this model, and analysis of the mapping from W to C, then to C', and then back to $\hat{W}$ suggests various text entry designs. The mapping from W to C can be classified into two types depending on whether the mapping is a one-to-one correspondence or otherwise. For example, in the case of English entry using a full keyboard, the mapping is one to one; on the other hand, in the case of one-key with disambiguation (see Chap. 5), in which, for example, "sky" can be encoded by "7-5-9," the mapping is multiple to one. There could be mappings of multiple to multiple, for example, when word completion is used: an entry code sequence in which C = "amb" could correspond to W = "ambiguous," "ambitious," etc., whereas W = "ambiguous" would correspond to multiple codes such as C = "am," "amb," or "ambig."

The mapping from C to C' can also be classified into two types, in this case depending on whether the entry system assumes mistakes are made by the user. Many widely used text entry systems assume C' will be equal to C, i.e., that users do not make mistakes. In reality, of course, users make mistakes, but the decoder assumes these are correct entries. If the possibility of mistakes is considered when the description to $\hat{W}$ is made, then the mapping from C to C' is a multiple-to-multiple correspondence. Then, as C is ambiguous with regard to C', W becomes ambiguous as regards C'.

Taking all this into account, entry methods can be classified into those with or without ambiguity. When the entry design is without ambiguity, the entry method is *nonpredictive*. When there is ambiguity, the entry method is *predictive*.

In the case of nonpredictive entry, the entry is generally made character by character. Decoder software is trivial or even unnecessary, because $C = C'$ corresponds to $\hat{W}$ on a one-to-one basis. The designer still has to design a code for each character, though. This concerns other factors such as the displacements of user actions or the length of the code. A text entry system is designed by measuring these factors using some evaluation function. Let us denote any such factor as $F(C = c)$ for a given code c. The evaluation function for a code is then described by the formula

$$\text{Eval}(C) = \sum_{c} F(C = c)P(C = c), \tag{2.1}$$

where $P(C = c)$ means the probability of a code c. As C and W have a one-to-one correspondence, this is equal to $P(W = w)$, which denotes the probability of a certain language fragment w occurring. This $P(W)$ is called the *language model*. Thus, designing a good code C concerns $P(W)$. One typical measure of $F(C = c)$ is the number of keystrokes needed for each character, which gives KSPC or KSPW (defined in Chap. 5, Section 5.2; examples of code evaluation for various keypads are shown in Section 5.4).

With predictive entry, the entry unit can be character-based, word-based, or phrase-based, but character-based methods are now rare. In addition, entry by completion is a kind of predictive entry. Predictive entry proceeds by repeating the following three steps:

Step 1. The user enters C' into the decoder using word or phrase units.

Step 2. The text entry system looks for corresponding target candidates in a system dictionary attached to the software. The candidates are sorted in some relevant order and then displayed to the user.

Step 3. The user chooses his preferred target from among the candidates. For example, in the case of one-key with disambiguation, the user enters "7-5-9" (both C, C') to enter "sky" (W), and then the system will present all words corresponding to "7-5-9" in a list: "sky," "sly," "ply," ($\hat{W}$), etc. The user chooses "sky" from the list.

For implementation of a predictive entry system, the system requires a database consisting of the dictionary and the language model. Such an additional database can be very large, depending on the vocabulary size and the language model. For these cases, advanced data structures, especially for dictionaries used for predictive entry, have been reported (Aoe, 1989).

The efficiency of the entry is measured not only by the efficiency of the code, but also by the decoder's efficiency in estimating $\hat{W}$. One typical strategy to do this decoding as well as possible is to maximize the conditional probability of the occurrence of W under $C' = c'$[2]:

$$\hat{W} = arg \max_{W} P(W|C' = c'). \qquad (2.2)$$

This model suggests that for the construction of the candidate list in Step 2, the candidates w are sorted in the descending order of $P(W = w|C' = c')$. In fact, this $P(W = w|C' = c')$ is difficult to measure, because the record of C' is not present in corpora. Therefore, it is transformed by using Bayes' theorem. Since $P(C' = c')$ is constant when W varies, the estimation problem is transformed as follows:

$$\hat{W} = arg \max_{W} P(C' = c'|W)P(W). \qquad (2.3)$$

This formula indicates that W is estimated by two terms: $P(W)$, the language model as noted previously, and $P(C' = c'|W)$, which is the *typing model*. When the system assumes no user mistakes, $P(C' = c'|W)$ is equal to $P(C = c|W)$. Moreover, when W corresponds to C through multiple-to-one mapping, as in the case of one-key with disambiguation, $P(C = c|W)$ becomes 1.0 and the equation becomes as simple as

$$\hat{W} = arg \max_{W} P(W). \qquad (2.4)$$

This means that decoding can be done only by evaluating how well the decoded sequence resembles the true language. This is the model used in most of today's predictive entry methods. However, we can see from this that there are further possibilities regarding how we estimate $P(C' = c'|W)$.

Like the design of the decoder software, the code design is important. By using the information theoretic tool, the efficiency of the code can be measured from the complexity of word W given $C' = c'$; this is formally defined as the conditional entropy $H(W|C')$:

$$H(W|C') = -\sum_{c'} H(W|C' = c')P(C' = c'), \quad \text{where} \qquad (2.5)$$

$$H(W|C' = c') = -\sum_{w} P(W = w|C' = c') \log P(W = w|C' = c').$$

$H(W|C')$ represents the number of bits required to encode W given a user entry C'. Therefore, the smaller $H(W|C')$ is, the less complex the choice of W will be. When there is no ambiguity, $H(W|C')$ becomes zero. Note how similar this is to Formula (2.1) by considering $F(C = c)$ as equivalent to $H(W|C = c')$. Some examples of evaluating codes by conditional entropy are given in Chap. 5, Section 5.4.

From Formula (2.5), we also see that the main terms related to construction of the decoder and code evaluation concern the language model $P(W)$ and the typing model $P(C' = c'|W)$. This chapter presents various language models $P(W)$.

---

[2]   The expression $argmax_{x} f(x)$ gives the value of x where the function $f(x)$ takes the maximum value.

2.3   *N*-GRAM MODELS

Assume that $W = w_1, w_2, \ldots, w_n$, where w_i denotes a word: for some entry systems w_i can be a character, but the same discussion essentially applies. Also, let $w_{i,j}$ denote w_i, $w_{i+1}, \ldots, w_{j-1}, w_j$. In the following, $P(X = x)$ is denoted as $P(x)$ for simplicity.

The simplest way to model language is to assume that a unit w independently occurs or occurs based on the sequence occurring just before. The latter case can be modeled by a typical sequence model called the *Markov model*. In Markov models, given a sequence $w_1, w_2, \ldots, w_{i-1}$, the next word w_i is assumed to occur based on the limited length k of the previous history. Such a model is called a *kth-order* Markov model.

Having $k = 0$ assumes that no history influences the occurrence of the next word. In this case, $P(W)$ is modeled as

$$P(W) \approx \prod_{i=1}^{n} P(w_i). \tag{2.6}$$

This model is called a unigram model and is a special case of Markov models. Suppose we are using the simplest entry model as in Formula (2.4), i.e., the entry system tries to maximize $P(W)$ for any user entry. Then, for example, with a word-based entry method using one-key with disambiguation, when the user enters "7-5-9," the software sorts the word candidates in Step 2 (explained in the previous section) according to the word probability. Further, in the case of phrase-based entry, suppose multiple words are entered in a sequence like "8-4-3-0-7-5-9-0" (with the intention to enter "the sky" with 0 indicating the word border, see Chap. 5). The system decodes this to get all two-word possibilities of w_i and w_{i+1} corresponding to "8-4-3-0-7-5-9-0" and then sorts them according to the value $P(w_i)P(w_{i+1})$.

Returning to the general Markov model, when $k \geq 1$, the model assumes that w_i depends only on the previous occurrences of $w_{i-k}, \ldots, w_{i-1}$, which is expressed as

$$P(w_i \mid w_{i-k, i-1}) \approx P(w_i \mid w_1, w_2, \ldots, w_{i-1}) \tag{2.7}$$

$P(W)$ is then transformed as follows:

$$\begin{aligned} P(W) &= P(w_1, w_2, \ldots, w_n) \\ &= P(w_1) P(w_2 \mid w_1) \cdots P(w_n \mid w_1, \ldots, w_{n-1}) \\ &\approx P(w_1) P(w_2 \mid w_1) P(w_3 \mid w_{1,2}) \cdots P(w_k \mid w_{1, k-1}) P(w_{k+1} \mid w_{1,k}) \cdots P(w_n \mid w_{n-k, n-1}) \\ &= P(w_1) \cdots P(w_k \mid w_{1,k-1}) \prod_{i=k+1}^{n} P(w_i \mid w_{i-k,i-1}). \end{aligned} \tag{2.8}$$

Specifically, when $k = 2$,

$$P(W) = P(w_1)\prod_{i=2}^{n} P(w_i \mid w_{i-1}). \tag{2.9}$$

This is called the *bigram* model and is one of the most frequently used language models in research concerning the text entry domain. Another possible model is the second-order Markov model, which is often called the *trigram* model. Such Markov models in general are often called *n-gram* models.

In the case of word-based entry using the bigram model, for example, when the user enters "7-5-9" using word-based one-key entry with disambiguation, the proposed word with the highest rank will be the word with the largest $P(w_i \mid w_{i-1})$. Given previously entered text such as "very blue," the word "sky" could be the best candidate because it is likely that $P(\text{"sky"} \mid \text{"blue"}) > P(\text{"ply"} \mid \text{"blue"})$. In the case of phrase-based entry using a trigram model, if the entry is "8-4-3-0-7-5-9-0" (with intended entry being "the sky") and the previous text was "fly in," then the two-word candidates are sorted based on the score $P(w_i \mid \text{"fly"}, \text{"in"})P(w_{i+1} \mid w_i, \text{"in"})$.

Such phrase-based entry is still rarely used for European languages, but phrase-based entry systems are widely used in Japanese and Chinese. For example, a Chinese code can be "Woxiangmaishuiguo" (I want to buy fruit), which is a whole sentence. The transformation from this code to the final Chinese text 我想买水果 is done as one, by chunking the code into every possible word unit, replacing every chunk by words, sorting those candidates according to the probability depending on the language model, and presenting them to the user. Here, the maximization of $P(W)$ is done through dynamic programming.

For the actual calculation of $P(W)$, we need the joint probabilities of words $P(w_{i-k,i})$. This is estimated from a relevant corpus. The simplest estimation is by the relative frequency; i.e., $C(w_{i-k,i})/N$, where $C(ws)$ indicates the frequency of word sequence ws in the corpus and N indicates the total number of occurrences of sequences of length ws. Even though this is the most frequently used estimation, bear in mind that this is only one rough way to estimate the probability. The main point of the statistical model is to *predict unseen text*. Thus, the model has to take every possible occurrence of language into consideration. One way to do so is to introduce a global hypothesis (model) concerning language and fit the model as well as possible to the corpus. Under statistical processing, one possible hypothesis is to assume a global distribution of word occurrence, of which the simplest is the multinomial distribution, i.e., assume words occur randomly just like the outcome of a coin flip. Fitting the distribution to the corpus through maximum likelihood estimation then gives the relative frequency. Other possibilities for the global statistical distribution are Zipf's law (Zipf, 1949) or Mandelbrot's distribution (Mandelbrot, 1952; Bell *et al.*, 1990).

Even when such a global distribution is introduced, though, the model often does not sufficiently incorporate unseen text: for example, the relative frequency method will assign zero to all words not occurring in the corpus. The probability of an unseen word appearing for the first time in a user entry then becomes zero, and the whole $P(W)$ becomes zero. As the order of the Markov model becomes higher, the number of possible word chains becomes exponentially larger and the problem becomes more serious. This problem is often called the *zero-frequency* or *data-sparseness* problem, since it is due to the difficulty of defining the complete set of words used in a language.

Various solutions were proposed for this problem, which are generally called *smoothing* methods. Among the easiest of these are the *discounting* methods, in which some portion of the frequency for each word is taken away for redistribution to zero-frequency words. A more sophisticated group of methods are the *back-off* methods, in which higher order probabilities are estimated from lower order probabilities. Related to this is a group of methods called *Good – Turing* methods (Good, 1953; Gale & Sampson, 1995). For a more detailed explanation of smoothing methods, see Manning and Schutze (1999).

As *n*-gram models are the most used worldwide as regards entry systems, let us see how much the entry efficiency improves when *n* is increased from unigram to trigrams. We compare the performance for the entry method on a mobile-phone-like keypad (see Chap. 5, Fig. 5.2). We tested three types of entry system: one-key with disambiguation without completion, one-key with disambiguation with completion from the first three characters, and the same with completion from the first two characters. For example, to enter "school," "7-2-4-6-6-5" is the entry in the first case, "7-2-4" is the entry in the second case, and "7-2" is the entry in the third case. For this experiment, 1 year's worth of issues of the *Wall Street Journal* was used, which was separated into 103 Mbytes of training data and 1 Mbyte of test data. Rare words that occurred fewer than 20 times were eliminated to limit the whole vocabulary size to about 28,000 words. The zero-frequency problem is solved by the Good – Turing estimator.

The results are shown in Fig. 2.2. The horizontal axis shows the length of the *n*-grams, from unigram ($k = 0$) to trigram ($k = 2$). The vertical axis shows the average

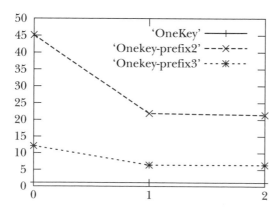

FIGURE

2.2

Average ranking decrease when longer *n*-grams are used.

ranking of the target word for an entry (K_{scan}, defined in Chap. 5). Three lines are shown, each corresponding to one of the three types of entry method. For the first type, the entry worked reasonably well even when unigram models were used. When there was a large degree of ambiguity, as with the second and third types of entry, use of the bigram greatly improved entry efficiency. Therefore, when n-gram models are used, the bigram model already provides a good approximation. At the same time, users will sense the difference between a system using unigrams and one using bigrams. Beyond the trigram model, however, the improvement leveled off. Thus, even though the trigram model improves the language model, and thus the entry method is more efficient using the trigram model, the user might not be explicitly aware of this improvement. Overall, bigram or trigram is the best choice when constructing an entry method based on n-grams.

2.4 HIDDEN MARKOV MODEL

This section introduces language models that incorporate language latent features underlying surface language sequences. A representative model is the hidden Markov model (HMM). Such language models are especially important for phrase-based entry methods.

As noted, phrase-based methods are still rarely used for European languages, though there are exceptions (Shieber & Baker, 2003) that could lead to greater use of phrase-based entry. In contrast, for Japanese and Chinese, the history has been from character to word, and then to phrase, and phrase-based entry systems are nowadays the common standard (see Chap. 11). The advantage of entry by a larger unit is greater entry speed, because most of the time required in predictive entry is for scanning and selecting candidates. With a phrase-based method, the user needs select only once if the text entry system proposes a top-ranked candidate that matches the target. In contrast, a word-based method requires multiple selections.

Moreover, simple Markov models are sometimes problematic, especially for higher order models, because the size of the database representing the language model can become large. This was a serious problem when computers were far more primitive than today and had only a small amount of memory. Similarly, current mobile phones have limited computing resources compared with those of desktop computers. Also, as noted, the zero-frequency problem is greater for higher order models.

One way to solve these problems is to use an HMM, in which we assume a hidden sequence formed of a reduced number of elements underlying the surface word level and model that hidden sequence by a Markov model. One typical hidden sequence is the part of speech (POS) attached to each word. For example, instead of asking what word comes after the word "blue," we ask what POS appears after the *adjective*.

Let us denote a hidden sequence as $T = t_1, t_2, \ldots, t_n$, where t_i denotes an element of the hidden sequence corresponding to w_i. Let's introduce the term t_0 as a sentinel for simplicity $P(W)$ can then be similarly transformed as in the previous section:

$$P(W) = \sum_T P(W, T)$$

$$= \sum_T P(w_{1,n}, t_{0,n}) \qquad (2.10)$$

$$= \sum_T P(t_0) P(t_1 \mid t_0) P(t_2 \mid t_0, t_1) \cdots P(t_n \mid t_{0,n-1}) \cdot$$

$$P(w_1 \mid t_{0,n}) P(w_2 \mid t_{0,n}, w_1) P(w_3 \mid t_{0,n}, w_{0,2}) \cdots P(w_n \mid t_{0,n}, w_{1,n-1}). \qquad (2.11)$$

Two assumptions are introduced here. The first is that the occurrence of w_i depends only on t_i:

$$P(w_i \mid w_1, \ldots, w_{i-1}, t_{0,n-1}) \approx P(w_i \mid t_i). \qquad (2.12)$$

The second is that the hidden sequence is modeled as a Markov sequence:

$$P(t_i \mid t_{0,i-1}) \approx P(t_i \mid t_{i-1}). \qquad (2.13)$$

There are other variations, such as assuming a higher order Markov model for the sequence of T (such as a trigram) or considering the actual neighboring occurrence of surface word w_i (Charniak, 1993). With these two approximations, the right-hand side of Formula (2.11) becomes

$$P(W) = \sum_T \prod_{i=1}^{n} P(w_i \mid t_i) P(t_i \mid t_{i-1}). \qquad (2.14)$$

Given a word sequence, multiple POS sequences could correspond to each word. For all combinations of such a sequence, $\prod_{i=1}^{n} P(w_i \mid t_i) P(t_i \mid t_{i-1})$ is calculated and added to obtain $P(W)$.

An example is shown in Fig. 2.3 for the case in English of when "8-4-3-0-7-5-9-0" ("the sky") is entered after "fly in." Suppose there are three candidates for "8-4-3," which are "the," "tie" (verb), and "tie" (noun) and two candidates for "7-5-9," which are "sky" (noun) and "sly" (adjective). There are branches connecting the POSs, and probabilities are shown for the first three. Note that the probability of a link between preposition and verb is lower than for those between preposition and noun or article. Also, note that the sum of probabilities on branches going out from

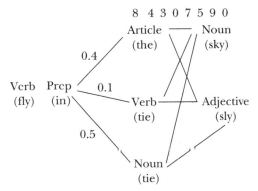

8 4 3 0 7 5 9 0

FIGURE 2.3   Example of HMM calculation for phrase-based one-key entry with disambiguation.

"prep (in)" should become 1.0. The probability of "the sky" coming after "fly in" is calculated by

$$P(\text{article}\,|\,\text{prep})\,P(\text{"the"}\,|\,\text{article})\,P(\text{noun}\,|\,\text{article})\,P(\text{"sky"}\,|\,\text{noun}),$$

whereas that of "tie sly" is obtained by

$$P(\text{verb}\,|\,\text{prep})\,P(\text{"tie"}\,|\,\text{verb})\,P(\text{adjective}\,|\,\text{verb})\,P(\text{"sly"}\,|\,\text{adjective})$$
$$+\,P(\text{noun}\,|\,\text{prep})\,P(\text{"tie"}\,|\,\text{noun})\,P(\text{adjective}\,|\,\text{noun})\,P(\text{"sly"}|\text{adjective}),$$

because there are two paths in the graph that can be taken to generate "in tie sly."

This illustration suggests that Formula (2.14) can be calculated recurrently. In order to see this, we denote $S_i(x) = P(w_{1,i}, t_i = x)$, where x is an element of the POS corresponding to t_i. We see that

$$P(w_{1,i}) = \sum_x P(w_{1,i}, t_i = x). \tag{2.15}$$

Then,

$$
\begin{aligned}
S_{i+1}(y) &= P(w_{1,i+1}, t_{i+1} = y) \\
&= \sum_x P(w_{1,i+1}, t_i = x, t_{i+1} = y) \\
&= \sum_x P(w_{1,i}, t_i = x)\,P(w_{i+1}, t_{i+1} = y\,|\,w_{1,i}, t_i = x) \\
&\approx \sum_x P(w_{1,i}, t_i = x)\,P(w_{i+1}, t_{i+1} = y\,|\,t_i = x) \\
&= \sum_x S_i(x)\,P(w_{i+1}, t_{i+1} = y\,|\,t_i = x).
\end{aligned}
\tag{2.16}
$$

Transformation (2.16) is based on Markov assumptions (2.12) and (2.13). Therefore, the calculation of $S_{i+1}(y)$ is reduced to $S_i(x)$. This means the maximization of $P(W)$ for various W can also be done through dynamic programming.

The calculation requires that the corpus be tagged by POS. A direct way to do this is to use manually tagged corpora. However, the construction cost of manually tagged corpora is very high and the available amount is quite small (only about 1 month of newspaper articles for any language). Also, a manually constructed corpus could lead to consistency problems. Another choice is to use public POS tagging software (called taggers). Some examples are Brill's tagger for English, ICTCLAS software for Chinese, and Chasen for Japanese. In fact, these programs do not have 100% accuracy, thus results include mistakes. However, the best taggers have recently achieved accuracy of more than 97%, some even over 99%, using much more sophisticated language technologies. Thus, such products from the NLP domain are useful for constructing a basic database for the purpose of a user interface.

Such sophisticated methods can also be used for text entry tasks. The HMM presented here is based on only a rigid approximation such as in (2.12) and (2.13). A model that is more flexible regarding which proximity features to consider recently appeared (Gao *et al.*, 2006), while another possibility is to use techniques such as the conditional random fields model (Lafferty *et al.*, 2001). However, a user test is needed to determine whether the use of such sophisticated models for interactive entry systems is justified.

2.5   ADAPTIVE MODELS

So far, the discussion has concerned the creation of a language model from a corpus and its use to design a means of text entry. The language models we have considered were built offline. Another possibility when using decoder software is to construct a language model online, i.e., dynamically adapt the language model to the text that is entered.

In fact, there is another option situated between the nonadaptive method and the dynamic adaptive methods presented so far: offline modification of the initial language model using domain corpora. We then have two techniques to consider when designing the adaptation: offline and online adaptation. The task of offline adaptation is to combine two heterogeneous language models, one obtained from a huge corpus and the other obtained from a fairly large domain-specific corpus. One way to do this is by interpolation, taking the weighted sum of probabilities obtained from different corpora such as in Yuan *et al.* (2005). Technologically, this is similar to techniques for offline construction of language models as explained in Section 2.3 as smoothing. Thus, in this section, we focus on online adaptation.

Evidence of how such adaptive models might work is provided by users' editorial behavior in which the word reuse rate is very high (Tanaka-Ishii *et al.*, 2003). When a

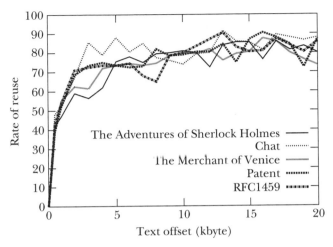

FIGURE

2.4
Reuse rate of vocabulary along with text offset.

Document	Unigrams	Bigrams
The Adventures of Sherlock Holmes	1958	6164
Chat (in English by two people)	1424	5399
The Merchant of Venice	1926	6655
Patent (English)	1235	4426
RFC1459 (protocol manual)	1507	5765
WSJ article	2519	7183

TABLE

2.1
Number of different *n*-grams in various 10,000-word documents.

word is randomly picked from a sequence, we can group the word into two categories: *reused* or *unused*. Unused words are those appearing for the first time in the text and reused words have already appeared. Figure 2.4 shows the reuse rate shift (vertical axis) for various types of text as a function of the text offset (horizontal axis) counted at every 1000-byte point. At the very beginning of the text, the reuse rate was 0%, of course, and then it increased as the text proceeded toward the end. Interestingly, this increase leveled off at about 70 to 80% for all of the text samples. These results suggest that context is provided by 70 to 80% of the vocabulary and the story evolves through the rest. From this observation, we would expect a typical user to reuse text equivalent to about 70 to 80% of the vocabulary only after an offset of several kilobytes.

It is also known that a characteristic of a specific user's document is the small vocabulary size compared with that for the same amount of text taken from a newspaper. For example, Table 2.1 shows how many different unigrams and bigrams were contained in 10,000-word chunks from various types of text. Compared with the values for an article in the *Wall Street Journal* (*WSJ*) at the bottom, we see how limited a text of specific context can be. This does not mean, however, that a user's overall vocabulary is small. Each person has a large general language model, but only part of it is used to communicate a specific context.

This tendency toward a small vocabulary in a user corpus suggests that language modeling by adaptation is efficient, because the smaller the domain size and the vocabulary, the smaller the language model becomes, making estimation easier.

At the same time, bear in mind that the total size of a uniform user document is small. For example, the total number of words in a typical programming textbook is around 80,000. In contrast, newspapers easily exceed the level of a million words per year: the *Wall Street Journal* contains over 5 million words each year. Therefore, the size of the existing corpus and that of a personal document are clearly not commensurate. This means that by employing a user corpus only, we cannot obtain a sufficient amount of data to construct a good language model.

Therefore, we should use two corpora at the same time:

+ A large general corpus for developing the static initial language model. This could be any static language model previously presented.

+ A document of specific context to adapt the initial language model dynamically.

Therefore, in the following sections, two online adaptive language models are introduced. With such models, each time a user selects a candidate, the language model is updated according to the user's action.

2.5.1   Move to Front

The move-to-front (MTF) model was first proposed in the field of text compression. It has been applied to text entry, especially in commercial systems.

With MTF, the most recent candidate selected by the user for a given input becomes the best candidate. After the user selects the nth best candidate in Step 3 in Section 2.2, it will be proposed as the best candidate when the same code sequence is entered the next time. For example, suppose the user entered "7-5-9," and the word "sky" was proposed as the fifth best candidate. If the user selected "sky," it will be the top candidate the next time the user enters "7-5-9."

This model works well when the degree of ambiguity is limited. When it becomes large, however, the user frequently has to change preferences according to the context. For example, if the entry system uses the entry by word completion method, in which the ambiguity is usually high, the user could write text involving the words "technical" and "technology" and these two words will both appear among the candidates when the user entry is "tech." If the user selects "technology," then the next time the user enters "tech" the system will propose "technology" as the best candidate, even though the user may want to enter "technique." As a result, the user often has to change his preference. To overcome this problem, the model must take the surrounding words into account. The next section describes such a model.

2.5.2 PPM: Prediction by Partial Match

Text prediction follows a process very similar to that of text compression, except that the codes in text compression are binary, rather than for human use. There is a tight relationship between text compression and efficient entry: code sequences that compress well are efficient in text entry. Various studies have been done on dynamic ways to compress text, and one of the methods that provide the best compression rate is PPM (Bell *et al.*, 1990).

PPM was originally proposed to make use of higher order context prediction in arithmetic coding. Broadly put, PPM interpolates the *n*-gram counts in a user corpus with initial statistics, denoted as $P_{init}(w)$. The following formula describes PPM, for some arbitrary k_{max}:

$$P(w_i) = u_{-1}P_{init}(w_i) + u_0 P_{uc}(w_i) + \sum_{k=1}^{k_{max}} u_k P_{uc}(w_i \mid w_{i-k,i-1}). \qquad (2.17)$$

In the original PPM model for text compression, $P_{init}(w)$ was set to a unique value ($1/N$, where N is the total number of words to be coded). When applied to text entry, in which there are both a large corpus and a small user corpus, $P_{init}(w)$ can be regarded as the estimation obtained from the large initial corpus, while $P_{uc}(w)$ is obtained from the user corpus (Tanaka-Ishii, 2006). According to PPM, with N_{uc} being the total occurrence of words in the user corpus seen so far, and $C(ws)$ being the occurrence of the word ws in the user corpus seen so far, P_{uc} is calculated as

$$P_{uc}(w_i) = \frac{C(w_i)}{N_{uc}}, \qquad (2.18)$$

$$P_{uc}(w_i \mid w_{i-k,i-1}) = \frac{C(w_{i-k,i})}{C(w_{i-k,i-1})}. \qquad (2.19)$$

Finally, u_k is a weighting probability that is multiplied with $P_{uc}(w_i | w_{i-k,i-1})$; the results of this multiplication are then added to obtain the final $P(w_i)$. In PPM, u_k is defined using the *escape probability* e_i:

$$u_k = (1 - e_k) \prod_{i=k+1}^{k_{max}} e_i, \quad -1 \le k < k_{max}$$

$$u_{k_{max}} = 1 - e_{k_{max}}.$$

In this formula, the weight of each successively lower order is reduced by the escape probability. The escape probability is defined depending on the user corpus seen so far. One of the simplest definitions of escape probability is

$$e_k = \frac{1}{C(w_{i-k,i-1}) + 1}. \tag{2.20}$$

This method is called PPMA. There are other sophisticated ways to define escape probabilities, such as PPMB, PPMC, PPMX, and PPMZ. For more information on these methods see Bell *et al.* (1990).

Intuitively, higher order *n*-grams are incorporated into the language model if it exists; if it does not exist, statistics are obtained by lower order *n*-grams. For example, if "the clear blue sky" appears frequently, then the entry of "7-5-9" will be considered to have a high probability of "sky" if the previously entered text was "the clear blue." If no such statistics are available, statistics from within the initial language are used. PPM is similar to the smoothing techniques explained at the end of Section 2.3, except that it is a dynamic method.

The effect of adaptation is shown by a small example. Figure 2.5 shows the relation between the quantity of learning data (horizontal axis, in number of words) and the number of keystrokes per word (vertical axis) (Tanaka-Ishii, 2007). Two of the lines show the results for Phone and TMK4 from Table 5.2 in Chap. 5. Here, the entry method of one-key with disambiguation with completion was used. The horizontal line slightly above 5.5 keystrokes per word indicates the baseline, which is the average number of keystrokes needed to process a single word with a full keyboard (including spaces).

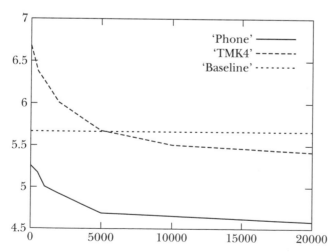

FIGURE   Adaptation by PPM. *WSJ* unigram model adapted using PPMA.

2.5

The number of keystrokes is the sum of the keystrokes per word required for the input and selection operations (KSPW of Chap. 5, Section 5.2). The keystrokes for selection were counted as n when choosing the nth candidate. In predicting words, there are multiple points at which the target word can be chosen. For example, if the word "technology" appears as the second best choice after the user has typed in "8-3" on a phone keypad, the user can either select the target at this point or type in another "2", indicating "c", and increase the target's rank. The automatic routine chooses the target only after it has appeared as the best candidate; otherwise, the routine continues to accept new inputs for the word. When the full length of the word has been entered, the target word with the highest current ranking is chosen.

The data used for the experimental evaluations described here were a unigram model obtained from the *Wall Street Journal* (30 Mega bytes), which was used as the initial language model, and computer magazine articles, which were used as the user documents.

When there were no learning data, entry with four buttons (TMK4) required far more keystrokes than the baseline value. After only 5000 words were learned, however, the number of keystrokes fell below the baseline. This tendency was even more stressed for user documents written with a more limited vocabulary.

The adaptive model shown here can be considered an adaptive version of the n-gram models explained in Section 2.3. The HMM can also be extended to make it adaptive, because the basis of the HMM is also an n-gram model. However, our group's previous work (Tanaka-Ishii *et al.*, 2001), in which we integrated PPM with HMM, showed that n-gram adaptation at the latent POS level does not work very well, no matter which adaptive model is used. This can be understood from the fact that a POS chain is less variant with respect to different users.

Overall, though, MTF and PPM are techniques with which we may be able to construct better text entry software.

2.6   CONCLUDING REMARKS

This chapter has briefly described the language models used in current entry systems. The huge amounts of language data now available have provided an important tool that can be used to raise the efficiency of entry systems.

Recent entry methods can be summarized as character-based nonpredictive methods or as word/phrase-based predictive methods with/without completion using nonadaptive/adaptive methods. All of these can be modeled by Shannon's noisy channel model, and we have considered the most basic and important language models for designing them. If a nonpredictive entry method is to be designed, the language models presented in this chapter provide methods to estimate character probabilities to be considered as well as other human factors. If a predictive entry method is designed, methods to construct the initial language model and whether to incorporate adaptation should be defined. As for the initial model, if only word-based prediction is required, then an *n*-gram model in bigram or trigram will usually suffice. If phrase-based prediction is required, then at least an HMM should be implemented. When adaptation is incorporated, there are two possibilities: offline adaptation and online adaptation. Most of these methods are already used for one language or another, except for phrase-based entry with completion. The main problem holding back phrase-based entry with completion is how to estimate the user's intention so as to limit the number of candidates.

An important area for future studies will be the typing model $P(C' \mid W)$. Though small, some studies on user mistakes are leading to practical applications. For example, JustSystems, Inc. (http://www.justsystems.co.jp/), released Japanese-entry software that dynamically acquires mistyped words and puts them into a software dictionary. Further extension of such results applied to predictive entry methods will be an interesting area for future work.

REFERENCES

Aoe, J. (1989). An efficient digital search algorithm by using a double-array structure. *IEEE Transactions on Software Engineering, 15*, 1066–1077.

Bell, T., Cleary, J., & Witten, I. H. (1990). *Text compression*. Upper Saddle River, NJ: Prentice Hall.

Charniak, E. (1993). *Statistical language learning*. Cambridge, MA: MIT Press.

Gale, W., & Sampson, G. (1995). Good – Turing frequency estimation without tears. *Journal of Quantitative Linguistics, 2*, 217–237.

Gao, J., Suzuki, H., & Yu, B. (2006). Approximation lasso methods for language modeling. In *Proceedings of the 21st International Conference on Computational Linguistics and 44th Annual Meeting of the Association for Computational Linguistics* (pp.225–232). Morristown, NJ: Association for Computational Linguistics.

Good, I. (1953). The population frequencies of species and the estimation of population parameters. *Biometrika, 40*, 237–264.

Jelinek, F. (1997). *Statistical methods for speech recognition*. Cambridge, MA: MIT Press.

Lafferty, J., MaCallum, A., & Pereira, F. (2001). Conditional random fields: Probabilistic models for segmenting and labeling sequence data. In *International Conference on Machine Learning*. Williams College Massachusetts, 28th June–1st July 2001.

Mandelbrot, B. (1952). An informational theory of the statistical structure of language. In *Symposium on Applications of Communication Theory* (pp.486–500). London: Butterworth.

Manning, C. D., & Schutze, H. (1999). *Foundations of statistical natural language processing*. Cambridge, MA: MIT Press.

Shieber, S., & Baker, E. (2003). Abbreviated text input. In *International Conference on Intelligent User Interfaces* (pp.293–296). Miami, USA, January 12–15th 2003.

Tanaka-Ishii, K. (2007). Predictive text entry techniques using adaptive language models. *Journal of Natural Language Engineering*. In press.

Tanaka-Ishii, K., Hayakawa, D., & Takeichi, M. (2003). Acquiring vocabulary for predictive text entry through dynamic reuse of a small user corpus. In *Proceedings of the 41st Annual Meeting for Association of Computational Linguistics* (pp.407–414). Morristown, NJ: Association for Computational Linguistics.

Tanaka-Ishii, K., Inutsuka, Y., & Takeichi, M. (2001). Personalization of text input systems for mobile phones. In *Proceedings of the Sixth Natural Language Processing Pacific Rim Symposium, November 27–30, 2001. Hitotsubashi Memorial Hall, National Center of Sciences, Tokyo, Japan, 2001* (pp.177–184).

Yuan, W., Gao, J., & Suzuki, H. (2005). An empirical study on language model adaptation using a metric of domain similarity. In *International Joint Conference on Natural Language Processing* (pp.957–968). New York: Springer–Verlag.

Zipf, G. (1949). *Human behavior and the principle of least effort*. Reading, MA: Addison–Wesley.

3 Measures of Text Entry Performance

Jacob O. Wobbrock   University of Washington, Seattle, WA, USA

3.1 INTRODUCTION

When people encounter a new text entry method, the first question they usually ask is, "How fast is it?" Although speed is a key feature of any text entry method, there is much more that can and should be said. Clearly, accuracy is important and is not entirely independent of speed. Even so, there are different kinds of accuracy, such as accuracy *during* input, when errors may be made and corrected, and accuracy *after* input, when the entered text is considered complete. But do speed and accuracy tell us everything? What can we say about how learnable a method is, or how efficient? What measures are applicable to keyboard typing or stylus-based gestures? People are sometimes surprised at how much can be said about the performance of a text entry method. Certainly, we can capture and quantify a great deal more than just speed and accuracy.

This chapter presents numerous empirical measures of text entry performance. These measures are, for the most part, *method-agnostic,* applicable to a variety of text entry methods. Speed is one example of a method-agnostic measure. Other measures presented near the end of the chapter are *method-specific,* inherent to keyboard typing, selector movement, or gestural methods.

Although this chapter does not focus on experimental or methodological issues (see Chap. 4), it is important to note that the meaning of an empirical measure is dependent upon the manner in which the text entry data are captured. For example, entry rates must be regarded differently when one is composing text versus copying it, since the former may involve substantial thinking time and other considerations that are difficult to measure. Therefore, copying text is usually preferred when evaluating text entry methods in laboratory settings (MacKenzie & Soukoreff, 2002a). Even for copying text, however, some studies have required participants to maintain synchronicity with the source text, disallowing incorrect characters (Venolia & Neiberg, 1994; Isokoski & Kaki, 2002; Evreinova *et al.,* 2004; Ingmarsson *et al.,* 2004), while others have disabled backspace and other error correction mechanisms (Matias *et al.*, 1996; MacKenzie & Zhang, 1999). As we might imagine, these rather artificial limitations may adversely affect participants' entry and error rates.

Owing to its naturalness and widespread use, the *unconstrained text entry evaluation paradigm* (Soukoreff & MacKenzie, 2001, 2003; Wobbrock & Myers, 2006d) is the experimental methodology assumed by most measures in this chapter. In these evaluations, a short *presented string* is shown to participants who enter it using the method under investigation. A participant's entered result is called the *transcribed string*. This process is repeated over many trials. During transcription, all printable characters are accepted as legitimate entries, and backspace is used as the sole means of error correction. No error beeps or other intrusions affect the fluid entry of text, and participants are simply told to "proceed quickly and accurately" (Soukoreff & MacKenzie, 2003) in an effort to balance speed and accuracy without unduly favoring one over the other. Log files are written that provide a record of the *input stream,* which is the sequence of actions (i.e., keystrokes, gestures, and so on) taken by participants during transcription. This input stream is then parsed and interpreted according to the measures presented in the rest of this chapter.

3.2   AGGREGATE MEASURES

Aggregate text entry measures refer to those that characterize a method's performance *on the whole.* These are contrasted with character-level measures, explained in Section 3.3. In particular, this section focuses on method-agnostic aggregate measures, mainly dealing with entry rates, error rates, and various measures of efficiency.

3.2.1   Entry Rates

Although characterizing the entry rate of a text entry method is mostly straightforward, a few nuances and alternatives exist that warrant some discussion. This section reviews various speed-related measures and highlights their differences.

Words per Minute (WPM)

Words per minute (WPM) is perhaps the most widely reported empirical measure of text entry performance. Since about 1905, it has been common practice to regard a "word" as 5 characters, including spaces (Yamada, 1980)[1]. Importantly, the WPM measure does not consider the number of keystrokes or gestures made *during* entry,

---

[1] Note that different text entry communities have different definitions of many common terms, including the term "word." For example, speech-based text entry researchers define "words" as actual spoken words, not 5 characters. See Chap. 8 for a discussion of speech-based text entry.

but only the length of the resulting transcribed string and how long it takes to produce it. Thus, the formula for computing WPM is:

$$\text{WPM} = \frac{|T| - 1}{S} \times 60 \times \frac{1}{5}.$$ (3.1)

In Eq. (3.1), T is the final transcribed string entered by the subject, and $|T|$ is the length of this string. As stated, T may contain letters, numbers, punctuation, spaces, and other printable characters, but not backspaces. Thus, T does not capture the text entry *process*, but only the text entry *result*. The S term is seconds, measured from the entry of the first character to the entry of the last, including backspaces. The "60" is seconds per minute and the "1/5" is words per character.

Sometimes researchers prefer to report entry rates in characters per second (CPS). Although this is less common than WPM, the measure is a simple transformation of WPM, since the first ratio in Eq. (3.1) is in CPS.

The "−1" in the numerator deserves special mention and is often neglected by researchers when reporting entry rates. As stated, the S term in Eq. (3.1) is measured from the entry of the first character to the entry of the last. Consider this example from MacKenzie (2002b):

```
the quick brown fox jumps over the lazy dog (43 chars)
^                                             ^
t = 0 sec                                     t = 20 sec
```

It would be incorrect to calculate CPS as 43/20, since timing begins with the entry of the first character. Thus, the proper CPS calculation is $(43 - 1)/20$. Of course, multiplying this ratio by $60 \times 1/5$ gives us WPM.

Adjusted Words per Minute (AdjWPM)

In the unconstrained text entry evaluation paradigm, participants can enter text freely and must therefore strike a balance between speed and accuracy[2]. From Eq. (3.1), it is clear that errors made and then corrected *during* text entry reduce WPM, since it takes time to make and correct errors and WPM considers only the length of the transcribed string. In contrast, errors *remaining* in the transcribed string, so-called *uncorrected errors*, are at odds with speed, since participants can go faster if they leave more errors. A way of penalizing WPM in proportion to the number of uncorrected errors is to compute an adjusted entry rate (Matias *et al.*, 1996; Wobbrock *et al.*, 2006):

$$\text{AdjWPM} = \text{WPM} \times (1 - U)^a.$$ (3.2)

---

[2] To help participants in this regard, experimenters may suggest that participants enter text "as if they were writing an e-mail to a colleague" or other such guideline.

In Eq. (3.2), U is the uncorrected error rate ranging from 0.00 to 1.00, inclusive. The variable a might be called the "penalty exponent" and is usually set to 1.0, but may be increased in order to more severely penalize WPM in light of uncorrected errors. For example, if we have 10% uncorrected errors, our adjusted WPM will be 90% of the raw WPM if $a = 1.0$, but only 81% of the raw WPM if $a = 2.0$. For an example of using AdjWPM in a longitudinal study, see prior work (Wobbrock *et al.*, 2006).

Because of the rather arbitrary nature of AdjWPM, some experimenters (Lewis, 1999) have insisted that participants correct *all* errors during entry, thereby eliminating uncorrected errors and enabling WPM to be a single measure of performance. In these studies, trials that contain uncorrected errors may be discarded and replaced with additional trials. Such trials should, however, be reported separately as a percentage of all trials performed.

Keystrokes per Second (KSPS)

As noted, the calculation of WPM and AdjWPM do not take into account what happens *during* text entry. To do this, it is also useful to view text entry activity as a process of data transfer from the user to the computer. We can then characterize the "data rate." For example, some speech recognition systems may enter long chunks of text very quickly, but also make many errors. These systems often support rapid error correction with a designated phrase such as "scratch that." Users may retry certain phrases many times before the system correctly recognizes them, but WPM will not capture all of this activity. Instead, we can use keystrokes per second (KSPS) according to the following formula:

$$\text{KSPS} = \frac{|IS| - 1}{S}.\tag{3.3}$$

In Eq. (3.3), IS is the input stream, which contains all entered characters, including backspaces. As in Eq. (3.1), the timing for S in seconds is assumed to begin with the entry of the first character and end with the entry of the last. The use of the word "keystrokes" in this measure should not be taken strictly, as the measure is still applicable to nontyping text entry methods[3]. (The term might instead be "bytes per second" (BPS), but in many of today's character sets, characters are no longer single bytes, so this term is not preferred.)

As an example, consider the following input stream in which "<" symbols indicate backspaces and transcribed letters are in bold:

```
tha<e p<quik<ck brwn<<own t<fox  (31 keystrokes)
 ^                          ^
t = 0 sec                   t = 10 sec
```

---

[3] For historical reasons and because of its relationship to the *keystrokes per character* (KSPC) performance measure (see Section 3.2.2), KSPS uses the word "keystrokes" to refer to any token in the input stream, whether it was generated by a literal keystroke or not. Although numerous text entry methods are *not* keystroke-based methods, they still generate an input stream of characters, spaces, and backspaces, and thus KSPS applies just fine.

This input stream results in the transcribed string "the quick brown fox". The proper KSPS calculation for this input stream is $(31 - 1)/10 = 3.0$. Note that this differs from a calculation of CPS: $(19 - 1)/10 = 1.8$.

Using KSPS, researchers can estimate an "empirical upper bound" by assuming that all entered characters are correct. Such a calculation tells us how fast a method might be (in CPS) if its accuracy during entry were improved to 100%. For an example use of KSPS (referred to as BPS), see prior work (Wobbrock *et al.*, 2004).

Gestures per Second (GPS)

If KSPS is the data rate of a method, then gestures per second (GPS) is the "action rate." At first blush, the term "gestures" may seem applicable only to stroke-based text entry, but it should be interpreted more broadly. Here, a "gesture" is an atomic action taken during the text entry process. What constitutes an "atomic action" is dependent upon the method under investigation. For a stroke-based method, it would be any individual unistroke. For a stylus keyboard, it would be a stylus tap. For a physical keyboard, it would be an attempt to strike a key. For a speech recognition system, it would be an utterance. All of these are examples of gestures. Notably, the actions themselves do not have to be text-producing. For example, tapping a sticky SHIFT key on a stylus keyboard may be consider a gesture, even though SHIFT itself does not produce a character. Since different methods will require different gestures, it is important that researchers who use this measure report exactly what they consider a gesture to be.

The GPS measure tells us how fast the user is taking actions. We also therefore introduce the concept of a "nonrecognition," which we define as "any unproductive gesture." This may be an unrecognized unistroke, a stylus tap on "dead space" between virtual keys, a missed physical key, or an unrecognized utterance. We will represent nonrecognitions as "ø". With this understanding, we can define GPS as:

$$\text{GPS} = \frac{|IS_\varnothing| - 1}{S}. \tag{3.4}$$

In Eq. (3.4), $IS_\varnothing$ stands for the input stream *including all actions*. Text entry experiments can capture these actions by adding them to performance logs. For physical gestures like striking a key, video analysis can be used to discover actions, including nonrecognitions (i.e., missed keys).

Consider this example, in which "ø" represents a nonrecognition and "•" represents SHIFT:

```
•Tha<øe p<quiøk<ck brwn<<own t<foxø  (35 gestures)
 ^                               ^
 t = 0 sec                       t = 10 sec
```

The proper GPS calculation is $(35 - 1)/10 = 3.4$. It should now be clear that GPS $\geq$ KSPS $\geq$ CPS for a given text entry trial.

Learning Curves

Another common use of entry rates is to graph WPM over time and model the points according to the power law of learning (Card *et al.*, 1983)[4]. Such models take the following form:

$$\text{WPM} = aX^b. \tag{3.5}$$

In Eq. (3.5), X is the variable "time," usually a session number, and a and b are fitted regression coefficients. The value for a is "initial performance" and the value for b, often below 0.5, determines the steepness of the curve. The result of fitting such curves allows us to estimate performance in future sessions, especially if the goodness of fit (R^2) is high. For additional discussion, see the following examples: MacKenzie and Zhang (1999), Isokoski and MacKenzie (2003), Lyons *et al.* (2004), Wobbrock and Myers (2006a), and Wobbrock *et al.* (2006).

3.2.2   Error Rates

It may come as no surprise that measuring error rates in unconstrained text entry experiments is trickier than measuring entry rates. There are multiple error metrics, but most are concerned with the distinction between errors *during* entry ("corrected errors") and errors *after* entry ("uncorrected errors").

Keystrokes per Character (KSPC)—Performance Measure

One way to quantify errors during text entry is to use the keystrokes per character (KSPC) performance measure (Soukoreff & MacKenzie, 2001)[5]. This measure is a simple ratio of the number of entered characters (including backspaces) to the final number of characters in the transcribed string. The formula for calculating KSPC is:

$$\text{KSPC} = \frac{|IS|}{|T|}. \tag{3.6}$$

---

[4] See Chap. 4, Section 4.4, for experimental issues concerning learning curves and longitudinal studies.

[5] This is not to be confused with the KSPC *characteristic measure* (see Sections 3.2.3 and 5.2), which describes the inherent efficiency of a method as the number of key or button presses required to generate a character. Note that like KSPS, the KSPC performance measure does not require a keystroke-based method. All that is required to use this measure effectively is a text entry method that generates a character-level input stream containing tokens like letters, spaces, and backspaces.

As in Eq. (3.3), IS includes all characters, including backspaces. To use our previous example:

```
tha<e p<quik<ck brwn<<own t<fox (31 keystrokes)
```

The transcribed string is "the quick brown fox", which contains 19 characters. Thus, our KSPC accuracy ratio is $31/19 = 1.63$. Note that lower KSPC is better and 1.0 represents "perfect entry." For an example use of KSPC, readers are referred to prior work (Wobbrock *et al.*, 2003b).

A limitation of the KSPC performance measure is that it makes no distinction between backspaced characters that were initially correct and backspaced characters that were initially incorrect (Soukoreff & MacKenzie, 2004). In the example above, the first "wn" in "brwn" were, in some sense, correct, but erased in order to enter the omitted "o". The "wn" are treated as any other incorrect letters, even though they were entered correctly by the participant. Much more complicated procedures are needed to correctly differentiate corrected-and-wrong and corrected-but-right characters. Such procedures require a *character-level* error analysis of the input stream (see Section 3.3.3).

Gestures per Character (GPC)

An extension of KSPC is gestures per character (GPC). As with GPS, we regard a "gesture" as any atomic action taken during the text entry process, and a "nonrecognition" to be any unproductive gesture. Researchers should report GPS and GPC with clear definitions of what they consider a gesture. The GPC measure gives us an indication of the accuracy during entry *including futile actions*. The formula for GPC is:

$$\text{GPC} = \frac{|IS_{\varnothing}|}{|T|}. \tag{3.7}$$

In Eq. (3.7), $IS_{\varnothing}$ encodes all characters, backspaces, nonrecognitions, and other actions. To use our previous example in which "•" represents SHIFT:

```
•Tha<øe p<quiøk<ck brwn<<own t<foxø (35 gestures)
```

The transcription is "The quick brown fox". Thus, GPC is $35/19 = 1.84$. That is, nearly two gestures (i.e., actions) were required for every character that ended up in the transcribed string. Thus, GPC is also some measure of efficiency, since entry methods that require more actions per character will have a higher GPC, even if the accuracy of participants taking those actions is reasonable. For an example use of GPC, see prior work (Wobbrock *et al.*, 2003b).

Minimum String Distance (MSD)

Thus far, we have considered accuracy during text entry, but what about the accuracy of the resultant transcribed string? For this, we may use the *minimum string distance*

```
MSD(P, T)
 1   D ← new matrix of dimensions |P| + 1, |T| + 1
 2   for i ← 0 to |P| do
 3       D[i, 0] ← i
 4   for j ← 0 to |T| do
 5       D[0, j] ← j
 6   for i ← 1 to |P| do
 7       for j ← 1 to |T| do
 8           D[i, j] ← MIN(D[i − 1, j] + 1,
 9                         D[i, j − 1] + 1,
10                         D[i − 1, j − 1] + P[i − 1] ≠ T[j − 1])
11   return D[|P|, |T|]
```

FIGURE

3.1

Algorithm for computing the minimum string distance. In this case, the ≠ comparison returns integer "1" if **true** and integer "0" if **false**. Adapted from Soukoreff and MacKenzie (2001) and Wobbrock and Myers (2006d).

statistic (Levenshtein, 1965; Wagner & Fischer, 1974; Soukoreff & MacKenzie, 2001). The MSD statistic gives us the "distance" between two strings in terms of the lowest number of error-correction operations required to turn one string into the other. The error-correction operations available to us are *inserting* a character, *deleting* (or *omitting*) a character, and *substituting* a character (Damerau, 1964; Morgan, 1970; Gentner *et al.*, 1984). Consider the following presented (P) and transcribed (T) strings:

```
P: the quick brown fox
T: tha quck browzn fox
```

Manual inspection shows us that we have a substitution of "a" for "e", an omission of "i", and an insertion of "z". So for this example, MSD = 3. However, sometimes the MSD result is not so clear:

```
P: quickly
T: qucehkly
```

What is the MSD in this case? Fortunately, an algorithm exists to compute the MSD for us (Fig. 3.1). As parameters, the algorithm takes the presented and transcribed strings.

Using the MSD algorithm, we discover that "quickly" and "qucehkly" can be equated with no fewer than three operations[6]. We can compute an MSD error rate according to the following equation (Soukoreff & MacKenzie, 2001):

$$\text{MSD error rate} = \frac{\text{MSD}(P, T)}{\text{MAX}\left(|P|, |T|\right)}. \tag{3.8}$$

---

[6] Determining *which* three operations is another matter, requiring a character-level error analysis. See Section 3.3.2.

Correct (C)	All correct characters in the transcribed text.
Incorrect-not-fixed (INF)	All incorrect characters in the transcribed text.
Incorrect-fixed (IF)	All characters backspaced during entry.
Fix (F)	All backspaces.

TABLE   Character classes used in computing corrected, uncorrected, and total error rates.

3.1

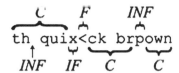

FIGURE   An example phrase showing character classifications according to the four categories

in Table 3.1. Adapted from Soukoreff and MacKenzie (2003). Used with permission.

3.2

As Soukoreff and MacKenzie (2001) explain, the denominator uses the longer of the two strings so that (a) the measure does not exceed 1.00, (b) participants do not receive undue credit for entering less text than contained in the presented string, and (c) an appropriate penalty is incurred if more text is entered than is contained in the presented string. Thus, for "quickly" and "qucehkly", our error rate is $3/8 = 0.375$.

Corrected, Uncorrected, and Total Error Rates

One drawback of using KSPC for accuracy during entry and MSD for accuracy after entry is that they are not easily combined. Recent work has therefore set out to devise a unified error metric. The result was the development of corrected, uncorrected, and total error rates (Soukoreff & MacKenzie, 2003). These three error rates depend on classifying all entered characters into one of four categories (Table 3.1).

Consider the classification example shown in Fig. 3.2. Automating these classifications is straightforward because we do not need to know *which* characters belong to each category, but simply *how many* characters do. Characters belonging to the F and IF classes can be counted by making a backward pass over the input stream. The size of the INF class is equal to $\text{MSD}(P, T)$. The size of the C class equals $\text{MAX}(|P|, |T|) - \text{MSD}(P, T)$.

Similar to the KSPC performance measure, the IF class contains *all* backspaced characters, regardless of their initial correctness. In Fig. 3.2, if the "x" were a "c" it would still belong to the IF class. This is one limitation of these aggregate error metrics that is remedied by character-level error analyses (see Section 3.3.3).

Using these character classes, we can define our three error rates. The corrected error rate supersedes the KSPC performance measure. It is calculated with Eq. (3.9):

$$\text{corrected error rate} = \frac{\text{IF}}{\text{C} + \text{INF} + \text{IF}}. \tag{3.9}$$

The uncorrected error rate supersedes the MSD error rate and is calculated using Eq. (3.10):

$$\text{uncorrected error rate} = \frac{\text{INF}}{\text{C} + \text{INF} + \text{IF}}. \qquad (3.10)$$

The total error rate is merely the sum of Eqs. (3.9) and (3.10):

$$\text{total error rate} = \frac{\text{IF} + \text{INF}}{\text{C} + \text{INF} + \text{IF}}. \qquad (3.11)$$

In practice, it is common for corrected errors to vastly outnumber uncorrected errors. This can make the total error rate rather uninformative, since it will mostly reflect corrected errors. Furthermore, evaluators must be careful to point out that higher corrected errors decrease speed, but higher uncorrected errors increase speed. A rapid method that creates many corrected errors, has efficient error correction, and leaves few uncorrected errors can still be considered a successful method, since it produces accurate text in relatively little time.

Cumulative and Chunk Error Rates

Thus far, we have considered error metrics from the unconstrained text entry evaluation paradigm. However, many user test software programs and typing tutors prior to 2001 neither used the unconstrained paradigm nor analyzed errors in this way. Instead, many of these programs (Matias *et al.,* 1996) disallowed error correction all together and simply treated an error as any character out of sync with the presented text. This gave rise to what has been called the *cumulative error rate.* Consider again our example:

```
P: the quick brown fox
T: tha quck browzn fox
     x    xxxxxxxx
```

In this case, 19 characters were presented, and of those entered, 9 disagree in a pairwise comparison. Thus, the cumulative error rate is $9/19 = 47.4\%$.

Clearly, however, the second block of errors—the eight-error "chunk"—was precipitated by the omitted "i" in "quck". Thus, Matias *et al.* (1996) defined the *chunk error rate* to account for this by treating error chunks as single errors, thus permitting a more realistic automated analysis. The chunk error rate for the above example would be $2/19 = 10.5\%$. However, we can see a drawback of the chunk error rate, since a third error has been engulfed by the same chunk: the inserted "z" in "browzn" deserves to be counted as a separate error, but the chunk error rate would fail to do so. At this point, we can appreciate the development of the previous error rates designed to accommodate the unconstrained text entry evaluation paradigm.

3.2.3   Efficiency Measures

Various measures also exist that describe a method's efficiency. The first of these presented in this section is a characteristic (or "model") measure. The others are empirical measures based on text entry experiments.

Keystrokes per Character (KSPC)—Characteristic Measure

The KSPC *characteristic measure* (MacKenzie, 2002c) quantifies how many key presses are required to generate a single character in a text entry method. This is not the same as the KSPC performance measure (see Section 3.2.2), which is a ratio of entered characters to transcribed characters (Soukoreff & MacKenzie, 2001). As before, the term "keystrokes" should be interpreted broadly. For example, a hypothetical stroke-based stylus method that requires two distinct unistrokes to generate each character would have a characteristic KSPC of 2.0.

MacKenzie (2002b) provides numerous examples to illustrate the calculation of the KSPC characteristic measure. Entering lowercase letters on a standard Qwerty keyboard has a KSPC of 1.0000, since each key corresponds to a single letter. The multitap method used on most mobile phones uses only eight keys for letters (keys 2–9) and a ninth key (often the 0 key) for SPACE. Its KSPC is 2.0342. The disambiguating phone keypad technique *T9* (www.tegic.com) resolves phone key sequences into their most likely words without requiring multiple presses of the same key. Its KSPC is 1.0072. Word prediction and completion techniques have KSPCs under 1.0000 since multiple letters may be entered in single actions (e.g., tapping a candidate word with a stylus).

How are these figures for KSPC calculated? The answer depends on the type of method being considered, but all calculations require a *language model*. For our purposes, a language model contains single letters, letter pairs, or entire words along with a count of how many times those entities were observed in a corpus of text (Table 3.2).

When the entry of letters is independent of previously entered letters, the "letter model" will do. For each letter in the model, we append the number of keystrokes required to generate that letter in the text entry method being considered. The formula for the KSPC characteristic measure is:

$$\mathrm{KSPC} = \frac{\sum_{c \in C} (K_c \times F_c)}{\sum_{c \in C} F_c}. \tag{3.12}$$

In Eq. (3.12), c is a single character in the letter model C, K_c is the number of keystrokes required to enter c, and F_c is the frequency count for c.

When the entry of a letter depends on the previously entered letter, we must use the letter-pair model. (Letter pairs are also sometimes called letter digraphs or letter

Letter model	Letter-pair model	Word model
_ 90563946	e_ 18403847	the 6187925
a 32942557	_t 14939007	of 2941789
b 6444746	th 12254702	and 2682874
c 12583372	he 11042724	to 2560344
d 16356048	s_ 10860471	a 2150880

TABLE

3.2

Examples of three language models used to calculate KSPC. Underscores ("_") represent SPACE. Frequency counts are from the British National Corpus. Adapted from MacKenzie (2002c).

digrams.) Selection keyboards that allow a user to move a selector over an on-screen depiction of keys with successive presses of directional keys require the letter-pair model, since the number of key presses required for each letter depends on the letter from which we start (i.e., the previous letter). In this case, Eq. (3.12) still applies, but c is now a letter-pair and C contains all $27 \times 27 = 729$ letter-pairs in the model.

When the result of a key press depends on word-level context, the word model must be used to calculate KSPC. To each word and frequency count in the model (Table 3.2), we append the number of keystrokes required to generate that word, including a trailing space. The KSPC calculation is then:

$$
\text{KSPC} = \frac{\sum\limits_{w \in W} (K_w \times F_w)}{\sum\limits_{w \in W} (C_w \times F_w)}.
\tag{3.13}
$$

In Equation (3.13), w is a word in the word model W, K_w is the number of keystrokes required to enter w, F_w is the frequency count for w, and C_w is the number of characters in w. Both K_w and C_w assume the presence of a trailing space after the word.

The KSPC characteristic measure is one model-based way of quantifying the efficiency of a text entry method. The following sections describe other measures of text entry efficiency based on text entry experiments.

Correction Efficiency

The efficiency of error correction can be captured with the *correction efficiency* metric (Soukoreff & MacKenzie, 2003). This metric is defined using the character classes from Section 3.2.2. Correction efficiency is defined as:

$$
\text{correction efficiency} = \frac{\text{IF}}{\text{F}}.
\tag{3.14}
$$

As Eq. (3.14) shows, the correction efficiency metric is the ratio of incorrect-fixed characters to the fix keystrokes that correct them. For basic keyboard typing, this metric will be 1.00, since characters can be created and erased in single key presses. However, other methods may allow multiple characters to be erased with a single fix, such as the Fisch in-stroke word completion technique (Wobbrock & Myers, 2006b), which allows word suffixes to be erased with a special backspace stroke. As a second example, consider speech recognition systems, which often allow multiple words to be erased with a single command like "scratch that," which could be considered a single fix "keystroke."

Participant Conscientiousness

Although it is not an efficiency metric per se, *participant conscientiousness* is related to correction efficiency (Soukoreff & MacKenzie, 2003). The metric compares the number of errors corrected to the total number of errors made, indicating how meticulous participants were in correcting errors as they entered text. The formula for participant conscientiousness is:

$$\text{participant conscientiousness} = \frac{IF}{IF + INF}. \tag{3.15}$$

Utilized and Wasted Bandwidth

The KSPS data rate (see Section 3.2.1) viewed text entry as the process of data transfer from the user to the computer. Along with the KSPS data rate, we can characterize the *utilized bandwidth* of a method (Soukoreff & MacKenzie, 2003)—the proportion of transmitted keystrokes that contribute to the correct aspects of the transcribed string:

$$\text{utilized bandwidth} = \frac{C}{C + INF + IF + F}. \tag{3.16}$$

Accordingly, the *wasted bandwidth* is defined as its complement:

$$\text{wasted bandwidth} = \frac{INF + IF + F}{C + INF + IF + F}. \tag{3.17}$$

Cost per Correction (CPC)

To more finely characterize error correction, we can use the *cost per correction* metric (Gong & Tarasewich, 2006). This metric was developed to capture the relative cost of error corrections in light of the fact that some errors go unnoticed until after a few additional characters have been entered. Consider these three input streams in which

correction sequences have been grouped in parentheses, spaces have been added for
clarity, and erroneous letters have been made bold:

```
(pui<<<) quick
(p<) q (r<r<) uick
(p<) q (v<) u (j<) ick
```

Gong and Tarasewich (2006) term the above sequences in parenthesis *corrections*. A
single correction[7] consists of consecutive chunks of backspaced letters and the backspaces that remove them. In the first sequence, one error, the "p", inspires the removal
of the following "ui", resulting in a single correction block of six keystrokes. In the second sequence, the "p" is an initial error immediately corrected, but two attempts at "u"
result in "r"; this sequence therefore has two correction blocks. The third sequence
contains three separate correction blocks separated by transcribed characters.

   Using the notion of a "correction" and the keystroke classes defined previously
(see Section 3.2.2), cost per correction (CPC) is defined as:

$$CPC = \frac{IF + F}{corrections}.$$ (3.18)

Applying Eq. (3.18)[8] to the first sequence results in a CPC of $(3 + 3)/1 = 6$. For the second sequence, we have $(3 + 3)/2 = 3$. For the third sequence, we have $(3 + 3)/3 = 2$.
These results correspond to intuition, which suggests that the "damage done" by the first
sequence's error is greater than that of the second or third sequence.

3.3   CHARACTER-LEVEL MEASURES

Thus far, we have considered measures that produce results for an entire input
stream or transcribed string. Importantly, many of our measures have utilized only
counts of letters (e.g., number of backspaced letters) without regard to *what those letters
are*. For example, the IF character class may contain numerous already-correct characters that have been either mistakenly or purposefully erased (Soukoreff & MacKenzie,
2004). For finer grained analyses that differentiate among individual characters, we
must use *character-level analyses*. Such analyses are generally more complicated than

---

[7] Although Gong and Tarasewich (2006) use the term "correction," I find this term easily confused
    with a single backspace. Instead, I prefer the term "correction sequence" or "correction block."

[8] Gong and Tarasewich (2006) include a third term in the numerator that represents "control key-
    strokes" used to produce any letters in correction blocks. I omit this term because the example
    sequences are method-agnostic and devoid of any method-specific control keys (e.g., NEXT in
    Multitap).

aggregate analyses, particularly in the case of errors. This section gives an overview of method-agnostic character-level measures.

3.3.1 Intra- and Intercharacter Time

The character-level measure somewhat analogous to entry rate (see Section 3.2.1) is *intracharacter time,* or the time to make a single character. Exactly how this value is measured will depend on the type of method under investigation, but most text entry methods support some notion of this measure. In a unistroke method, for example, the intracharacter time is the time from *pen down* to *pen up.* This measure has been used to compare unistroke character speeds in Graffiti and EdgeWrite (Wobbrock *et al.,* 2003b). For a continuous-stroking method like Quikwriting (Perlin, 1998), the intracharacter time is from when the stylus exits and returns to the center "hub" area. In a typing-based method, we could measure times from *key down* to *key up,* although as others have pointed out (Rumelhart & Norman, 1982), the full time to strike a key must include the time to move to the key before it can be depressed. The use of high-speed video can make it possible to identify the intracharacter times involved in keyboard typing, although this is a labor-intensive process.

The formula for calculating the average intracharacter time from a time-stamped input stream *IS* is

$$\text{intracharacter time} = \frac{\sum_{i=1}^{|IS|}\left(\text{character-end}_i - \text{character-start}_i\right)}{|IS|}. \tag{3.19}$$

In Eq. (3.19), the character-start$_i$ and character-end$_i$ values are time stamps for the ith character in the input stream. The first character in *IS* is at index $i = 1$.

Accordingly, we can also define the *intercharacter time,* which tells us how long participants delay between the end of one character and the beginning of the next. For example, world-champion typists, who can type up to 200 WPM, have average interkeystroke intervals of about 60 ms, which is close to the neural transmission time between the brain and fingers (Rumelhart & Norman, 1982). The intercharacter time can also be useful in spotting learning or recall difficulties in gestural alphabets, since novices may pause at length when trying to remember how to make certain characters (Wobbrock *et al.,* 2005a).

The formula for the average intercharacter time is

$$\text{intercharacter time} = \frac{\sum_{i=2}^{|IS|}\left(\text{character-start}_i - \text{character-end}_{i-1}\right)}{|IS| - 1}. \tag{3.20}$$

Note that Eq. (3.20) requires that we have at least two input stream characters.

ALIGN (*P*, *T*, *D*, *x*, *y*, *P'*, *T'*, **ref** *alignments*)
1   **if** $x = 0$ **and** $y = 0$ **then**
2   *alignments* $\leftarrow^+$ (*P'*, *T'*) // add a new aligned pair
3   **return**
4   **if** $x > 0$ **and** $y > 0$ **then**
5   **if** $D[x, y] = D[x - 1, y - 1]$ **and** $P[x - 1] = T[y - 1]$ **then**
6   ALIGN(*P*, *T*, *D*, $x - 1, y - 1, P[x - 1] + P', T[y - 1] + T'$)
7   **if** $D[x, y] = D[x - 1, y - 1] + 1$ **then**
8   ALIGN(*P*, *T*, *D*, $x - 1, y - 1, P[x - 1] + P', T[y - 1] + T'$)
9   **if** $x > 0$ **and** $D[x, y] = D[x - 1, y] + 1$ **then**
10   ALIGN(*P*, *T*, *D*, $x - 1, y, P[x - 1] + P'$, "-" + *T'*)
11   **if** $y > 0$ **and** $D[x, y] = D[x, y - 1] + 1$ **then**
12   ALIGN(*P*, *T*, *D*, $x, y - 1$, "-" + *P'*, $T[y - 1] + T'$)

FIGURE

3.3

Algorithm for computing the optimal alignments of *P* and *T*. Adapted from MacKenzie and Soukoreff (2002b) and Wobbrock and Myers (2006d).

3.3.2   Uncorrected Errors in Transcribed Strings

Recall the three MSD error-correction operations: *insertion, omission,* and *substitution* (see Section 3.2.2). Although the MSD algorithm tells us how many of these corrections (and hence, errors) separate two strings, it does not tell us *which* errors exist or for which characters. For that, we need a character-level error analysis for transcribed strings (MacKenzie & Soukoreff, 2002b; Wobbrock & Myers, 2006d). Consider our earlier example:

```
P: quickly
T: qucehkly
```

Previously, we determined that the MSD = 3. What might these three errors be? We could have a substitution of "c" for "i", another of "e" for "c", and an insertion of "h". Or we could have an omission of "i" and insertions of "e" and "h". Might there be other sets of three errors? How can we know?

The answer lies in using the *D* matrix filled in by the MSD algorithm (see Section 3.2.2) to produce pairs of *P* and *T* that reflect the different error corrections that result in the MSD value. These pairs are called the *optimal alignments* of *P* and *T*, and they can be discovered using the algorithm shown in Fig. 3.3.

The algorithm in Fig. 3.3 takes as parameters the presented string *P*, transcribed string *T*, the filled MSD matrix *D* (see Fig. 3.1), integers *x* and *y* (initialized with the lengths of *P* and *T*, respectively), and strings *P'* and *T'*, initially empty. The last parameter is a reference to the set of optimal alignments, which is initially empty but serves as the return value once filled.

Using the ALIGN algorithm, we receive the following optimal alignment pairs of "quickly" and "qucehkly":

```
P₁: qu-ickly
T₁: qucehkly
```

```
P₂: qui-ckly
T₂: qucehkly
P₃: quic-kly
T₃: qucehkly
P₄: quic--kly
T₄: qu-cehkly
```

In the alignment pairs, hyphens in *P* indicate insertions in *T*; hyphens in *T* indicate omissions from *P*; and different letters in corresponding positions indicate substitutions. The alignments show us that there are four sets of three errors that result in $MSD = 3$. Since it is impossible to know which set reflects the user's actual intentions, we can simply weight each error by the number of alignments in which it occurs. For example, two alignments show a substitution of "c" for "i"; we can therefore treat this as a 50% chance that "c" was substituted for "i". Accordingly, we can tally character-level errors for each character in our alphabet. This information can help designers target problematic characters and fix them. A problematic character may be a unistroke gesture that is commonly misrecognized or confused with another, or mini-Qwerty keys that are too close together and often accidentally interchanged.

3.3.3   Corrected Errors in Input Streams

The character-level error analysis in the previous section gives fine-grained results for each letter of the alphabet, but it has a major drawback: it considers only presented and transcribed strings, ignoring the text entry process captured by input streams.

Recent work has attempted to extend the character-level error analysis to the input stream by dealing with *corrected* character-level errors, not just uncorrected errors (Wobbrock & Myers, 2006d). In many text entry studies, the number of corrected errors (i.e., backspaced letters) is much greater than the number of uncorrected errors left in the transcribed string. Therefore, a character-level error analysis of the input stream has access to a great deal more character-level data than analyses of just presented and transcribed strings. The algorithms for automatically detecting and classifying character-level input stream errors are lengthy and complicated, and interested readers are referred to them elsewhere (Wobbrock & Myers, 2006d). The remainder of this section gives examples of corrected character-level errors for illustration.

Corrected-and-Wrong, Corrected-but-Right

We have previously noted that the IF class of backspaced characters is just a count of erroneous letters and therefore may include already-correct letters. An input stream character-level error analysis can separate corrected-and-wrong from corrected-but-right characters. Consider the following example:

```
 P: quickly
IS: pui<<<quickly
```

In this input, the "p" is corrected-and-wrong, but the first "ui" is corrected-but-right. At the character level, the "p" is classified as a corrected substitution for "q", and the "ui" is corrected-but-right.

Separating corrected-and-wrong from corrected-but-right requires the determination of the target letter in P that the participant is entering. This is a complicated issue that involves many ambiguities. However, in the majority of cases, we can use some fairly reliable assumptions to simplify the challenges involved. For more information in this regard, readers are referred elsewhere (Wobbrock & Myers, 2006d).

Corrected Substitutions and Confusion Matrices

As we saw in the previous example, corrected substitutions occur whenever a character that does not match the target character is initially entered but later erased. Consider this example:

```
P: quickly
IS: qv<w<vickly
```

This input shows trouble entering the "u" in "quickly". The participant first entered a "v", then erased it only to enter a "w", and then erased *that* only to enter a "v" again. Presumably the participant gave up, choosing to leave the final "v" and move on. Here, the first "v" and the "w" are corrected substitutions, while the last "v" is an uncorrected substitution.

Both uncorrected and corrected substitutions can be graphed in a *confusion matrix* (Grudin, 1984; MacKenzie & Soukoreff, 2002b; Wobbrock & Myers, 2006d). In a confusion matrix, one axis holds target characters, another axis holds produced characters, and a third axis holds the count of such entries. Figure 3.4 shows an example from a real text entry study (Wobbrock *et al.*, 2003a):

Corrected Insertions

Sometimes characters are initially inserted but then removed. In such cases, we have corrected insertions:

```
P: quickly
IS: qxu<<uickly
```

In this example, it seems likely that the "x" was inserted before the "u", and then noticed and corrected. The "x" is therefore a corrected insertion, and the first "u" is corrected-but-right.

Corrected Omissions

A character that is initially omitted but later entered is a corrected omission. Consider:

```
P: quickly
IS: qic<<uickly
```

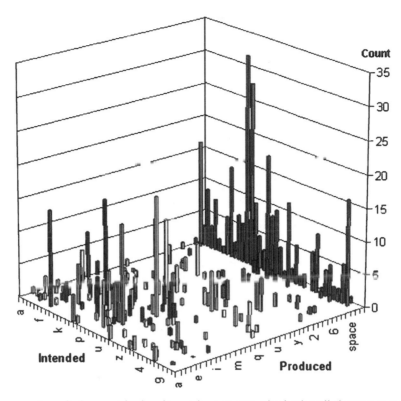

FIGURE

3.4

A confusion matrix showing various counts. The back wall shows nonrecognitions that occurred for different attempted characters. Adapted from Wobbrock and Myers (2006d). Used with permission.

Here, it seems that the "u" was initially omitted, but later replaced after backspacing the "ic". Thus, "u" is a corrected omission, and the "ic" are corrected-but-right.

Although these corrected character-level errors seem straightforward, numerous nuances and tricky cases exist. Interested readers are referred to the fuller discussion available elsewhere (Wobbrock & Myers, 2006d).

3.4   MEASUREMENTS FROM LOG FILES

This chapter has thus far been primarily concerned with text entry experiments in which participants transcribe a presented string. Such laboratory studies are extremely useful for eliciting results in controlled settings. But what about real-world use? How can we assess a text entry method as it is used in the field? What if a particular method requires substantial learning beyond that which is possible or desirable in a single session or even multisession study? When faced with these questions, some text entry researchers have used extensive log file analysis.

Real-world text entry logs are messy. They may contain thousands or even millions of character entries, thoughtful pauses, long delays, and sudden bursts of activity and numerous nonprintable character codes (e.g., cursor arrow keys). Accordingly, the types of measurements available to researchers from real-world log files usually involve comparisons of counts or ratios.

One extended analysis logged all desktop keystrokes for four PC users over a period of 2 months (MacKenzie & Soukoreff, 2002a). The log file analysis counted each type of keystroke and reported relative percentages for each key. Interesting findings included the affirmation that SPACE is indeed the most common key (11.29%), that BACKSPACE is second most common (7.10%), and SHIFT, DOWN ARROW, and DELETE figure prominently in the results.

Another log file study of extended use focused on using a trackball as a writing device and keyboard replacement (Wobbrock & Myers, 2006c). As part of a trackball text entry method called *Trackball EdgeWrite,* users can complete entire words with simple extensions to their trackball unistrokes. However, the positions of the word completions take time to learn. Thus, extended logging of one participant with a spinal cord injury over 11 weeks was used to capture real-world learning. The results showed that 43.9% of the participant's text was entered using word completion and that undone completions accounted for only 7.7% of all completions performed, suggesting reasonable accuracy.

Of course, many more measures are possible from the analysis of real-world text entry logs. Which measures are most important will depend on the methods under investigation and the questions being asked by researchers or developers. Of course, permission should be obtained from participants before logging their text!

3.5   METHOD-SPECIFIC MEASURES

This chapter has been devoted mainly to method-agnostic measures so as to remain relevant to as many text entry methods as possible. However, some useful measures are specific to certain types of text entry methods. Those measures are covered briefly in this section.

3.5.1   Keyboard Typing

Typing on a physical keyboard has been studied extensively (Rumelhart & Norman, 1982; Grudin, 1984). Although substitutions, insertions, and omissions characterize a large percentage of typing errors (Gentner *et al.*, 1984), other errors also appear frequently in typing. For example, a *transposition error* occurs when adjacent characters are swapped:

```
P: special
T: speical
```

In the example above, the "ci" in "special" have been swapped as "ic", constituting a transposition error. In one study, researchers observed about one transposition error for every 1800 typed characters (Rumelhart & Norman, 1982). Reportedly, a large percentage of transposition errors, about 76%, occur across hands.

Another typing error is a *doubling error,* which occurs when a word that contains a double letter has the wrong letter doubled. An example is:

```
P: school
T: scholl
```

Alternation errors are similar to doubling errors but with an alternating sequence of characters. For example·

```
P: these
T: thses
```

A *homologous error* occurs when the wrong hand is used with the otherwise correct finger and key position. This type of error is thought to be more common in novice typists than in expert typists.

A *capture error* occurs "when one intends to type one sequence, but gets 'captured' by another that has a similar beginning" (Norman, 1981; Rumelhart & Norman, 1982). Capture errors occur at the word level, as in the following examples from Rumelhart and Norman (1982):

```
P: efficiency
T: efficient
P: incredibly
T: incredible
P: normal
T: norman
```

Another word-level error is a *phonetic swap,* such as in the following examples:

```
P: their
T: there
P: your
T: you're
```

These are high-level errors that are unlikely to occur in short transcription typing, but may occur when participants are composing text or transcribing long documents. Most studies that analyze these types of errors simply report the number or rate of occurrences and give salient examples.

3.5.2   Selection-Based Methods

Selection-based methods are those that show on-screen options, such as letters in a virtual keyboard, and allow users to select from among them. Selections may be performed *directly*, such as when tapping with a stylus or clicking with a mouse, or *indirectly*, such as when moving a selector with directional arrow keys and entering the highlighted letter by pressing a separate select button.

Deviation in Direct Selection

For *direct* selection-based methods, we can analyze the distribution of selection points relative to target centers and target sizes. Then we can compare deviations. A deviation value of 0% means that the selection points each hit their targets at the ideal locations (e.g., the very centers of virtual keyboard keys). A value of 100% means that the selection points were at their full allowable range (e.g., the borders of virtual keyboard keys):

$$\text{deviation} = \frac{\sum_{t \in T} \sum_{i=1}^{|P_t|} \frac{\sqrt{(x_i - x_t)^2 + (y_i - y_t)^2}}{S_t}}{\sum_{t \in T} |P_t|}. \tag{3.21}$$

In Eq. (3.21), t is a target in the set of all targets T and P_t is the set of selection points (x_i, y_i) intended for target t, which has its center at (x_t, y_t). The S_t term indicates the radius of target t, which for simplicity is abstracted as a circle. The range of Eq. (3.21) is 0% to 100%, assuming all selection points fall within their intended targets. If some selection points fall outside their intended targets, the upper end of the range is unbounded. Participants who are selecting targets with 90% deviation are much closer to missing than participants who are selecting at 45% deviation. An important aspect of this formula is that it is target-relative and therefore capable of comparing results obtained from different targets.

Selector Movement for Indirect Selections

Measures that can be reported for *indirect* selection-based methods are concerned with the amount and manner of selector movement. An example of an indirect selection-based method is the three-key date stamp method (MacKenzie, 2002a; Wobbrock *et al.*, 2006), in which one key moves a selector left, another moves it right, and a third selects the current letter (Fig. 3.5).

A study of three-key text entry methods found that *typamatic keystrokes*, which are those produced by automatic key repeat when a key is held down, comprise a large percentage of keystroke behavior (MacKenzie, 2002a). In one three-key method,

FIGURE

3.5

A three-key indirect selection-based method. The selector, which can be moved left and right, is currently over the letter "e". Image adapted from Wobbrock *et al.* (2006). Used with permission.

typamatic events comprised 77% of the observed keystrokes. In another, they comprised 42%. The selector movement was also analyzed for *movement efficiency,* since participants often overshot their intended letter. In one three-key method, participants moved the selector 13.7% more than optimal; in another, they moved it 27.7% more than necessary.

Another study examined two indirect selection-based methods used for joystick text entry on game consoles (Wobbrock *et al.*, 2004). The first was a selection keyboard. With this method, the joystick moves a selector up, down, left, and right over the keys of a virtual keyboard, and a joystick button selects the highlighted letter. Novice participants were found to move the selector about 47.6% more than necessary, in part because the keyboard employed wrap-around in both dimensions, but participants rarely used this feature. A second method was the classic in-place date stamp method familiar from high-score screens in arcade games. With this method, participants "rolled" the stamp about 21.4% more than necessary.

3.5.3 Stroke- or Gesture-Based Methods

A key trade-off when moving from selection-based methods to stroke- or gesture-based methods is in moving from *recognition* to *recall.* That is, with selection-based methods, users can recognize what actions to take based on their view of what selections are available. With strokes or gestures, however, users must remember when, how, and what actions to perform. Thus, some of the method-specific measures for gesture- based methods are often concerned with how usable, guessable, and memorable the gestures are.

Immediate Usability, Inherent Accuracy, and Memorability

MacKenzie and Zhang (1997) studied the *immediate usability* of Graffiti in four parts. First, they compared the shapes of Graffiti letters to Roman letters, finding 80.8% of them to be similar[9]. They called this value Graffiti's *inherent accuracy.* Second, they

---

[9] This value is not weighted by letter frequency. With letter-frequency weighting, this value is 79.2%.

exposed participants for 1 minute to a Graffiti character chart, after which participants entered each Graffiti letter five times without the chart or concern for speed. In this task, participants were 81.8% accurate. Third, they allowed participants 5 minutes of freeform practice with Graffiti, retesting them afterward as before. Accuracy increased to 95.8%. A fourth and final assessment came 1 week later when participants were brought back for a final test without additional exposure. This measure can be said to be Graffiti's *memorability* and remained at an impressive 95.8%.

Guessability

Wobbrock *et al.* (2005b) investigated the *guessability* of EdgeWrite gestures. Whereas the immediate usability procedure gave participants some initial exposure and practice, the guessability assessment did not. Twenty participants were recruited to simply guess how they would make each letter of the alphabet with their index finger on a touchpad, with the constraint that their strokes would pass through any of the four corners of the touchpad square, since this is how EdgeWrite letters are defined. Participants had no prior knowledge or exposure to EdgeWrite whatsoever.

Guessability itself was calculated by comparing participants' guesses to the existing EdgeWrite alphabet, effectively determining how many guesses would have been accommodated by the existing alphabet:

$$G = \frac{\sum_{s \in S} |P_s|}{|P|}.$$

(3.22)

In Eq. (3.22), G is the guessability of a symbol set S (e.g., a stroke alphabet), s is an individual symbol in S (e.g., a unistroke for "a"), P is the set of all proposals (i.e., guesses), and P_s is the set of proposals that were correct for symbol s. Using this formula, the guessability of EdgeWrite was calculated to be 51.0%. The guesses provided by participants were then collected as a *new* EdgeWrite alphabet. After resolving conflicts, this new alphabet accommodated 80.1% of participants' guesses.

3.6   DISCUSSION OF MEASURES

In this chapter, we have discussed a number of text entry measures and studies that have used them. We have reviewed aggregate measures for speed and accuracy, character-level measures, extended log file measures, and method-specific measures. However, not all measures can or should be reported for all evaluations. So when should we use which measures?

At the very least, text entry studies should report entry rate as WPM and accuracy as uncorrected errors. Neither of these essential measures should be reported without the other, since as we noted previously, they exist as trade-offs. Corrected errors are also of interest and should generally be reported, but it is important to differentiate them from uncorrected errors since corrected errors reduce WPM but uncorrected errors often increase it.

Studies of gestural methods or other methods that have clear notions of *gestures* (or *actions*) should consider reporting GPS and GPC. Studies of novices learning gestural methods should consider beginning with an assessment of guessability or immediate usability. These studies may also want to report character-level errors, particularly substitutions, and show confusion matrices in which peaks reveal commonly misrecognized or humanly confused gestures. Any other methods in which the process of making each letter differs substantially may want to report character-level errors.

Longitudinal studies should always report learning curves of WPM over sessions. They should pay particular attention to any crossover points that may occur.

Keystroke-based methods should report both performance KSPC and characteristic KSPC and compare them. They may also want to report intercharacter time, typamatic events, and typing-specific errors. Of course, other nonkeypad methods can report the KSPC performance measure as well.

Some studies will require extended learning and real-world use. In such studies, extended log file analyses will be appropriate, showing counts and ratios for different text entry events over a period of weeks or months.

Certainly there are more measures conceivable than could fit in this chapter. Different measures may be more appropriate for East Asian text entry, for example. Researchers and developers should feel encouraged to invent new measures that are targeted specifically to their method of interest. As with all measures, the important thing is that they are relevant, reproducible, and rigorous. When reported in the literature, they should be well defined and precise enough that readers can reuse the measures in their own work.

3.7   FURTHER READING

An excellent place to start is the line of work by William Soukoreff and I. S. MacKenzie (Soukoreff & MacKenzie, 2001, 2003, 2004). For character-level analyses, see MacKenzie and Soukoreff (2002b) and Wobbrock and Myers (2006d). For examples of extended log-file-based studies, see MacKenzie and Soukoreff (2002a), Magnuson and Hunnicutt (2002), and Wobbrock and Myers (2006c). A study that reports many of the measures described in this chapter for both selection-based and gestural methods is Wobbrock *et al.* (2004).

REFERENCES

Card, S. K., Moran, T. P., & Newell, A. (1983). *The psychology of human–computer interaction.* Hillsdale, NJ: Erlbaum.

Damerau, F. (1964). A technique for computer detection and correction of spelling errors. *Communications of the ACM, 7,* 171–176.

Evreinova, T., Evreinov, G., & Raisamo, R. (2004). Four-key text entry for physically challenged people. *Adjunct Proceedings of the 8th ERCIM Workshop on User Interfaces for All (UI4ALL '04), 28–29 June 2004, Vienna.*

Gentner, D. R., Grudin, J. T., Larochelle, S., Norman, D. A., & Rumelhart, D. E. (1984). A glossary of terms including a classification of typing errors. In W. E. Cooper (Ed.), *Cognitive aspects of skilled typewriting* (pp.39–43). New York: Springer-Verlag.

Gong, J., & Tarasewich, P. (2006). A new error metric for text entry method evaluation. *Proceedings of the ACM Conference on Human Factors in Computing Systems (CHI '06), 22–27 April 2006, Montréal* (pp.471–474). New York: ACM Press.

Grudin, J. T. (1984). Error patterns in skilled and novice transcription typing. In W. E. Cooper (Ed.), *Cognitive aspects of skilled typewriting* (pp.121–143). New York: Springer-Verlag.

Ingmarsson, M., Dinka, D., & Zhai, S. (2004). TNT—a numeric keypad based text input method. *Proceedings of the ACM Conference on Human Factors in Computing Systems (CHI '04), 24–29 April 2004, Vienna* (pp.639–646). New York: ACM Press.

Isokoski, P., & Kaki, M. (2002). Comparison of two touchpad-based methods for numeric entry. *Proceedings of the ACM Conference on Human Factors in Computing Systems (CHI '02), 20–25 April 2002, Minneapolis* (pp.25–32). New York: ACM Press.

Isokoski, P., & MacKenzie, I. S. (2003). Combined model for text entry rate development. *Extended Abstracts of the ACM Conference on Human Factors in Computing Systems (CHI '03), 5–10 April 2003, Ft. Lauderdale, FL* (pp.752–753). New York: ACM Press.

Levenshtein, V. I. (1965). Binary codes capable of correcting deletions, insertions, and reversals. *Doklady Akademii Nauk SSSR 163,* 845–848.

Lewis, J. R. (1999). Input rates and user preference for three small-screen input methods: Standard keyboard, predictive keyboard, and handwriting. *Proceedings of the Human Factors and Ergonomics Society 43rd Annual Meeting, 27 September–1 October 1999, Houston* (pp.425–428). Santa Monica, CA: Human Factors and Ergonomics Society.

Lyons, K., Starner, T., Plaisted, D., Fusia, J., Lyons, A., Drew, A., & Looney, E. W. (2004). Twiddler typing: One-handed chording text entry for mobile phones. *Proceedings of the ACM Conference on Human Factors in Computing Systems (CHI '04), 24–29 April 2004, Vienna* (pp.671–678). New York: ACM Press.

MacKenzie, I. S. (2002a). Mobile text entry using three keys. *Proceedings of the 2nd Nordic Conference on Human–Computer Interaction (NordiCHI '02), 19–23 October 2002, Århus, Denmark* (pp.27–34). New York: ACM Press.

MacKenzie, I. S. (2002b). A note on calculating text entry speed. Unpublished work. Available online at *http://www.yorku.ca/mack/RN-TextEntrySpeed.html*

MacKenzie, I. S. (2002c). KSPC (keystrokes per character) as a characteristic of text entry techniques. *Proceedings of the 4th International Symposium on Human–Computer*

Interaction with Mobile Devices and Services (Mobile HCI02), 18–20 September 2002, Pisa (pp.195–210). Berlin: Springer-Verlag.

MacKenzie, I. S., & Soukoreff, R. W. (2002a). Text entry for mobile computing: Models and methods, theory and practice. *Human–Computer Interaction, 17*, 147–198.

MacKenzie, I. S., & Soukoreff, R. W. (2002b). A character-level error analysis technique for evaluating text entry methods. *Proceedings of the 2nd Nordic Conference on Human–Computer Interaction (NordiCHI '02), 19–23 October 2002, Århus, Denmark* (pp.243–246). New York: ACM Press.

MacKenzie, I. S., & Zhang, S. X. (1997). The immediate usability of Graffiti. *Proceedings of Graphics Interface 1997, 21–23 May 1997, Kelowna, BC* (pp.129–137). Toronto: Canadian Information Processing Society.

MacKenzie, I. S., & Zhang, S. X. (1999). The design and evaluation of a high-performance soft keyboard. *Proceedings of the ACM Conference on Human Factors in Computing Systems (CHI '99), 15–20 May 1999, Pittsburgh* (pp.25–31). New York: ACM Press.

Magnuson, T., & Hunnicutt, S. (2002). Measuring the effectiveness of word prediction: The advantage of long-term use. *Speech, Music and Hearing, 43*, 57–67.

Matias, E., MacKenzie, I. S., & Buxton, W. (1996). One-handed touch-typing on a QWERTY keyboard. *Human–Computer Interaction, 11*, 1–27.

Morgan, H. L. (1970). Spelling correction in systems programs. *Communications of the ACM, 13*, 90–94.

Norman, D. A. (1981). Categorization of action slips. *Psychological Review, 88*, 1–15.

Perlin, K. (1998). Quikwriting: Continuous stylus-based text entry. *Proceedings of the ACM Symposium on User Interface Software and Technology (UIST '98), 1–4 November 1998, San Francisco* (pp.215–216). New York: ACM Press.

Rumelhart, D. E., & Norman, D. A. (1982). Simulating a skilled typist: A study of skilled cognitive–motor performance. *Cognitive Science, 6*, 1–36.

Soukoreff, R. W., & MacKenzie, I. S. (2001). Measuring errors in text entry tasks: An application of the Levenshtein string distance statistic. *Extended Abstracts of the ACM Conference on Human Factors in Computing Systems (CHI '01), 31 March–5 April 2001, Seattle* (pp.319–320). New York: ACM Press.

Soukoreff, R. W., & MacKenzie, I. S. (2003). Metrics for text entry research: An evaluation of MSD and KSPC, and a new unified error metric. *Proceedings of the ACM Conference on Human Factors in Computing Systems (CHI '03), 5–10 April 2003, Ft. Lauderdale, FL* (pp.113–120). New York: ACM Press.

Soukoreff, R. W., & MacKenzie, I. S. (2004). Recent developments in text-entry error rate measurement. *Extended Abstracts of the ACM Conference on Human Factors in Computing Systems (CHI '04), 24–29 April 2004, Vienna* (pp.1425–1428). New York: ACM Press.

Venolia, D., & Neiberg, F. (1994). T-Cube: A fast, self-disclosing pen-based alphabet. *Proceedings of the ACM Conference on Human Factors in Computing Systems (CHI '94), 24–28 April 1994, Boston* (pp.265–270). New York: ACM Press.

Wagner, R. A., & Fischer, M. J. (1974). The string-to-string correction problem. *Journal of the Association for Computing Machinery, 21*, 168–173.

Wobbrock, J. O., Aung, H. H., Myers, B. A., & LoPresti, E. F. (2005a). Integrated text entry from power wheelchairs. *Journal of Behaviour and Information Technology, 24*, 187–203.

Wobbrock, J. O., Aung, H. H., Rothrock, B., & Myers, B. A. (2005b). Maximizing the guessability of symbolic input. *Extended Abstracts of the ACM Conference on Human Factors in Computing Systems (CHI '05), 2–7 April 2005, Portland, OR* (pp.1869–1872). New York: ACM Press.

Wobbrock, J. O., & Myers, B. A. (2006a). Trackball text entry for people with motor impairments. *Proceedings of the ACM Conference on Human Factors in Computing Systems (CHI '06), 22–27 April 2006, Montréal* (pp.479–488). New York: ACM Press.

Wobbrock, J. O., & Myers, B. A. (2006b). In-stroke word completion. *Proceedings of the ACM Symposium on User Interface Software and Technology (UIST '06), 15–18 October 2006, Montreux, Switzerland* (pp.333–336). New York: ACM Press.

Wobbrock, J. O., & Myers, B. A. (2006c). From letters to words: Efficient stroke-based word completion for trackball text entry. *Proceedings of the ACM SIGACCESS Conference on Computers and Accessibility (ASSETS '06), 23–25 October 2006, Portland, OR* (pp.2–9). New York: ACM Press.

Wobbrock, J. O., & Myers, B. A. (2006d). Analyzing the input stream for character-level errors in unconstrained text entry evaluations. *Transactions on Computer–Human Interaction (TOCHI)*, 13(4), 458–489.

Wobbrock, J. O., Myers, B. A., & Aung, H. H. (2004). Writing with a joystick: A comparison of date stamp, selection keyboard, and EdgeWrite. *Proceedings of Graphics Interface 2004, 17–19 May 2004, London, ON* (pp.1–8). Waterloo, ON: Canadian Human–Computer Communications Society.

Wobbrock, J. O., Myers, B. A., & Hudson, S. E. (2003a). Exploring edge-based input techniques for handheld text entry. *Proceedings of the 3rd International Workshop on Smart Appliances and Wearable Computing (IWSAWC '03).* In *23rd International Conference on Distributed Computing Systems Workshops (ICDCSW '03), 19–22 May 2003, Providence, RI* (pp.280–282). Los Alamitos, CA: IEEE Computer Society.

Wobbrock, J. O., Myers, B. A., & Kembel, J. A. (2003b). EdgeWrite: A stylus-based text entry method designed for high accuracy and stability of motion. *Proceedings of the ACM Symposium on User Interface Software and Technology (UIST '03), 2–5 November 2003, Vancouver, BC* (pp.61–70). New York: ACM Press.

Wobbrock, J. O., Myers, B. A., & Rothrock, B. (2006). Few-key text entry revisited: Mnemonic gestures on four keys. *Proceedings of the ACM Conference on Human Factors in Computing Systems (CHI '06), 22–27 April 2006, Montréal* (pp.489–492). New York: ACM Press.

Yamada, H. (1980). A historical study of typewriters and typing methods: From the position of planning Japanese parallels. *Journal of Information Processing, 2*, 175–202.

4 Evaluation of Text Entry Techniques

CHAPTER

I. Scott MacKenzie   York University, Toronto, ON, Canada

4.1   INTRODUCTION

New methods of text entry appear with great frequency these days. This is due in large part to the recent and heightened interest in pen-based computing, mobile computing, and short message service (SMS) messaging on mobile phones. The statistics for SMS messaging are particularly staggering: world volumes are now in excess of 1 billion messages per day (*Economist,* 2004)! In that such quantities of text are entered using the small and limited keypad on mobile phones, it is no wonder that researchers are investigating new techniques for the efficient entry of text.

However, there is an unfortunate reluctance on the part of researchers to engage the user community as a final and essential step in the creative process. Great ideas too often remain inadequately tested or untested. To simply invent a new text entry technique and then declare it is fast, efficient, and easy to learn, without testing such claims with users, falls short of the standards of research expected today.

The focus in this chapter is the evaluation of text entry techniques. Our goal is, first, to build a case for the need for evaluation and, second, to lay out strategies and methodologies to do it. We begin with two examples from the literature in which evaluations were not performed, but where a need was clearly evident.

In reviewing a new and interesting text entry technique in 1988, Potosnak wrote, "no tests (other than analyses comparing the number of wipes to number of keystrokes required on traditional keyboards) have been reported to determine performance or preference effects with this keyboard" (Potosnak, 1988, p. 491). The design referred to is the *Wipe-Activated Keyboard,* patented in 1980 and presented in *IEEE Computer* in 1982 (Montgomery, 1980, 1982). An evaluation was not reported, and this deficiency in the research did not escape the scrutiny of Potosnak. The idea, shown in Fig. 4.1, was for a keyboard with a flat touch-sensitive surface and no moving parts. The design also included a nonstandard letter arrangement to facilitate an

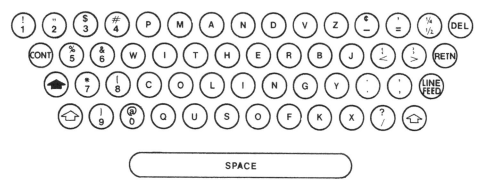

Montgomery Wipe-Activated Keyboard (from Montgomery, 1982).

alternative interaction: wiping. Letters may be entered in the usual way—by touch-tapping keys with one's finger—or with wiping gestures where consecutive letters are neighbors.

The letters were arranged to maximize opportunities for wipe-activated input for the most common words in English, as verified in Fig. 4.1 for THE, OF, AND, TO, IN, IS (one wipe each); THEY, THEIR, THEM (one wipe plus one tap each); and so on. Despite building a working prototype, the inventor acknowledged that the design was "yet to be tested" (Montgomery, 1982, p. 18)[1].

The example above is by no means unique. More recently, within the discipline of human–computer interaction (HCI), *Quikwriting* was developed as a gesture-based text entry technique using a stylus (Perlin, 1998). The idea involves a 3 × 3 grid on which characters are entered with gestures beginning in a central home zone and moving through one or two adjoining zones, returning to the home zone (see Fig. 4.2). The symbols in the top center and bottom center zones invoke different modes. Letters that occur more frequently in English are given the shortest gestures. For example, "i" in Fig. 4.2 is entered by moving in and out of the bottom right zone. Less frequent letters have longer gestures ("k" requires a move into the upper left zone, then across to the upper right zone, and finally back to home).

The inventor wrote, "while we have yet not done systematic user testing, anecdotal experience to date is consistent: Users well practiced in both *Graffiti* and *Quikwriting* consistently find the latter to be about three times faster" (Perlin, 1998, p. 216)[2]. "Three times faster" combined with the "quick" self-reference in Quikwriting leaves

---

[1]   To this author's knowledge, no user test has ever been performed on this keyboard, nor has it appeared in any commercial product.

[2]   Graffiti is the stylus-based single-stroke per symbol text entry method used on Palm's Personal Digital Assistants (www.palm.com).

FIGURE

4.2

Quikwriting input of "quick" (based on Perlin, 1998).

little doubt as to the promise of this text entry technique. Yet no formal or informal empirical results were given. A follow-on, independent evaluation of Quikwriting was performed, however, with walk-up entry rates measured at just 4 words per minute (WPM) (Isokoski & Raisamo, 2004). Entry speed increased to 16 WPM, but only after 5 hours of practice. Considering that human handwriting speeds are 20+ WPM (Bailey, 1996, p. 287), "quick" is not a word that comes to mind for Quikwriting. Empirical tests of Graffiti, on the other hand, report entry speeds in the range of 7–10 WPM initially, with rates rising above 20 WPM with practice (Fleetwood *et al.*, 2002; Koltringer & Grechenig, 2004; MacKenzie *et al.*, 2006). It remains a challenge to reconcile the just-cited empirical results with the anecdotal report in the original publication.

What do you think of Quikwriting or the Wipe-Activated Keyboard? They are interesting ideas, for sure. Will they support fast and accurate text entry? Will they do so with modest practice or do they require prolonged practice? What are the expected entry speeds or error rates? Will users like the techniques or will they find them frustrating? How do they compare to alternative text entry techniques? Are there aspects of the designs that could be modified in some way to improve performance? The questions just posed are the central motivation in this chapter. While analysis through modeling might assist in predicting answers to these questions (Card *et al.*, 1978, 1980; MacKenzie, 2003), the final, incontestable answer lies in the community of people that ultimately employ a technique: users. Waiting for the collective response of the public following deployment of a product is risky, albeit not unheard of

(Cooper, 1999)[3]. A more reliable and safer approach is to engage a subset of the user community as participants in an empirical evaluation of the text entry technique in question. Let us see what this entails.

4.2   COMPARATIVE EVALUATION OF TEXT ENTRY TECHNIQUES

A word has crept into the title of this section that is missing in the chapter's title: "comparative." Indeed, evaluation in the absence of comparison is of limited value. When a new text entry technique is proposed, it is usually offered as an improvement over an existing technique, e.g., a new method for handwritten input or a new keyboard for keyed input. At the very least, comparing a new technique with an established technique with known performance characteristics serves as a check on the methodology. That is, if a similar and accepted result is reported for an established technique, then a differential result for a new technique in the same evaluation is given greater credence than if the latter result were reported alone. A slightly different motivation is simply to establish which of two or more design alternatives is better. In any event, a comparative evaluation is recommended.

The framework for a comparative evaluation is an experiment conforming to established standards and methods in the field of experimental psychology. After all, we are dealing with humans interacting with technology. In a sense, HCI is the beneficiary of this more mature field with a history of refined methods of experimentation involving humans. Answering research questions, such as in the preceding section, using a concocted methodology, customized and tailored as might seem reasonable, falls short of good research. In experimental psychology, it is sometimes stated that research questions must pass the "ROT" test (Martin, 2004). Questions must be repeatable, observable, and testable. "Repeatable" refers to the need to describe the apparatus and procedure with sufficient detail to allow others to repeat the research, to verify or refute results. "Observable" refers to the need to test human responses that are directly measurable, such as the time to enter a phrase of text. "Testable" refers to the need to pose questions about numbers; e.g., is the speed of entry faster for one technique than another? Meeting the testable criterion is more difficult for research questions of a qualitative nature, since users' feelings, opinions, or attitudes are not directly measurable. In this case, the accepted approach is to solicit responses from users via a questionnaire. If the responses use a numeric rating scale, e.g., from 1, strongly agree, to 5, strongly disagree, then the testable criterion is met by analyzing the coded responses.

---

[3] The mockery made of the handwriting recognition on Apple's Newton by cartoonist Garry Trudeau in *Doonesbury* is a specific example (see MacKenzie & Soukoreff, 2002b).

In the following sections, the steps in performing a comparative evaluation of a text entry technique are given.

4.2.1 Preexperimental Testing

The first order of business is to build a working prototype. With a working prototype, the user enters text, with the result appearing for inspection on a display. For research, it is best to keep the design separate from target applications such as e-mail clients or word processors. An example of a handwriting recognition prototype system, created by the author, is shown in Fig. 4.3.

Once a prototype is operational, substantial preexperimental testing is possible—to rid the code of bugs and to refine the design until satisfactory performance is achieved. Since entry speed is the performance variable of greatest interest, it is important to get a rough sense of the technique's potential early on. A good way to do this is to measure the time to enter a phrase of text and to compute entry speed in words per minute. A common phrase for this purpose is

the quick brown fox jumps over the lazy dog

FIGURE
4.3

A working prototype. In this case, text is entered using handwriting recognition with results appearing in a text field in the prototype software.

The phrase contains 43 letters, including spaces, and, notably, each letter of the English alphabet. How fast can this phrase be entered? No need to get fancy at this stage. Timing with a wall clock or wristwatch will suffice. If the phrase is entered in, say, 45 seconds, then the entry speed is $(43/5)/(45/60) = 11.4$ WPM. Dividing the number of characters by 5 yields "words," and dividing the number of seconds by 60 yields "per minute[4]."

Such a cursory evaluation as just described exceeds that reported in the two papers cited at the beginning of this chapter, and, arguably, there is no excuse for this. Even a short paper or poster presentation should give at least preliminary expectations in terms of text entry speeds achievable with simple tests as just described.

As a precaution, we note that the inventor or researcher is so close to the design and interaction requirements that the entry rates achieved by that individual may not reflect those achievable by a broader community of users. Therefore, it is recommended to have arms-length users try the technique. The results may be surprising!

The prototype in Fig. 4.3 is actually software running on a desktop computer. While such mock-ups are relatively simple to implement and convenient to test, the results obtained are limited. Certainly, the data are better than no data at all; but, it is important to remember that the physical affordances of the intended device may be very different (e.g., a mobile phone or PDA). Testing, at some point, should be performed on a device similar to the final product in shape, size, weight, and so on. In the same vein, we, as researchers, need to be aware of the important role of aesthetic qualities in the overall success of products. It is not just entry speed!

4.2.2   The Evaluation Task

Early on in the development and testing of the prototype, focus shifts to the ensuing experimental evaluation. An important consideration is the task: will users create their own text or will they copy text provided to them? The distinction is important. Although text creation is closer to typical usage and, thus, improves the external validity of the experiment, this approach generally is not appropriate for an empirical evaluation. This is explained as follows.

First, we introduce "focus of attention" (FOA). Consider an expert touch-typist using a Qwerty keyboard to copy text from a nearby sheet of paper. This is a text-copy

---

[4]   It has been a convention since about 1905 to standardize the computation of text entry speed in "words per minute," in which a word is defined as five keystrokes (Yamada, 1980, p. 182). This includes letters, spaces, punctuation, and so on. Although some researchers use actual word size (e.g., James & Reischel, 2001), this is inappropriate since it allows entry speed to be inflated by testing with phrases containing predominantly short words. It also hinders comparisons between languages with different mean word sizes.

task. Because the typist is an expert, she attends to only the source text. This is a single FOA task. However, if input is via a stylus and soft keyboard, the typist must also attend to the keyboard because a soft keyboard cannot be operated "eyes free." Therefore, stylus typing in a text-copy task, even for expert users, is a two-FOA task. If the typist is less than expert and corrects errors, she must look at the display to monitor results. This is now a three-FOA task: the typist attends to the display, to the keyboard, and to the source text. Clearly, the feedback channel is overburdened in a three FOA task.

So, why are text-copy tasks preferred over text-creation tasks if the former increase the attention demand? There are several reasons. One is that text creation tasks are likely to include behaviors not required of the interaction technique per se. Examples include pondering ("What should I enter next?") or secondary tasks (e.g., fiddling with system features). The measurement of text entry performance—particularly speed—is compromised if such behaviors are present.

A second difficulty with text-creation tasks is identifying errors—it is difficult to know exactly what was intended if the text is generated by the user. Even if the message content is known a priori, errors in spelling or memory recall may occur, and these metalevel mistakes are often indistinguishable from errors due to the interface itself.

A third difficulty is the loss of control over the distribution of letters and words entered. The task should require the subject to enter a representative number of occurrences of characters or words in the language. However, it is not possible to control for this if the subject is generating the text.

The main advantage of a text-creation task is that it mimics typical usage. The disadvantages just cited, however, are significant enough that most researchers choose a text-copy task, despite the increased FOA. One way to mitigate the effects of increased FOA is to dictate the source text through the audio channel, although other compromising issues arise (Ward *et al.*, 2000).

A carefully designed experiment may capture the strengths of both a text-creation task and a text-copy task. One technique is to present subjects with short, easy-to-memorize phrases of text. Subjects are directed to read and memorize each phrase before entering it. Memorization is enforced by hiding the source text during entry. Entry in this manner benefits from the desirable property of a text-creation task, namely, reduced FOA. As well, the desirable properties of a text-copy task are captured, that is, control over letter and word frequencies and measurement of behaviors limited to the text-entry task. There are numerous examples of this approach in the literature (e.g., Alsio & Goldstein, 2000; MacKenzie *et al.*, 1994; MacKenzie & Zhang, 1999; Rau & Skiena, 1994).

As for the choice of text to enter, a custom set of phrases may be used, for example, as appropriate for non-English users (Majaranta *et al.*, 2003), or a standard set of phrases may be employed. MacKenzie and Soukoreff (2003) developed a phrase set for this purpose. The set contains 500 short phrases of English text. Phrases vary from 16 to 43 characters (mean length 28.6 characters). The letter frequency correlation with an English corpus is high at $r = 0.954$. This phrase set, sometimes with a few modifications, has proven useful, as other researchers have used it in their evaluations (Agarwal & Simpson, 2005; Gong *et al.*, 2005; Hwang *et al.*, 2005; Koltringer & Grechenig, 2004;

Lyons *et al.*, 2004; Read, 2005; Spakov & Miniotas, 2004; Wigdor & Balakrishnan, 2004; Wobbrock *et al.*, 2004).

4.2.3   Data Collection and Display

Assuming the experimental task is the input of phrases of text, the prototype software must be modified to include the phrases, perhaps reading them from a file, and presenting them to users for input. Random selection and presentation are probably the best choice. It is at this stage that the software should include data collection and display. An example created by the author is shown in Fig. 4.4. The top field contains a

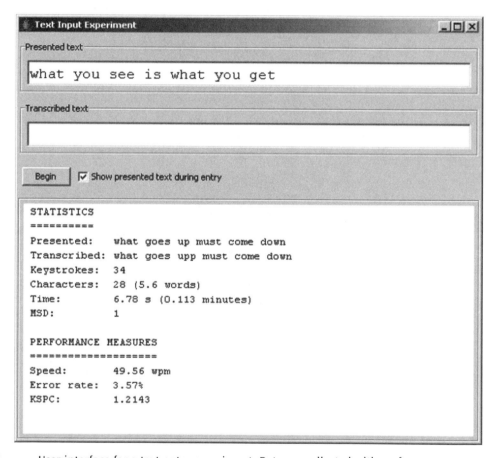

FIGURE   User interface for a text-entry experiment. Data are collected with performance
4.4   statistics displayed following each entered phrase. Note that the statistics and
performance measures are for the previous phrase entered and appear after
ENTER is detected, signaling the end of the phrase.

phrase of text to enter, the "presented text." Below that is the "transcribed text." An optional checkbox toggles between hiding and showing the presented text during entry.

The software for the interface in Fig. 4.4 is not tied to any particular text entry method. Some customization is needed depending on the method's input mechanism and output display. Variations on this approach appear in the form of screen snaps in several published evaluations (e.g., MacKenzie, 2002; MacKenzie *et al.*, 2001; Oniszczak & MacKenzie, 2004; Pavlovych & Stuerzlinger, 2003; Soukoreff & MacKenzie, 2003). A distinguishing feature of the software is the immediate presentation of performance data upon detection of ENTER at the end of each entered phrase.

The performance measures in Fig. 4.4 are for entry speed (words per minute), error rate (%), and keystrokes per character (the number of keystrokes divided by the number of characters produced). These are important summary statistics but others may be as important for different entry methods. Showing these in a pop-up or integrated window after each phrase facilitates demonstration of a text entry method and also helps in an experiment, for example, to maintain the interest and motivation of users.

The data for the statistics and performance measures in Fig. 4.4 were gathered by the experimental software and saved in a file for subsequent analyses. For this purpose, it is useful to save two streams of data. Figure 4.5 shows an excerpt of an "sd1" file, wherein low-level, raw data are written ("sd" is for "summary data"). For each phrase, both the presented and the transcribed text are shown as a time stamp and key code for each keystroke. Of course, this file may be customized as appropriate for the entry technique. In an eye typing experiment, for example, we found it useful also to log time stamps for "read-text events"—shifts in the point of gaze to review the transcribed text field (Majaranta *et al.*, 2003).

We save higher level summary data in an "sd2" file, in which each line has summary statistics on a per-phrase basis, rather than on a per-keystroke basis. In Fig. 4.6, the variables are shown in a header line, with the measurements following in a series of lines, one per phrase entered in a block of testing.

It is also useful to add columns in the data files to identify the participant, the entry technique, the block number, and so on, although this information also may be coded in the file name.

4.3   EXPERIMENT DESIGN

At this point, we have a prototype that adequately implements the text entry technique of interest and perhaps some variations on the technique. The prototype also includes mechanisms to present phrases of text to users, to collect data, and perhaps to display summary results after each phrase of entry. It is time to experimentally evaluate the text entry technique and compare it with design alternatives. In this section we identify the steps for this.

```
what goes up must come down
what goes upp must come down
0       w
130     h
240     a
350     t
510     space
841     g
941     o
1071    e
1241    s
1412    space
1642    u
1872    p
2133    p
2533    space
2744    m
2944    u
3024    s
3154    t
3485    space
3945    d
4086    o
4296    m
4777    backspace
4937    backspace
5067    backspace
5227    c
5337    o
5468    m
5668    e
5828    space
5998    d
6098    o
6309    w
6509    n
6779    enter
#
```

FIGURE
4.5

Example summary data file for one phrase (sd1). The first two lines contain the presented and transcribed text, respectively. The remaining lines contain time stamps (in milliseconds) and key codes. Note the presence of presses of BACKSPACE to correct input. The data are for the phrase in the bottom of Fig. 4.4.

```
keystrokes, characters, time, msd, wpm, er, kspc
26,   26,   5.65,   1,   55.23,   3.85,   1.0
24,   24,   4.68,   0,   61.59,   0.0,    1.0
29,   29,   5.1,    0,   68.26,   0.0,    1.0
30,   30,   5.52,   1,   65.24,   3.33,   1.0
36,   36,   6.42,   0,   67.29,   0.0,    1.0
28,   28,   4.81,   2,   69.9,    6.9,    1.0
34,   28,   6.78,   1,   49.56,   3.57,   1.2143
```

FIGURE

4.6

Example summary data file for one block of phrases (sd2). The first line is a header identifying the summary statistics in subsequent lines. The last line shows the summary statistics for the phrase in Fig. 4.4.

4.3.1   Participants

Users tested in an experiment are called "participants[5]." Most empirical evaluations of text entry techniques include a dozen or so participants, although the exact number to use is debatable. If too few participants are used, large performance differences may occur, but these may not be statistically significant. If too many participants are used, small performance differences of no practical interest may show statistical significance. The best advice, perhaps, is to study the literature and use approximately the same number of participants as found in other research using a similar methodology (Martin, 2006, p. 215).

Ideally, participants are selected randomly from the population of people in the intended community of users. In practice, participants are solicited from the pool of people conveniently available, for example, students at a local university or colleagues at work. Obviously, if the research is aimed as a specific community, such as children or the handicapped, then participants must be solicited accordingly. In some cases, prescreening is necessary if, for example, users with a specific level of expertise or experience with aspects of the interaction are required. This includes having no prior exposure, if such is important in the evaluation. In any event, it is customary to describe the participants by collecting and reporting demographic data in the form of counts, means, or ranges. Examples include age, gender, and prior or current experience using computers or related devices. Additional data may be sought as deemed appropriate, such as handedness, use of corrective lenses, or experience with handwriting recognition or SMS messaging.

---

[5]   Prior to about 1996, the term "subjects" was used. The shift to "participants" reflects a degree of respect and gratitude for the contribution made by those who assist in research by participating as subjects.

4.3.2   Procedure

What will participants do in your experiment? No doubt, they will enter phrases of text. But, how many phrases? Was the text entry technique demonstrated by you, the investigator, beforehand? Did the investigator use any aides in explaining or demonstrating the technique? Were practice phrases allowed before data collection? Were the phrases organized in blocks or sessions with rest breaks between? These questions need to be considered and reported. (Remember the "R" in ROT?)

A particularly important aspect of the procedure is the instructions given to participants. What were participants trying to do? Were they to proceed "as quickly as possible," "as quickly and accurately as possible," or "without making mistakes" or were instructions worded in some other manner? Was it possible to correct errors? Were participants *required* to correct errors or required *not* to correct errors, or was some degree of discretion permitted? There is no single correct answer to these questions, as the instructions given and procedure used depend on the text entry technique and on the objectives in the experiment. Essential, however, is the need to report accurately on the procedure used in the experiment.

One further point on instructions is warranted. Use the same instructions for all participants. Sounds simple enough, but when instructions are given, participants often ask for clarification. It is important to constrain such discussions to ensure all participants proceed similarly. Sometimes instructions are read to participants to enforce consistency. In any event, it is important not to bias some participants by giving them additional information that may cause them to act differently from other participants.

On the potential to bias participants, it also worth commenting on the demeanor of the investigator during testing and while greeting the participants and introducing the research. The investigator should strive to make participants feel comfortable. A nervous manner or an attitude of indifference are sure to affect the way participants take to the task. Be calm, neutral, and encourage participants to feel comfortable.

4.3.3   Experimental Variables

It is important and useful to think about and organize your experiment around two classes of variables: independent variables and dependent variables.

Independent Variables

Independent variables are the conditions tested. They are so named because they are under control of the investigator, not the participant; thus, they are "independent" of the participant. The term "independent variable" is synonymous with "factor." The settings of the variable or factor are called "levels." For example, if three keyboard layouts were compared, say, Qwerty, Alphabetical, and New, the factor is "keyboard layout" and the levels are "Qwerty," "Alphabetical," and "New." Perhaps there is also an interest in the effects of two different sizes of keyboards. In this case, there is an additional factor, "keyboard size," with two levels, "small" and "large." Combining these two factors, the design is referred to as a 3×2 design. This nomenclature signals that there are two factors, with three levels on the first and two levels of the second, six test conditions in all.

Dependent Variables

Dependent variables are the measured behaviors of participants. They are dependent because they "depend on" what the participants do. The most obvious example is text entry speed, measured, for example, in words per minute. Note in the preceding sentence the distinction between the variable ("text entry speed") and the units for the variable (words per minute). For clarity, it is important to distinguish the two.

Make sure the measurement is clear. When did the timing for a phrase begin? When did it end? Did timing begin with the first character or with a START button or some other signal before the first character? Did timing end with the last character or by pressing ENTER after the last character? If timing begins with the first character and ends with the last character, then, arguably, the first character should not count, since timing excludes the time leading up to the entry of the first character. The important point is to clearly describe the measurement of all dependent variables.

The other dependent variable of common interest is "accuracy" or error rate, usually reported as the ratio of incorrect characters to total characters. As it turns out, error rate is tricky to measure, since error-ridden passages often contain a confusing and conflicting collection of insertion errors, deletion errors, substitution errors, transposition errors, and so on. The reader is directed to previous work that adequately describes the measurement and categorization of text entry errors (Gentner *et al.*, 1983; MacKenzie & Soukoreff, 2002a; Matias *et al.*, 1996; Soukoreff & MacKenzie, 2001, 2003, 2004) as well as to Chap. 3 herein.

In addition to coarse measures of speed and accuracy, researchers often devise new dependent measures as appropriate for an entry technique under investigation, as noted earlier for read-text events as a dependent variable in an eye typing experiment (Majaranta *et al.*, 2003). As another example, consider Wigdor and Balakrishnan's (2003) *TiltText*, a technique for mobile phone text entry that uses the orientation of the device to resolve the ambiguity of letters on keys on the mobile phone keypad. In addition to conventional error rate analyses, they defined and used "button error" and "tilt error" as dependent variables. Button errors were the ratio of errors due to pressing the wrong button, and tilt errors were the ratio of errors due to tilting the device in the wrong direction. McQueen, MacKenzie, and Zhang's (1995) *PiePad* is a gesture-based entry method for numeric entry. Gestures were stylus strokes conforming to a clock metaphor: right for 3, down for 6, left for 9, and so on. In addition to analyzing the time to make gestures, they defined and used "preparation time" and "scripting time" as dependent variables. Preparation time was the time between gestures, from stylus up after the previous character to stylus down for the current character. Scripting time was the gesturing time, from stylus down to stylus up.

Devising specialized dependent variables is particularly useful for text entry methods that use word prediction or other language-based acceleration techniques. As users engage acceleration opportunities, they exhibit a variety of behaviors that can be measured. In evaluating a stylus-based predictive system, MacKenzie *et al.* (2006) logged all stylus strokes and taps, but also categorized these by function, as shown in Fig. 4.7. The various stroke categories served as useful dependent variables in examining participants' usage patterns with the available acceleration aides.

Read-text events, button errors, tilt errors, preparation time and scripting time, keystroke savings, and so on are examples of dependent variables devised by researchers to gain insight into performance nuances of an entry technique. As one final comment, if a dependent variable is a count of the occurrence of an observable event, then it is useful to normalize it by converting the count into a ratio, for example, the number of such events *per character of input*. This facilitates comparisons across conditions and potentially across studies. If, for example, we are interested in participants' error-correcting behavior and decide to use presses of the BACKSPACE key as a dependent variable for such, then it is more instructive to analyze and report on "BACKSPACE key presses per character" than the raw counts of presses of the BACKSPACE key.

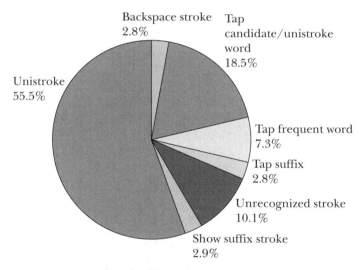

FIGURE

4.7
Seven categories of stylus strokes or taps used as dependent variables in the evaluation of a handwriting recognition system with predictive aides (from MacKenzie *et al.*, 2006).

Other Variables and Internal vs External Validity

While consideration of the test conditions, or independent variables, is crucial in the design of an experiment, researchers need to be aware of three other types of variables: random, control, and confounding. Any circumstance that could affect performance is potentially an independent variable in an experiment: standing vs sitting vs lying down, before lunch vs after lunch, quiet vs noisy, sun lighting vs room lighting vs dim lighting vs no lighting, left-handed users vs right-handed users, males vs females, big keys vs small keys, keys that click vs keys that do not click, and so on. There is no limit to the possibilities. There are three choices: (a) to engage a circumstance as an independent variable, (a) to ignore a circumstance and expect that it varies in a random and representative way within the experiment (random variable), or (c) to limit a circumstance to one setting throughout the experiment (control variable). The first choice was discussed above. Of the random or control choices, there is a trade-off. This is best articulated in terms of two important concerns in experimental research: internal validity and external validity. *External validity* refers to the extent to which the effect observed is generalizable to other persons and situations. *Internal validity* is the extent to which the effect observed is due to the test conditions. To clarify, "effect observed" is the difference observed in a dependent variable across the settings of an independent variable, for example, observing an entry speed of 12 WPM for method A compared to 15 WPM for method B. Was the difference due to the methods or to something else (internal validity)? Is the same outcome likely with other people in other situations (external validity)? Table 4.1 summarizes.

The third type of additional variable to consider is a confounding variable. A confounding variable is any circumstance that varies systematically with an independent variable. There are no advantages to confounding variables. They are an insidious defect in an experiment, and all researchers need to be wary of the possible presence of them. Here is an example. Let us say two keyboard layouts are compared and one is found to perform better on a dependent variable. If the keys were larger on one keyboard than on the other, then "key size" is a confounding variable because it varies systematically with "keyboard layout" (large for one, small for the other). Perhaps the effect observed was due to key size, not to keyboard layout. The solution is to ensure that the keys are the same size on the two keyboards or to include key size as an independent variable and to test both keyboard layouts with both key sizes.

Variable	Advantage	Disadvantage
Random	Improves external validity by using typical situations and people	Compromises internal validity by introducing additional variability in the measured behaviors
Control	Improves internal validity since differences in measured behaviors are more likely due to the test conditions	Compromises external validity by limiting responses to a specific circumstance or a specific type of person

TABLE

4.1

Relationship between random and control variables and internal and external validity.

4.3.4 Within-Subjects vs Between-Subjects Designs

If the evaluation is comparative, as is typically the case, then there is at least one factor in the experiment and this factor has at least two levels. The levels are the test conditions. If all participants are tested on all levels of a factor, the design is called a "within-subjects design" or a "repeated-measures design." In other words, the measurements gathered under one condition are repeated on the same participants for the other condition(s). The alternative to a within-subjects design is a between-subjects design. In this case, each participant is tested under one condition only. One group of participants is tested under condition A, a separate group under condition B, and so on.

There are a number of issues to consider in deciding whether an experimental factor should be assigned within subjects or between subjects. Sometimes there is no choice. For example, "handedness" might be a factor in an experiment in which a text entry technique is thought to have a bias favoring, say, right-handed users over left-handed users. In this case, handedness must be assigned between subjects, because a participant cannot be both left handed and right handed! Conversely, if an experiment seeks to investigate the acquisition of skill over multiple blocks of practice, then "practice" is a factor in the experiment, with levels "block 1," "block 2," and so on. Clearly, the only option for practice is within subjects. No two ways about it!

In many situations, however, there is a choice. If so, a within-subjects design is generally preferred because effects due to the disposition of participants are minimized. Such effects are likely to be consistent across conditions. For example, a participant who is predisposed to be meticulous will likely exhibit such behavior consistently across experimental conditions. This is beneficial because the variability in measurements is more likely due to differences among test conditions than to behavioral differences between participants (if a between-subjects design were used).

Despite the above-noted advantage of a within-subjects design, a between-subjects design is sometimes preferred due to interference between conditions. If the conditions under test involve conflicting motor skills, such as typing on keyboards with different arrangements of keys, then a repeated-measures design may be a poor choice because the required skill to operate one keyboard may inhibit, block, or otherwise interfere with the skill required for the other keyboard. Such a factor may be assigned between subjects (see MacKenzie *et al.*, 2001, for an example).

If interference is not anticipated, or if the effect is minimal and easily mitigated through a few minutes of practice when a participant changes conditions, then a within-subjects design is the best choice.

4.3.5 Counterbalancing

An additional effect must be accounted for in within-subjects designs: learning. For example, if two techniques, A and B, are compared and all participants used technique A first, followed by B, then an improvement with B might occur simply because participants benefited from practice on A[6]. The solution is counterbalancing, or splitting the participants into groups, testing half on A, first followed by B, and half on B first, followed by A. Learning effects, if any, should cancel. Counterbalancing is useful for more than two conditions also, and in this case grouping is done according to a Latin Square. The most common arrangements are shown in Fig. 4.8. Note that in each case a condition appears precisely once in each row and column. For a balanced Latin Square, it is also true that each condition occurs before and after each other condition an equal number of times, thus improving the balance (see Fig. 4.8d).

Obviously, the number of groups required must divide evenly into the total number of participants. If three conditions are counterbalanced over 15 participants, each group has 5 participants.

4.3.6   Testing Research Questions

The "T" in ROT (see above) is for testable. Not only must research questions be repeatable and observable (we have dwelled on these in detail already), they must be testable. In text entry research, we often just want to know if a new entry technique is any good or if it is better than an existing or alternative technique. Fair enough, but "Is it good?" and "Is it better than…?" are not testable questions. We can evaluate techniques and ask participants their opinions, and this is certainly part of the process; but, usually, "good" or "better than" follows from the outcome on observable, measurable behaviors. That is, if participants enter text using method A "faster than" or "with fewer errors than" method B, it is usually true that their opinions align with their performance.

So, testable research questions are usually of the form "Is method A *faster than* method B?" or "Is method A *more accurate than* method B?" However, we are not quite there yet. Let us say we develop a new text entry technique ("A") and conduct an experiment according to the steps above, comparing the new technique with an alternative method ("B"). The data collected reveal 14.5 WPM for method A and 12.7 WPM for method B. Method A is about 15% faster than method B. Fair enough, but where is the test? The test lies in establishing whether the difference is significant or just a chance outcome. Since we are testing humans, variability in responses is inevitable. If the experiment were run again, no doubt the results would be slightly different. But, how much different? Would method B be faster? Clearly, this is a concern.

To answer the question, "Is method A faster than method B?" we use a statistical test called an analysis of variance (ANOVA)[7]. It is a test to determine if two or more mean scores are the same based on the variance in the constituent measures. More

---

[6]   The alert reader will notice that learning, as just described, is a confounding variable.

[7]   If only two means are compared, then a "*t* test" is the same as an ANOVA. In practice, usually more than two conditions are compared (as, for example, six in the 3×2 design discussed earlier), so the discussion here uses an ANOVA.

(a) A B   (b) A B C

    B A   C A B

                      B C A

(c) A B C D   (d) A B C D

    D A B C   B D A C

    C D A B   D C B A

    B C D A   C A D B

FIGURE   Latin Squares. (a) 2 by 2, (b) 3 by 3, (c) 4 by 4, (d) balanced 4 by 4. The distinguishing

4.8   feature in the balanced Latin Square is that each condition occurs an equal number
                of times before and after each other condition.

precisely, an ANOVA is a test of a null hypothesis, in this case "The entry speed for method A *is the same as* that for method B." Let us see how this is done. Consider the two hypothetical data sets in Fig. 4.9. The outcome in both cases is the same, 14.5 WPM for method A and 12.7 WPM for method B.

Figure 4.10 illustrates the difference in the data sets. An important embellishment in the charts is error bars showing, in this case, ± 1 standard deviation in the constituent measures. Standard deviation is the square root of the variance. Even though the variance is tested, the standard deviation is more commonly articulated, since it has the same units as the mean. Either way, the error bars in Fig. 4.10 clearly show the increased dispersion in the responses of the participants in example b. Further indication of this is evident by comparing the individual participant measures in Figs. 4.9a and 4.9b.

The ANOVA is performed with a statistics program, the full details of which are beyond the scope of this chapter. For the data in Fig. 4.9a, an ANOVA produces a table as in Fig. 4.11[8]. In a research paper, the results would appear somewhat as follows: "The text entry speeds were 14.5 WPM for method A and 12.7 WPM for method B, suggesting about a 15% performance advantage for method A. The difference was statistically significant ($F_{1,9} = 19.0$, $p < 0.005$), as determined using an analysis of variance."

The ANOVA result is given in parentheses. First, the *F* statistic appears along with the degrees of freedom for the effect and the residual sources of variation (method = 1, method * subject = 9, respectively). Following the *F* statistic is *p*, the probability that the hypothesis is true. (Remember that the hypothesis is expressed in the null form; namely, that there is no difference.) For example a, evidently there is only a 0.0018 probability that the entry speed for method A is the same as that for method B. That is pretty low;

---

[8]   Created by *Statview*, now marketed as *JMP* (www.jmp.com).

(a)	Example #1		
	Participant	Method	
		A	B
	1	15.3	12.7
	2	13.6	11.6
	3	15.2	12.1
	4	13.3	11.5
	5	14.0	13.0
	6	14.1	15.0
	7	14.0	14.0
	8	15.0	11.6
	9	15.2	12.5
	10	15.1	12.6
	Mean	14.5	12.7
	SD	0.73	1.12

(b)	Example #2		
	Participant	Method	
		A	B
	1	17.3	12.7
	2	13.6	10.6
	3	15.2	12.1
	4	10.3	7.5
	5	16.6	14.5
	6	14.1	15.5
	7	10.0	15.0
	8	15.0	9.6
	9	18.2	15.5
	10	15.1	13.6
	Mean	14.5	12.7
	SD	2.71	2.72

FIGURE

4.9

Hypothetical data sets for a text entry experiment. The mean entry speeds are the same in both data sets. In (a) the difference is significant. In (b) the difference is not significant. SD is the standard deviation in the measures used to compute the mean. See text for discussion.

thus we reject the hypothesis and conclude that the difference in the means is statistically significant. The threshold for significance is typically any value of p lower than 0.05 or a 1 in 20 chance. Instead of reporting a precise value, p is rounded to the more conservative of the thresholds 0.05, 0.01, 0.005, 0.001, 0.0005, or 0.0001. So, in this case, p is rounded from 0.0018 to 0.005. By the way, the difference in the entry speed for method A and method B in example b was not statistically significant ($F_{1,9} = 3.83$, $p > 0.05$).

As a final note, "statistically significant" does not imply that the difference is important, useful, or meaningful. Whether a 15% performance advantage is important for design success or commercial viability is not within the purview of statistical tests.

4.4   LEARNING

We spoke earlier about learning as a behavior to balance out, to cancel, as though it were an undesirable human condition. While learning can confound other effects in within-subjects designs, the human trajectory in skill acquisition is often the most crucial aspect of a text entry method. How quickly can a method be learned, and with

(a)

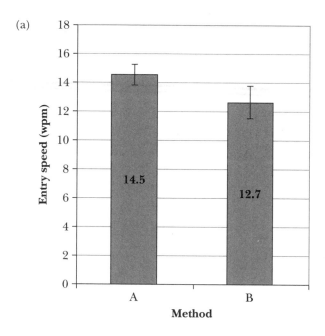

(b)

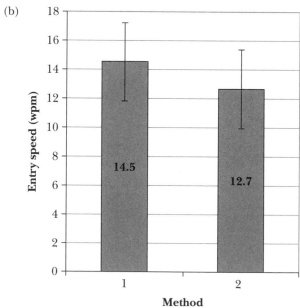

FIGURE

4.10

Charts for data in Fig. 4.9. The vertical lines on the bars show ±1 standard deviation in the measures forming the means. See text for discussion.

ANOVA Table for entry speed (wpm)

	DF	Sum of squares	Mean square	F-value	P-value	Lambda	Power
Subject	9	7.840	.871				
Method	1	17.672	17.672	19.007	.0018	19.007	.979
Method * Subject	9	8.368	.930				

FIGURE

4.11

ANOVA table for data in Fig. 4.9a.

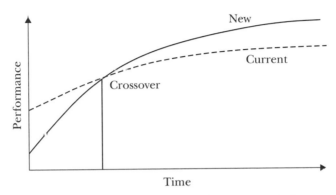

FIGURE

4.12

Improved performance with practice. A new technique outperforms an existing technique, but not initially.

what performance outcomes? Are the intended users consumers with high expectations for immediate usability? Are they high-use experts willing to invest considerable effort in learning the method? In recognition of this diversity in the user community, researchers often investigate learning in their research program.

The trajectory of human's learning a skill is shown in Fig. 4.12. As our emphasis is on comparative evaluation, two curves are shown, one for a new technique and one for a current or alternative technique serving as a point of comparison.

The curves show a performance metric, perhaps text entry speed, plotted against the time invested in learning the techniques. Curves following a power function are shown, but logarithmic scales are sometimes used for the axes, and this produces a plot with straight lines (e.g., Card *et al.*, 1978). The curves reveal a crossover point, wherein one technique, after sufficient practice, outperforms the other.

The equation for the performance–time relationship in Fig. 4.12 is built using linear regression, by regressing the observed performance data on the block or session number in which the data were gathered. Gathering the data is labor intensive because a longitudinal study is required, wherein testing proceeds over a prolonged period of time. This is shown in Fig. 4.13 for an experiment comparing text entry speeds for two soft keyboard layouts over 20 sessions of practice (MacKenzie & Zhang, 1999).

(a)

Session	Entry speed (wpm)	
	QWERTY	OPTI
1	28.44	16.98
2	29.98	21.06
3	31.56	24.80
4	32.62	27.26
5	33.20	29.18
6	34.52	31.04
7	34.14	33.08
8	34.68	34.16
9	35.66	34.72
10	36.77	35.89
11	36.95	37.22
12	37.36	38.75
13	38.50	39.95
14	38.65	40.73
15	39.12	40.68
16	39.00	41.85
17	39.20	42.74
18	39.85	43.55
19	40.16	43.91
20	40.30	44.29

(b)

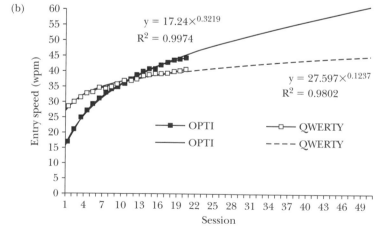

$y = 17.24 \times^{0.3219}$
$R^2 = 0.9974$

$y = 27.597 \times^{0.1237}$
$R^2 = 0.9802$

■— OPTI   □— QWERTY
—— OPTI   ---- QWERTY

FIGURE

4.13

Power law of learning for an experiment comparing two soft keyboard layouts. (a) Data. (b) Learning curves and extrapolations to the 50th session (from MacKenzie & Zhang, 1999).

The equation for each condition is shown beside its curve in Fig. 4.13b. The equation is in the power form and is derived using a statistics application or a spreadsheet such as Microsoft *Excel*. The crossover phenomenon in Fig. 4.12 appears at the 10th session in Fig. 4.13. An extrapolation beyond the period of practice is also shown, although this obviously bears increasing inaccuracy the farther it extends beyond the test period.

While the plots in Fig. 4.13b are instructive, often the most significant point is the first one—the measured performance during initial exposure to the technique. This point reflects the walk-up usability (a.k.a. immediate usability) of the technique. Researchers are often seeking to develop a text entry technique that improves on a current, established, but less-than-ideal technique. If there is a community of users familiar with the current technique, it is a tough sell to convince them to switch. Performance advantages of a new technique are often expected with minimal effort. In view of this researchers have developed evaluation methodologies designed specifically to capture the immediately usability of a technique, for example, by limiting and tightly controlling participants exposure to the technique. In one experiment, participants were given just 1 minute of exposure before performance measures were gathered (MacKenzie & Zhang, 1997). A second round of testing was done following an additional 5 minutes of exposure. Others have adopted similar evaluation methods (Koltringer & Grechenig, 2004; MacKenzie & Zhang, 2001; Wobbrock *et al.*, 2005).

4.5   SUMMARY AND FURTHER READING

This chapter on evaluation techniques has been crafted in the language of text entry research. It has also been pared down for delivery in a single chapter. Indeed, there is considerably more to evaluation than can fit in this space. We have, for example, not commented on the potential problems of asymmetric skill transfer in within-subjects designs or post hoc comparison tests to determine which conditions differ significantly from which others (when more than two conditions are tested). Other issues in experiment design are just as important, such as participant consent, the method of selecting participants, and sequencing of conditions in more complex experiment designs. Two references on experimental methods the author finds particularly useful are the *Publication manual of the American Psychological Association* (American Psychological Association, 2001) and Martin's *Doing psychology experiments* (Martin, 2004). It is also worthwhile just to study research papers that present experimental evaluations that are comparative and empirical, both in text entry and on other topics in human–computer interaction.

Quite a few papers are cited in the pages above, but, in closing, there are a few others to consider that present experimental methodologies for text entry that include learning models similar to Fig. 4.13 (Bellman & MacKenzie, 1998; Isokoski & Raisamo, 2004; Lyons *et al.*, 2006; MacKenzie *et al.*, 2001; McQueen et al., 1995; Wigdor & Balakrishnan, 2003; Wobbrock *et al.*, 2006).

REFERENCES

Agarwal, A., & Simpson, R. (2005). User modeling for individuals with disabilities: a pilot study of word prediction. *Proceedings of the 7th International ACM SIGACCESS Conference on Computers and Accessibility—ASSETS '05* (pp.218–219). New York: ACM Press.

Alsio, G., & Goldstein, M. (2000). Productivity prediction by extrapolation: Using workload memory as a predictor of target performance. *Behaviour & Information Technology, 19*, 87–96.

American Psychological Association (2001). *Publication manual of the American Psychological Association (5th ed.).* Washington, DC: APA.

Bailey, R. W. (1996). *Human performance engineering: Designing high quality, professional user interfaces for computer products, applications, and systems (3rd ed.).* Upper Saddle River, NJ: Prentice Hall.

Bellman, T., & MacKenzie, I. S. (1998). A probabilistic character layout strategy for mobile text entry. *Proceedings of Graphics Interface '98* (pp.168–176). Toronto: Canadian Information Processing Society.

Card, S. K., English, W. K., & Burr, B. J. (1978). Evaluation of mouse, rate-controlled isometric joystick, step keys, and text keys for text selection on a CRT. *Ergonomics, 21*, 601–613.

Card, S. K., Moran, T. P., & Newell, A. (1980). The keystroke-level model for user performance time with interactive systems. *Communications of the ACM, 23*, 396–410.

Cooper, A. (1999). *The inmates are running the asylum.* Indianapolis: Sams.

Economist (2004). Je ne texte rien. *The Economist, 10 July, Vol. 372* (p.85).

Fleetwood, M. D., Byrne, M. D., Centgraf, P., Dudziak, K. Q., Lin, B., & Mogilev, D. (2002). An evaluation of the text-entry in Palm OS: Graffiti and the virtual keyboard. *Proceedings of the Human Factors and Ergonomics 46th Annual Meeting—HFES 2002* (pp.617–621). Santa Monica, CA: Human Factors and Ergonomics Society.

Gentner, D. R., Grudin, J. T., Larochelle, S., Norman, D. A., & Rumelhart, D. E. (1983). A glossary of terms including a classification of typing errors. In W. E. Cooper (Ed.), *Cognitive aspects of skilled typewriting* (pp.39–44). New York: Springer.

Gong, J., Haggerty, B., & Tarasewich, P. (2005). An enhanced multitap text entry method with predictive next-letter highlighting. *Extended Abstracts of the ACM Conference on Human Factors in Computing Systems—CHI 2005* (pp.1399–1402). New York: ACM Press.

Hwang, S., Geehyuk, L., Jeong, B., Lee, W., & Cho, H. (2005). FeelTip: Tactile input device for small wearable information appliances. *Extended Abstracts of the ACM Conference on Human Factors in Computing Systems—CHI 2005* (pp.1475–1478). New York. ACM Press.

Isokoski, P., & Raisamo, R. (2004). Quikwriting as a multi-device text entry method. *Proceedings of the Third Nordic Conference on Human–Computer Interaction—NordiCHI 2004* (pp.105–108). New York: ACM Press.

James, C. L., & Reischel, K. M. (2001). Text input for mobile devices: Comparing model prediction to actual performance. *Proceedings of the ACM Conference on Human Factors in Computing Systems—CHI '01* (pp.365–371). New York: ACM Press.

Koltringer, T., & Grechenig, T. (2004). Comparing the immediate usability of Graffiti 2 and virtual keyboard. *Extended Abstracts of the ACM Conference on Human Factors in Computing Systems—CHI 2004* (pp.1175–1178). New York: ACM Press.

Lyons, K., Starner, T., & Gane, B. (2006). Experimental evaluation of the Twiddler one-handed chording mobile keyboard. *Human–Computer Interaction, 21*(4), 343–392.

Lyons, M. J., Chan, C.-H., & Tetsutani, N. (2004). MouthType: Text entry by hand and mouth. *Proceedings of the ACM Conference on Human Factors in Computing Systems—CHI 2004* (pp.1383–1386). New York: ACM Press.

MacKenzie, I. S. (2002). Mobile text entry using three keys. *Proceedings of the Second Nordic Conference on Human–Computer Interaction—NordiCHI 2002* (pp.27–34). New York: ACM Press.

MacKenzie, I. S. (2003). Motor behaviour models for human–computer interaction. In J. M. Carroll (Ed.), *HCI models, theories, and frameworks: Toward a multidisciplinary science* (pp.27–54). San Francisco: Morgan Kaufmann.

MacKenzie, I. S., Chen, J., & Oniszczak, A. (2006). Unipad: Single-stroke text entry with language-based acceleration. *Proceedings of the Fourth Nordic Conference on Human–Computer Interaction—NordiCHI 2006* (pp.78–85). New York: ACM Press.

MacKenzie, I. S., Kober, H., Smith, D., Jones, T., & Skepner, E. (2001). LetterWise: Prefix-based disambiguation for mobile text entry. *Proceedings of the ACM Conference on User Interface Software and Technology—UIST 2001* (pp.111–120). New York: ACM Press.

MacKenzie, I. S., Nonnecke, R. B., Riddersma, S., McQueen, C., & Meltz, M. (1994). Alphanumeric entry on pen-based computers. *International Journal of Human–Computer Studies, 41,* 775–792.

MacKenzie, I. S., & Soukoreff, R. W. (2002a). A character-level error analysis technique for evaluating text entry methods. *Proceedings of the Second Nordic Conference on Human–Computer Interaction—NordiCHI 2002* (pp.241–244). New York: ACM Press.

MacKenzie, I. S., & Soukoreff, R. W. (2002b). Text entry for mobile computing: Models and methods, theory and practice. *Human–Computer Interaction, 17,* 147–198.

MacKenzie, I. S., & Soukoreff, R. W. (2003). Phrase sets for evaluating text entry techniques. *Extended Abstracts of the ACM Conference on Human Factors in Computing Systems—CHI 2003* (pp.754–755). New York: ACM Press.

MacKenzie, I. S., & Zhang, S. X. (1997). The immediate usability of Graffiti. *Proceedings of Graphics Interface '97* (pp.120–137). Toronto: Canadian Information Processing Society.

MacKenzie, I. S., & Zhang, S. X. (1999). The design and evaluation of a high-performance soft keyboard. *Proceedings of the ACM Conference on Human Factors in Computing Systems—CHI '99* (pp.25–31). New York: ACM Press.

MacKenzie, I. S., & Zhang, S. X. (2001). An empirical investigation of the novice experience with soft keyboards. *Behaviour & Information Technology, 20,* 411–418.

Majaranta, P., MacKenzie, I. S., Aula, A., & Raiha, K.-J. (2003). Auditory and visual feedback during eye typing. *Extended Abstracts of the ACM Conference on Human Factors in Computing Systems—CHI 2003* (pp.766–767). New York: ACM Press.

Martin, D. W. (2004). *Doing psychology experiments (6th ed.)*. Belmont, CA: Wadsworth.

Matias, E., MacKenzie, I. S., & Buxton, W. (1996). One-handed touch typing on a QWERTY keyboard. *Human–Computer Interaction, 11*, 1–27.

McQueen, C., MacKenzie, I. S., & Zhang, S. X. (1995). An extended study of numeric entry on pen-based computers. *Proceedings of Graphics Interface '95* (pp.215–222). Toronto: Canadian Information Processing Society.

Montgomery, E. B. (1980). Data input system. U.S. Patent 4,211,497. U.S. Patent Office.

Montgomery, E. B. (1982). Bringing manual input into the 20th century: New keyboard concepts. *Computer, 15*, 11–18.

Oniszczak, A., & MacKenzie, I. S. (2004). A comparison of two input methods for keypads on mobile devices. *Proceedings of the Third Nordic Conference on Human–Computer Interaction—NordiCHI 2004* (pp.101–104). New York: ACM Press.

Pavlovych, A., & Stuerzlinger, W. (2003). Less-Tap: A fast and easy-to-learn text input technique for phones. *Proceedings of Graphics Interface 2003* (pp.97–104). Toronto: Canadian Information Processing Society.

Perlin, K. (1998). Quikwriting: Continuous stylus-based text entry. *Proceedings of the ACM Symposium on User Interface Software and Technology—UIST '98* (pp.215–216). New York: ACM Press.

Potosnak, K. M. (1988). Keys and keyboards. In M. Helander (Ed.), *Handbook of human–computer interaction* (pp.475–494). Amsterdam: Elsevier.

Rau, H., & Skiena, S. (1994). Dialing for documents: An experiment in information theory. *Proceedings of the ACM Symposium on User Interface Software and Technology—UIST '94* (pp.147–154). New York: ACM Press.

Read, J. (2005). The usability of digital ink technologies for children and teenagers. *People and Computers XIX: Proceedings of HCI 2005* (pp.19–25). Berlin: Springer-Verlag.

Soukoreff, R. W., & MacKenzie, I. S. (2001). Measuring errors in text entry tasks: An application of the Levenshtein string distance statistic. *Extended Abstracts of the ACM Conference on Human Factors in Computing—CHI 2001* (pp.319–320). New York: ACM Press.

Soukoreff, R. W., & MacKenzie, I. S. (2003). Metrics for text entry research: An evaluation of MSD and KSPC, and a new unified error metric. *Proceedings of the ACM Conference on Human Factors in Computing Systems—CHI 2003* (pp.113–120). New York: ACM Press.

Soukoreff, R. W., & MacKenzie, I. S. (2004). Recent developments in text-entry error rate measurement. *Extended Abstracts of the ACM Conference on Human Factors in Computing Systems—CHI 2004* (pp.1425–1428). New York: ACM Press.

Spakov, O., & Miniotas, D. (2004). On-line adjustment of dwell time for target selection by gaze. *Proceedings of the Third Nordic Conference on Human–Computer Interaction—NordiCHI 2004* (pp.203–206). New York: ACM Press.

2 PART
Entry Modalities and Devices

Ward, D. J., Blackwell, A. F., & MacKay, D. J. C. (2000). Dasher: A data entry interface using continuous gestures and language models. *Proceedings of the ACM Symposium on User Interface Software and Technology—UIST 2000* (pp.129–137). New York: ACM Press.

Wigdor, D., & Balakrishnan, R. (2003). TiltText: Using tilt for text input to mobile phones. *Proceedings of the ACM Symposium on User Interface Software and Technology—UIST 2003* (pp.81–90). New York: ACM Press.

Wigdor, D., & Balakrishnan, R. (2004). A comparison of consecutive and concurrent input text entry techniques for mobile phones. *Proceedings of the ACM Conference on Human Factors in Computing Systems—CHI '04* (pp.81–88). New York: ACM Press.

Wobbrock, J. O., Aung, H. H., Rothrock, B., & Myers, B. A. (2005). Maximizing the guessability of symbolic input. *Extended Abstracts of the ACM Conference on Human Factors in Computing Systems—CHI 2005* (pp.1869–1872). New York: ACM Press.

Wobbrock, J. O., Myers, B. A., & Aung, H. H. (2004). Writing with a joystick: A comparison of date stamp, selection keyboard, and EdgeWrite. *Proceedings of the 2004 Conference on Graphics Interface—GI 2004* (pp.1–8). Toronto: Canadian Information Processing Society.

Wobbrock, J. O., Myers, B. A., & Rothrock, B. (2006). Few-key text entry revisited: Mnemonic gestures on four keys. *ACM Conference on Human Factors in Computing Systems—CHI 2006* (pp.489–492). New York: ACM Press.

Yamada, H. (1980). A historical study of typewriters and typing methods: From the position of planning Japanese parallels. *Journal of Information Processing, 2,* 175–202.

5 Text Entry Using a Small Number of Buttons

CHAPTER

I. Scott MacKenzie   York University, Toronto, ON, Canada
Kumiko Tanaka-Ishii   University of Tokyo, Tokyo, Japan

5.1   INTRODUCTION

This chapter focuses on systems in which the user enters text by pressing keys or buttons and in which more than one character or letter is assigned to each button. Such keyboards are ambiguous because there is uncertainty as to the intended symbol when a key is pressed. There is recent worldwide interest in such *ambiguous keyboards* because of mobile computing, for which space is limited. Also, such keyboards widen the communications possibility for users with physical disabilities who have insufficient motor facility to operate a full-size keyboard (see Chap. 15).

Even though ambiguous keyboards have a reduced complement of keys, users still require access to a large set of characters, including the alphabet, numbers, symbols, and editing keys. Bear in mind that the standard PC keyboard has about 100 keys, yet can produce closer to 800 symbols with the use of modifier keys such as SHIFT, CONTROL, or ALT. So, in this sense, the standard PC keyboard is also ambiguous.

Two general methods enable access to a large set of characters; these differ depending on who performs the disambiguation. First, there is the *multi-tap method* or *non-predictive method*, in which the user disambiguates using multiple strokes to uniquely indicate a character. In the case of a full-size keyboard, additional strokes such as those applied through the CONTROL or SHIFT key are a kind of multi-tap entry. Although the multi-tap method is as old as the typewriter, the concept received new attention when text entry on a phone keypad was first considered in the 1970s (Smith & Goodwin, 1971).

The second approach uses a *predictive method,* in which the system disambiguates and presents a list of ordered candidates from which the user chooses. Prediction in English was first studied in the 1950s as a general problem in information theory (Shannon, 1951) and somewhat later in 1970s as applied to text entry using a phone keypad (Desautels & Soffer, 1974; Rabiner & Schafer, 1976). In addition, predictive entry methods for English were proposed in the 1980s as a typing aid (Darragh *et al.*, 1992). The first concept of text entry by prediction, though, occurred in the 1960s in

Japan by Kurihara (Kurihara & Kurosaki, 1967; Kurihara, 1970), where the language uses thousands of characters. When computers were introduced in Japan, the first problem was how to enter thousands of characters using a keyboard designed for European languages. Entry by prediction is now widely used throughout Japan and China and is spreading to many applications in European languages.

Conceptually, key ambiguity lies in a continuum (see Fig. 5.1). At one extreme, we have a keyboard with a dedicated key for each symbol in the language (Fig. 5.1a),

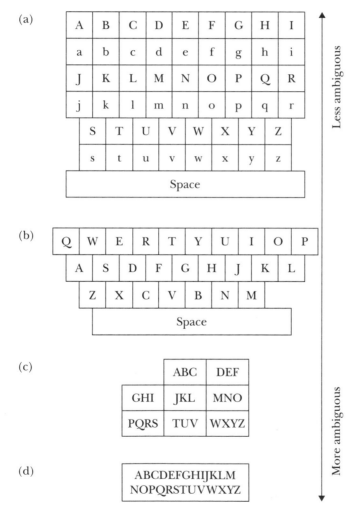

FIGURE
5.1

Key-ambiguity continuum. (a) Fictitious alphabetic keyboard with distinct keys for upper- and lower-case letters. (b) Qwerty keyboard. (c) Standard telephone keypad. (d) Hypothetical single-key keyboard, which, to be useful, would require either many mode keys or a near-psychic disambiguation algorithm.

while at the other we have just one key that maps to every symbol in the language (Fig. 5.1d). The Qwerty keyboard (Fig. 5.1b) and telephone keypad (Fig. 5.1c) represent two relevant points in the continuum.

This continuum suggests many other possibilities in keyboard design. Basically, two decisions are required: how many keys to include and the assignment of symbols to keys. Usually, the number of keys (or buttons in devices like cell phones) depends on the physical limits of the device. The second decision is more critical. Clearly, the assignment governs the entry efficiency regardless of whether the entry method is predictive or non-predictive.

This chapter introduces various ambiguous keyboards and explores how the efficiency of such keyboards is measured. To this end, we describe text entry methods for mobile phones and then present a general measure of each method's efficiency.

5.2   MOBILE PHONE KEYPAD AND ENTRY METHODS

With about 1 billion SMS messages sent per day, today's mobile phone keypad (see Fig. 5.2) is one of the world's most common devices for text entry.

The 12-key keypad consists of number keys 0–9 and two additional keys (* and #). Characters A–Z are spread over keys 2–9 in alphabetic order. The placement of

FIGURE

5.2

Standard 12-key telephone keypad. The 26 letters of the English alphabet are assigned to keys 2 through 9. The SPACE character is typically assigned to the 0 key.

characters is similar on most mobile phones, as it is based on an international standard. The SPACE character is typically assigned to the 0 key or sometimes to the # key. Since there are fewer keys than the 26 needed for the letters A–Z, three or four letters are grouped on each key and, so, ambiguity arises. As noted above, text entry using a mobile phone keypad is possible using non-predictive or predictive methods. With a multi-tap, or non-predictive method, the user disambiguates the meaning of the entry through multiple keystrokes.

With a typical multi-tap method in English, the user presses each key one or more times to specify the input character. For example, the 2 key is pressed once for A, twice for B, and three times for C. There is the additional problem of segmentation, when a character is on the same key as the previous character, for example, the word "ON" because both O and N are on the 6 key. To enter "ON" the user presses 6 three times for "O", segments, then presses 6 twice more for "N". Segmentation is performed using a timeout (e.g., 1.5 seconds on Nokia phones) or by pressing a "time-out kill" key (e.g., the down-arrow key). The user decides which strategy to use.

A multi-tap method can be designed in another way. With the *matrix* method, each character requires two strokes, the first to select the desired character, and the second to indicate the rank of that character on the key. For example, to enter C, the user presses 2 first and then 3, indicating that C is the third character on key 2. Thus, for every character, the user presses exactly two keys. This method requires that the number of characters assigned to a key is less than the total number of keys. The matrix method is a common method for Japanese entry on mobile phones.

The second way to enter characters is by prediction. In this method, disambiguation is performed first by the system and the user then selects the target from candidates shown by the computer. This is realized by providing the system with linguistic knowledge via a large amount of text data. Specifically, the user enters text by repeating the following process:

Step 1.   The user enters a *code* sequence of the target text.

Step 2.   The text entry system *decodes* the code by looking for corresponding targets in a dictionary associated with the software. It sorts the candidates in a relevant order using linguistic knowledge and displays them for the user. (The technological aspects of ordering candidates are explained in detail in Chap. 2.)

Step 3.   The user chooses the target from among the candidates.

A well-known method within this framework is *one-key with disambiguation*. The technique has been used since the 1970s (e.g., Rabiner & Schafer, 1976), although today it is most commonly associated with *T9* by Tegic Communications, Inc. (www.tegic.com). With *T9*, each key is pressed only once. For example, to enter "THE," the user enters 8-4-3-0 (see Fig. 5.2). The 0 key, for SPACE, delimits words and terminates disambiguation of the preceding keys. *T9* compares the word possibilities to a linguistic database to guess the intended word.

Naturally, multiple words may have the same key sequence. In these cases the most common is the default. A simple example follows using the well-known "quick brown fox" phrase (words are shown top to bottom, most probable at the top):

```
843   78425  27696  369   58677   6837  843   5299   364
the   quick  brown  fox   jumps   over  the   jazz   dog
tie   stick  crown        lumps   muds  tie   lazy   fog
vie                                     vie
```

Of the nine words in the phrase, eight are ambiguous, given the key sequence. For seven of the eight, however, the intended word is the most probable word. The intended word is not the most probable word just once, with "jazz" being more probable in English than "lazy." In this case, the user must press a "NEXT" key (e.g., down arrow) to obtain the desired word (i.e., lazy = 5299N0). Evidently, the term "one-key" in "one-key with disambiguation" is an oversimplification!

Another commonly used method using prediction is *entry by completion*. Entry by completion is associated with commercial software, such as available from CIC Corp. (www.cic.com) or ZI Corp. (www.zicorp.com). Completion is also common in mobile phone entry systems in East Asian countries.

As an example of entry by completion, when entering "quick," instead of entering the whole word, the user may enter only "qui" and then the whole word is guessed by the system. The candidate list in this case would include words other than "quick," such as "quit" and "quiche."

Entry by completion can be combined with one-key with disambiguation. In the case of "quick," the user proceeds with the intention of entering 7-8-4-2-5, but receives complete-word candidates as entry proceeds, for example, after entering 7-8-4 or even 7 only. Entering 7-8-4 results in multiple words that begin with this combination: "still," "suggest," "quite," "sugar," "suit," "stick," etc. Note that ambiguity is greater when completion is used. Still, if the guesses are good, the user might need fewer keystrokes: the number of keystrokes may be less than the length of the word.

Generally, in both non-predictive and predictive methods, there is a trade-off between the degree of ambiguity and entry efficiency, with efficiency governed by the keyboard design. For example, if a phone keypad assigned A through Q to the digit 0 and R through Z to keys 1 to 9, respectively, the entry efficiency will be further limited no matter which entry method is adopted. To help clarify and quantify the trade-off, we next introduce evaluation metrics.

5.3   CHARACTERISTIC MEASURES FOR AMBIGUOUS KEYBOARDS

Design is defined as achieving goals within constraints (Dix *et al.*, 2004, p. 193). The "goal" in designing text entry methods is always to create a "better" method. Since empirical evaluation with users always follows design (sometimes occurring substantially later or not at all; see examples at the beginning of Chap. 4), researchers often use a model for the conjectured benefits of a design. For the research leading to the designs described in this section, the model hinges on a statistic—such as KSPC (MacKenzie, 2002), keystroke savings (Higginbotham, 1992; Koester & Levine, 1998), or word collisions (www.eatoni.com)—that captures the benefits in terms of the keystroke requirements of the technique. We here introduce several measures based on statistics.

The first is KSPC/KSPW, an acronym for "keystrokes per character/word." KSPC and KSPW are metrics to characterize keyboards with reduced keys or those using predictive aids[1]. KSPC and KSPW represents the number of key presses, or keystrokes, on average, to produce a character or word of text on a given keyboard using a given interaction technique in a given language.

Specifically,

$$\text{KSPC} = \Sigma_c \, K(c) P(c), \tag{5.1}$$

where $P(c)$ describes the probability of characters and $K(c)$ describes the number of keystrokes required to enter a character.

When a predictive method is used, both KSPC and KSPW can be calculated. In Japanese and Chinese, there are phrase-based entry systems (see Chap. 11), but here we limit the discussion to the most commonly used word-based entry. In the case of KSPW, the definition is

$$\text{KSPW} = \Sigma_w \, K(w) P(w), \tag{5.2}$$

where $K(w)$ indicates the number of keystrokes required to enter w and $P(w)$ indicates the probability of word w (Tanaka-Ishii *et al.*, 2002). This KSPW is transformed into $\text{KSPC}_{\text{word}}$ measured by word units (MacKenzie, 2002) by dividing KSPW by $\Sigma_w |w| \, P(w)$, where $|w|$ denotes the length of w. In both cases, $K(w)$ is further divided into two stages of entry: the first corresponds to the word typeface (for example, 5-2-9-9 to enter "lazy") and the other to the selection of the word (two scans for the word "lazy" in our "quick brown fox" example above). We use $K_{\text{code}}(w)$ to denote the former and $K_{\text{scan}}(w)$ to denote the latter.

One benefit of $\text{KSPC}_{\text{word}}$ for the word case is that it can be compared with non-predictive methods. On the other hand, KSPW allows us to determine the per-word entry efficiency, which is more direct in predictive entry by word units.

Both $\text{KSPC}_{\text{word}}$ and KSPW are somewhat simplistic because neither reflects the attention demands or movement requirements of the technique. Such a problem is

---

[1] The term "KSPC" is used here with a meaning slightly different from that in Chap. 3. As used here, KSPC (as well as KSPW, K_{code}, and K_{scan}) is a *characteristic measure,* relating to inherent properties of a keyboard. KSPC, as used in Chap. 3, is a *performance measure,* relating to the keystrokes actually used in producing text.

partly solved by separately analyzing $K_{\mathrm{code}}(w)$ and $K_{\mathrm{scan}}(w)$, thus clarifying the degree of ambiguity upon entry. Per-word $K_{\mathrm{scan}}(w)$ on average represents the average ranking of the target word:

$$K_{\mathrm{scan}} = \Sigma_w K_{\mathrm{scan}}(w)P(w). \tag{5.3}$$

This forms part of Formula (5.2) (the rest is the per-word average of $K_{\mathrm{code}}(w)$, denoted as K_{code} in the following). This average ranking can be measured more finely by the average complexity of word W (for example, "lazy"), predicted given an entry code T (for example, 5299). Such complexity is formally defined as conditional entropy (Bell *et al.*, 1990; Tanaka-Ishii *et al.*, 2002):

$$H(W|T) = -\Sigma_{w,t} P(w,t) \log P(w|t), \tag{5.4}$$

where t denotes the entry to get the word w. $H(W|T)$ represents the number of bits required to encode W given a user entry T. Therefore, the smaller $H(W|T)$ is, the less the effort to choose W. When there is no ambiguity, $H(W|T)$ is 0.0.

Calculating the measures above requires a keystroke model for the interaction method and also a language model to estimate the word and character probabilities. This is typically in the form of a token-frequency list appended with the required keystrokes to enter each word. The tokens may be words, single letters, digrams, trigrams, and so on; however, a word-frequency list is the most convenient, particularly for predictive entry techniques (see Chap. 2). The list is a reduction of a corpus and is, arguably, "representative" of a language. For the calculations presented in this chapter, we used a word-frequency list derived from the British National Corpus, the same list described by Silfverberg *et al.* (2000). The list contains the 9022 most common words in English, with frequencies totaling 67,962,112.

5.4   MOBILE PHONE KEYPAD VARIANTS

Due to the SMS messaging phenomenon noted earlier and to the difficulties in entering text on a mobile phone keypad, substantial research has emerged in recent years on alternative text entry techniques with reduced-key keyboards. Some examples are given in Fig. 5.3.

The phone keypad in Fig. 5.3a is "Qwerty-like." Hwang and Lee (2005) assigned letters to keys while trying to mimic the arrangement in Qwerty keyboards. The rationale is that users require less visual scan time to find letters if the arrangement is familiar. This, combined with placing letters on nine keys (rather than eight, as on a phone keypad) and slightly reworking the assignment, is intended to improve the disambiguation process and, hence, improve performance. Ryu and Cruz's (2005) efforts in Figs. 5.3b and 5.3c are similarly motivated: use a few more keys and reassign

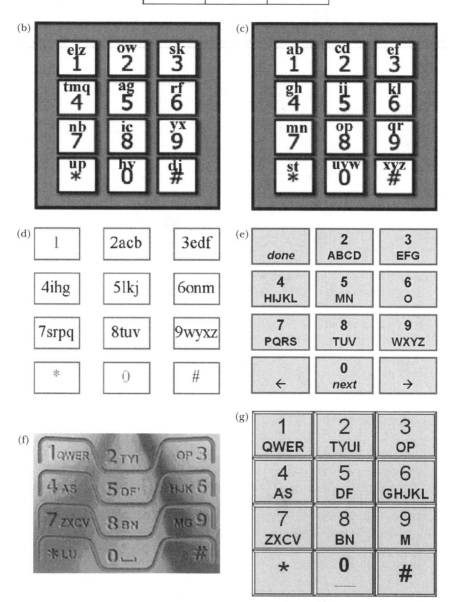

FIGURE 5.3   Mobile phone keypad variants. (a) Qwerty-like phone keypad (Hwang & Lee, 2005). (b) LetterEase (Ryu & Cruz, 2005). (c) FLpK (Ryu & Cruz, 2005). (d) LessTap (Pavlovych & Stuerzlinger, 2003). (e) ACD (Gong & Tarasewich, 2005). (f) EQ3 (eatoni.com). (g) QP10213.

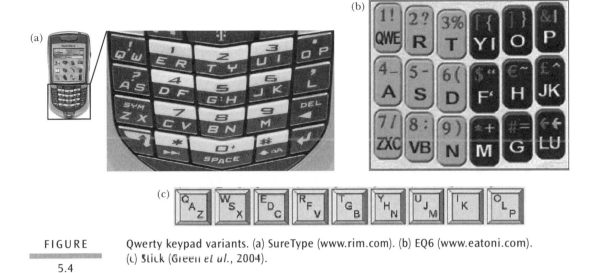

FIGURE

5.4

Qwerty keypad variants. (a) SureType (www.rim.com). (b) EQ6 (www.eatoni.com). (c) Stick (Green *et al.*, 2004).

letters to improve disambiguation. LetterEase in Fig. 5.3b does not use a familiar letter arrangement, whereas the fewer-letters-per-key (FLpK) design in Fig. 5.3c uses an alphabetical assignment. As with the Qwerty-like design of Hwang and Lee, it is thought that the familiar letter assignment will reduce the time to visually scan the layout in search of intended letters.

LessTap in Fig. 5.3d maintains the key and letter groupings of the phone keypad, while rearranging letters within keys. The goal, again, is to improve disambiguation. Gong and Tarasewich's (2005) alphabetically constrained design (ACD) in Fig. 5.3e uses the same 8 keys as a phone keypad, but with a strict alphabetic assignment. EQ3 by Eatoni (www.eatoni.com) in Fig. 5.3f uses 10 keys with a Qwerty-like assignment of letters. First author MacKenzie proposes the QP (Qwerty phone) design in Fig. 5.3g. It strictly adheres to the three-row Qwerty letter assignment, while using the phone keypad's top three rows of keys. The thought, again, is for a reduced visual scan time. For this design, an exhaustive search was performed using every possible assignment of letters, within these constraints. Of the 15,120 possibilities, enumeration 10,213 produces the lowest KSPC, hence the somewhat uninspired name of QP10213 for the design.

Figure 5.4 gives three interesting designs that do not utilize the three-column key arrangement in a phone keypad. Figure 5.4a is RIM's SureType keyboard (www.rim.com). Letters are assigned on 14 keys in a Qwerty arrangement. Figure 5.4b is Eatoni's EQ6, which assigns letters to 18 keys in a Qwerty-like arrangement. The G, L, and U letters are out of sequence to improve disambiguation. Figure 5.4c is the Stick of Green *et al.* (2004), which places letters on 9 keys in a single row. The P key is the lone outlier from the standard Qwerty arrangement.

One interesting research direction is to reduce the key complement below that of a phone keypad. Some examples are shown in Fig. 5.5. The TouchMe4Key of Tanaka-Ishii *et al.* (2002) in Fig. 5.5a is a predictive text entry system placing letters on four keys in alphabetic order within keys. The layout in Fig. 5.5b is the AKKO system for the motor impaired (Harbusch & Kuhn, 2003). The letter assignments were selected using a genetic algorithm that optimized the length of candidate word lists based on a built-in dictionary. The designs in Figs. 5.5c through 5.5f are some example arrangements assigning letters alphabetically to one, two, four, or six keys, respectively. They are denoted LnK, for letters on "*n*" keys.

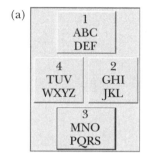

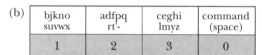

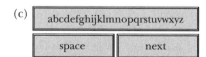

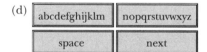

FIGURE 5.5 Fewer key keypad variants. (a) TouchMeKey4 (Tanaka-Ishii *et al.*, 2002). (b) AKKO (Harbusch & Kuhn, 2003). (c) Letters on one key. (d) L2K. (e) L4K. (f) L6K.

5.5   EVALUATING KEYBOARDS

The 17 designs in Figs. 5.2 through 5.5 are brought together for comparison in Table 5.1 along with the standard Qwerty keyboard as a point of reference. The entries are ordered by *T factor*, which is 1 plus the number of keys bearing letters. "One plus" reflects the need to include an additional key for SPACE, which constitutes about 18% of text entry in English. We use this convention to maintain consistency with Tegic's *T9*—"text on nine keys," which includes eight keys for letters (see Fig. 5.2) and a ninth key for SPACE. So, *T* factors range from 2 (Fig. 5.5c) to 27 for Qwerty. The columns Design and Figure refer to the discussions and figures above. The column Letter assignment notes, in a rough sense, the type of letter-to-key arrangement in each design. The last four columns show the statistics explained in Section 5.3. Two KSPC statistics are given for each entry method discussed earlier: one for multitap and the other for one-key with disambiguation. The last two columns show the degree of ambiguity when one-key with disambiguation is adopted.

Globally, there is a trade-off between the *T* factor and KSPC. This holds for both the non-predictive and the predictive cases. Figure 5.6 is offered as a visual improvement over the *T* factor and KSPC columns in Table 5.1. Here we clearly see a trade-off

Design	Figure	Letter arrangement	*T* factor	KSPC Multitap	KSPC One-key	Degree of ambiguity Average ranking K_{scan}	Degree of ambiguity Conditional entropy
L1K	5c	na	2	10.36647	20.05379	104.40538	6.36152
L2K	5d	ABC	3	5.14570	1.54712	3.96924	2.42934
AKKO	5b	Optimized	4	3.96958	1.09967	1.54090	1.05670
TMK4	5a	ABC	5	3.10980	1.05118	1.27776	0.63402
L4K	5e	ABC	5	3.52515	1.06697	1.36346	0.74735
L6K	5f	ABC	7	3.13954	1.02884	1.17902	0.43003
Phone	2	ABC	9	2.02422	1.00641	1.03479	0.11878
LessTap	3d	Optimized	9	1.49148	1.00641	1.03479	0.11878
ACD	3e	ABC	9	1.84078	1.00575	1.03122	0.09679
QP10213	3g	Qwerty	10	2.09677	1.00431	1.02337	0.08656
Stick	4c	Qwerty-like	10	1.59582	1.00545	1.05844	0.19253
QLPK	3a	Qwerty-like	10	1.32646	1.00537	1.03396	0.10037
EQ3	3f	Qwerty-like	11	1.84373	1.00227	1.01231	0.04446
FLpK	3c	ABC	13	1.43832	1.00597	1.03242	0.10547
LetterEase	3b	Optimized	13	1.21377	1.00265	1.01466	0.05514
SureType	4a	Qwerty	15	1.40525	1.00195	1.01059	0.04204
EQ6	4b	Qwerty-like	19	1.39502	1.00010	1.01701	0.06665
Qwerty	—	Qwerty	27	1.00000	1.00000	1.00000	0.00000

TABLE   KSPC and ambiguity for various keyboard designs and letter arrangements.

5.1

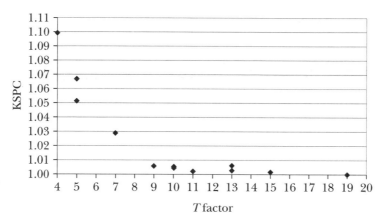

FIGURE

5.6

Trade-off between KSPC and T factor using data from Table 5.1. KSPC statistics are for one-key with disambiguation text entry.

in researchers' efforts to reduce the number of keys (T factor) and the ensuing KSPC. To show this relationship clearly, the L1K, L2K, and Qwerty entries are omitted in the chart. Despite this, KSPC figures are so close as to appear superimposed for T factors 9 (three entries) and 10 (three entries).

Another observation from Table 5.1 is that predictive methods reduce keystrokes. This is seen by comparing the columns under KSPC, one for multi-tap and the other for one-key with disambiguation. We see that the reduction in K_{code} is superior to the increase required for K_{scan} unless ambiguity is extreme, as in the L1K case.

As most points in Fig. 5.6 are close to 1.00, we offer an example of the impact of the ambiguity and the need to occasionally press NEXT to obtain the correct word. If a keyboard design has, say, KSPC = 1.012, the result is an additional 12 keystrokes per thousand. It does not sound like much, but let us see. In English, the average word size is 4.5 characters, or 5.5 characters counting spaces. So, the overhead is 1 additional keystroke for every $1000/5.5/12 = 15$ words, such keystroke serving to select an alternative word from an ambiguous set. From a performance perspective, the problem is that users do not know when ambiguity will occur, except for common words or words frequently entered. As an input strategy, then, users typically attend to the display at the end of each word to determine if the correct word has appeared. And therein lurks the "attention demand" limitation of KSPC noted above.

Table 5.1 includes three measures concerning the degree of ambiguity: KSPC (for one-key with disambiguation), average ranking per word (K_{scan}), and conditional entropy. Figure 5.7 plots KSPC and average ranking for conditional entropy for each keyboard design. The horizontal axis shows the number of bits and the vertical axis shows the number of keystrokes. Both lines monotonically increase (almost linearly) as the conditional entropy is increased. We see here how the three scores globally

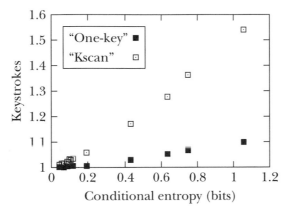

FIGURE

5.7

Correlation of KSPC and average ranking ambiguation text entry with conditional entropy.

correlate. Thus, KSPC and K_{scan} are globally governed by the complexity of candidates. Precisely speaking, though, KSPC in one-key with disambiguation includes K_{code}. The K_{code} component trades off with K_{scan} (see next section for a more explanation), so the conditional entropy sometimes is not exactly correlated with KSPC. In such cases, the conditional entropy, or K_{scan}, helps for a closer analysis.

Using such measures, the design is judged from the viewpoint of keystrokes. With multi-tap, there is no ambiguity and the user's actions are relatively uniform, so the KSPC number directly reflects the user's cognitive load. Therefore, among the keyboards with a T factor of 9 (for example), LessTap is the best. With the predictive entry methods, the keyboard should be judged by KSPC and the other measures directly showing the degree of ambiguity, although globally KSPC provides a good approximation. When the T factor is 9, we see that ACD is the best, which differs from the multitap case.

5.6   ENTRY BY COMPLETION

Entry by completion applies to either multi-tap or one-key with disambiguation. With multi-tap, entry changes from non-predictive to predictive: the system presents a list of candidates and the user selects from among them. The interesting design point is the keystroke reduction. This is an important benefit for users who enter text on mobile devices or for the disabled with reduced motor facility.

In this section, we discuss completion with the mobile phone keypad (summarized in the seventh row in Table 5.1, labeled Phone), for which the entry method is one-key

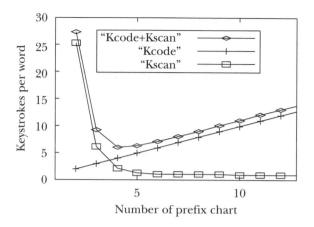

Number of prefix chart

FIGURE   Minimum points for the number of keystrokes on a phone keypad.

5.8

with disambiguation with completion. The same discussion applies to entry methods on other keypads with completion, either multi-tap or one-key with disambiguation. As mentioned, a commercial version of such an entry system is manufactured by ZI Corp. Many entry systems for Japanese and Chinese also use this entry method.

Entry by completion is realized by entering the prefix and then selecting from among the candidates. Keystrokes are reduced by combining these two actions. Importantly, there is a trade-off between these two actions in terms of candidate complexity. The more of the prefix entered, the smaller the candidate list becomes, thus making it easier for the user to make a selection.

Figure 5.8 illustrates this for a ZI-like case in English. The x axis shows the length of the prefix (K_{code}) of the word and the y axis shows the keystrokes per word. To show the relationship clearly, the case with $K_{code} = 1$ is omitted in the chart. There are three lines in the figure. One plots $y = x$ ("+" markers), indicating the increasing value of K_{code}. Another (square markers) indicates the average ranking of the candidate for a given prefix length (K_{scan}). Clearly, the greater K_{code} is, the smaller K_{scan} becomes. The third (diamond markers) represents the keystrokes KSPW, the total of K_{code} and K_{scan}, with a minimum as a trade-off between K_{code} and K_{scan}. This line asymptotically approaches one of the two other lines at each end.

With a ZI-like keypad, the number of keystrokes is minimal at $K_{code} = 4$, where $K_{scan} = 2.13$. As the average length of an English word is 4.5 characters (excluding spaces), this means the user should enter almost the entire word to maximize the reduction in the number of keystrokes. For any other entry method using completion, the same discussion holds. For example, for Qwerty, the minimal point is at $K_{code} = 4$ (with $K_{scan} = 1.535$ to choose the candidate), and for TMK4 it is at $K_{code} = 5$ (with $K_{scan} = 2.619$). Curiously, for Qwerty, the minimal point is at the same word-beginning length as for the mobile phone, indicating that the degree of ambiguity is still large for cases with limited word-beginning length.

Another analysis is to compare methods with the same T factor. As shown in Table 5.1, ACD has less candidate complexity than Phone. However, ACD's minimal point is $K_{code} = 4$ with $K_{scan} = 2.23$, larger than that of a phone ($K_{scan} = 2.13$). Thus, a phone keypad is better if completion is used. Consequently, the degree of ambiguity when using completion is useful as a design aid.

In practice, the situation is more complicated. The above explanation assumes that the word-beginning length is predefined at a fixed value. However, the user may change the length while watching the candidates presented by the software. Such a decision affects the number of candidates shown at a time. These complicating factors are more finely modeled and measured by MacKenzie (2002), in which the minimal point is calculated using KSPC for list sizes of 1, 2, 5, and 10 on a Qwerty keyboard. These device options should be taken into consideration in exploring design scenarios.

5.7   SUMMARY AND FURTHER READING

Different keyboards can be designed for different tasks. Even though commercial de facto standard keyboards have predominated in the past, keyboard efficiency has become more important with the widespread adoption of ambiguous keyboards. We have explained ways to measure entry efficiency and expect the application of these techniques to lead to a better keyboard design.

For related work on ambiguous keyboards, the reader is directed to several sources, including Dunlop's five-key watch-top text entry system (Dunlop, 2004), Wobbrock and Myers' four-key gesture-based system (Wobbrock & Myers, 2006), and several eight- and nine-key designs described by Arnott and Javed (1992) and Lesher *et al.* (1998).

REFERENCES

Arnott, L. J., & Javed, Y. M. (1992). Probabilistic character disambiguation for reduced keyboards using small text samples. *Augmentative and Alternative Communications, 8,* 215–223.

Bell, T., Cleary, J., & Witten, I. H. (1990). *Text compression.* Upper Saddle River, NJ: Prentice Hall.

Darragh, J. J., Witten, I. H., & Long, J. (1992). *The reactive keyboard.* Cambridge, UK: Cambridge University Press.

Desautels, E. J., & Soffer, S. B. (1974). Touch-tone input techniques: Data entry using a constrained keyboard. *Proceedings of the 1974 Annual Conference* (pp.245–253). New York: ACM Press.

Dix, A., Finlay, J., Abowd, G., & Beale, R. (2004). *Human–computer interaction (3rd ed.)*. London: Prentice Hall.

Dunlop, M. (2004). Watch-top text-entry: Can phone-style predictive text entry work with only 5 buttons? *Proceedings of Mobile HCI 2004* (pp.342–346). Heidelberg: Springer-Verlag.

Gong, J., & Tarasewich, P. (2005). Alphabetically constrained keypad designs for text entry on mobile phones. *Proceedings of the ACM Conference on Human Factors in Computing Systems—CHI 2005* (pp.211–220). New York: ACM Press.

Green, N., Kruger, J., Faldu, C., & Amant, R. S. (2004). A reduced QWERTY keyboard for mobile text entry. *Extended Abstracts of the ACM Conference on Human Factors in Computing Systems—CHI 2004* (pp.1429–1432). New York: ACM Press.

Harbusch, K., & Kuhn, M. (2003). Towards an adaptive communication aid with text input from ambiguous keyboards. *Proceedings of the 11th Conference of the European Chapter of the Association for Computational Linguistics—EACL 2003*. Cambridge, MA: MIT Press.

Higginbotham, D. J. (1992). Evaluation of keystroke savings across five assistive communication technologies. *Augmentative and Alternative Communications, 8*, 258–272.

Hwang, S., & Lee, G. (2005). Qwerty-like 3×4 keypad layouts for mobile phone. *Extended Abstracts of the ACM Conference on Human Factors in Computing Systems—CHI 2005* (pp.1479–1482). New York: ACM Press.

Koester, H. H., & Levine, S. P. (1998). Model simulation of user performance with word prediction. *Augmentative and Alternative Communications, 14*, 25–35.

Kurihara, T. (1970). Kana-Kanji Conversion (I). *Technology reports of Kyushu University, 42(6)*, 880–884, in Japanese. Hakata: Kyushu University.

Kurihara, T. & Kurosaki, Y. (1967). On the Transformation Process of Phonetic Sentences into Ideographic Sentences. *Technology reports of Kyushu University, 39(4)*, 659–664, in Japanese. Hakata: Kyushu University.

Lesher, G. W., Moulton, B. J., & Higginbotham, D. J. (1998). Optimal character arrangements for ambiguous keyboards. *IEEE Transactions on Rehabilitation Engineering, 6*, 415–423.

MacKenzie, I. S. (2002). KSPC (keystrokes per character) as a characteristic of text entry techniques. *Proceedings of the Fourth International Symposium on Human–Computer Interaction with Mobile Devices* (pp.195–210). Heidelberg: Springer-Verlag.

Pavlovych, A., & Stuerzlinger, W. (2003). Less-Tap: A fast and easy-to-learn text input technique for phones. *Proceedings of Graphics Interface 2003* (pp.97–104). Toronto: Canadian Information Processing Society.

Rabiner, L. R., & Schafer, R. W. (1976). Digital techniques for computer voice response: Implementations and applications. *Proceedings of the IEEE, 64*, 416–433.

Ryu, H., & Cruz, K. (2005). LetterEase: Improving text entry on a handheld device via letter reassignment. *Proceedings of the 19th Conference of the Computer–Human Interaction Special Interaction Group (CHISIG) of Australia* (pp.1–10). New York: ACM Press.

Shannon, C. E. (1951). Prediction and entropy of printed English. *Bell System Technical Journal, 30,* 51–64.

Silfverberg, M., MacKenzie, I. S., & Korhonen, P. (2000). Predicting text entry speed on mobile phones. *Proceedings of the ACM Conference on Human Factors in Computing Systems—CHI 2000* (pp.9–16). New York: ACM Press.

Smith, S. L., & Goodwin, N. C. (1971). Alphabetic data entry via the touch tone pad: A comment. *Human Factors, 13,* 189–190.

Tanaka-Ishii, K., Inutsuka, Y., & Takeichi, M. (2002). Entering text with a four-button device. *Proceedings of the 19th International Conference on Computational Linguistics, Vol. 1* (pp.1–7). Morristown, NJ: Association for Computational Linguistics.

Wobbrock, J. O., & Myers, B. A. (2006). Few-key text entry revisited: Mnemonic gestures on four keys. *Proceedings of the ACM Conference on Human Factors in Computing Systems—CHI 2006* (pp.489–492). New York: ACM Press.

6 English Language Handwriting Recognition Interfaces

Charles C. Tappert and Sung-Hyuk Cha Pace University, New York, NY, USA

6.1 INTRODUCTION

Handwriting has been an excellent means of communication and documentation for thousands of years, and this chapter deals with handwriting recognition as a method of entering text into a computer. Handwriting is a learned skill, but because it has a long history and is learned in early school years, many consider it more natural than the alternative learned skill of text entry by either standard or virtual keyboards. Nevertheless, keyboarding is usually considerably faster than handwriting recognition of standard alphabets (Zhai & Kristensson, 2003). With the increase in text entry on mobile computing devices, however, shorthand alphabets and other shorthand notations, such as chat room abbreviations, have been explored with the aim of increasing the speed and recognition rate of handwritten text input.

In this chapter we deal with the recognition of English handwriting and begin by discussing the English handwriting styles used for computer input, the fundamental property of handwriting, and what makes handwriting recognition difficult. For simplicity, we focus our discussions on the alphabetic characters and omit detailed coverage of punctuation, numbers, and other symbols required for complete working systems. We also omit dealing with correcting and editing the input where the current trend is to use gestures and editing symbols (see Chap. 7).

We briefly discuss offline handwriting recognition, which falls in the area of optical character recognition (OCR), for which only the static information is available. Here we cover line, word, and character segmentation and character recognition technologies. Because this book deals primarily with real-time text entry, we discuss more thoroughly the area of online handwriting recognition in which pen movements are tracked. Here we describe the dynamic information and the digitizer equipment that captures it and then cover the usual recognition strategies and especially those that deal with the problems of segmentation and dynamic writing variation. We then describe shorthand techniques for speed writing, including shorthand alphabets and other shorthand for words and phrases. We briefly discuss some of the

English writing styles for computer input (Tappert *et al.*, 1990).

commercial handwriting systems for laptop and handheld computers. Finally, we present a case study and suggestions for further reading.

6.1.1   English Handwriting Styles for Computer Input

The common pattern recognition problems for English text entry, presented in Fig. 6.1, include hand-printed (discrete) characters written in boxes for filling forms, spaced discrete characters, run-on discrete in which the characters can touch and overlap, pure cursive writing, and a mixture of discrete and cursive writing. Available handwriting recognition products are highly accurate with careful hand printing, and some products are available that recognize cursive script and mixed hand printing and cursive, their accuracy being dependent on the writing style and the regularity and clarity of the writing.

6.1.2   Fundamental Property of Writing

What makes handwritten communication possible is that differences between different characters are more significant than differences between different drawings of the same character, and this might be considered the *fundamental property of writing* (Tappert *et al.*, 1990). Interestingly, for English hand printing this property holds within the subalphabets of uppercase, lowercase, and digits, but not across them. Figure 6.2 shows an example of the uppercase "I" (the one in the word "LION"), the lowercase "l", and the number "1" all drawn the same way, with a single vertical stroke, and the upper- and lowercase "O" and the digit "0" drawn the same way, with an oval.

I'll meet you at 1130 in LION HALL.

FIGURE
6.2
Different characters with the same shape.

The most general solution to this problem is to handle it the way humans do—by using the context to puzzle out the meaning. With a machine this is usually done in a *postprocessing* (after recognition) phase that uses syntax and possibly semantics to resolve ambiguities.

6.1.3   What Makes Recognition Difficult

Perhaps the most difficult problem for both humans and machines is careless and, in the extreme, almost illegible writing, and size and slant variation can also be included here. This problem is most severe for similarly shaped characters, and the Roman alphabet has a number of similar letter pairs, such as "U" and "V". A general solution to this problem involves sophisticated recognition algorithms as well as syntax and semantics to resolve ambiguities. In later sections we describe in more detail the machine recognition difficulties for real-time input.

6.2   OFFLINE HANDWRITING RECOGNITION

Offline handwriting recognition, often referred to as optical character recognition, is performed after the writing is completed by converting the handwritten document into digital form. The advantage of offline recognition is that it can be done at any time after the document has been written, even years later. The disadvantage is that it is not done in real time as a person writes and therefore not appropriate for immediate text input.

Applications of offline handwriting recognition are numerous: reading postal addresses, bank check amounts, and forms. Furthermore, OCR plays an important role for digital libraries, allowing the entry of image textual information into computers by digitization, image restoration, and recognition methods.

Offline handwriting systems generally consist of four processes: acquisition, segmentation, recognition, and postprocessing (Fig. 6.3). First, the handwriting to be recognized is digitized through scanners or cameras. Second, the image of the document is segmented into lines, words, and individual characters. Third, each character is recognized using OCR techniques. Finally, errors are corrected using lexicons or spelling checkers.

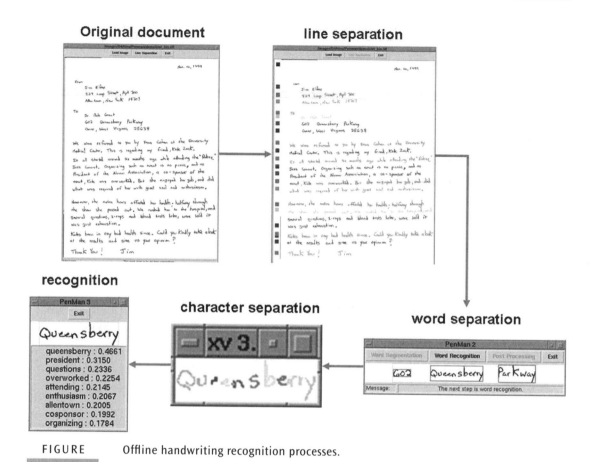

FIGURE   Offline handwriting recognition processes.

6.3

Offline handwriting recognition systems are less accurate than online systems because only spatial information is available for offline systems, while both spatial and temporal information is available for online systems. One promising approach, however, is to estimate the dynamic trajectory information from the offline handwriting and then use online recognition algorithms (Plamondon & Srihari, 2000).

6.3   ONLINE HANDWRITING RECOGNITION

6.3.1   Dynamic Information

In *online*, or *real-time*, handwriting recognition the machine recognizes the writing while the user writes. In contrast to offline systems, online systems capture the temporal or

FIGURE

6.4

Examples of "S" versus "5". The leftmost drawing looks like an S, the next could be either, the third a 5, and the two-stroke one on the right a 5.

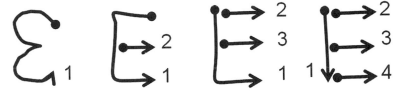

FIGURE

6.5

Stroke number variation for the letter "E" (one to four strokes). Stroke direction is indicated by a dot at the start of a stroke, and stroke order by the number at the end of a stroke.

dynamic information of the writing: the *number* of strokes, the *order* of the strokes, the *direction* of the writing of each stroke, and the *speed* of writing within each stroke. A *stroke* is the writing from pen down to pen up. Because it uses the dynamic as well as the static information, online can be more accurate than offline recognition. In English, uppercase handprint averages about two strokes per letter and lowercase about one stroke, while cursive writing averages less than one stroke per letter.

This dynamic information can be helpful in distinguishing between similarly shaped characters, such as "5" versus "S" (Fig. 6.4). If the character is drawn with two strokes, it is almost always a 5. Also, a one-stroke 5 can often be identified by the dynamic information of the pausing or slowing down at the corners even if they are not drawn sharply (the pen tip velocity is not indicated in the figure).

However, the dynamic information can also complicate the recognition process because the machine has to handle many variations of the characters. Also, some variations, like the one-stroke 5, may be similar to variations of other characters. The large number of possible variations that can occur is readily illustrated with the letter "E", which can be written with one (in cursive fashion), two, three, or four strokes (Fig. 6.5) and with various stroke orders and directions; and despite these writing variations, the resulting handwritten letters can appear essentially the same.

The four-stroke E, consisting of one vertical and three horizontal strokes, has 384 variations (4! = 24 different stroke orders multiplied by $2^4 = 16$ for the two possible stroke directions for each of the four strokes). In fact, any four-stroke character can be written in these 384 possible ways.

Further complications can be caused, for example, by connected strokes (Fig. 6.6). The first drawing shows what might have been intended as a four-stroke E, but resulted

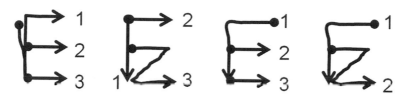

FIGURE   Examples of connected strokes and other variations.

6.6

in a three-stroke E because the first two strokes are connected by essentially retracing the first stroke. The second drawing also shows what might have been intended as a four-stroke E, but resulted in a three-stroke one because the last two strokes are connected like a Z. The third drawing shows another three-stroke variation, and the fourth shows a connected-stroke variation of it. Thus, the problem of the number of strokes and the two writing directions of each stroke is multiplied by the number of different ways that strokes can be drawn and connected in real handwriting.

6.3.2   Digitizer Equipment

For online recognition, unlike for offline recognition, special equipment is required during the writing process. Tablet digitizers (electronic tablets), available since the 1950s, allow the capture of handwriting and drawing by accurately recording the x–y coordinate data of pen-tip movement. The advent of pen computers in the 1980s combined digitizers and flat displays, allowing the same surface to handle both input and output to provide immediate electronic ink feedback of the digitized writing and mimicking the familiar pen-and-paper paradigm to provide a "paperlike" interface (for more information on digitizer equipment see the tutorial papers listed under Further Reading).

With a pen computer, or a pen-enabled computer, users can not only use the pen (writing stylus) as a mouse but also write or draw as they would with pen and paper. Keyboard entry can be mimicked by touching sequences of buttons on a "soft" keyboard displayed on the screen or, alternatively, handwriting can be inputted that is then automatically converted to ASCII code.

6.3.3   Recognition Strategies

There are many trade-offs in designing a handwriting recognition system. At one extreme, the designer puts no constraints on the user and attempts to recognize the user's normal writing. At the other extreme, the writer is severely constrained, restricted to write in a particular style such as hand printing and further restricted to write strokes in a particular order, direction, and graphical specification.

Because the computers and tablet digitizers were rather primitive when the first digitizers appeared in the late 1950s and 1960s, much of the early work employed simple character segmentation and recognition techniques and required the user to write the characters in a prescribed manner with respect to their stroke number, order, and direction. Later systems tended to be more flexible in that they attempted to handle most of the ways the alphabet characters are usually written. Some systems allowed the user to train the system to recognize a user's particular way of drawing each character. Many of these were actually hybrid systems, allowing a user to train the system but also recognizing the common variations in the untrained, or so-called walk-up, mode.

For PDAs and other small devices in which limited computing power prohibits the use of complex techniques like syntax and semantics, special strategies are used to simplify the recognition problems. Because computing power was also limited in the 1960s, when the early systems were developed, many of these special strategies are simply those developed in that earlier era. Some of these strategies require writer (user) cooperation. For example, to distinguish between digits and alphabetics, the strategy might compel the writer to use different regions of the writing surface for different subalphabets. Or, similar to using the shift key on a typewriter, the writer can use a special symbol to put the machine into uppercase, lowercase, or digit mode.

PDAs might also limit the user to a predefined alphabet, possibly a shorthand alphabet (see below), to simplify shape recognition. Such simplifications are, of course, at the sacrifice of naturalness and usability. The more powerful machines, like laptops, can use a general solution to the shape recognition problem by employing sophisticated recognition algorithms such as dynamic programming, Markov models, and Affine transformations (see the references under Further Reading for a discussion of these algorithms).

Segmentation

A key problem in handwriting recognition, hand printing as well as cursive writing, is character *segmentation* (separation). While extreme in cursive writing, in which several characters can be made with one stroke, this problem remains significant with hand printing because the characters can consist of one or more strokes, and it is often not clear which strokes should be grouped together. Segmentation ambiguities include the well-known *character-within-character* problem in which, for example, a hand-printed lowercase "d" might be recognized as "cl" if drawn with two strokes that are somewhat separated from one another.

Pre-recognition solutions, those applied prior to recognition, involve a combination of writer control and *preprocessing* (machine processing prior to recognition). These techniques include the writer giving an explicit signal to the machine that a character is completed, the writer pausing between characters and the preprocessor detecting a sufficient pause and producing a time-out signal, the writer drawing characters in predefined boxes and the preprocessor grouping the strokes within a box, the writer lifting the pen either alone or in combination with a time-out signal, and the writer geographically spacing the characters and the preprocessor measuring sufficient spatial separation (see the tutorial papers listed under Further Reading).

Other methods involve the machine recognition of the writing. The *stroke code* method is the most popular of these methods, in which the machine recognizes each stroke immediately after the pen is lifted (see Tappert *et al.*, 1990, and the other survey articles). For multiple-stroke characters the resulting stroke codes are then combined to recognize the whole character. This method is commonly used for Chinese characters because the number of different characters far exceeds the number of different stroke shapes used to form the characters, and the recognition component then needs deal only with a relatively small library of stroke shapes, rather than with a large library of character shapes. This method is also used for English *run-on* writing in which the characters can touch or overlap one another. The recognized strokes are then grouped into characters using topological information. In English uppercase, for example, a vertical stroke could be the first stroke of a B, D, E, F, H, I, K, M, N, P, R, or T. Postprocessing (machine processing after shape recognition), such as dictionary lookup and language statistics, can assist this complex segmentation-recognition process.

Perhaps the simplest segmentation method is to use an alphabet of only single-stroke characters. This is a simple pre-recognition method that can also be viewed as the reduced (trivial) case of the stroke code method in which each stroke is a character.

Dynamic Writing Variation

Dynamic writing variation is the various ways—in stroke number, order, and direction—that characters can be drawn. In some countries, like Japan, there is considerable homogeneity in writing dynamics because children are taught to write each character in a specific way. In other countries, like the United States, writing variation is greater. As we saw earlier with the various ways of writing "E", dynamic variation can be a serious problem, and it becomes even more complex when combined with the segmentation problem. The simplest way to handle wide dynamic variation is not to allow it. Thus, many systems, especially the early ones, prescribe the limited ways each character can be written, and for the system to work, the writer must conform to these variations.

When allowing many variations, one solution is for the machine to reorder the strokes into a normalized form, for example from left to right and top to bottom, and writing direction could be handled similarly. For example, a four-stroke E would be reordered into the vertical stroke followed by the three horizontal ones from top to bottom. Other methods are to incorporate the more common variations and either to inform the users what they are or simply to let them adapt to the system by trial and error. The earlier mentioned techniques of using stroke codes or single-stroke alphabets can also be used to solve this problem.

Ideal Recognition System

The ideal recognition system is one that supports handwritten input of all the Unicode characters (the characters of basically all languages can be represented by the 16-bit Unicode) and does not impose any constraints on what and where the user writes. The user should also be able to intermingle text with graphics and gestures, and the recognizer should be able to distinguish these kinds of input. A currently common handwriting recognition method is to incorporate a hidden Markov model into a complex stochastic language model (Hu *et al.*, 1996), and the application of other techniques like support vector machines is being explored (Bahlmann *et al.*, 2002). Even though recent advances in handwriting recognition are promising, further research is warranted since the above goals have yet to be achieved.

6.4   SHORTHAND

We focus here on online shorthand systems that have been developed for text input on small consumer devices like PDAs that have limited computing power. *Shorthand* is "a method of writing rapidly by substituting characters, abbreviations, or symbols for letters, words, or phrases" and can be traced back to the Greeks (Panati, 1984).

6.4.1   Shorthand Alphabets

The first widely used Latin shorthand system was devised in 63 BC by Marcus Tullius Tiro, Cicero's secretary, to record speeches in the Roman senate (Panati, 1984). Many Romans, including Julius Caesar, favored shorthand, and this system remained in use for over a thousand years. The Tironian alphabet is shown in Fig. 6.7.

During the Middle Ages shorthand became associated with witchcraft and fell into disrepute, and it was not until the late 12th century that King Henry II revived the use of Tironian shorthand. It is interesting that many famous writers throughout history preferred shorthand—Cicero's orations, Martin Luther's sermons, and Shakespeare's and George Bernard Shaw's plays were all written in a style of shorthand.

The use of shorthand in the field of handwriting recognition is well known. Some of the earliest instances of its use are in the field of CAD/CAM applications in which symbols were used to represent various graphical items and commands. Later, shorthand was used to represent scientific symbols and notations, and Pitman shorthand was also implemented. Other systems used special alphabets and symbols for online character recognition, and we present and discuss several of these systems. Note that, in addition to shape and orientation, online systems can also use the dynamic information such as stroke direction to differentiate among symbols.

FIGURE

6.7

Tironian alphabet, 63 BC (Panati, 1984).

Several shorthand alphabets have been designed for pen computers. Some of these, such as the Allen (1993) and Goldberg (1997) alphabets, are *geometric short-hands* based on geometrical figures such as circles, ovals, straight lines, and combinations of these (Glatte, 1959). Several of the precomputer alphabets, such as the Stenographie (Daniels & Bright, 1996) alphabet from 1602 and the Moon (Gove, 1986) alphabet from 1894, were of similar geometric design. The symbols of these systems are well separated from each other, which facilitates machine recognition and, within the design constraints, a few of the alphabet symbols can usually be made similar to their Roman counterparts. While the symbols of these alphabets are easy for a machine to recognize, the disadvantage is that the writer must remember the

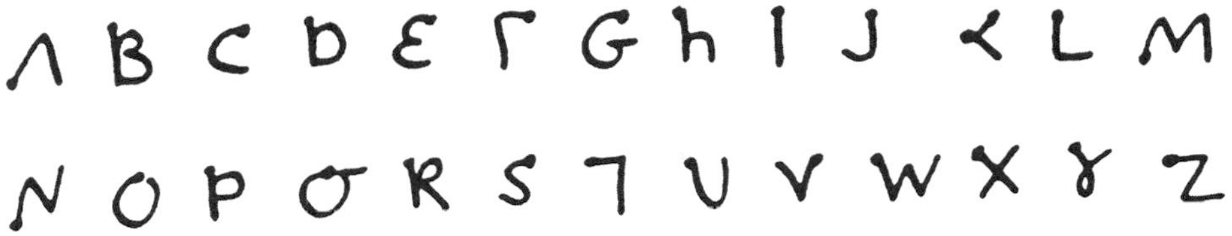

Λ B C D Ɛ Γ G h I J < L M

N O P σ R S ⏀ U V W X ɣ Z

(a) Graffiti Alphabet (Palm Computing).

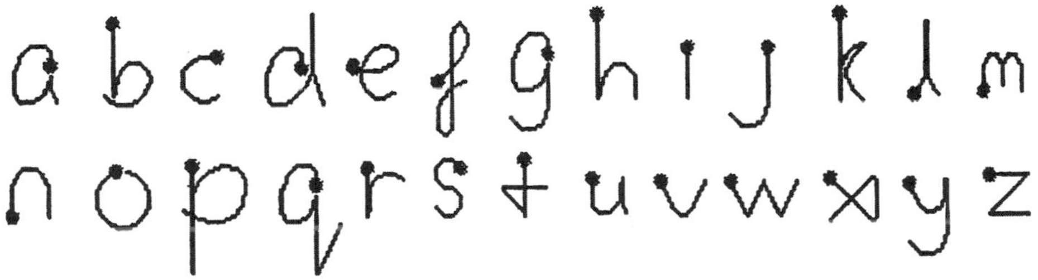

a b c d e f g h i j k l m

n o p q r s t u v w x y z

(b) Papyrus Allegro Alphabet (Papyrus Associates, 1995).

FIGURE 6.8   Short alphabets used in commercial PDA devices. (a) Graffiti alphabet (Palm Computing). (b) Papyrus Allegro alphabet (Papyrus Associates, 1995).

unique way to draw each symbol and consistently draw each symbol accurately. The basic shapes are simple so they can be drawn quickly, and to optimize for writing speed, the alphabet can be designed so that the simplest shapes are assigned to the letters used most frequently. Perhaps because the symbols would be difficult to learn and remember by the general population, these alphabets have not been used successfully in commercial handwriting recognition devices.

Two special predefined alphabets currently used in PDA devices are shown in Fig. 6.8. For simplicity we include them here under shorthand alphabets even though their high correspondence with the Roman alphabet may not qualify them as such. The Graffiti alphabet (Palm Computing, 1996) is used in the popular Palm OS devices, notably the PalmPilot and Handspring models, and the Papyrus Allegro alphabet (Papyrus Associates, 1995) is used in Microsoft Windows devices[1]. These alphabets, and Allegro perhaps more so than Graffiti, are easy to learn because of their high correspondence to the Roman alphabet. Even with this high correspondence, however, one does need to learn the prescribed way of writing each letter.

---

[1] The EdgeWrite alphabet (Wobbrock, 2005), designed for motor-impaired users entering text on small devices, also has a high correspondence to the Roman alphabet.

Company/system	Writing style
Palm Computing/Graffiti[a]	Special shorthand alphabet
Microsoft/Papyrus Allegro	Special shorthand alphabet
Communications Intelligence Corp./Jot	Relatively unconstrained hand printing
Microsoft	Relatively unconstrained hand printing and cursive

[a] A few years ago Palm switched from Graffiti to Graffiti2, which is basically Jot licensed from Communications Intelligence Corp.

TABLE   Current commercial online handwriting systems for English.

6.1

6.4.2   Shorthand for Words and Phrases

Chat room and user-defined abbreviations can further increase the speed of text entry in applications like sending e-mail in which such abbreviations can occur frequently. Huber *et al.* (2005) developed a preliminary system using such abbreviations and indicated that using such handwriting input on small PDA interfaces might be faster than the keyboard input.

6.5   COMMERCIAL ONLINE SYSTEMS

Several of the current commercial online handwriting systems are shown in Table 6.1. Graffiti and Allegro, as discussed above, are shorthand systems used in PDAs. The Jot handwriting recognition system is used in both PDAs and the more powerful pen-enabled laptops. The relatively unconstrained Microsoft system, which is perhaps the most sophisticated system in use today, is available only in the pen-enabled laptops because the algorithms employed require substantial memory and computing power. Because the techniques used in these product systems are proprietary to the companies that produce the products, they are not available for discussion.

6.6   CASE STUDY

We briefly trace here the likely design decisions that led to the creation of the Graffiti and Allegro alphabets. The first design decision was to choose a small alphabet by using only one case rather than attempting to recognize both upper- and lowercase and by using a small number of writing variations per letter (preferably only one). Allegro followed this design decision precisely but Graffiti allowed most alphabet letters to be drawn in several ways (not shown in Fig. 6.8a).

The second design decision was to recognize each stroke upon pen lift (stroke code method) and to use only one stroke per character so that each character (now a stroke) is recognized immediately. Again, Allegro followed this design precisely but Graffiti allowed a two-stroke "X", although there is also a one-stroke X variation (not shown in Fig. 6.8a).

The third design decision was to use a high correspondence with the Roman alphabet. The resulting alphabets are easier to learn than the basic-shape alphabets described above in the section on shorthand alphabets, but at the sacrifice of distinctiveness (separability of shapes for easy machine recognition) and of speed of entry. Allegro followed this design rather closely by drawing the T and X with one stroke rather than using the usual crossing second stroke and by omitting the dots on the I and J. Graffiti, on the other hand, has a number of letters that are only partially like their Roman counterparts. The design of Allegro was also more consistent by modeling all lowercase letters of the Roman alphabet, whereas Graffiti modeled the uppercase Roman alphabet except for the lowercase H.

The fourth design decision was to use separate writing areas for the letters and the digits to avoid confusion of the similarly shaped symbols from these subalphabets. These design decisions resulted in alphabets that are easy to learn and also rather easy to recognize using techniques that can be implemented on limited computing devices like PDAs.

6.7   FURTHER READING

For further information on handwriting recognition we recommend the books and conference proceedings by Downton and Impedova (1997), Lee (1999), and Liu *et al.* (2003) and the tutorial papers by Suen *et al.* (1980), Tappert *et al.* (1990), Schomaker (1998), Subrahmonia and Zimmerman (2000), and Plamondon and Srihari (2000). The three major conferences on handwriting recognition, for which information can be found on the Internet, are the International Workshop on Frontiers in Handwriting Recognition (IWFHR), the Conference of the International Graphonomics Society (IGS), and the International Conference on Document Analysis and Recognition (ICDAR). Two Web sites with extensive information are also worth mentioning: Jean Ward's online character recognition bibliography (http://users.erols.com/rwservices/biblio.html) and the Handwriting Recognition Group of the Nijmegen Institute for Cognition and Information (http://hwr.nici.kun.nl/).

REFERENCES

Allen, G. (1993). Data input grid for computer. U.S. Patent 5,214,428. U.S. Patent Office.

Bahlmann, C., Haasdonk, B., & Burkhardt, H. (2002). On-line handwriting recognition with support vector machines—a kernel approach. *Proceedings of the 8th International Workshop on Frontiers in Handwriting Recognition, 6–8 August 2002, Niagara-on-the-Lake, ON, Canada* (pp.49–54).

Daniels, P. T., & Bright, W. (Eds.) (1996). *The world's writing systems*. Oxford: Oxford University Press.

Downton, A. C., & Impedova, S. (Eds.) (1997). *Progress in handwriting recognition*. Singapore: World Scientific.

Glatte, H. (1959). *Shorthand systems of the world*. New York: Philosophical Library.

Goldberg, D. (1997). Unistrokes for computerized interpretation of handwriting. U.S. Patent 5,596,656. U.S. Patent Office.

Gove, P.B. (Ed.) (1986). *Webster's third new international dictionary*. Springfield, MA: Mirriam–Webster.

Hu, J., Brown, M. K., & Turin, W. (1996). HMM based on-line handwriting recognition. *IEEE Transactions on Pattern Analysis and Machine Intelligence, 18,* 1039–1045.

Huber, W. B., Hanson, V. L., Cha, S.-H., & Tappert, C. C. (2005). Facilitating pen computing through common chatroom abbreviations. *Proceedings of the Conference on Human Factors in Computing Systems—CHI '05*. New York: ACM Press.

Lee, S.-W. (1999). *Advances in handwriting recognition*. Singapore: World Scientific.

Liu, Z.-Q., Cai, J.-H., & Buse, R. (2003). *Handwriting recognition: Soft computing and probabilistic approaches*. New York: Springer-Verlag.

Palm Computing (1996). PalmPilot: Graffiti reference card.

Panati, C. (1984). *The browser's book of beginnings*. Boston: Houghton Mifflin.

Papyrus Associates (1995). *Recognition by Papyrus for Microsoft Windows: User reference guide*. Redmond, WA: Microsoft Corp.

Plamondon, R., & Srihari, S. N. (2000). On-line and off-line handwriting recognition: A comprehensive survey. *IEEE Transactions on Pattern Analysis and Machine Intelligence, 22,* 63–84.

Schomaker, L. (1998). From handwriting analysis to pen–computer applications. *Electronics and Communication Engineering Journal,* 93–102.

Subrahmonia, J., & Zimmerman, T. (2000). Pen computing: challenges and applications. *Proceedings of the 15th International Conference on Pattern Recognition, 2,* 60–66. Los Alamitos, CA: IEEE Computer Society.

Suen, C. Y., Berthod, M., & Mori, S. (1980). Automatic recognition of handprinted characters—The state of the art. *Proceedings of the IEEE, 68,* 469–487.

Tappert, C. C., Suen, C. Y., & Wakahara, T. (1990). The state-of-the-art in on-line handwriting recognition. *IEEE Transactions on Pattern Analysis and Machine Intelligence, 12,* 787–808.

Wobbrock, J. O. (2005). A robust design for accessible text entry. *Proceedings of the 7th International ACM SIGACCESS Conference on Computers and Accessibility, 9–12 October 2005, Baltimore, MD* (pp.31–32).

Zhai, S., & Kristensson, P.-O. (2003). Shorthand writing on stylus keyboard. *Proceedings of the Conference on Human Factors in Computing Systems—CHI.* New York: ACM Press.

7 Introduction to Shape Writing

CHAPTER

Shumin Zhai IBM Almaden Research Center, San Jose, CA, USA
Per Ola Kristensson Linköpings Universitet, Linköping, Sweden

7.1 INTRODUCTION

The previous chapter (Chap. 6) gives an overview of two types of pen-based text input methods. One is based on conventional handwriting scripts (Tappert et al., 1990) and the other is based on artificial or novel character sets such as Graffiti and Unistrokes (Goldberg & Richardson, 1993). Pen-stroke gestures[1] can also be used in many other ways for text entry. For example, traditional shorthand systems use a large set of pen-stroke symbols to represent phonemes or syllables (Kreitzman, 1998).

This chapter introduces "shape writing"—a novel form of writing that uses pen strokes on graphical keyboards to write text. We first describe the basic concept of shape writing, followed by the human-performance considerations and rationales that guided its iterative design and development process in the past few years (Zhai & Kristensson, 2003; Kristensson & Zhai, 2004). We conclude the chapter by analyzing shape writing in relation to the multiple dimensions of goodness of text entry.

7.2 THE BASIC CONCEPT OF SHAPE WRITING

Shape writing, also known as shorthand-aided rapid keyboarding (SHARK), is a writing method designed to enable users to enter text efficiently at a faster rate than previously possible on mobile phones, handheld computers, and other mobile devices. It can also be used with external tablets connected to desktop computers for those who need an effective alternative to two-handed touch-typing on a physical keyboard.

---

[1] "Gesture" in the conventional sense of the word is richer and broader than what is typically referred to in the user interface field. The input actions described in this chapter should be more appropriately called pen strokes, pen marks, pen-stroke gestures, or digital ink. However, given the wide adoption of the term "pen gesture" in the field, we do not differentiate it from the more accurate terms.

FIGURE

7.1

The word "the" as an ideal *sokgraph* and a user's actual pen input. The dot indicates the start of the pen stroke.

Unlike the handwriting systems covered in the previous chapter, which rely on predefined symbols (based on either widely practiced scripts or novel symbols), shape writing is defined on and used with a graphical keyboard.

The basic concept of shape writing is rather simple. A shape-writing system (our current system is named ShapeWriter) displays a graphical keyboard to the user. Instead of tapping each individual letter key explicitly and precisely, the user slides the pen over all the letter keys in a word sequentially on the graphical keyboard. Figure 7.1 shows the ideal trace (left) and one actual and acceptable input stroke (right) for the word "the." The user's pen trace can deviate and sometimes not even cross some of the intended keys as long as it is closer to the intended word's ideal trace than any other word traces in a lexicon.

The ideal trace is called a *sokgraph* (shorthand on keyboard as a graph) (Kristensson & Zhai, 2004). In other words, a sokgraph is the continuous trace that is formed by serially connecting the center points of the keys on a graphical keyboard for a string of letters (normally a word). For shape writing, a graphical keyboard is simply an array of characters arranged either in the traditional Qwerty layout or in an optimized layout. To shape write a word, the user draws a pen stroke on the keyboard that approximates the sokgraph of the word. Once the pen stroke terminates (by lifting the pen for example), the shape-writing system in principle compares the pen stroke on the keyboard with all sokgraphs generated from a lexicon and returns the closest match. Figure 7.2 shows ShapeWriter in action—a user is shape writing the word "writing" on an optimized keyboard layout. Shape writing is inherently error tolerant, allowing noises such as hand tremors or faster and more "sloppy" writing.

7.3   INFORMATION AND CONSTRAINTS

Text entry can be viewed as a communication system through which information is transmitted from the user to the computer (see Fig. 2.1 in Chap. 2 for an explicit illustration of Shannon's noisy channel model). With shape writing the writer encodes his message (a word) with geometric shapes defined on a letter map (the graphical keyboard). Such a process is "noisy" both because one often has to cross

FIGURE   ShapeWriter on a Tablet PC.

7.2

irrelevant letters in order to reach the intended letter and because the writer can be sloppy and miss some relevant letters. In other words the stroke drawn is often imperfect. The shape writing recognizer decodes the message from the code + noise and outputs the message (the word).

The reason a shape-writing system can decode the noisy "shape code" lies fundamentally in the regularities and redundancies in language (and word compositions in particular). In fact, in his seminal paper that laid the mathematical foundation of modern communication systems (the information theory) Shannon (1948) introduced his work by first examining the constraints and redundancy in the English language. The statistical regularities in natural language form the basis for much of today's speech recognition and other language processing technologies (see Chap. 2 for a general introduction to language modeling). The most basic way of capturing the lexical level of language regularities is the notion of a lexicon that consists of all permissible letter combinations, including words, parts of words, names, and acronyms. The use of a lexicon is a critical aspect of shape writing. Using lexical constraints a shape-writing system allows many irrelevant letters to be crossed and still have the intended word returned. Taking Fig. 7.2 as an example, the letters intended to be crossed were "w-r-i-t-i-n-g," but the actual pen stroke crosses "w-r-t-o-s-i-s-e-t-e-s-i-n-g." ShapeWriter can still return the word "writing" because the lexical constraints eliminate all illegitimate letter strings. Consequently, ShapeWriter takes advantage of the regularities of word formation and recognizes the user's pen stroke on the keyboard with flexibility and error tolerance. An intended word can still be recognized although irrelevant letters between intended letters are crossed or even if some of the letters in a word are missed by the pen stroke.

To give a sense of the amount of lexical constraint existing in a natural language, such as English, consider only words with the length of five letters. The letter permutations of a five-letter string would be in the range of tens of millions. This number is even greater if we can consider permutations of letter strings with different lengths. In practical writing an individual's active vocabulary is several orders of magnitude smaller. For instance, in the Enron e-mail corpus (Klimt & Yang, 2004) the most frequent e-mail sender wrote 8926 e-mails in 2 years, totaling around 400,000 words. But the number of unique words in all of his e-mails written is only 10,858. Hence the vast majority of letter combinations can be considered as shape-writing error tolerance "white space" (illegitimate letter combinations not in the lexicon).

A lexicon is only a special and limited form of language modeling for shape writing. Other types of either lower or higher order regularities, such as word level n-grams, can potentially also help to further relax the precision requirement of shape writing (see Chap. 2). Also, the smaller or more specific the lexicon is, the more flexibility and error tolerance shape writing can provide. This is a factor that can be taken advantage of in certain domains, for example, in medical applications.

7.4   SHAPE-WRITING RECOGNITION

Due to space limitations and the introductory nature of this article, we refer the reader to Kristensson and Zhai (2004) for a detailed presentation of shape-writing recognition, in particular, and the vast literature such as Duda *et al.* (2001) and Theodoridis and Koutroumbas (1999) for pattern-recognition technologies in general. Here we highlight only some specific characteristics of shape-writing recognition derived from the idiosyncrasies of the shape-writing paradigm.

7.4.1   Template-Based Recognition

Unlike the majority of the popular contemporary handwriting recognition methods that rely on data-training-based statistical pattern recognition (Tappert *et al.*, 1990) we chose a template-based approach in which the user's pen stroke is compared to each word's sokgraph template. The template-based approach allows new words to be added to the lexicon easily. For instance, by tapping a new word on the graphical keyboard the system can instantly build the template of the added word. In contrast a training-based statistical pattern recognition method may require the user to provide several sample pen strokes of the word. A template-based approach whose "orthography"—the canonical format of a script (Coulmas, 1989)—is clearly defined by the letter map is also more easily implemented for shape writing. For natural handwriting, there is often a great deal of variation for writing each letter all within the acceptable bounds (see Chap. 6).

7.4.2 Multichannel Recognition

Shape writing also poses some unique challenges to its recognition. One of them is the large number of sokgraphs to be recognized. The two primary features we decided to include in our recognition system to address the challenge are total shape similarity between the user's pen trace and the ideal sokgraph and the user's pen-trace location on the graphical keyboard in relation to the location of the letter keys of the intended word. These shape and location features are treated as parallel recognition channels that are integrated using a probabilistic approach. To improve recognition accuracy several weighting schemes are used within each channel and between the channels.

7.5 OUT-OF-LEXICON INPUT, AMBIGUITY, AND ERROR HANDLING

7.5.1 Handling Words outside the Lexicon

What happens if the user wants to shape write a word that is not in the lexicon? No matter how large the lexicon is or how closely the lexicon matches the individual user's writing vocabulary, occasionally the user may still need to write a word, such as a rare name, an acronym, or a foreign word, that is not prestored in the lexicon. Fortunately, shape writing is used atop a graphical keyboard. One can use the conventional graphical keyboard input method and tap one letter at a time to enter a new word. ShapeWriter will mark the tapped unknown word with, for example, a box (Fig. 7.3) to show the user that this is not a word in the lexicon. The user can choose to add the word to the lexicon so it can be shape written the next time.

7.5.2 Ambiguity

Due to the nature of mapping words onto a graphical keyboard, it is inevitable that the sokgraphs of some pairs of words are almost or completely identical. Our study (Kristensson & Zhai, 2004) shows that in a lexicon containing 20,000 words, 1117 pairs of words (5.6%) are identical in normalized shapes (independent of scale and location) on the ATOMIK (alphabetically tuned and optimized mobile interface

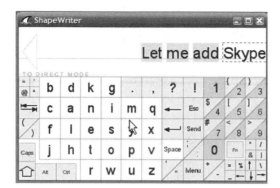

FIGURE

7.3

(a) A tapped word not in the lexicon is marked with a box and (b) the user can add the new word to the lexicon by clicking on it. Shown is the ATOMIK layout (Zhai *et al.*, 2002a) available in ShapeWriter.

keyboard) layout (see Fig. 7.3), for example, "root" vs "heel" and "ben" vs "buy." Many of these conflicts are not natural or complete English words. For example, the word "as" conflicts with "lo," "oz," "by," "ny," and "ft." If we consider only confusion pairs with the same starting and ending key positions, the number reduces to 493 (2.5%). Examples of confusion pairs with identical start and ending positions include "refuge" vs "refugee," "webb" vs "web," and "traveled" vs "travelled." Two hundred eighty-four of these confusion pairs are Roman numerals, such as "lxvi" vs "lxxxvi." Excluding Roman numerals there are 209 pairs of confusion in the 20,000 word lexicon (1.0%). The number of complete ambiguous word pairs on a Qwerty layout is only slightly higher (Kristensson & Zhai, 2004). Techniques for resolving ambiguity are discussed in the next section.

7.5.3   Error Recovery

As in all human skills, a text entry method operates on a speed–accuracy trade-off curve (Fig. 7.4). As one shape writes faster (to the left on Fig. 7.4), she is increasingly more likely to draw a shape that is closer to an unintended word than the intended word, resulting in an entry error.

Error recovery is a critical aspect of any text entry system design. It presents a problem that is very difficult to solve in speech recognition since it requires mode switching between dictation and command (for editing), both of which use voice. Errors occur even in the most common text entry method, two-handed touch typing on a keyboard, but there error correction is quite easy—hit the BACKSPACE key and retype. One can easily visualize the intensity of the use of the BACKSPACE key with a keyboard monitoring program (e.g., *RSI Guard*), which displays the hit plots on each individual key. Computer users who are not rigorously trained touch-typists can see that BACKSPACE is one of the most frequently hit keys.

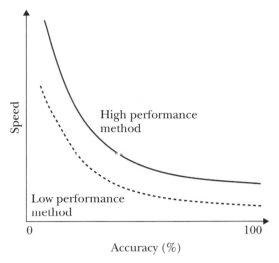

FIGURE

7.4
Hypothetical speed–accuracy trade-off curves of text entry.

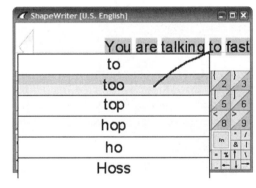

FIGURE

7.5
The user can correct an unintended word with Shape Writer by means of the alternative list.

In shape writing, the basic method of dealing with errors, due either to the small number of confusion pairs or to the deviation of the user's stroke from the intended sokgraph to an unintended one, is using the alternative list menu. If the user clicks on a displayed word, a correction menu is shown, in which alternative candidates are listed according to their probability of being the intended target word (Fig. 7.5). From a certain (simplified) motor action standpoint, two pen strokes (one for shape writing and one occasionally for menu selection) are still more efficient than writing a word with longhand, which on average consists of writing five letters with more than five strokes. With ShapeWriter one can also erase a word in the editor with, for example, a stroke crossing the word (Fig. 7.6) and rewrite.

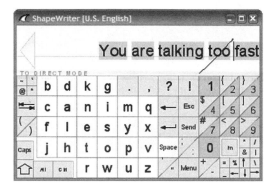

FIGURE
7.6

The user can delete an unwanted word with a stroke crossing the word. One can also cross out multiple words with one stroke.

7.6   HUMAN SENSITIVITY TO SHAPE AS AN ENCODING MODALITY AND THE PROGRESSION FROM TRACING TO DIRECT SHAPE WRITING

As mentioned earlier in relation to the communication model, shape writing uses geometric shapes as an encoding mechanism for words (see Fig. 7.9 for a few examples). Humans are very good at "geometric encoding." A mundane example is using shape as a mnemonic aid to memorize pass codes. For example, it is much more difficult to remember the number sequence 1478963 than to remember the keys forming a U shape on the telephone keypad as a password.

Quantitatively, one experiment on people's ability to learn, memorize, and reproduce sokgraphs showed that people could on average learn 10 to 15 sokgraphs in each hour of practice and correctly reproduce them later without seeing the keyboard (Zhai & Kristensson, 2003).

In practice, learning shape writing is expected to be more gradual and implicit, with the graphical keyboard serving as a map that guides pen movement. One does not have to memorize any sokgraph to begin shape writing. Instead, one traces the intended word from letter to letter by visual guidance from the graphical keyboard. The disadvantage of visual guidance-based input is that it is relatively slow since entering each letter requires closing the perception–action loop. The advantage, on the other hand, is that it makes shape writing easier to begin without needing to memorize a system of symbols as in other shorthand writing systems (see Chap. 6). Ease of use, or more appropriately the low requirement of learning, made graphical user interfaces (GUI) the standard way of interacting with computers today, although it is in fact slower than the earlier command-based interaction method at expert skill levels.

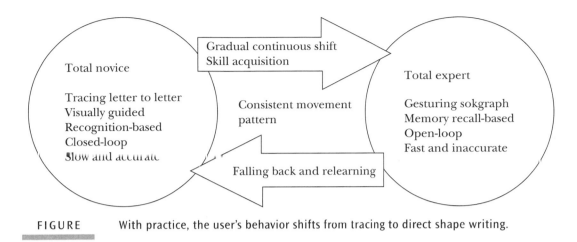

FIGURE 7.7   With practice, the user's behavior shifts from tracing to direct shape writing.

The transition from visual tracing to direct shape writing is modeless. After tracing a word a few times, the user begins to remember parts or the entire shape of the sokgraph of the word. In the same laboratory experiment mentioned earlier (Zhai & Kristensson, 2003), in which the interval of practice of each word was gradually increased, the study participants could completely remember the shape of a sokgraph after 7 to 15 trials of practice. Once parts or the entire shape is remembered, the user's performance shifts toward the expert end of direct shape writing (Fig. 7.7). As a result, the writing speed of the user increases due to two related factors: chunking (Miller, 1956; Buxton, 1986) and open-loop behavior. Chunking means the user does not have to plan, search, and execute the pen strokes from letter to letter on the graphical keyboard as separate units. Instead, the user plans and executes several letters or the entire word as one shape. The action is open-loop in the sense that much of the behavior is driven by memory recall rather than visual guidance, as in all skilled and rapid performance. In our "stress tests," if a user practices and repeats a sentence until all the shapes of the words in the sentence are remembered, the shape-writing speed can reach beyond 100 words per minute.

Obviously, the longer the word, the more practice it will take to remember the entire shape of its sokgraph. Before that, the user is somewhere in between the two ends of shape-writing expertise: complete visual tracing vs complete direct shape writing (Fig. 7.7). Common segments or syllables of a long word may be chunked and these parts can be directly gestured. For less common segments, the user may rely more on visual guidance of the graphical keyboard. Forgetting a sokgraph is also possible, which means the user has to fall back to the novice behavior of visual tracing, which gives the user an opportunity to rehearse the shape of the sokgraph again. See Fuchs (1962) for an early observation of the progression and regression of human motor skills in general.

What bridges the novice end to the expert end of shape-writing performance is that their actual movement actions are consistent. The same (consistent) movement pattern is used both in novice tracing behavior and in expert recall-based direct shape writing. Psychology research has shown that a key to developing automaticity or less attention-demanding performance in human behavior (Schneider & Shiffrin, 1977) is consistency. The concept of facilitating novice-to-expert transition can also be related to Kurtenbach and Buxton's inspiring work and their compelling articulation of marking menus (Kurtenbach *et al.*, 1993; Kurtenbach & Buxton, 1994). They observed that the disconnection between the novice GUI menu operations and the expert hot-key-based operation prevents a natural transition from novice to expert. As an alternative solution they designed marking menus, which are pie menus with a delayed pop-up of the menu items. Users make angular pen marks to select the menu items with (in case of a novice) or without (in case of an expert) the guidance of the pie menu display.

There is an interesting difference between marking menus and shape writing (particularly in its later design) in how the novice-to-expert transition is designed. Via the delayed pop-up display, marking menus enforce a binary transition from novice to expert behavior. A novice pauses and waits for the delayed menu display to pop up, whereas an expert would not wait for the pop-up but produce the angular pen marks from memory. Shape writing takes a more subtle approach—the transition is more gradual and controlled by the user rather than by the interface. With shape writing, the keyboard is always displayed. The user can choose to look at the keyboard a lot, a little, or not at all. It is conceivable that the marking menu approach "pushes" the user to jump to the expert mode sooner, while the shape writing approach is less forceful, less explicit, but less rapid in helping the user to progress toward an open-loop mode. We feel the more subtle approach is necessary for shape writing due its large vocabulary size. Understanding and devising effective methods to aid the novice-to-expert transition is an important but underinvestigated HCI research topic.

7.7 EFFICIENCY AND LAYOUT MATTERS

Shape writing's high efficiency comes from several related factors. First and foremost, it is a form of speed writing in that it enables writing one word with one stroke. "Natural" handwriting is longhand, articulating one letter at a time. The weighted average length of English words is 4.7 letters (according to our analysis based on the American National Corpus, http://americannationalcorpus.org/), with each letter's articulation complexity on par with a sokgraph of a common (often short) word. Figure 7.8 shows the sokgraphs of the words "shape writing is fun" on the ATOMIK and Qwerty layout.

The second efficiency factor is due to the "intelligence" built into shape-writing recognition. Since ShapeWriter takes advantage of the constraints of the total shape of sokgraphs it allows the user to deviate from the precise trajectory. The user can be as "sloppy" as the white space allows, enabling the user to trade a certain amount of accuracy for speed.

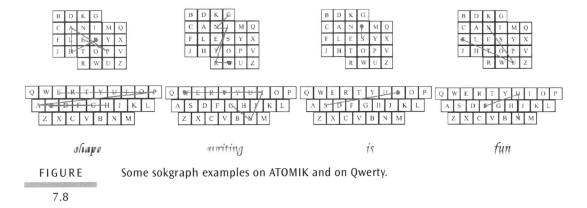

FIGURE

7.8

Some sokgraph examples on ATOMIK and on Qwerty.

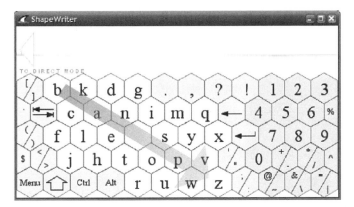

FIGURE

7.9

Classic ATOMIK layout with ABC to Z order tuning illustration.

The third efficiency factor comes from layout optimization. Shape writing is in principle independent of layout and, indeed, can use any number of layouts. The subjectively familiar layout is the Qwerty layout invented in the 1860s for minimizing mechanical jamming (Yamada, 1980). However, touch-typing uses motor memory instead of visual spatial memory so the learning advantage of Qwerty as a map for shape writing is not as great as one might think. The disadvantage of using Qwerty for shape writing is the loss of potential efficiency and greater difficulty in long-term learning. We have experimented with a class of optimized layout called ATOMIK (Zhai & Smith, 2001; Zhai *et al.*, 2002a). We started with the classic ATOMIK optimized for tapping (Fig. 7.9) as a more efficient shape-writing map. Sokgraphs defined on ATOMIK are both more efficient and easier to remember because the sokgraphs are more diverse than those defined on Qwerty, which tend to zigzag in a similar fashion (see Fig. 7.8) for many words due to the fact that common consecutive letters tend to be arranged on the opposite sides of the Qwerty layout (see Chap. 1 for a short review and Yamada, 1980, for a thorough review of Qwerty design). Two mechanisms in the

FIGURE

7.10

The ATOMIK layout revised for shape writing with ABC to Z order tuning illustration.

ATOMIK layout help a novice user find the letters. First, due to the optimization effect the next letter needed is more likely to be in the vicinity of the current pen position. Second, letters from A to Z tend to run from the upper left to lower right corner of the ATOMIK layout, giving the novice user another clue for finding a particular letter (Figs. 7.9 and 7.10) (Smith & Zhai, 2001).

There are a few aspects of ATOMIK that were improved specifically for shape writing, resulting in a revised ATOMIK layout (Fig. 7.10). As shown in Figs. 7.9 and 7.10, the D and K keys are swapped so that the common suffix ED is more distant from the common suffix ING. Hexagon keys are changed to the simpler and cleaner squared keys. In the classic ATOMIK layout (Fig. 7.9) keys were hexagonal to maximize tapping efficiency, which is no longer needed for shape writing. Similarly, the space key is moved off the center since spaces are automatically filled after every sokgraph is recognized. The last row is slightly shifted to the left to make the layout more compact and some sokgraphs less stretched.

Keyboard optimization research (Getschow et al., 1986; Lewis et al., 1992; MacKenzie & Zhang, 1999; Zhai et al., 2000; Smith & Zhai, 2001) has focused on the core Roman letter set. Auxiliary keys in fact also matter to the overall efficiency and usability of the keyboard. The main rationale for the auxiliary keys in the revised ATOMIK in Fig. 7.10 is as follows: $ is close to the number keys, since it is usually followed by digits. The % key is below the number keys, since it is usually placed after digits. Similar pairs such as "{ }" and "[]" are aligned and grouped together. Similar keys \ | / are aligned and grouped. Arrow keys are set according to convention (location and shape). The Caps, SHIFT, Ctrl, Alt, and Fn keys cause a state change as soon as a stylus lands on them, even if the user is in the middle of drawing a stroke and lands on one accidentally. To minimize unintentional activation of these keys, they are made slightly smaller with a gap between them and the adjacent keys. The smaller

Fn and Ctrl keys also make the user more careful and deliberate to trigger "command strokes"—sokgraphs starting from a command key so they will be interpreted as a command. For example, Ctrl-C-O-P-Y issues a "copy" command rather than entering the word "copy." The Fn key is placed as close to the numeric keys as possible, so that function shortcuts such as F1 and F3 are more separated. Ctrl is placed more to the center (swapped with Alt) for a similar reason.

7.8   THE MULTIPLE DIMENSIONS AND GUIDELINES OF EFFICIENT TEXT ENTRY

Developing effective text entry methods is a challenging task, partly because the goodness of the solution is multidimensional. In our view, there are at least the following dimensions that can be desirable in a text entry method: high performance (high product of speed and accuracy), ease of entry/ease of learning, low effort, mobility, and fun. In this section we discuss shape writing along these dimensions of goodness as design guidelines.

To achieve perfection in all of these dimensions in one method is an impossible task, since some of them can be contradictory in design choices. The relative importance of each of these dimensions depends on application requirements and individual preference. Our primary goal of developing ShapeWriter is to enable mobile devices to take on common personal computing tasks efficiently (e.g., e-mail, text messaging, note taking), which dictated the trade-offs we made, described as follows.

7.8.1   High Performance

High performance should not be measured by high speed only, but rather by a high speed–accuracy trade-off curve (Fig. 7.4). High performance is one of our primary goals in developing shape writing. This was achieved due to the shorthand nature, the built-in "intelligence" and error tolerance, and the layout optimization. The relative ease of error correction should also contribute to average performance.

7.8.2   Ease of Entry and Ease of Learning

This dimension is typically at odds with the first. For example, character-based longhand writing is easy to begin for any literate user, but it is not high performance. On the other hand, traditional shorthand writing (such as Pitman or Gregg's system) can give very high speed, but they require the user to memorize a large number of symbols to begin, making its learning requirement impractical for ordinary computing and communication use. One of the core ideas in shape writing is to bridge ease of entry with high performance. One can start with no memory at all (tracing) and gradually move to (partially and increasingly) memory recall-based high-performance gesturing. Interestingly, the standard desktop text entry method, two-handed touch-typing, can afford quite high performance but its learning requirement would be hardly acceptable if it were a new computer user interface that had not been widely adopted. Learning shape writing is much easier than learning touch-typing.

7.8.3   Effortless

A good text entry solution should require as little effort as necessary. Effort in fact can be further divided along multiple subdimensions of human performance: motor, perceptual, and cognitive. A method can optimize for one of the subdimensions at the cost of another. For example, by dynamically positioning letter keys according to context as in Dasher (Ward *et al.*, 2000), the amount of stylus moment for text entry can be minimized. The cost of dynamically arranging letters, however, is the greater perceptual effort needed to constantly monitor the changing letters. Such a trade-off of motor effort with perceptual effort could well be justified for some applications, for example, interfaces for users with certain types of motor impairments. In contrast, methods like Unistrokes (Goldberg & Richardson, 1993) and Graffiti can be potentially eyes-free but they require much more motor effort since they are fundamentally longhand methods (character-level writing). Shape writing balances the motor and perceptual effort with a stationary layout augmented with fluid pen strokes. In our early implementation of shape writing, named SHARK at the time (Zhai & Kristensson, 2003), an important goal was making shape-writing scale and location independent so an expert user did not have to look at the keyboard at all if the sokgraph is remembered completely. This was achieved by limiting shape writing to only a small set of common words. For all other words, the user was expected to tap one letter at a time. The Zipf's law effect was expected to skew the impact of the small number of common words and therefore speed up the average writing time. A cost to this hybrid approach, we later realized, could be cognitive: the user has to decide between shape writing the whole word or tapping individual letters. We hence decided to expand shape writing to all words needed (Kristensson & Zhai, 2004), although it means that a certain degree of visual monitoring of the strokes on the keyboard is needed since scale and location independence cannot be guaranteed for such a large number of words. This perceptual cost is much lower than that of conventional stylus tapping requiring high precision taps within each individual key. Overall, the design of ShapeWriter minimizes the user's motor effort without demanding an unacceptable level of perceptual and cognitive effort.

7.8.4   Mobility

Today's research interest in developing new text entry methods is largely driven by the need to carry out computing and communication functions on small, handheld mobile devices. A small and flexible form factor, with a small footprint and a near-zero start-up time (including the time of setting up the device in case of an external attachment solution), is desirable. An extreme case is one-handed (or no hand at all) input while walking or driving (which is probably unsafe in any case). Speech offers a unique advantage in this regard and is making inroads into these extreme mobile conditions, such as command systems in cars, but suffers other problems such as error correction difficulty for large vocabularies and cognitive load if used as a dictation method (Karat *et al.*, 1999). Shape writing requires one hand (if the device is rested on a surface) or both hands (with one holding the device). The size of ShapeWriter is scalable. How human performance of shape writing precisely changes with the keyboard size requires future research. Previous research on path-steering performance shows that the best motor control performance is achieved at a scale in which finger joints and hand–wrist carry out the motion (Accot & Zhai, 2001).

7.8.5   Fun and Aesthetics

Ultimately, users' subjective experience of using a text entry method dictates the market demand. Not all the factors that make an interface fun and enjoyable are well understood today. All of the previous four dimensions (high performance, ease of learning, low effort, and mobile form factor) can contribute to a fun shape-writing experience. In addition, simple and clean visual design, effective feedback, and fluid stroking actions may also contribute to a fun experience. More explicitly, we have also developed a practice game embedded in ShapeWriter so the user can master shape-writing skills in a playful mode (Fig. 7.11). In this game, balloons carrying different words float upward and are popped when the user enters the correct sokgraph for each word. The words that appear in the game are driven by an expanding rehearsal interval (Landauer & Bjork, 1978; Zhai & Kristensson, 2003) so the practice impact is optimized. There is also an autoplay mode in the game in which ShapeWriter draws the sokgraphs automatically so the user can learn by watching. The benefit of "observational practice" has been shown in human motor control research (Kohl & Shea, 1992).

Since the many dimensions of an efficient text entry interface sometimes conflict with one another there will probably never exist a single text entry method that addresses all needs in all situations for all users. Many of the recently developed methods, such as EdgeWrite (Wobbrock *et al.*, 2003), offer unique strengths and hence may find particular applications. Shape writing is an evolving novel technology and we are conducting more empirical and analytical studies, which may give us more insights for further improvement. Clearly, we have made various design trade-offs in order to address as many important dimensions of goodness as possible. In its current form ShapeWriter is already practical enough for writing daily e-mail and parts of this article (when a tablet is available), but much more can be done to further improve it. Obviously shape writing also needs to be adapted to languages other than English. This is relatively easy for alphabetical languages. For nonalphabetical languages such

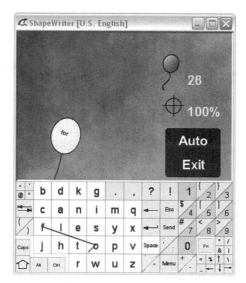

FIGURE   An embedded ShapeWriter game based on memory research.

7.11

as Chinese, many creative steps are needed, since Chinese characters[2] are not easily parsed into regular elements (see Chap. 6 of Coulmas, 1989, for an introduction to Chinese writing). An indirect approach is to use *pinyin,* the Roman-letter-based phonetic equivalent of Chinese characters, which is how Chinese is entered into computers today by most users in mainland China (see Chap. 11 for a general introduction to Chinese, Japanese, and Korean input). Unfortunately there are numerous homophonic characters corresponding to each phonetic spelling. This is solved typically by displaying multiple choices for the user to choose, which demands additional visual attention and slows down the input speed due to the perceptual and cognitive burden on the user (Wang *et al.,* 2001).

Finally, we present some questions as food for thought. First, what can be the highest possible performance in articulating words through shape writing as we have developed it or through some variant form of it in the future? There is no straightforward theoretical estimate on this due to the lack of an empirical law on stroke gesturing that can be used in the way Fitts' law is used to estimate tapping on a graphical keyboard (Lewis, 1992; Soukoreff & MacKenzie, 1995; Zhai *et al.,* 2002b). As a reference point 150 to 160 words per minute is the recommended rate for easily understandable speech, such as recording books on tape (Williams, 1998). Speech is also a form of muscle articulation although not by hand. Can shape writing be improved to

---

2   Unlike Roman characters, Chinese characters, or *zi,* are at a higher level than alphabet but lower than words. The closest counterpart to a Chinese zi in English is a syllable, although most Chinese characters have more defined semantics than English syllables.

the point that it is as fast as this level of speech? Another interesting and difficult question is how a text entry technology or some of its components may or may not be adopted (see Chap. 1 for a review of the history of the typewriter and other technologies). In economics there has been a lively debate between David (1985, 1998–2000) and Liebowitz and Margolis (1990, 1996) regarding "Qwertynomics"—the path-dependence theory that a suboptimal rather than the optimal technology can be locked into the society. The various writing systems of the world, as a very special type of technology in different civilizations, in fact also underwent complicated creation (often by borrowing from other cultures), evolution, or extinction processes that were shaped by economical (efficiency), compatibility with previous practice, and sociopolitical (such as nationalism) factors (Coulmas, 1989). Many interesting and important lessons can be learned there in order to influence the future of the digital mobile society with creative technology solutions.

7.9 FURTHER READING

Zhai and Kristensson (2003) present the initial motivation, implementation, and experimentation of shape writing on graphical keyboards. Kristensson and Zhai (2004) describe the rationale and implementation of a large-scale shape-writing system. Zhai *et al.* (2005) give an overview of both shape writing and ATOMIK, the preceding project that led to the creation and development of shape writing.

REFERENCES

Accot, J., & Zhai, S. (2001). Scale effects in steering law tasks. *Proceedings of CHI 2001: ACM Conference on Human Factors in Computing Systems, CHI Letters 3,* 1–8.

Buxton, W. (1986). Chunking and phrasing and the design of human–computer dialogues. *Proceedings of the IFIP World Computer Congress* (pp.475–480). Amsterdam: North Holland Publishers.

Coulmas, F. (1989). *The writing systems of the world.* Oxford: Blackwell.

David, P. A. (1985). Clio and the economics of QWERTY. *American Economic Review, 75,* 332–337.

David, P. A. (1998–2000). *Path dependence, its critics, and the quest for 'historical economics'* (No. JEL-codes: A1 B0 C4 D9 N0 O3). Stanford, CA: Stanford University.

Duda, R. O., Hart, P. E., & Stork, D. G. (2001). *Pattern classification.* New York: Wiley.

Fuchs, A. H. (1962). The progression–regression hypothesis in perceptual–motor skill learning. *Journal of Experimental Psychology, 29,* 39–53.

Getschow, C. O., Rosen, M. J., & Goodenough-Trepagnier, C. (1986). A systematic approach to design a minimum distance alphabetical keyboard. *Proceedings of the RESNA (Rehabilitation Engineering Society of North America) 9th Annual Conference, Minneapolis, MN* (pp.396–398).

Goldberg, D., & Richardson, C. (1993). Touching-typing with a stylus. *Proceedings of INTERCHI, ACM Conference on Human Factors in Computing Systems* (pp.80–87). New York: ACM Press.

Karat, C.-M., Halverson, C., Horn, D., & Karat, J. (1999). Patterns of entry and correction in large vocabulary continuous speech recognition systems. *Proceedings of CHI '99: ACM Conference on Human Factors in Computing Systems* (pp.568–574). New York: ACM Press.

Klimt, B., & Yang, Y. (2004). Introducing the Enron corpus. *Proceedings of the Conference on Email and Anti-Spam (CEAS), Mountain View, CA.*

Kohl, R. M., & Shea, C. H. (1992). Pew (1966) revisited: Acquisition of hierarchical control as a function of observational practice. *Journal of Motor Behavior, 24,* 247–260.

Kreitzman, A. (1998). The history of shorthand. *Journal of Court Reporting,* July.

Kristensson, P.-O., & Zhai, S. (2004). SHARK2: A large vocabulary shorthand writing system for pen-based computers. *Proceedings of the ACM Symposium on User Interface Software and Technology* (pp.43–52). New York: ACM Press.

Kurtenbach, G., & Buxton, W. (1994). User learning and performance with marking menus. *Proceedings of CHI: ACM Conference on Human Factors in Computing Systems* (pp.258–264). New York: ACM Press.

Kurtenbach, G., Sellen, A., & Buxton, W. (1993). An empirical evaluation of some articulatory and cognitive aspects of "marking menus." *Human–Computer Interaction, 8,* 1–23.

Landauer, T. K., & Bjork, R. A. (1978). Optimum rehearsal patterns and name learning. In M. M. Gruneberg, P. E. Morris, & R. N. Sykes (Eds.), *Practical aspects of memory* (pp. 625–632). London: Academic Press.

Lewis, J. R. (1992). *Typing-key layouts for single-finger or stylus input: initial user preference and performance* (Technical Report No. 54729). Boca Raton, FL: International Business Machines Corp.

Lewis, J. R., Kennedy, P. J., & LaLomia, M. J. (1992). *Improved typing-key layouts for single-finger or stylus input* (Technical Report No. TR 54.692). Boca Raton, FL: International Business Machines Corp.

Liebowitz, S., & Margolis, S. E. (1996). Typing errors. *Reason Magazine,* http://reason.com/9606/Fe.QWERTY.shtml.

Liebowitz, S. J., & Margolis, S. E. (1990). The fable of the keys. *Journal of Law and Economics, 33(1),* 1–25.

MacKenzie, I. S., & Zhang, S. X. (1999). The design and evaluation of a high-performance soft keyboard. *Proceedings of CHI '99: ACM Conference on Human Factors in Computing Systems* (pp.25–31). New York: ACM Press.

Miller, G. A. (1956). The magical number seven, plus or minus two: Some limits on our capacity for processing information. *Psychological Review, 63,* 81–97.

Schneider, W., & Shiffrin, R. M. (1977). Controlled and automatic human information processing. I. Detection, search, and attention. *Psychological Review, 84,* 1–66.

Shannon, C. E. (1948). A mathematical theory of communication. *Bell System Technical Journal, 27,* 379–423, 623–656.

Smith, B. A., & Zhai, S. (2001). Optimised virtual keyboards with and without alphabetical ordering—A novice user study. *Proceedings of INTERACT 2001—IFIP International Conference on Human–Computer Interaction, Tokyo, Japan* (pp.92–99).

Soukoreff, W., & MacKenzie, I. S. (1995). Theoretical upper and lower bounds on typing speeds using a stylus and keyboard. *Behaviour & Information Technology, 14,* 379–379.

Tappert, C. C., Suen, C. Y., & Wakahara, T. (1990). The state of the art in on-line handwriting recognition. *IEEE Transactions on Pattern Analysis and Machine Intelligence, 12,* 787–808.

Theodoridis, K., & Koutroumbas, K. (1999). *Pattern recognition.* San Diego: Academic Press.

Wang, J., Zhai, S., & Su, H. (2001). Chinese input with keyboard and eye tracking—An anatomical study. *Proceedings of CHI 2001—ACM Conference on Human Factors in Computing Systems* (pp.349–356). New York: ACM Press.

Ward, D., Blackwell, A., & MacKay, D. (2000). Dasher—A data entry interface using continuous gesture and language models. *Proceedings of the 13th ACM Symposium on User Interface Software and Technology (UIST)* (pp.129–136). New York: ACM Press.

Williams, J. R. (1998). Guidelines for the use of multimedia in instruction. *Proceedings of the Human Factors and Ergonomics Society 42nd Annual Meeting* (pp.1447–1451). Santa Monica, CA: HFES.

Wobbrock, J. O., Myers, B. A., & Kembel, J. A. (2003). EdgeWrite: a stylus-based text entry method designed for high accuracy and stability of motion. *Proceedings of the ACM Symposium on User Interface Software and Technology* (pp.61–70). New York: ACM Press.

Yamada, H. (1980). A historical study of typewriters and typing methods: From the position of planning Japanese parallels. *Journal of Information Processing, 2,* 175–202.

Zhai, S., Hunter, M., & Smith, B. A. (2000). The Metropolis keyboard—An exploration of quantitative techniques for virtual keyboard design. *Proceedings of the 13th Annual ACM Symposium on User Interface Software and Technology (UIST)* (pp.119–218). New York: ACM Press.

Zhai, S., Hunter, M., & Smith, B. A. (2002a). Performance optimization of virtual keyboards. *Human–Computer Interaction, 17,* 89–129.

Zhai, S., & Kristensson, P.-O. (2003). Shorthand writing on stylus keyboard. *Proceedings of CHI 2003, ACM Conference on Human Factors in Computing Systems. CHI Letters, 5,* 97–104.

Zhai, S., Kristensson, P.-O., & Smith, B. A. (2005). In search of effective text input interfaces for off the desktop computing. *Interacting with Computers, 17(3),* 229–250.

Zhai, S., & Smith, B. A. (2001). Alphabetically biased virtual keyboards are easier to use—layout does matter. *Proceedings of CHI 2001: ACM Conference on Human Factors in Computing Systems* (pp.321–322). New York: ACM Press.

Zhai, S., Sue, A., & Accot, J. (2002b). Movement model, hits distribution and learning in virtual keyboarding. *Proceedings of CHI 2002: ACM Conference on Human Factors in Computing Systems. CHI Letters, 4,* 17–24.

8 | Speech-Based Interfaces

Sadaoki Furui   Tokyo Institute of Technology, Tokyo, Japan

8.1   INTRODUCTION

Speech is the primary, and most convenient, means of communication between people (Juang & Furui, 2000). Whether it is due to a technological curiosity to build machines that mimic humans or to the desire to automate work with machines, research in machine recognition of human speech, as the first step toward natural human–machine communication, has attracted much enthusiasm over the past 5 decades. The advent of powerful computing devices has given further ongoing hope to this pursuit, particularly in the past few years. While we are still far from having a machine that converses with a human like a human, many important scientific advances have been achieved, bringing us closer to the "Holy Grail" of automatic speech recognition by machine.

8.2   CATEGORIES OF SPEECH RECOGNITION TASKS

Speech recognition tasks may be classified into four categories, as shown in Table 8.1, according to two criteria: whether the system is targeting human-to-human utterances or human-to-computer utterances and whether the utterances have a dialogue or monologue style (Furui, 2003). The table lists typical tasks and data corpora that are representative of each category.

Category I targets human-to-human dialogues. Speech recognition research in this category aiming to produce minutes of meetings (e.g., Janin *et al.*, 2004) has recently started. Waibel and Rogina (2003) have been developing a meeting browser, which observes and tracks meetings for later review and summarization. Akita *et al.* (2004) have investigated techniques for archiving discussions. In their method, speakers are automatically indexed in an unsupervised way, and speech recognition is performed using the results of the indexing. Processing human–human conversational speech

	Dialogue	Monologue
Human to human	Conversations, meetings, interviews (Category I)	Broadcast news, lectures, presentations, voice mail (Category II)
Human to machine	Information retrieval, hotel/ airline reservations (Category III)	Dictation (Category IV)

TABLE   Categorization of speech recognition tasks.

8.1

under unpredictable recording conditions and vocabularies presents new challenges for spoken language processing.

A relatively new task classified into this category is the MALACH (Multilingual Access to Large Spoken Archives) project (Oard, 2004). Its goal is to advance the state-of-the-art technology for access to large multilingual collections of spontaneous conversational speech by exploiting an unmatched collection assembled by the Survivors of the Shoah Visual History Foundation. This collection presents a formidable challenge because of the heavily accented, emotional, and age-related characteristics of the survivors' spontaneous speech. Named entity tagging (tagging by names, prices, etc.), topic segmentation, and unsupervised topic classification are also being investigated.

Tasks belonging to Category II, which focus on recognizing human-to-human monologues, include transcription of broadcast news (e.g., Nguyen *et al.*, 1999), news programs, lectures, presentations (e.g., Furui, 2003), and voice mail (e.g., Hirschberg *et al.*, 2001). Speech recognition research in this category has recently become very active. Since utterances in Category II are made with the expectation that the audience will be able to correctly understand what is said in one-way communication, they are relatively easier to recognize than utterances in Category I. If high recognition performance can be achieved for the utterances in Category II, a wide range of applications such as making lecture notes, records of presentations, and closed captions; archiving and retrieving these records; and retrieving voice mail will be realized. Since almost no one can type Japanese sentences comprising a complex set of characters in real time, closed captioning systems using automatic speech recognition technology have been built and employed by several Japanese broadcast companies (e.g., Ando *et al.*, 2000).

Most of the practical application systems widely used now fall into Category III, recognizing utterances in human–computer dialogues, such as in airline information services tasks. DARPA (Defense Advanced Research Projects Agency)-sponsored projects, including ATIS (Pallet *et al.*, 1990) and Communicator (Gao *et al.*, 2001), have laid the foundations for these systems. Unlike the other categories, the systems in Category III are usually designed and developed after clearly defining the application/task. The machines that have been designed so far are, almost without exception, limited to the simple task of converting a speech signal into a word sequence and then determining from the word sequence a meaning that is "understandable." Here, the set of understandable messages is finite in number, each being associated with a particular action (e.g., route a call to a proper destination or issue a buy order for a particular stock). In this limited sense of speech communication, the focus is detection and recognition rather than inference and generation.

One of the typical tasks belonging to Category IV, which targets the recognition of monologues performed when people are talking to computers, is dictation (text entry). Many commercial software applications have been developed for such purposes. Various research has made clear that utterances spoken by people talking to computers, such as those in Categories III and IV, especially when the people are conscious of computers, are acoustically, as well as linguistically, very different from utterances directed toward other people, such as those in Categories I and II. Since the utterances in Category IV are made with the expectation that the utterances will be converted exactly into texts with correct characters, their spontaneity is much lower than those in Category III. Of the four categories, spontaneity is considered to be the highest in Category I and the lowest in Category IV. Attempts are now being made to automate the process of making minutes for meetings, a task which up to now has required a human typist and special phonetic typewriter. As described before, this task belongs to Category I. Since dictation and spoken dialogue are the most basic methods used for text entry, they will be extensively described in Sections 8.4 and 8.5.

Speech recognition tasks can also be classified according to whether they involve isolated word recognition or continuous speech recognition and whether the task requires a speaker-dependent or speaker-independent system. In the case of isolated words, the beginning and the end of each word can be detected directly from the energy of the signal. This makes word boundary detection (segmentation) and recognition much easier than if the words are connected. However, in real applications in which speech is contaminated by noise, it is not always easy to detect word boundaries by simply relying on the energy of the signal. Speaker-independent recognition is more difficult than speaker-dependent recognition, since the speech model must somehow be general enough to cover all types of voices and all possible variations in word pronunciation and yet sophisticated enough to discriminate between individual words. For a speaker-dependent system, training or adaptation of speech models is carried out by using utterances from each prospective user. In speaker adaptation, the system is bootstrapped with speaker-independent models and then gradually adapted to the specific characteristics of individual speakers/users.

8.3   PRINCIPLES OF SPEECH RECOGNITION

In the current state-of-the-art approach, human speech production as well as the recognition process is modeled through four stages, text generation, speech production, acoustic processing, and linguistic decoding, as shown in Fig. 8.1 (Furui, 2001). A speaker is represented as a transducer that transforms into speech the "text" of thoughts he/she intends to communicate (information source). Based on the

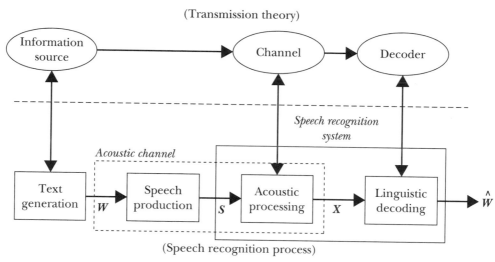

FIGURE   Structure of the state-of-the-art speech recognition system.

8.1

information transmission theory, this sequence of processes is compared to an information transmission system in which a word sequence W is converted into an acoustic observation sequence X, with a probability $P(W, X)$, through a noisy transmission channel, which is then decoded into an estimated sequence $\hat{W}$. The goal of recognition is then to decode the word string, based on the acoustic observation sequence, so that the decoded string has the maximum a posteriori (MAP) probability (Rabiner & Juang, 1993; Young, 1996), i.e.,

$$\hat{W} = \underset{W}{\mathrm{argmax}}\, P(W\,|\,X) \qquad (8.1)$$

Using Bayes' rule, Eq. (8.1) can be rewritten as

$$\hat{W} = \underset{W}{\mathrm{argmax}}\, P(X\,|\,W)P(W)/P(X) \qquad (8.2)$$

Since $P(X)$ is independent of W, the MAP decoding rule of Eq. (8.2) is converted into

$$\hat{W} = \underset{W}{\mathrm{argmax}}\, P(X\,|\,W)P(W) \qquad (8.3)$$

The first term in Eq. (8.3), $P(X|W)$, is generally called the acoustic model as it estimates the probability of a sequence of acoustic observations conditioned with the

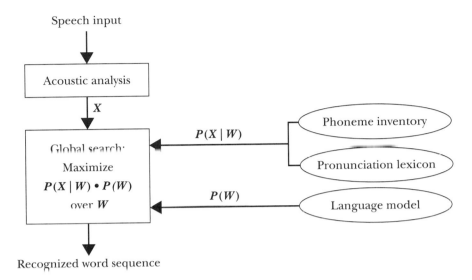

Speech input

Acoustic analysis

X

Global search:
Maximize
$P(X \mid W) \bullet P(W)$
over W

$P(X \mid W)$

Phoneme inventory

Pronunciation lexicon

$P(W)$

Language model

Recognized word sequence

FIGURE   Overview of statistical speech recognition.

8.2

word string. The second term, $P(W)$, is generally called the language model since it describes the probability associated with a postulated sequence of words. Such language models can incorporate both syntactic and semantic constraints of the language and the recognition task. Often, when only syntactic constraints are used, the language model is called a grammar.

The cepstrum, or cepstral coefficient, defined as the inverse Fourier transform of the short-time logarithmic amplitude spectrum, is typically used as the acoustic feature. The term *cepstrum* is essentially a coined word that includes the meaning of the inverse transform of the spectrum. The special feature of the cepstrum is that it allows for separate representation of the spectral envelope and fine structure. The lower order cepstral coefficients representing the spectral envelope are used in combination with their transitional coefficients, "delta and delta–delta cepstral coefficients" (Furui, 2001). In order to increase robustness against various speech variations by taking the human auditory characteristics into consideration, the logarithmic spectrum is usually resampled at Mel-scale frequency and converted into Mel frequency cepstral coefficients.

Hidden Markov models (HMMs) and statistical language models are usually employed as the acoustic and language models, respectively. Figure 8.2 shows the information flow of the MAP decoding process given the parameterized acoustic signal X. The likelihood of the acoustic signal $P(X|W)$ is computed using a composite HMM representing W constructed from simple HMM phoneme models joined in sequence according to word pronunciations stored in a dictionary (lexicon).

8.4   DICTATION SYSTEMS AND THEIR DIFFICULTIES

Dictation systems that use automatic speech recognition technology are now employed at many hospitals for making reports on medical examinations and records of radiograph diagnoses and observations. Although their performance is not as good as experienced human dictation-takers, the dictation systems are successfully used to reduce the cost of human labor. These dictation systems are also used by handicapped writers, such as reporters and novelists, who have difficulty in using typewriters.

In order to achieve high automatic recognition performance, users need to utter each sentence as clearly and fluently as possible, without inserting hesitations, pauses, or fillers, such as "um"s or "ah"s. Due to pronunciation errors and various factors described below, speech recognition errors cannot be avoided. Therefore, it is crucial to prepare a mechanism for easily correcting errors, which will in part determine the ease of using the systems. Since the speech recognition process uses language models for each sentence hypothesis, the recognition results cannot be fixed until the speaker has finished uttering the entire sentence. Therefore, the user cannot check speech recognition results continuously from the sentence beginning to the end, in parallel with the utterance input. Instead, the user must wait to check recognition results for a given sentence until after finishing the sentence input, which imposes a burden on user's memory. When recognition errors are found, they need to be corrected by keyboard, since isolated word utterances for correction are not easy to recognize. This reduces the convenience of using automatic speech recognition-based dictation systems. Due to these problems, the market for dictation systems/software has not yet been extended beyond the limited application domains described above.

There are several factors affecting the performance of current dictation systems. First, several factors have an impact on the quality of the input speech. These include the environmental conditions at the time of input (background noise, etc.), the type of microphone used, and the transmission channel bandwidth and compression if any (high bandwidth speech, landline and cell phone speech, etc.). Second, factors concerning the speakers themselves and the amount of training data available also affect performance. The speaker factors include physical and emotional states (under stress or ill), speaker cooperativeness, and familiarity with the system. Finally, system performance depends heavily on the input complexity.

Ideally, all these factors should be taken into account when designing evaluation paradigms or when comparing the performance of two systems on different types of input. The excellent performance obtained under artificially good conditions (quiet environment, high-quality microphone, and consecutive inputs of the training and test material) rapidly degrades in real-life situations. Therefore, it is important to make a profile of the acoustic environment in which the system is typically used. It is also important to know that for high noise conditions, such as higher than 60 dB(A), the Lombard effect (Furui, 2001) may change the level and voice of a speaker.

Increasing the robustness of speech recognition algorithms is crucial to making future dictation systems/software really useful.

8.5 SPOKEN DIALOGUE SYSTEMS AND THEIR DIFFICULTIES

As described in Section 8.2, spoken dialogue systems (SDSs) are now widely used mainly in telephone-based information and transaction services. Since these systems, like traditional dictation systems, are highly susceptible to variations in the speech signal caused by environmental and user variations, it is crucial to increase the robustness of these systems. The utterances in SDSs are in general more difficult to recognize than those encountered in dictation systems, since they are shorter and more spontaneous and have more disfluencies and fillers than those encountered in dictation systems. In addition, in contrast to dictation systems, it is very difficult to apply user-specific model adaptation to SDSs. This is mainly due to the fact that dictation systems usually involve a small number of users repeatedly using the system over a long period of time, whereas SDSs involve just the opposite: a very large number of individuals who often employ the system no more than once or twice. Finally, although recognition errors produced by dictation systems can be corrected by user-directed keyboard input, in an SDS environment errors need to be corrected using spoken utterances.

On the other hand, as described in Section 8.2, applications/tasks for SDSs are usually clearly defined, and therefore, in contrast to dictation systems, it is possible to correct speech recognition errors or guide users' utterances through dialogues using application/task-dependent constraints and to apply sophisticated strategies to achieve users' goals with a limited number of interactions. One of the difficulties posed by SDSs is that, even when the domain of a task is defined, the vocabulary related to this task may not necessarily be clear to the users. Furthermore, in many scenarios it may be impractical or even impossible to provide users with explicit information about supported vocabulary and out-of-vocabulary (OOV) words. Thus, how to correctly reject the OOVs spoken by users, instead of recognizing them as the closest words in the dictionary, presents another difficult but crucial issue.

There are two fundamental strategies currently employed to design SDSs: these are user-initiative strategies and system-initiative strategies. Since systems based on the former provide a higher degree of freedom for users, they are easier to use and more convenient than the latter if the system is functioning properly. However, when users have only a small amount of knowledge about the system, the latter strategy, in which systems make requests to users and users simply respond to them, often results in a more user-friendly system. Because the system-initiative strategy is more amenable to the handling of speech recognition errors, most commercial systems are based on this strategy. Ideally these systems should also incorporate shortcut strategies, since it is often tedious for frequent users to repeatedly go through an entire preset dialogue when they already know their objective. Because there are the pros and cons to each of the two strategies, mixed-initiative systems combining both are often designed.

8.6   EVALUATION OF SPEECH-BASED INPUT SYSTEMS

8.6.1   Introduction

Given the complexity of the human–computer interface, it is clear that evaluation protocols that address a large number of different types of speech-based input systems are required. The majority of research in the area of speech-based input system evaluation has concentrated on evaluating system components, such as measuring the word recognition accuracy for a speech recognizer, rather than on overall effectiveness measures for complete systems.

In order to give the reader information on how to evaluate the performance of speech-based input systems, this section first introduces various performance measures, followed by discussions of the parameters that affect the performance. The section then goes on to an evaluation framework, which includes high-level sophisticated metrics such as correction and transaction success.

To obtain a more detailed description of various evaluation techniques for speech-based input systems, readers are encouraged to refer to the handbook by Gibbon *et al.* (1998).

8.6.2   Classification of Evaluation Methods

Techniques for evaluating speech-based input methods/systems can be categorized as either subjective or objective. The former directly involves human subjects during measurement, whereas the latter, typically using prerecorded speech, does not directly involve human subjects. Objective methods have the advantage of producing reproducible results and of lending themselves to being automated; thus, they are also more economical. The problem with objective methods for speech-based input application evaluation is that it is difficult to create methods with the capacity to cope easily with the complex processes required for evaluating speech recognition or interaction systems. On the other hand, subjective methods are more suited to evaluating applications with higher semantic or dialogue content, but they suffer from the fact that human subjects cannot reliably perform quantitative measurement or handle fine-grained measurement scales. This is because, on average, a human subject uses gradation scales with 5 to 10 levels and no more.

In order to compare the performance of different speech recognition systems, quantitative comparisons should be carried out only on a common subset of capabilities.

In comparative testing, it is also necessary to normalize the difficulty of the task of each system. For this purpose, the following task-difficulty evaluation methods are used.

8.6.3   Evaluation of Speech Recognition Task Difficulty

In order to reduce the relevant number of words to select from, recognition systems are often equipped with some linguistic knowledge. This may vary from very strict syntax rules, in which the words that may follow one another are defined by explicit rules, to probabilistic language models, in which the probability of the output sentence is taken into consideration, based on statistical knowledge of the language. An objective measure of the freedom of the language model is the *perplexity*, which measures the average branching factor of the language model (Ney *et al.*, 1997). The higher the perplexity, the more words there are to choose from at each instant and hence the more difficult the task.

The perplexity (PP) is defined by

$$PP = 2^{H(L)}, \tag{8.4}$$

where $H(L)$ is the *entropy* of the language model per word, which is defined by

$$H(L) = -\sum_{w_1 \dots w_n} \frac{1}{n} P(w_1 \dots w_n) \log P(w_1 \dots w_n). \tag{8.5}$$

Here, $P(w_1 \dots w_n)$ is the probability of producing a word sequence $w_1 \dots w_n$ given the language model L. $H(L)$ indicates the amount of information (bits) necessary to specify a word produced by the language model. The perplexity defined above is often called language-model perplexity.

Performance of a speech recognition system depends not only on its task but also on texts of a test set, that is, a set of utterances to be used for a recognition test. Therefore, in order to evaluate the difficulty of the test set, the perplexity is often calculated for the test set, which is called *test-set perplexity* or *corpus perplexity*. If we can assume that the language is statistically ergodic, the entropy per word can be calculated as

$$H(L) = -\frac{1}{Q} \log P_{\mathrm{M}}\left(w_1 \dots w_Q\right), \tag{8.6}$$

where $P_{\mathrm{M}}(w_1 \dots w_Q)$ is the probability of producing the test-set word sequence $w_1 \dots w_Q$. Therefore, the test-set perplexity can be calculated as follows:

$$PP = 2^{H(L)} = P_{\mathrm{M}}\left(w_1 \dots w_Q\right)^{-\frac{1}{Q}}. \tag{8.7}$$

The above equations show that the test-set perplexity is the geometric average of the reciprocal probability over all Q words. Apart from the constant factor $(-1/Q)$, the perplexity is identical to the average conditional probability or likelihood. Therefore, minimizing the perplexity is the same as maximizing the log-likelihood function. Since the test set for recognition experiments should be separate from the corpus that is used to construct the language model, the language-model perplexity and the test-set perplexity are usually different.

When a formal grammar, such as a finite automaton and context-free grammar, is used as the language model, every partially parsed tree up to word w_i ($1 \leq i \leq Q$) is made, and the number of words that can follow the word w_i is calculated. The test-set perplexity is obtained as a geometric mean of the number of possible following words at each word w_i, assuming that every word is selected with equal probability.

The set of all words the recognition system has been designed to recognize is called the *vocabulary*, V_L. The vocabulary size is one of the measures indicating the task difficulty. The test vocabulary V_R is defined as the set of words appearing in the evaluation test. A word w is called out of vocabulary if it is present in the test vocabulary but not present in the recognizer's vocabulary. The *OOV rate* is defined as the ratio of the number of words in the test set that are not included in V_L to the total number of words in the test set. In general, the larger the test vocabulary size V_R and the larger the OOV rate, the more difficult the task is.

Although the perplexity and the OOV rate measure the test source's complexity from the recognizer's point of view, they refer to written (e.g., transcribed) forms of language only and completely disregard acoustic–phonetic modeling. The difficulty of the recognition task also depends on the length of the sentences (average number of words) and the average number of phonemes comprising each word. Therefore, task difficulty needs to be measured as a combination of various factors covering both linguistic and acoustic complexity.

8.6.4 Objective Evaluation of General Recognition Performance

Isolated Word Scoring

The *error rate* of speech recognition is defined as "the average fraction of items incorrectly recognized." Here, an item can be a word, a subword unit (e.g., a phone), or an entire utterance. For an isolated word recognition system, the error rate is defined as

$$E = N_E/N. \tag{8.8}$$

Here, N is the number of words in the test utterance and N_E the number of words incorrectly recognized. The latter can be subdivided into substitution error, N_S, and deletion (incorrect rejection) error, N_D:

$$N_E = N_S + N_D. \tag{8.9}$$

Sometimes the fraction of correctly recognized words, $C = 1 - E$, called *correctness*, is used:

$$C = \frac{N_C}{N} = \frac{N - N_S - N_D}{N}.$$ (8.10)

These measures do not include so-called insertions, since it is assumed that the beginning and the end of each word can be detected directly from the energy of the signal. However, in real applications in which speech is contaminated by noise, it is not always easy to detect word boundaries, and sometimes noise signals cause insertion errors. Therefore, under these real-world conditions, the same measure as that used in continuous word scoring, which will be described later, is also used in the isolated recognition task.

For isolated word recognizers, a measure more specific than the various contributions to the error rate, *a confusion matrix*, has also been used, in which the class of substitutions is divided into all possible confusions between words. The confusion C_{ij} is defined as the probability that word i is recognized as word j. The value C_{ii} is the fraction of times word i is correctly recognized. These probabilities are estimated by measuring the number of times the confusion took place,

$$C_{ij} = \frac{N_{ij}}{\sum_{i'} N_{i'j}},$$ (8.11)

where N_{ij} is the number of times word j was recognized on the input word i. The confusion matrix gives more detailed information than the error rates. Insertions and deletions can also be included in the matrix by adding a null word $i = 0$ (nonvocabulary word). Then, the row C_{0j} contains insertions, the column C_{i0} the deletions, and $C_{00} = 0$. Using this expanded confusion matrix, the error rate can be calculated from the diagonal elements, i.e., $E = 1 - \sum_i C_{ii} = \sum_{i \neq j} C_{ij}$. The elements C_{ij} for $i \neq j$ are called the off-diagonal elements.

Continuous Word Scoring

In continuous speech recognition, the output words are generally not time synchronous with the input utterance. Therefore, the output stream has to be aligned with the reference transcriptions. This means that classifications such as substitutions, deletions, correct words, and insertions can no longer be identified with complete certainty. The actual measurement of the quantities through alignment is difficult. The alignment process uses a dynamic programming algorithm to minimize the misalignment of two strings of words (symbols), the reference sentence and the recognized sentence. The alignment depends on the relative weights of the contributions of the three types of the errors: substitutions, insertions, and deletions. Hunt (1990) discussed the theory of word–symbol alignment and analyzed several experiments on alignment. Usually, the three types of errors have equal weights. Depending on the application, one can assign different weights to the various kinds of errors.

Thus, the total number of errors is the summation of three types of errors,

$$N_E = N_S + N_I + N_D, \tag{8.12}$$

where N_S, N_I, and N_D are the numbers of substitutions, insertions, and deletions, respectively. The error rate is therefore

$$E = \frac{N_E}{N} = \frac{N_S + N_I + N_D}{N}. \tag{8.13}$$

Note that this error measure can become larger than 1 in cases of extremely bad recognition. Often, one defines the *accuracy* of a system as

$$A = 1 - E = \frac{N - N_S - N_I - N_D}{N}. \tag{8.14}$$

Note that the accuracy is not just the fraction C of words correctly recognized, because the latter does not include insertions.

8.6.5 Objective Evaluation of Dictation and Spoken Dialogue Systems

Various commercial systems (software) for dictation using automatic speech recognition have been developed. The performance measures that can be used for evaluating these systems are:

1. Recognition accuracy.

2. Dictation speed: the number of words per minute that can be handled.

3. Error correction strategies: a good measure for the ease of error correction is the average time spent per correction.

Dictation systems can be compared to other systems and also to human performance. Error rate and dictation speed are the most obvious performance measures for the human benchmark.

Performance measures that can be used for evaluating spoken dialogue systems are:

1. Recognition accuracy.

2. OOV rejection: a good system correctly rejects OOV words and asks the users to rephrase, instead of wrongly recognizing them as vocabulary words. This is actually

a very difficult issue, since there is no perfect confidence measure for the recognition results.

3. Error recovery: both the system and the user are sources of errors. A good system allows the user to undo actions triggered by previous spoken commands.

4. Response time: important for good usability is the time it takes to respond to a spoken command, i.e., system reaction time. This is defined as the time from the end of the command utterance to the start of the action. Both the average time and the distribution of the response time are important parameters

5. Percentage of tasks successfully completed.

6. Average number of interactions required to complete a task successfully.

To learn more about the details of the issues involved in evaluating telephone-based spoken dialogue systems, readers are advised to refer to the textbook by Moeller (2005).

8.6.6 Subjective Evaluation Methods

In subjective evaluations, tests are designed in such a way that human subjects interact with the system. Subjective measures include level of intelligibility, general impression, annoyance, user friendliness, intuitiveness, level of difficulty, and subjective impression of system response time. The ultimate overall measure is: "Can the task be completed?" This is a measure that includes recognition, error recovery, situational awareness, and feedback. In this sense, the time required to complete the entire test might also be indicative of the quality of the system. General impressions of test subjects can be indicative of how the system performs.

8.7 CONCLUSION

Over 3 decades of research in spoken language processing have produced remarkable advances in automatic speech recognition and helped us take a big step toward natural human–machine communication. Signal processing techniques led to a better understanding of speech characteristics, and the introduction of a statistical framework not only makes the problem of automatic recognition of speech tractable but also paves the road to practical engineering system designs. Coupled with a finite state representation of a language, hidden Markov modeling has become the underpinning of most of today's speech recognition systems. To accomplish the ultimate goal of a machine that can communicate with people, however, a number of research issues are awaiting further study.

Technology development and evaluation are two sides of the same coin; we cannot make useful progress until we make a good measure of what progress is. However, since human–computer interfaces using speech are very complex, it is not easy to establish effective evaluation strategies. Although various investigations on evaluation methods have been conducted and various measures have been proposed, a truly comprehensive set of metrics has not yet been developed. Since the target of speech recognition is now shifting from clean, read speech to natural spontaneous speech contaminated by noise and distortions, evaluating a system's performance is becoming increasingly difficult.

The ultimate speech recognition-based interfaces need to be able to deliver satisfactory performance under a broad range of operating conditions and have an efficient way of representing, storing, and retrieving the "knowledge" required for a natural conversation (Furui *et al.*, 2004). However, with the current enthusiasm in research advances, we are optimistic that this Holy Grail of natural human–machine communication will soon be within our technological reach.

REFERENCES

Akita, Y., Nishida, M., & Kawahara, T. (2003). Automatic transcription of discussions using unsupervised speaker indexing. *Proc. IEEE Workshop on Spontaneous Speech Processing and Recognition, 13–16 April 2003, Tokyo* (pp.79–82).

Ando, A., Imai, T., Kobayashi, A., Isono, H., & Nakabayashi, K. (2000). Real-time transcription system for simultaneous subtitling of Japanese broadcast news programs. *IEEE Transactions on Broadcasting, 46,* 189–196.

Furui, S. (2001). *Digital speech processing, synthesis, and recognition, (2nd ed.).* New York: Dekker.

Furui, S. (2003). Toward spontaneous speech recognition and understanding. In W. Chou & B.-H. Juang (Eds.), *Pattern recognition in speech and language processing* (pp.191–227). New York: CRC Press.

Furui, S., Kikuchi, T., Shinnaka, Y., & Hori, C. (2004). Speech-to-text and speech-to-speech summarization of spontaneous speech. *IEEE Transactions on Speech and Audio, 12,* 401–408.

Gao, Y., Erdogan, H., Li, Y., Goel, V., & Picheny, M. (2001). Recent advances in speech recognition systems for IBM DARPA communicator. *Proceedings of Eurospeech2001, 3–7 September 2001, Aalborg, Denmark* (pp.503–506).

Gibbon, D., Moore, R., & Winski, R. (Eds.) (1998). Spoken language system assessment. In *Handbook of standards and resources for spoken language systems, Vol. III.* Berlin: Mouton de Gruyter.

Hirschberg, J., Bacchiani, M., Hindle, D., Isenhour, P., Rosenberg, A., Stark, L., Stead, L., Whittaker S., & Zamchick, G. (2001). SCANMail: Browsing and searching speech data by content. *Proceedings of Eurospeech2001, 3–7 September 2001, Aalborg, Denmark* (pp.2377–2380).

Hunt, M. (1990). Figures of merit for assessing connected-word recognizers. *Speech Communication, 9*, 329–336.

Janin, A., Ang, J., Bhagat, S., Dhillon, R., Edwards, J., Macias-Guarasa, J., Morgan, N., Peskin, B., Shriberg, E., Stolcke, A., Wooters, C., & Wrede, B. (2004). The ICSI Meeting project: Resources and research. *Proceedings of the NIST ICASSP 2004 Meeting Recognition Workshop, 17 May 2004, Montreal.*

Juang, B.-H., & Furui, S. (2000). Automatic recognition and understanding of spoken language—A first step toward natural human–machine communication. *Proceedings of the IEEE, 88*, 1142–1165.

Moeller, S. (2005). *Quality of telephone-based spoken dialogue systems.* New York: Springer.

Ney, H., Martin, S., & Wessel, F. (1997). Statistical language modeling using leaving-one-out. In S. Young & G. Bloothooft (Eds.), *Corpus-based methods in language and speech processing* (pp.174–207). Dordrecht: Kluwer Academic.

Nguyen, L., Matsoukas, S., Davenport, J., Liu, D., Billa, J., Kubala, F., & Makhoul, J. (1999). Further advances in transcription of broadcast news. *Proceedings of Eurospeech99, 5–9 September 1999, Budapest* (pp.667–670).

Oard, D. W. (2004). Transforming access to the spoken word. *Proceedings of the International Symposium on Large-Scale Knowledge Resources, 8–9 March 2004, Tokyo* (pp.57–59).

Pallett, D., Fisher, W., Fiscus, J., & Garofolo, J. (1990). DARPA ATIS test results, June 1990. *Proceedings of the Speech and Natural Language Workshop, 24–27 June 1990* (pp.114–121).

Rabiner, L. R., & Juang, B.-H. (1993). *Fundamentals of speech recognition.* Upper Saddle River, NJ: Prentice Hall.

Waibel, A., & Rogina, I. (2003). Advances on ISL's lecture and meeting trackers. *Proceedings of the IEEE Workshop on Spontaneous Speech Processing and Recognition, 13–16 April 2003, Tokyo* (pp.127–130).

Young, S. (1996). A review of large-vocabulary continuous-speech recognition. *IEEE Signal Processing Magazine, 13*, 45–57.

9 | Text Entry by Gaze: Utilizing Eye Tracking

CHAPTER

Päivi Majaranta and Kari-Jouko Räihä   University of Tampere, Tampere, Finland

9.1   INTRODUCTION

Text entry by eyes is essential for severely disabled people with motor disorders who have no other means of communication. By using a computer equipped with an eye-tracking device, people suffering from amyotrophic lateral sclerosis or the locked-in syndrome, for instance, can produce text by using the focus of gaze as a means of input.

In one sense, text entry by eye gaze is quite similar to any screen-based text entry technique, such as the on-screen keyboards used with tablet PCs. The interface is more or less the same, only the interaction technique for pointing and selecting changes. Instead of a stylus or other pointing device, eye gaze is used. However, this change in the interaction technique brings with it fundamental differences, giving rise to a number of design issues that make text entry by eye gaze a unique technique with its own set of research problems.

The fundamental reason for this is that the eye is a perceptual organ: eyes are normally used for observation, not for control. Nevertheless, gaze direction does indicate the focus of the viewer's visual attention (Just & Carpenter, 1976). Thus, despite eyes being primarily a perceptual organ, gaze can be considered as a natural means of pointing. It is easy to focus on items by looking at them (Stampe & Reingold, 1995). However, gaze provides information only about the direction of the user's interest, not the user's intentions. All on-screen objects touched by the eye gaze cannot be activated. Doing so would cause the so-called Midas touch problem (Jacob, 1991): everywhere you look something gets activated. At least one additional bit of information is needed to avoid the Midas touch, such as a click from a separate switch or an "eye press" by staring at a button for a predetermined amount of time ("dwell time").

The inaccuracy of the measured point of gaze presents another challenge. Most of the current eye-tracking devices achieve an accuracy of $0.5°$ (equivalent to a region of approximately 15 pixels on a 17-in. display with a resolution of 1024×768 pixels viewed from a distance of 70 cm). Even if eye trackers were perfectly accurate, the size of the fovea restricts the practical accuracy to about 0.5–1°. Everything inside the foveal region is seen in detail. Visual attention can be retargeted within the foveal region at will without actually moving the eyes. Thus, an absolute, pixel-level accuracy may never be reached by gaze pointing alone.

The accuracy of eye tracking is also very much dependent on successful calibration. Before an eye-tracking device can be used for gaze pointing, it has to be calibrated for each user. The calibration is done by showing a few (typically 5–12) points on screen and asking the user to look at them one by one. The camera takes a picture of the eye when the user looks at the calibration points. This enables the computer then to analyze any eye image while the user is looking at the screen and associate the image with screen coordinates.

In addition to the design challenges, gaze-based interaction also provides some new opportunities. Eyes are extremely fast. Eye movements anticipate actions: people typically look at things before they act on them (Land & Furneaux, 1997). Hence, eyes have the potential to enhance interaction.

We will continue by presenting different techniques for text entry by gaze, followed by a review of various evaluations concerning the speed of the entry by gaze and detailed design issues. We close by suggestions for further reading.

9.2   DIFFERENT APPROACHES TO TEXT ENTRY BY GAZE

Systems that utilize eye tracking for text entry have existed since the 1970s (Majaranta & Räihä, 2002). In fact, the first real-time applications using eye tracking in human–computer interaction were targeted at people with disabilities (Jacob & Karn, 2003). Eyes can be used for text entry in various ways. In this section we first focus on systems that utilize information from the gaze direction (direct gaze pointing). Then, a brief review of other ways of using the eyes is given.

9.2.1   Text Entry by Direct Gaze Pointing

The most common way to use gaze for text entry is direct pointing by looking at the desired letter. A typical setup has an on-screen keyboard with a static layout, an eye-tracking device that tracks the user's gaze, and a computer that analyzes the user's gaze behavior (see Fig. 9.1).

To type by gaze, the user *focuses* on the desired letter by looking at one of the keys on the on-screen keyboard. The system gives *feedback* on the focused item, for example, by highlighting the focused item or by moving a "gaze cursor" over the focused key. The focused item can be *selected* by using, for instance, a separate switch, a blink, a wink, or even a wrinkle or any other (facial) muscle activity. Muscle activity is typically

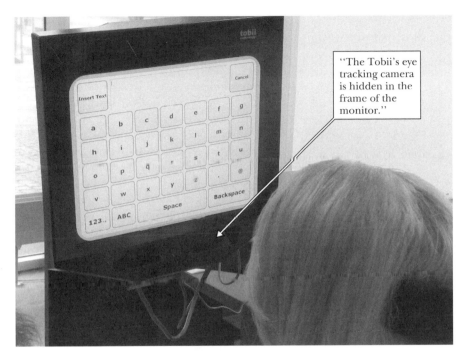

FIGURE

9.1

The Tobii eye-tracking device has a camera integrated into the frame of the monitor that shows the on-screen keyboard.

measured by electromyography (see, e.g., Surakka *et al.*, 2003), though blinks and winks can also be detected from the same video signal used to analyze eye movements.

For severely disabled people, *dwell time* is the best and often the only way of selection ("eye press"). A dwell means a prolonged gaze: the user needs to fixate on the key for longer than a predefined threshold (typically, 500–1000 ms) in order for the key to be selected. Requiring the user to fixate for a long time helps in preventing false selections, but it is uncomfortable for the user, as fixations longer than 800 ms are often broken by blinks or saccades[1] (Stampe & Reingold, 1995).

The inaccuracy of the measured point of gaze was a considerable problem especially in the early days of eye tracking. Therefore, the keys on the screen had to be quite large. For example, the first version of the ERICA system (Hutchinson *et al.*, 1989) had only six selectable items available on the screen at a time. The letters were organized in a tree-structured menu hierarchy. The user first selected a group of letters

---

[1] Our eyes usually are stable for only a brief period at a time. Such *fixations* typically last 200–600 ms (Jacob, 1995). *Saccades* occur between fixations when we move our eyes. Saccades are ballistic movements that last about 30–120 ms.

and then either another group of letters or the single target letter. Typing was slow, as it took from two to four menu selections to select a single letter. Letters were arranged in the hierarchy based on word frequencies, so that the expected number of steps for text entry was minimized (Frey *et al.*, 1990).

Layouts with large keys are still needed and used in today's systems. Even though the state-of-the-art eye trackers are fairly accurate, the so-called "low-cost systems" still do not reach the accuracy needed for a Qwerty keyboard. For example, the GazeTalk system (Hansen *et al.*, 2001) was developed with a standard Web camera in mind (Hansen *et al.*, 2002). It divides the screen into a 3×4 grid (see Fig. 9.2). The six cells on the bottom right contain the six most likely letters to continue the word that is being entered (shown in the two top left cells). The leftmost entry on the middle row provides a short-hand access to the eight most likely completions: by activating that button, the screen changes into one on which those words appear in the cells in the two bottom rows. If none of the suggested continuations (words or letters) is correct, the user has access to the "A to Z" button that appears in the bottom row of cells with the next hierarchical level, like in the ERICA system above.

Finally, even if the eye trackers were perfectly accurate, systems with large buttons are still useful. In addition to the accuracy limitations due to the size of the fovea, some medical conditions cause involuntary head movements or eye tremors, which prevent getting a good calibration (Donegan *et al.*, 2005).

FIGURE
9.2

The 3×4 on-screen grid of the GazeTalk system.

9.2.2   Text Entry by Eye Switches and Gaze Gestures

Voluntary eye blinks can be used as binary switches (see, e.g., Grauman *et al.*, 2003). For text entry, blinks are usually combined with a "scanning" technique (see Chap. 15), in which letters are organized into a matrix. The system moves the focus automatically by scanning the alphabet matrix line by line. The highlighted line is selected by an eye blink. Then the individual letters on the selected line are scanned through and again the user blinks when the desired letter is highlighted.

In addition to eye blinks, coarse eye movements can also be used as switches. The Eye-Switch Controlled Communication Aids by Ten Kate *et al.* (1979) used large (about 15°) eye movements to the left and to the right as switches. It, too, applied the scanning technique. The user could start the scanning by glancing to the left and select the currently focused item by glancing to the right.

I4Control (Fejtová *et al.*, 2004) can be considered to be a four-direction eye-operated joystick, as looking at any of the four directions (left, right, up, down) causes the cursor to move at that direction until the eye returns to the home position (center). The cursor can also be stopped by blinking. A blink emulates a click or double-click. Text entry by I4Control is achieved by moving the mouse cursor over the desired key on an on-screen keyboard and selecting the key by an eye blink.

The four different eye movements recognized by I4Control can be considered to be four switches, each activated by a different glance or eye gesture. Several eye gestures can also be combined into one operation, just as several key presses are used to enter a letter in the multitap method for mobile phones. This approach is used in VisionKey (Kahn *et al.*, 1999), in which an eye tracker and a keyboard display (Fig. 9.3, right) are attached to eyeglass frames (Fig. 9.3, left). As the key chart is attached in

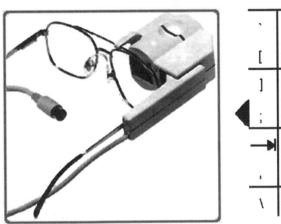
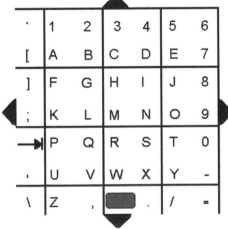

FIGURE
9.3

VisionKey is attached to eyeglass frames (left). It has a small screen integrated to it (right) (http://www.eyecan.ca).

front of the user's eye, it is important to make sure that plain staring at a letter does not select it. The VisionKey selection method avoids the Midas touch problem by using a two-level selection method, i.e., two consecutive eye gestures for activating a selection. To select a character, the user must first gaze at the edge of the chart that corresponds to the location of the character in its block. For example, if the user wants to select the letter "G", the user first glances at the upper right corner of the chart and then looks at the block where "G" is located (or simply looks at "G"). After a pre-defined dwell time the selected key is highlighted to confirm a successful selection.

Using eye blinks or gaze gestures (instead of direct gaze pointing) is needed by people who are able to move their eyes only in one direction or who have trouble fixating their gaze due to their medical condition (Chapman, 1991; Donegan *et al.*, 2005).

9.2.3   Text Entry by Continuous Gaze Gestures

The techniques presented in Section 9.2.2 made use of discrete, consecutive gaze gestures. Dasher (Ward & MacKay, 2002) is a zooming interface that is operated by

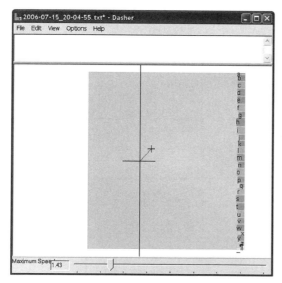 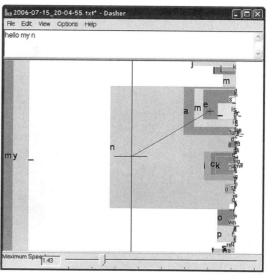

FIGURE

9.4

Dasher facilitates text entry by navigation through a zooming world of letters. In the initial state, the letters are ordered alphabetically on the right side of the screen (image on the left). As the user looks at the desired letter, its area starts to grow and simultaneously the language prediction system gives more space to the next most probable letters. In the image on the right, the user is in the middle of writing "name," with "n" already selected. Dasher is freely available online at http://www.inference.phy.cam.ac.uk/dasher/ and http://www.cogain.org.

continuous pointing gestures. At the beginning, the letters of the alphabet are located in a column on the right side of the screen (see Fig. 9.4). Letters are ordered alphabetically (Fig. 9.4, left). The user moves the cursor to point at the region that contains the desired letter by looking at the letter. The area of the selected letter starts to zoom in (grow) and move to the left, closer to the center of the screen (Fig. 9.4, right). Simultaneously, the language model of the system predicts the most probable next letters. The areas of the most probable letters start to grow (compared to other, not as probable, letters) within the chosen region. This brings the next most probable letters closer to the current cursor position, thus minimizing the distance and time to select the next letter(s). The letter is typed when it crosses the horizontal line on the center of the screen. Canceling the last letter is done by looking to the left; the letter then moves back to the right side of the screen.

Dasher's mode-free continuous operation makes it especially suitable for gaze as only one bit of information is required: the direction of gaze. No additional switches or dwell time are needed to make a selection or to cancel. Furthermore, instead of adding separate buttons or lists with the next most probable words, Dasher embeds the predictions into the writing process itself. Many successive characters can be selected by a single gesture, and often-used words are easier and faster to write than rare words. This not only speeds up the text entry process but also makes it easier: In a comparative evaluation, users made fewer mistakes with Dasher than with a standard Qwerty keyboard.

The continuous gestures used in Dasher make it a radically different technique compared to all the others we have discussed. Some gestures can essentially select more than one character (the selection point does not have to be moved, since the display moves dynamically), which can speed up text entry. The most likely characters occupy a large portion of the display space, so that gestures do not always need to be accurate. Dasher can be used with any input device that is capable of gesturing. It has been implemented on a pocket PC to be used by a stylus and can even be controlled by breathing using a special breath-mouse.

9.3 CASE STUDIES AND GUIDELINES

9.3.1 Entry Speed Evaluations

The speed of text entry by eye gaze depends on a number of factors. The evaluation methods and metrics discussed in the earlier chapters can be applied, but it is typical that even with the same basic technique, many parameters, such as the threshold for dwell-time selection, can be adjusted, and this affects the theoretical maximum speed obtainable by a technique. Also, learning to master text entry by eye typing requires a long learning period. Gips *et al.* (1996) report that "for people with severe disabilities it can take anywhere from 15 minutes to many months to acquire eye control skill to run the system." The speed of real experts has not been systematically measured for any of the eye-controlled text entry systems.

With on-screen keyboards and dwell-time selection (the most common setup), text entry can never be very fast. Assuming, for instance, a 500-ms dwell time (usually too short for all but the most experienced eye typists), and a 40-ms saccade from one key to the next, the maximum speed obtainable would be 22 WPM with error-free performance and no time for cognitive processing to search for the next key from the keyboard. Measured entry speeds have been significantly lower. A starting speed with a dwell time of 900 ms was on the order of 7 WPM in the controlled experiments reported by Majaranta *et al.* (2006), which is in line with previous results, e.g., those by Frey *et al.* (1990). However, performance improved slightly yet significantly during just four trials. Changing the dwell time to 450 ms had a remarkable effect of improving the text entry speed to about 10 WPM. Not surprisingly, the error rates increased, but were still on the order of 1% of all characters entered.

Hansen and Hansen (2006) experimented with text entry by gaze using a common, "off-the-shelf" video camera with the GazeTalk system. They observed text entry speeds of 3–5 WPM by untrained users using large (3 × 4) on-screen buttons. It is not surprising that systems requiring hierarchical navigation or multiple gestures are slower than on-screen Qwerty keyboards with accurate eye trackers, although the prediction and completion features can improve the text entry speed. Their use depends heavily on both individual styles and extended use, so they are difficult to evaluate without longitudinal studies.

The language of the text also has an effect on text entry speed. All the figures given so far are for English. GazeTalk and Dasher also support entering text in Japanese. Itoh *et al.* (2006) report on a typing speed of 22–24 Kanji characters per minute, with performance improving from 19 to 23–25 characters per minute over seven short trials over 3 days. Both systems reached these text entry rates.

The Dasher system does not have such intrinsic limitations for maximum text entry speed as the dwell-based systems. It is, in fact, the fastest of the current gaze-based text entry techniques. Ward and MacKay (2002) report that after an hour of practice, their users could write up to 25 WPM and experts were able to achieve 34 WPM. The results are based on only a few participants and a relatively short practice time. Controlled experiments with more participants and longitudinal studies with expert users would be interesting.

In addition to the standard metrics, some additional metrics that are pertinent just to text entry by eye gaze have been proposed (see, e.g., Majaranta *et al.*, 2006; Aoki *et al.*, 2006). Such metrics focus on gaze behavior and its interaction with text entry events.

9.3.2   Experiments for Guiding Design Decisions

General guidelines on feedback in graphical user interfaces may not be suitable as such for dwell-time selection. There is a noteworthy difference between using dwell time as an activation command compared to, for example, a button click. With a button click, the user makes the selection and defines the exact moment when the selection is made. Using dwell time, the user only initiates the action; the system makes the actual selection after a predefined interval. Furthermore, when using gaze for text entry, the locus of gaze is engaged in the input process: the user needs to look at the letter to type it. To review the text written so far, the user needs to move the gaze from the virtual keyboard to the typed text field. As discussed below, proper feedback can significantly facilitate the tedious task of text entry by gaze. Even a slight improvement in performance makes a difference in a repetitive task of text entry, in which the effect accumulates.

Majaranta *et al.* (2006) conducted three experiments to study the effects of feedback and dwell time on speed and accuracy during text entry by gaze. Results showed that the type of feedback significantly affects text entry speed, accuracy, gaze behavior, and subjective experience. For example, adding a simple audible "click" after each selection significantly facilitates text entry by gaze. Compared with plain visual feedback, the added auditory feedback increases text entry speed and improves accuracy. It confirms the selection by giving a sense of finality that does not surface through visual feedback alone. The participants' gaze paths showed that added auditory feedback significantly reduced the need to review and verify the typed text.

Spoken feedback is useful for novices using long dwell times: speaking out the letters as they are typed significantly helps in reducing errors. However, with short dwell times, spoken feedback is problematic since speaking a letter takes time. People tend to pause to listen to the speech, which introduces double-entry errors: the same letter is unintentionally typed twice (Majaranta *et al.*, 2006). This, in return, reduces the text entry speed.

Most participants preferred an audible click over spoken or plain visual feedback because it not only clearly marks selection but also supports the typing rhythm. Typing rhythm is especially important with short dwell times, where the user no longer waits for feedback but learns to take advantage of the rhythm inherent in the dwell time duration.

For novices using a long dwell time, it is useful to give extra feedback on the dwell-time progress. This can be done by animation or by giving two-level feedback: first on the focus and then, after the dwell time has run out, feedback on selection. Showing the focus first gives the user the possibility of canceling the selection before reaching the dwell-time threshold. Moreover, it is not natural to fixate on a target for a long time. Animated feedback helps in maintaining focus on the target. However, with short dwell times, there is no time to give extra feedback to the user. Two-level feedback (focus first, then selection) is especially confusing and distracting if the interval between the two stages is too short.

Majaranta *et al.* (2006) conclude that the feedback should be matched with the dwell time. Short dwell times require simplified feedback, while long dwell times allow extra information on the eye-typing process. One should also keep in mind that the same dwell time (e.g., 500 ms) may be "short" for one user and "long" for another. Therefore, the user should be able to adjust the dwell-time threshold as well as the feedback parameters and attributes.

The need to adjust parameters is of uttermost importance for people with disabilities. Donegan *et al.* (2005) emphasize that user requirements for gaze-based communication systems are all about choice. The system needs to be flexible in order to accommodate the varied needs of the users with varied disabilities. For example, due to the medical condition, the user may have involuntary head or eye movements that prevent accurate calibration. Thus, the size of the selectable objects on screen need to be adjustable. For text entry, this means that only a few letters can be shown on screen at a time, which in turn requires special keyboard layout designs and word prediction, if one wants to achieve an adequate text entry speed.

Many users with severe disabilities also have visual impairment of some kind. Thus, in addition to varying selection methods (blink, dwell time, switch), a wide range of text output styles is needed, including a choice of font, background colors, and supporting auditory feedback.

9.4   FURTHER READING

For understanding the prospects and problems of text entry by gaze, it is instrumental to know in more detail how eye-tracking devices work and to understand their limitations. The best general introduction to eye tracking is the book by Duchowski (2003). The proceedings of the biennial conference series on Eye Tracking Research and Applications are accessible through the ACM Digital Library. They give an up-to-date view of the current research.

Eye trackers have been used for a variety of purposes. Jacob (1993) and Jacob and Karn (2003) provide good general introductions to the application areas. Recent comprehensive taxonomies of the various applications have been published by Hyrskykari *et al.* (2005) and Hyrskykari (2006).

Text entry by gaze is intended for users with disabilities. There are also other gaze-controlled applications intended for the same user group. Many of these, as well as reports on user experiences and requirements, are made available through the Web site (www.cogain.org) of the COGAIN Network of Excellence on Communication by Gaze Interaction. The site also contains a catalog of different eye-tracking systems.

An alternative to eye tracking is head tracking, in which the camera follows a marker on the user's forehead. The cursor on the screen can be moved by moving the head, leaving the eyes free for observation instead of command and control. All the techniques discussed in this chapter also lend themselves to head control. Comparisons of gaze vs head control are given by Bates and Istance (2003) and Hansen *et al.* (2003). Gaze and head movements can also be used together (Gips *et al.*, 1993).

We have discussed a variety of techniques for text entry by eye gaze. There are many influential systems, often used by a large number of disabled users, that use similar techniques. These include at least the Eyegaze system by LC Technologies

(Cleveland, 1994), QuickGlance by EyeTech Digital Systems (Rasmusson *et al.*, 1999), and VISIOBOARD by MetroVision (Charlier *et al.*, 1997).

ACKNOWLEDGMENTS

This work was supported by the COGAIN Network of Excellence on Communication by Gaze Interaction.

REFERENCES

Aoki, H., Hansen, J. P., & Itoh, K. (2006). Towards remote evaluation of gaze typing systems. *Proceedings of COGAIN 2006* (pp.96–103). Available at http://www.cogain.org/results/reports/COGAIN-D3.1.pdf.

Bates, R., & Istance, H. O. (2003). Why are eye mice unpopular? A detailed comparison of head eye controlled assistive technology pointing devices. *Universal Access in the Information Society, 2,* 280–290.

Chapman, J. E. (1991). The use of eye-operated computer system in locked-in syndrome. *Proceedings of the Sixth Annual International Conference on Technology and Persons with Disabilities—CSUN '91, 20–23 March 1991, Los Angeles, CA.*

Charlier, J., Buquet, C., Dubus, F., Hugeux, J. P., & Degroc, B. (1997). VISIOBOARD: a new gaze command system for handicapped subjects. *Medical and Biological Engineering and Computing, 35,* 461–462.

Cleveland, N. (1994). Eyegaze human–computer interface for people with disabilities. *Proceedings of 1st Automation Technology and Human Performance Conference, Washington, DC.* Available at http://www.eyegaze.com/doc/cathuniv.htm.

Donegan, M., Oosthuizen, L., Bates, R., Daunys, G., Hansen, J. P., Joos, M., Majaranta, P., & Signorile, I. (2005). *D3.1 user requirements report with observations of difficulties users are experiencing.* Communication by Gaze Interaction (COGAIN), IST-2003-511598: Deliverable 3.1. Available at http://www.cogain.org/results/reports/COGAIN-D3.1.pdf.

Duchowski, A. T. (2003). *Eye tracking methodology: Theory and practice.* London: Springer-Verlag.

Fejtová, M., Fejt, J., & Lhotská, L. (2004). Controlling a PC by eye movements: The MEMREC project. In K. Miesenberger, J. Klaus, W. Zagler, & D. Burger (Eds.), *Proceedings of Computers Helping People with Special Needs: 9th international conference (ICCHP 2004). Lecture Notes in Computer Science, 3118,* 770–773.

Frey, L. A., White, K. P., Jr., & Hutchinson, T. E. (1990). Eye-gaze word processing. *IEEE Transactions on Systems, Man, and Cybernetics, 20,* 944–950.

Gips, J., DiMattia, P., Curran, F. X., & Olivieri, P. (1996). Using EagleEyes—An electrodes based device for controlling the computer with your eyes—to help people with special needs. In J. Klaus, E. Auff, W. Kremser, & W. Zagler (Eds.), *Interdisciplinary aspects on computers helping people with special needs* (pp.630–635). Vienna: Oldenburg.

Gips, J., Olivieri, C. P., & Tecce, J. J. (1993). Direct control of the computer through electrodes placed around the eyes. In M. J. Smith & G. Salvendy (Eds.), *Human–computer interaction: Applications and case studies* (pp.630–635). Amsterdam: Elsevier.

Grauman, K., Betke, M., Lombardi, J., Gips, J., & Bradski, G. R. (2003). Communication via eye blinks and eyebrow raises: Video-based human–computer interfaces. *Universal Access in the Information Society, 2,* 359–373.

Hansen, D. W., & Hansen, J. P. (2006). Eye typing with common cameras. *Proceedings of the Symposium on Eye Tracking Research & Applications—ETRA 2006* (p.55). New York: ACM Press.

Hansen, D. W., Hansen, J. P., Nielsen, M., Johansen, A. S., & Stegmann, M. B. (2002). Eye typing using Markov and active appearance models. In *Proceedings of the Sixth IEEE Workshop on Applications of Computer Vision—WACV '02* (pp.132–136). Los Alamitos, CA: IEEE Computer Society.

Hansen, J. P., Hansen, D. W., & Johansen, A. S. (2001). Bringing gaze-based interaction back to basics. In C. Stephanidis (Ed.), *Universal access in HCI: Towards an information society for all* (pp.325–328). Mahwah, NJ: Lawrence Erlbaum.

Hansen, J. P., Johansen, A. S., Hansen, D. W., Itoh, K., & Mashino, S. (2003). Command without a click: Dwell time typing by mouse and gaze selections. In M. Rauterberg, M. Menozzi, & J. Wesson (Eds.), *Proceedings of Human–Computer Interaction—INTERACT '03* (pp.121–128). Amsterdam: IOS Press.

Hutchinson, T. E., White, K. P., Martin, W. N., Reichert, K. C., & Frey, L. A. (1989). Human–computer interaction using eye-gaze input. *IEEE Transactions on Systems, Man, and Cybernetics, 19,* 1527–1534.

Hyrskykari, A. (2006). *Eyes in attentive interfaces: Experiences from creating iDict, a gaze-aware reading aid.* In *Dissertations in interactive technology,* No. 4, Department of Computer Sciences, University of Tampere. Published electronically in *Acta Electronica Universitatis Tamperensis, 531.* Available at http://acta.uta.fi/pdf/951-44-6643-8.pdf.

Hyrskykari, A., Majaranta, P., & Räihä, K.-J. (2005). From gaze control to attentive interfaces. *Proceedings of the 11th International Conference on Human–Computer Interaction—HCII 2005, Vol. 7, Universal access in HCI: Exploring new interaction environments.* CD-ROM. Mahwah, NJ: Lawrence Erlbaum Associates, Inc.

Itoh, K., Aoki, H., & Hansen, J. P. (2006). A comparative usability study of two Japanese gaze typing systems. *Proceedings of the Symposium on Eye Tracking Research & Applications—ETRA 2006* (pp.59–66). New York: ACM Press.

Jacob, R. J. K. (1991). The use of eye movements in human–computer interaction techniques: What you look at is what you get. *ACM Transactions on Information Systems, 9,* 152–169.

Jacob, R. J. K. (1993). Eye movement-based human–computer interaction techniques: Toward non-command interfaces. In H. R. Hartson & D. Hix (Eds.), *Advances in human–computer interaction, Vol. 4* (pp.151–190). Norwood, NJ: Ablex Publishing.

Jacob, R. J. K. (1995). Eye tracking in advanced interface design. In W. Barfield & T. A. Furness (Eds.), *Virtual environments and advanced interface design* (pp.258–288). New York: Oxford University Press.

Jacob, R. J. K., & Karn, K. S. (2003). Eye tracking in human–computer interaction and usability research: Ready to deliver the promises (section commentary). In J. Hyönä, R. Radach, & H. Deubel (Eds.), *The mind's eye: Cognitive and applied aspects of eye movement research* (pp.573–605). Amsterdam: Elsevier.

Just, M. A., & Carpenter, P. A. (1976). Eye fixations and cognitive processes. *Cognitive Psychology, 8,* 441–480.

Kahn, D. A., Heynen, J., & Snuggs, G. L. (1999). Eye-controlled computing: The VisionKey experience. *Proceedings of the Fourteenth International Conference on Technology and Persons with Disabilities—CSUN '99, 15–20 March 1999, Los Angeles, CA.*

Land, M. F., & Furneaux, S. (1997). The knowledge base of the oculomotor system. *Philosophical Transactions: Biological Sciences, 352,* 1231–1239.

Majaranta, P., & Räihä, K.-J. (2002). Twenty years of eye typing: Systems and design issues. *Proceedings of the Symposium on Eye Tracking Research & Applications—ETRA 2002* (pp.15–22). New York: ACM Press.

Majaranta, P., MacKenzie, I. S., Aula, A., & Räihä, K.-J. (2006). Effects of feedback and dwell time on eye typing speed and accuracy. *Universal Access in the Information Society, 5,* 199–208.

Rasmusson, D., Chappell, R., & Trego, M. (1999). Quick Glance: Eye-tracking access to the Windows95 operating environment. *Proceedings of the Fourteenth International Conference on Technology and Persons with Disabilities—CSUN '99.* Los Angeles.

Stampe, D. M., & Reingold, E. M. (1995). Selection by looking: A novel computer interface and its application to psychological research. In J. M. Findlay, R. Walker, & R. W. Kentridge (Eds.), *Eye movement research: Mechanisms, processes and applications* (pp.467–478). Amsterdam: Elsevier.

Surakka, V., Illi, M., & Isokoski, P. (2003). Voluntary eye movements in human–computer interaction. In J. Hyönä, R. Radach, & H. Deubel (Eds.), *The mind's eye: Cognitive and applied aspects of eye movement research* (pp.473–491). Amsterdam: Elsevier.

Ten Kate, J. H., Frietman, E. E. E., Willems, W., Ter Haar Romeny, B. M., & Tenkink, E. (1979). Eye-switch controlled communication aids. *Proceedings of the 12th International Conference on Medical & Biological Engineering, 19–24 August 1979, Jerusalem, Israel.*

Ward, D. J., & MacKay, D. J. C. (2002). Fast hands-free writing by gaze direction. *Nature 418,* 838.

3 | Language Variations

PART

10 Writing System Variation and Text Entry

Kumiko Tanaka-Ishii   University of Tokyo, Tokyo, Japan
Renu Gupta   University of Aizu, Aizu, Japan

10.1   INTRODUCTION

Through Parts I, II, and IV of this book, the default language used for text entry tasks is English. This is because computers were first developed for the U.S. market and so the English interface was incorporated by default. However, in many parts of the world, text entry on computers, mobile phones, and PDAs is not done in English but in languages such as Arabic, Chinese, Hindi, and Russian, through scripts that are dissimilar to that of English. Given the variety of languages and scripts used throughout the world, such variation should be taken into consideration when designing devices and related software. Part III is therefore dedicated to a discussion of language and script variation as it pertains to text entry.

Part III is structured as follows. In this chapter, we describe the typology for writing systems proposed by Daniels (1996); in this typology, scripts can be categorized into six types of systems—logosyllabary, syllabary, abjad, alphabet, abugida, and featural—each of which raises a different set of text entry issues. The second half of this chapter examines issues in an alphabetic writing system. Since English is an alphabetic writing system, one assumes that text entry problems have been more than adequately covered in other chapters, but scripts such as Cyrillic (for Russian) also fall within this group, presenting small but not trivial problems for text entry.

The remaining chapters in Part III cover the five nonalphabetic writing systems. Chapter 11 is concerned with the logosyllabary in Chinese, Japanese, and Korean. Although Japanese uses syllabaries and Korean is primarily a featural system, the scripts used to write these languages cannot be discussed without considering their use of Chinese characters (a logosyllabary), which is why they are included in Chap. 11. Chapters 12 and 13 cover the two remaining writing systems—abugidas and abjads, respectively.

10.2   VARIATION IN WRITING SYSTEMS

Any discussion of text entry has to separate languages from scripts. Since languages can be classified according to similarities based on historical evolution, structure, or geographical proximity, and writing can be defined as "a set of visible or tactile signs used to represent units of language" (Coulmas, 1996), it may seem that a script typology would follow the language classification. The perception that writing is secondary to speech is reinforced by many linguists following Saussure (1993) and Bloomfield (1933) (for alternative views, see Harris, 1995, 2000; Vachek, 1989). However, scripts do not always map onto language classifications. For example, although Farsi, which is spoken in Iran, belongs to the Indo-European language family, like English, it is written in the Arabic script; on the other hand, Turkish, which does not belong to the Indo-European language family, uses the Roman script. Languages as diverse as Vietnamese in Vietnam and Bahasa in Indonesia have adopted the Roman script for their languages. Hence, we need to distinguish between languages and scripts.

In reality, several factors affect the choice of script for a language. This is best seen in examples of digraphia, where two scripts may be used for the same language (Grivelet, 2001). A language like Serbo-Croat is written in the Cyrillic script by Serbians, who are Orthodox, whereas Croatians, who are Catholic, use the Roman script (Magner, 2001). Similar instances of dual scripts for the same language can be found in South Asia, where languages like Sindhi and Punjabi are written in the Perso-Arabic script in Pakistan, but in India abugidas, such as Devanagari and Gurmukhi, are used. In these cases, the primary factor in script choice is religious affiliation but other factors can also dictate which script is used. Geographical location can affect script choice, as is the case with Konkani, an Indian language; since Konkani did not have a script of its own, speakers would write it in the script of the neighboring state, which could be Devanagari, Kannada, or the Roman script. Yet another factor is education: in north India, women were taught Hindi in the Devanagari script, whereas men used the Perso-Arabic script.

The arbitrary link between language and script is so great that whole systems are artificially replaceable. For example, as a result of government policy, the writing system in Turkey was changed from Arabic to Roman, and Hangeul was introduced as the Korean writing system in the 15th century.

Since text entry concerns language, it might be possible to construct intelligent text entry software by considering the linguistic characteristics of the languages. However, text entry above all is concerned with the writing system, because text entry is used to produce written text. Thus, any discussion of language variation regarding text entry should be based on a typology of scripts or writing systems rather than a language typology.

Given the large number of scripts in the world, it is necessary to group them so that they can be studied in a systematic manner. Scripts are usually classified based on the linguistic unit that the symbols represent. In the typology proposed by Saussure (1993), writing systems are divided into two categories: those using ideograms and those using phonograms. The most popular classification of scripts is a tripartite division that Daniels (1996) ascribes to Taylor (1883), but which has been popularized by Gelb (1952). In this classification, writing systems can be divided into three types: logography, syllabary, and alphabet. Although this classification added syllabaries as a separate writing system, it excluded large sets of scripts, namely, the Semitic scripts (Arabic and Hebrew), the scripts of South and Southeast Asia (e.g., Devanagari and Thai), and Korean Hangeul.

Gelb's focus was the evolution of writing systems from the logography through the syllabary to the alphabet, and these other scripts were positioned between syllabaries and alphabets. Hebrew and Arabic were considered "consonantal syllabaries," while South Asian and Southeast Asian scripts were "quasisyllabaries" (Gelb, 1952). There is hence considerable confusion about both the status of and the labels for these scripts. So, for example, the scripts in South and Southeast Asia have been variously termed "semialphabetic" (Vaid & Gupta, 2002), "semi-syllabic" (Vaid & Padakannaya, 2004), and "alphasyllabaries" (Bright, 1999). Since these labels imply a subsidiary status for these writing systems, Daniels (1992, 1996) resurrected the terms "abjad" and "abugida" for the Semitic and South/Southeast Asian writing systems, respectively. In addition, he created a typology for writing systems that is not evolution-based but lists six main writing systems, according them equivalent status. Part III of this book is, therefore, based on the typology set up by Daniels (1996), which recognizes the following six types of writing systems.

Logosyllabary—The primary example is the Chinese writing system. Japanese and Korean are also logosyllabaries to a certain degree because they incorporate Chinese characters in the written language. In a logosyllabary, a character denotes individual morphemes or a word. Due to this feature, thousands of characters are used in writing systems of this type.

Syllabary—Examples are the Japanese kana, Cree and Cherokee in North America, and Vai in Africa. In a syllabary, a character represents a syllable, but phonetically similar syllables do not have a similar graphical shape. For example, in Japanese kana, there is no graphical similarity between the syllables か(ka) and き (ki), even though they share the same consonant (/k/).

Abugida—Examples are Devanagari and Thai, used in India and Southeast Asia, respectively. In this writing system, the consonant character contains an inherent vowel (such as a schwa) and the other vowels are indicated by modifying the base consonant character. Creating a character can be a complex matter of adding other consonants, vowels, and tones. For example, the following is a character in Khmer produced from six key presses, in which each part is produced by a stroke chained by the operator "+":

ស + ◌្ + ត + ◌្ + រ + ◌ី → ស្ត្រី

Abjad—This type of writing system is a consonantary, such as Arabic, which is used not just in the Middle East but in a wide swathe from Albania to Malaysia because of religious links with Islam. The writing system has two characteristics. First, the consonants are represented by symbols but vowels play a secondary role. A second distinct characteristic is that the reading/writing direction is from right to left.

Featural—An example is Korean Hangeul. The phonogram letters are combined into a syllable block and the character shapes are related to distinctive features of the sound. For example, Hangeul jamos of similar shape, such as ⊏ , and Ε , both represent apical sounds.

Alphabet—Examples are English, Russian, and Turkish. The characters denote consonants and vowels.

Although alphabetic writing systems might seem dominant, millions of people write using nonalphabetic systems. In terms of sheer numbers, World Internet Statistics (2006) reports that Asia ranks the highest, with 380 million users (56.4% of the population), while the highest usage growth is seen in the Middle East (454.2% growth). China ranks second worldwide, with 123 million users, who represent 10.9% of Internet users, while Japan is third, with 86 million users (8.4%), followed by India with 50 million users (5%). The need to support languages other than alphabetic languages is clearly substantial.

10.3   TEXT ENTRY PROBLEMS IN DIFFERENT WRITING SYSTEMS

Text entry hardware and software in any writing system should address at least the following questions.

Input device—What is the best device for entering the script? How can a script be entered on an existing device?

Standards and compatibility—What is the character standard? If there are multiple standards, are they compatible?

Environmental settings—How can a user configure the language environment? Can the user easily switch between different languages and scripts?

Accuracy and efficiency—Is the resulting text accurate? For example, are accents retained? How efficient is the entry method?

Answers to these questions are readily available for English (and related scripts) because it is the default language for current interfaces. In languages and scripts that are different from English, text entry becomes an issue. For example, the Qwerty keyboard that was specifically designed to input English characters on the typewriter is easily adapted to other alphabetic scripts, such as Cyrillic, but the same method cannot be adopted for Chinese, which uses thousands of characters.

Of the six types of writing systems, this difficulty is especially severe for three categories: logosyllabary, abugidas, and abjads. The problems are summarized below and the solutions applied in each of these categories are discussed in more detail in Chaps. 11, 12, and 13.

Logosyllabary—discussed in Chap. 11.

Since Chinese and Japanese use thousands of characters that do not fit on the standard keyboard, a text entry system that enables the user to produce numerous characters had to be devised. The earliest solution consisted of a machine that used a combination of trays for the characters and levers to manipulate the trays. The modern solution is predictive entry, and predictive methods of all kinds have been mostly developed in East Asia.

Abugida—discussed in Chap. 12.

Although abugidas have a limited number of base symbols (about 50 to 70), the individual symbols change their shapes when combined with other symbols. The number of combinations can run into hundreds of different resulting block shapes. For tonal languages especially, such as Thai and Lao, the number of combinations increases because tones are explicitly incorporated in the symbols. On early typewriters, the normal and shift modes together were used to accommodate the basic symbols and diacritics, but sufficient block combinations could not be provided on the keyboard, therefore each component was shown linearly as an approximation. With the use of computers, this problem has been solved, but as seen in the Khmer example given in the previous section, multiple keystrokes are still required to produce a character.

Abjad—discussed in Chap. 13.

Abjads also have a limited number of characters. For example, Arabic has 28 characters, Farsi adds 4 consonants to the Arabic alphabet, and Urdu adds 8. There are three major problems in abjads concerning text entry software. The first is the appearance of the resulting text. Some Arabic letters are cursive and thus have to be joined. Character shapes depend on the position of the character, which can be initial, medial, final, or isolated. The second problem is the writing direction. Characters are written from right to left, but numerals are written from left to right. The third problem is the consonantary feature. The resulting text lacks information about vowels and the ambiguity of a chunk remains high. This poses problems when incorporating language technology. For example, if predictive entry is to be used, a lack of proper disambiguation will prevent precise prediction of the following word.

In the three remaining writing systems—alphabet, syllabary, and featural—text entry does not present the same degree of difficulty and, hence, they are discussed in conjunction with other writing systems. Alphabetic writing systems are taken up in the second half of this chapter, starting with the next section. Text entry in both syllabaries and featural writing systems is incorporated in Chap. 11, because the most prominent cases of a language using syllabary and featural writing systems with respect to advanced entry techniques are Japanese and Korean, respectively, and they cannot be explained without reference to their use of Chinese characters. Briefly, the text entry solution for syllabary and featural writing systems can be considered similar to that for an alphabet. Thus, Chap. 11 provides concrete examples of solutions for syllabary and featural systems along with those for a logosyllabary. Consequently, entry problems regarding language variation—both general issues and specific examples—are covered in Part III based on Daniels' typology.

If an entry system has to be constructed for a new script, this can be done by referring to an example from another script that belongs to the same writing system. For example, Vai and Japanese kana belong to the same writing system (syllabary), so the entry methods used for the two scripts can influence each other.

In addition, it would be interesting to apply an entry method developed for one type of writing system to another type. For example, predictive methods developed for logosyllabary writing systems are now used worldwide because the emergence of mobile devices has made the "too many characters for too few keys" a common problem regardless of the script. Similarly, an abugida writing system uses hundreds of combinations of resulting blocks, so predictive entry is a useful solution. This problem exists in other writing systems; Korean, a featural writing system, also combines Hangeul blocks and, as we will explain in Section 10.4.1, the same problem arises in alphabetic scripts that use diacritics.

10.4　ALPHABETIC SCRIPTS

The area where alphabetic writing systems are used is vast: in addition to Europe and North and South America, it includes Turkey, Russia, parts of Asia such as the Philippines and Vietnam, and parts of Africa such as places where the Comorian and Mandinka languages are used. Since the default linguistic features of most user interfaces for computer keyboards, mobile phones, and PDAs are currently based on English, with some modifications, the interface can be adapted to other scripts that are based on the Roman alphabet; in addition to East and West European languages, this includes languages for which the Roman script has been introduced as the national writing standard, such as Turkish and Vietnamese. Moreover, although scripts such as Cyrillic (for Russian), Armenian, and Greek look very different from the Latin alphabet, they belong to the same writing system, namely the alphabet, although the symbols may differ. Consequently, a large number of people use an alphabetic writing system.

Alphabetic scripts have the following characteristics.

✦ Each written symbol corresponds to a consonant or a vowel.

✦ The alphabet therefore consists of a limited number of characters.

✦ Characters are written in a linear sequence (in contrast to abugidas and abjads in which markers can appear nonlinearly).

The limited number of characters fits easily onto a standard Qwerty keyboard, which was originally designed for English typewriters. The conventional keyboard is sufficient for both upper- and lowercase letters, as well as numbers, punctuation marks, and special symbols. Also, since the symbols can be written only linearly, the sole task of the text entry software is to translate the signal into the character code before rendering the symbols on the screen.

Computer encoding of this type of writing system for the English (i.e., Roman) alphabet plus diacritics has used 8-bit character encoding under ISO-8859, making use of the 8th bit saved in the ASCII code. The most popular is the encoding known as Latin 1, still popular in Western Europe. Similar versions, namely, Latin 2, 3, and 4, include other diacritics. Recently, all characters have been equally incorporated into Unicode in the form of 2-byte characters.

Consequently, there have been no significant problems concerning text entry within alphabetic systems compared with logosyllabaries, abugidas, and abjads. An English interface can be easily converted for other alphabetic systems through slight modifications. All the technologies introduced in Parts I, II, and IV of this book can be similarly accommodated to fit other alphabetic scripts.

Still, adapting an English interface to another alphabetic language can involve two issues. One is how to accommodate diacritics, such as the tilde in Spanish or the accents in French. The other concerns languages with different sets of symbols, such as Russian. These two types of scripts are examined in the next two subsections.

10.4.1   Roman Scripts with Diacritics

French, German, and Spanish are alphabetic scripts that use the Roman alphabet but modify some letters through diacritics, such as accents, umlauts, tildes, and cedillas. A diacritical mark or a diacritic is added to a letter to alter the pronunciation of a word or to distinguish between similar words; it can appear above or below the letter to which it is added or in another position. However, such marks are not always diacritical. For example, in English, the tittle (dot) in the letters i and j is not a diacritical mark, but part of the letter itself. Further, a mark may be diacritical in one language, but not in another; for example, in Catalan, Portuguese, and Spanish, u and ü are considered the same letter, while in German, Estonian, Hungarian, and Turkish, they are considered separate letters.

Under the norms of text entry, such modification can be handled in two ways:

✦ A character with a diacritic can be considered a different character from the original character without the diacritic. If only a few characters have a diacritic, these characters can be considered as an addition to the normal alphabet. For text entry, this approach means that each character with a diacritic is assigned to a particular key of the keyboard.

✦ A character with a diacritic can be treated as a combination of a Latin character and a diacritic. In this case, diacritics can be assigned to separate keys and a character with a diacritic can be entered through multiple keystrokes. This method becomes similar to that for an abugida in which the resultant character is built from components.

For most languages, the first solution is generally used for two reasons: first, each character with a diacritic can be encoded separately, and second, it is easier from the developer's perspective. However, there are exceptions, like in Czech, which contains many characters with diacritics: all vowels plus the consonants C, D, N, R, S, T, and Z can have diacritics. In the default text entry method for Czech, such characters are entered by first typing the diacritic and then the alphabetic symbol. Also, even in languages with direct entry, nonnative speakers prefer to use a combination of a diacritic mark and alphabetic symbol because they are not familiar with the keyboard layout for characters with diacritics. For example, the French é can be obtained by entering an apostrophe (') after e.

To illustrate how text entry works in a Roman script with diacritics, we have used the example of Turkish. Although Turkish is structurally different from English, the language is represented well by the Roman script. Turkish uses 29 letters, of which 8 are vowels. The alphabet differs slightly from the English: it does not include w, q, or x, but uses ç, ğ, ö, ş, ü, and ı (i without a dot). Thus, the entire alphabet is Aa Bb Cc Dd Ee Ff Gg Ğğ Hh Iı İi Jj Kk Ll Mm Nn Oo Öö Pp Rr Ss Şş Tt Uu Üü Vv Yy Zz.

The standard keyboard layout for the Turkish alphabet for entry on a PDA's soft keyboard is shown in Fig. 10.1. We see how similar it is to the English keyboard, with only slight modifications to accommodate Turkish characters with diacritics. Note that the character set includes w, q, and x so that entry in English is possible.

For mobile phones, SMS is popular in Turkey. The assignment of letters on a mobile phone depends on the brand. However, for all current products, the Turkish

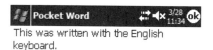

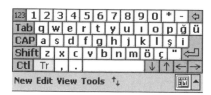

FIGURE   Turkish standard keyboard layout shown as a soft keyboard on a PDA.

10.1

letters are available, assigned in alphabetical order to the 2 to 9 buttons, with three to five letters assigned to each digit. A layout example is shown in Fig. 10.2. The standard method for entering text is by the multitap method. For example, to type the letter ü, a user clicks on the 8 button three times: first t appears, then u, and then ü. Some recent mobile phones also offer a predictive function such as one-key with disambiguation and word completion.

Thus, even in a language as different as Turkish, the text entry technologies developed for English can be applied. The same applies to other Latin alphabetic scripts that use diacritics.

10.4.2   Non-roman scripts

Although Russian and Greek use a set of symbols different from that of English, text entry in these scripts does not present much of a problem. Since these scripts are based on an alphabetic writing system, there is a limited set of symbols that can be accommodated on a standard keyboard designed for English. In fact, it may be easier to deal with an entirely different set of symbols than to design input devices for scripts that include characters with diacritics, when the diacritics increase the number of characters to be accommodated. In an alphabetic script that uses a different set of symbols, the alphabet can be redefined to best fit the language. Therefore, the number of characters usually remains small and all characters can be handled uniquely. The main issue for text entry is to change the character mapping given the entry signal.

One major difference between scripts with diacritics and non-Roman scripts lies in their encoding. In non-Roman scripts, all characters are encoded by 2 bytes, whereas Roman scripts that use diacritics are encoded by 1 byte as Latin 1 to 4. However, with the emergence of other characters to be encoded, for which every encoding requires at least 2 bytes, no technical problems remain with respect to 2-byte encoding.

1	2 ABCÇ	3 DEF
4 GĞHIi	5 JKL	6 MNOÖ
7 PQRSŞ	8 TUÜV	9 WXYZ
*	0	#

FIGURE   A popular Turkish mobile phone assignment.

10.2

Russian is representative of a non-Roman alphabetic script. The Cyrillic alphabet now consists of 33 letters. (The number of characters in the alphabet defined as the national standard has changed historically as rarely used characters have been removed.) The current alphabet on a standard Russian keyboard is shown in Fig. 10.3; again, this is a PDA's soft keyboard. Note how this assignment is completely different from the layout for English on the Qwerty keyboard; for example, the Cyrillic A is not assigned to the same key as the English A but is based on the convention for Russian typewriters. This phonetically different assignment of two languages onto the standard full keyboard does not cause a major problem, and there are many expert touch-typists who can switch between typing in Russian and English. Although there is a keyboard that maps Cyrillic symbols to English symbols, the most popular keyboard layout has become the one shown in Fig. 10.3.

Regarding mobile phones, SMS is popular throughout Russian-speaking areas. The characters are assigned to each digit from 2 to 9 in alphabetical order, just as for English. The keyboard layout on a mobile phone keypad depends on the product, but a popular assignment is shown in Fig. 10.4; in this case, 32 characters are accommodated (Ё, a rarely used character, has been dropped from digit 3). Here, as the number of characters assigned to each digit ranges from 3 to 5, several key presses are needed for a character. This problem is alleviated by an alternative key assignment,

FIGURE   Standard Russian keyboard layout.

10.3

1	2 А Б В Г	3 Д Е Ж З
4 И Й К Л	5 М Н О	6 П Р С
7 Т У Ф Х	8 Ц Ч Ш Щ Ъ	9 Ы Ь Э Ю Я
*	0	#

FIGURE   Most popular Russian character assignment for a mobile phone.

10.4

such as that in a Motorola mobile phone, on which only three or four characters are assigned to each digit.

Similar solutions have been used in Greece and for other alphabetic scripts that use non-Roman symbols. As we have explained, while text entry solutions have tended to be developed around English norms, the technologies for English text entry systems can be easily applied to such scripts.

10.5   CONCLUDING REMARKS

Convenient text entry is the key to modern electronic communication. To enable this, the differences among scripts must be taken into consideration so that devices are designed to accommodate the language of each user. Even though languages and scripts might seem to vary as much as people, Daniels suggests that all scripts can be grouped under six categories. Such a typology provides a useful bird's-eye view and will help to generate a more universal technology.

10.6   ACKNOWLEDGMENTS

The parts of this section concerning the Turkish, Russian, and Czech languages were written based on the kind comments provided by Ms. Yeşim Yazıcı (Project Chief, HP Pelzer Pimsa Otomotiv A.Ş.), Associate Professor Vitaly Klyuev (Aizu University), and Associate Professor Vladislav Kubon (Charles University Prague), respectively. We are grateful for their help.

REFERENCES

Bloomfield, L. (1933). *Language*. New York: Rinehart & Winston.

Bright, W. (1999). A matter of typology: Alphasyllabaries and abugidas. *Written Language and Literacy, 2,* 45–55.

Coulmas, F. (1996). *The Blackwell encyclopedia of writing systems*. Oxford: Blackwell.

Daniels, P. (1992). The syllabic origin of writing and the segmental origin of the alphabet. In P. Downing, S. Lima, & M. Noonan (Eds.), *The linguistics of literacy* (pp.83–110). Amsterdam: John Benjamins.

Daniels, P. (1996). The study of writing systems. In P. Daniels & W. Bright (Eds.), *The world's writing systems* (pp.3–17). New York: Oxford University Press.

Gelb, I. (1952). *A study of writing*. Chicago: University of Chicago Press.

Grivelet, S. (2001). Introduction to digraphia: Writing systems and society. *International Journal of the Sociology of Language, 150,* 1–10.

Harris, R. (1995). *Signs of writing.* London: Routledge.

Harris, R. (2000). *Rethinking writing.* Bloomington: Indiana University Press.

Magner, M. (2001). Digraphia in the territories of the Croats and Serbs. *International Journal of the Sociology of Language, 150,* 11–26.

Saussure, F. (1993). 3eme Cours de Linguistique Générale (2de partie: la langue) de Ferdinand Saussure, notes taken by E. Constantin. Elmsford, NY: Pergamon.

Taylor, I. (1883). *The alphabet: An account of the origin and development of letters.* London: Kegan Paul, Trench.

Vachek, J. (1989). *Written language revisited.* Amsterdam: John Benjamins.

Vaid, J., & Gupta, A. (2002). Exploring word recognition in a semi-alphabetic script: The case of Devanagari. *Brain and Language, 81,* 679–690.

Vaid, J., & Padakannaya, P. (2004). Introduction to the special issue of Reading and Writing: An Interdisciplinary Journal. *Reading and Writing: An Interdisciplinary Journal, 17,* 1–6.

World Internet Statistics (2006). *http://www.internetworldstats.com/stats.htm*

11 | Text Entry in East Asian Languages

CHAPTER

Kumiko Tanaka-Ishii University of Tokyo, Tokyo, Japan
Ming Zhou Microsoft Research, Redmond, WA, USA
Jin-Dong Kim University of Tokyo, Tokyo, Japan

11.1 INTRODUCTION

Chinese and Japanese are the two major languages in which ideograms are used in writing. In addition, while the Korean writing system is based on phonograms, the language is historically strongly influenced by the ideogram culture. This chapter describes text entry in these East Asian languages, a primary characteristic of which lies in ideograms.

A characteristic of a language that uses ideograms is that every morpheme—the smallest unit carrying meaning—corresponds to a distinct character, and so the number of characters in the language becomes large. In both Chinese and Japanese, the standard character set includes more than 6000 characters. In the case of Korean, ideograms correspond to Korean syllabic phonograms, of which there are also more than 10,000. Although, if rarely used and ancient ideograms are included, the number of characters exceeds 100,000.

When computers were introduced, the greatest problem for users of these languages was how to enter such a large number of characters with keyboards designed for European languages. In the case of Korean, in which the syllabic phonograms are systematically represented as a combination of a small set of phonemic characters, the entry is naturally performed by assigning these characters to keys of the standard keyboards. However, in Japan and China, the writing system is based on ideograms, and efforts to deal with this difficulty contributed greatly to the development of predictive entry methods. Most users of Chinese or Japanese on computers now enter text using predictive methods.

The problem of too many characters for too few keys has become a worldwide problem with the spread of mobile machines such as cell phones and even smaller devices (see Chap. 5). Moreover, text entry based on predictive methods using computers is important for assistive technology (see Chap. 15), because entry using a small number of keys can help the disabled, whose freedom of physical motion limits the ability to enter text. In this way, research on predictive technology done in East Asia has led the way toward what has become a universal entry technology.

For European languages, current technology for predictive entry is based mainly on entry using phonetics. However, in East Asia, the ideogram culture generated another type of entry, apart from that based on phonetics: entry based on character shapes. As people using these languages have always had to search for the meaning and reading of particular ideograms, there is a rich culture of looking up ideograms through shape-based methods. Some of the systems that have been developed are efficient enough to enable the entry of text at high speed.

The main focus of this chapter is to introduce representative and mainstream technologies based on such East Asian cultural norms. The available methods can be classified into three types: direct entry methods without using a predictive method and two predictive entry methods using either a phonetically based or a shape-based approach. These three types of entry method are widely used to represent Korean, Japanese, and Chinese, respectively; note, though, that all three types are used in and are well developed for all three languages. This chapter is structured accordingly.

A great variety of entry systems have been studied in the user interface domain with the goal of enabling East Asian language entry for each of the devices introduced in Part II of this book. For an ideogram culture, the key question we must answer concerning the different devices now becoming available is how to best incorporate the basic entry methods into each device. Here, we focus on this main issue and leave it to our readers to further investigate specific systems according to their interests.

We first describe the three languages from the viewpoint of the writing system before we go on to introduce actual text entry methods.

11.2   LANGUAGE DESCRIPTION

Chinese, Japanese, and Korean are the three main languages spoken in East Asia. With regard to writing systems, East Asia is a rich source of material for studying the contrast between phonogram and ideogram systems: Chinese is written using only ideograms, whereas Korean uses mostly phonograms, and Japanese uses both ideograms and phonograms. In addition, even though Korean uses mostly phonograms, the ideogram culture remains alive and plays a significant role in daily life.

Altogether, more than 120,000 characters are used in these three languages. The standard sets listed in Table 11.2, such as GB2312 in Chinese, JISX 0208-1990 in Japanese, and KS X 1005-1 in Korean, are mostly included in Unicode. However, while the Unicode system allows us to write using a combination of fonts from different languages, different entry systems have been adopted for each of the East Asian languages. To use these entry systems, the reader has to understand the writing system used in each language, so we will briefly explain these.

11.2.1 Chinese

The Chinese language is written using only Chinese ideogram characters called hanzi. Chinese has two different character sets. One is the traditional Chinese character set, used in Taiwan and Hong Kong, and the other is the simplified Chinese character set, used in mainland China and Singapore. Simplified characters are created mainly by reducing the number of strokes and simplifying the form of commonly used traditional Chinese characters. Two examples of such simplification are shown in the first two columns of Table 11.1, with characters in the first column being the simplification of the characters shown in the second column. A considerable number of characters have been simplified, but these two character sets still include many identical characters.

Different character encodings in computers are used for traditional Chinese characters and simplified Chinese characters. These different encodings are listed in Table 11.2. Among these, GB2312 is the national standard used in mainland China,

Chinese simplified	Chinese traditional	Japanese	Korean	Meaning
学	學	学	學	to study
电	電	電	電	electricity

TABLE
11.1

Examples of Chinese, Japanese, and Korean characters.

Language	Encoding	Number of characters
Chinese (simplified)	GB2312	6763
Chinese (traditional)	BIG5	13868
Chinese	GBK	20902
Chinese	GB18030	27484
Japanese	JISX 0208-1990	6879
	level 1	3489 (2965 ideograms, other phonograms, symbols)
	level 2	3390 (ideograms and radicals)
Japanese	JIS X 0213	11223
Korean	KS X 1001	2350 syllabic phonograms, 4888 ideograms
Korean	KS X 1005-1	11,172 syllabic phonograms and 334 jamos

TABLE
11.2

Character encoding in each language.

and it has been designed to include enough ideograms to support daily communication. However, the total number of Chinese characters is much larger than the number included in this standard. For example, the *Kangxi Zidian* (the *Kangxi Dictionary,* which is more than 300 years old) contains 47,035 Chinese characters. For the purpose of encoding these additional characters, other standards have been created, such as GBK and GB18030 (Table 11.2, the fourth and fifth rows).

The characteristics of Chinese make Chinese entry a nontrivial problem. Above all, written Chinese language has a very vague definition of what a word is, which is due to the writing being based on an ideogram sequence without the word border indicated in text. A Chinese word is usually one to three characters in length, but there are also longer words. There is no standard lexicon (definition of words). In fact, linguists often disagree on whether a character string qualifies as a word. Sentence segmentation is therefore very ambiguous and error prone. For instance, 原子组合成分子时 can be segmented into 12 or more results.

There is a standardized phonetic system called pinyin, which was defined in the 1950s based on Mandarin, the Beijing dialect. This phonetic Chinese has 406 syllables, each with up to 5 tones (1386 tonal syllables). While each syllable maps to 17 characters on average, the word Yi, for example, maps to 131 different characters.

The situation regarding entry systems for Chinese is more complicated than for Japanese or Korean, though, because China has many dialects. The phonetic systems of other dialects deviate so greatly from Mandarin that two people speaking different dialects might not be able to communicate at all. Despite this, ideograms are shared throughout the nation, and regardless of their native dialect, people can read Chinese writing. In other words, although something written in Chinese is pronounced completely differently depending on the dialect, the meaning remains the same.

This situation has led to a rich culture of various ways to encode and enter ideograms based on character shapes, as well as the development of entry systems based on the standard pinyin phonetic system. This is a significant characteristic of Chinese, compared with Japanese and Korean, in which phonetic entry systems are mainly used. We will further discuss these intriguing shape-based entry systems of Chinese later on.

11.2.2   Japanese

A notable characteristic of the Japanese language is the use of a writing system consisting of both phonograms and ideograms. The ideogram system was imported from China in ancient times, and Japanese phonograms were derived from certain Chinese characters.

The Japanese sound system roughly consists of five vowels and nine principle consonants plus five voiced consonants. Japanese phonograms, called kana, transliterate these sounds, each kana representing a sound formed of a pair of a consonant and a vowel, which can be considered a syllable. A kana character can be transcribed through a combination of letters of similar sound from the Roman alphabet. The principal

Consonants

w	r	y	m	h	n	t	s	k	φ	/	
わ	ら	や	ま	は	な	た	さ	か	あ		a
wa	ra	ya	ma	ha	na	ta	sa	ka	a		
	り		み	ひ	に	ち	し	き	い		i
	ri		mi	hi	ni	ti	si	ki	i		
ん	る	ゆ	む	ふ	ぬ	つ	す	く	う		u
n	ru	yu	mu	hu	nu	tu	su	ku	u		
	れ		め	へ	ね	て	せ	け	え		e
	re		me	he	ne	te	se	ke	e		
を	ろ	よ	も	ほ	の	と	そ	こ	お		o
wo	ro	yo	mo	ho	no	to	so	ko	o		

Vowels

Phonograms:
(kana)
roman:

にほんご
ni ho n go

Ideograms:
(kanji)
means:

日 本 語
Japanese

FIGURE 11.1   Principal part of the Japanese phonogram kana table and its Roman transcription.

part of the kana table, including the Roman transcriptions of each kana, is shown on the left side of Fig. 11.1. An example of a Japanese word, *nihongo*, written as both a phonogram and an ideogram sequence, is shown on the right.

The Japanese writing system also uses ideograms, called kanji, each of which can be transliterated by kana that correspond to the reading of each ideogram. Roughly speaking, ideograms are used to represent content words, whereas phonograms are used for both content words and function words. Such function words make the Japanese language agglutinative; that is, short function words are attached after each content word to indicate its role within the sentence (such as subject or object). Similar to Chinese, no word border is clearly shown within the writing system, as the borders are rather clear with ideogram parts indicating the main part of the content word.

In modern times, as in China, the ideograms used in Japan have been simplified. This simplification was done independent of the Chinese standardization policy, so Japanese ideogram sets differ from those of Chinese. Even with such different sets, however, Japanese and Chinese use many common characters, such as the two examples shown in the third column of Table 11.1.

The current Japanese character encoding, defined by the Japanese Industry Standards (JIS) organization, consists of 6879 characters (Table 11.2). As well as ideograms, this set includes phonograms and other related symbols. Different computer encodings have been designed for this character set, the three most representative being JIS, Shift-JIS and EUC. Ancient and rarely used characters were also standardized (in 2000) in the JIS X 0213 encoding, which includes more than 10,000 ideograms.

In Japanese, unlike Chinese, the same phonetic system is shared by all Japanese people since the phonogram system coexists with the writing system. Dialects do not deviate greatly from standard Japanese. Therefore, almost all Japanese entry systems are based on standard phonetics. Shape-based entry is less common and considered merely a complement to phonetic entry.

11.2.3   Korean

In Korea, most people currently use only phonograms called Hangeul[1], the native writing system of Korea. Hangeul is a phonetic writing system using jamos, a type of phonemic letters, like the Roman alphabet. Jamo, 자모(字母), literally means "the mother of characters" and is used as the building block to compose Hangeul characters, which are syllabic phonograms. Figure 11.2 shows the jamos of consonants and vowels. The figure also shows the Hangeul syllable blocks for the word Hangeul and how to compose them using jamos.

A Hangeul syllabic phonogram consists of an initial, a medial, and a final (which is optional). The initial is one of the 19 consonants or consonant clusters, the medial is one of the 21 vowels or diphthongs, and the final is one of the 27 consonant or consonant clusters. Figure 11.2 shows only the principal 14 consonants and 10 vowels. The other consonant clusters or diphthongs are made by combining the principal jamos. The number of all possible Hangeul syllabic phonograms is thus 11,172 $(19 \times 21 \times (27 + 1))$.

Although Hangeul is the prime writing system for Korean, a significant number of Korean words—50 to 60%—are derived from Chinese root words (Lee, 2002). Thus, using equivalent ideograms, called hanja, instead of or together with Hangeul syllabic phonograms is often regarded as useful for reducing reading ambiguity. For

(hangeul)

FIGURE   Hangeul jamos and two syllabic phonograms for Hangeul.

11.2

---

[1]   It is better known as Hangeul, but we use the name recommended by the Korean Standards body.

example, ideograms are still found in newspapers and academic writing. Korean ideogram character sets are defined independent of Chinese policy, and the shapes of the characters are almost the same as those of Chinese traditional characters with a few exceptions. Two examples are shown in the fourth column of Fig. 11.1.

KS X 1001 (previously known as KS C 5601-1987) is the most widely used Korean character encoding. It includes the most frequently used 2350 Hangeul syllabic phonograms and 4888 ideograms. The most popular computer encoding, called EUC-KR, is based on KS X 1001. There is significant opposition to the use of this character set, however, due to two drawbacks: it includes only 2350 syllables of 11,174 and it does not provide any way of decomposing a syllable into corresponding jamos, which disrupts systematic processing of Hangeul script. KS X 1005-1 (included in Unicode) is the alternative Korean character set. It addresses the drawbacks of KS X 1001 by including all the 11,174 modern Hangeul syllables and also 334 jamos (including jamos of middle Korean and jamo combinations) to support the composition of syllable blocks.

11.3 NONPREDICTIVE METHODS

In China and Japan, nonpredictive methods were considered in the early days of text entry studies, even though these required dealing with thousands of characters. The earliest solution was the construction of a huge Chinese keyboard that allowed direct entry of Chinese characters. It resulted in a machine that used a combination of trays for the characters and levers to manipulate the trays. People also devised ways to map characters onto a full keyboard to enable direct entry. One way is to encode a character as a combination of keys on a full keyboard. Given such a code set, the user must memorize a code for every ideogram before becoming able to enter text. Therefore, the number of users will always be limited to relatively few experts.

To understand how hard direct entry is, consider the T-code method (also called the two-stroke method) for Japanese (Yamada, 1980, 1983). T-code describes an ideogram with two strokes. The full keyboard is divided into two sections, left and right, as shown in Fig. 11.3. Each ideogram requires 2 keys from each section. As there are 20 keys in each section, this amounts to $20 \times 20 \times 4$ (left–left, left–right, right–right, right–left) = 1600 ideograms. Of course, this does not cover a sufficient number of Japanese characters, but the most frequently used ones can be processed. One code assignment for entry with the right–left case is shown in the right-hand side of the Fig. 11.3. To enter the character "出", the user enters "u" (second row, second column of the right section of the keyboard, which is indicated by the inner 5×4 table placed in the second row, third column of the 5×4 outer table) and then "e" (second row, third column of the left section of the keyboard, which is indicated by the outer 5×4 table). There are three other lists for left–left, right–right, and left–right, and the user can enter characters based on these tables. Curiously, entry by T-code is one

The table indicating the second stroke by the left section (ex. `出' requires 2nd row, 3rd column key = `e')

The table indicating the first stroke by the right section (ex. `出' requires 2nd row, 2nd column key = `u')

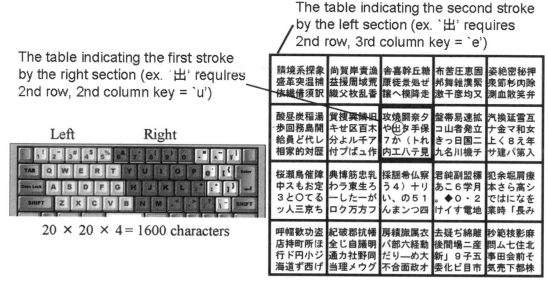

T-code (Japanese). Keyboard division and right–left character assignment.

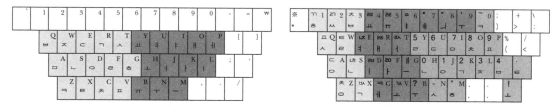

FIGURE 11.4

2- and 3-beolsik keyboard layouts for Korean.

of the most efficient and fastest entry methods once the tables are memorized. However, the hurdle of memorizing the tables is too high for most users. Nowadays, the majority of people use a predictive method, as we will explain in the next section.

In contrast, for Korean, as explained in Section 11.2.3, which is systematically formulated by decomposition into a small set of jamos, the U.S. ASCII keyboard layout with jamos assigned to the alphabet keys is the most typical entry method.

Since Hangeul is written using 24 jamos, the jamos are perfectly accommodated within the alphabet area of the U.S. ASCII layout. The left-hand side of Fig. 11.4 shows the most widely used keyboard layout for Hangeul entry, called *two-beolsik,* in which 24 jamos and the two most frequently used diphthongs are assigned to alphabet keys. Two-beolsik literally means "two-set system," in which there is a set for consonants

FIGURE
11.5

Chunjiin and EZ layouts for Hangeul entry on a mobile phone.

and one for vowels (colored differently). The consonant jamos are assigned to the left-hand side and the vowel jamos are assigned to the right, so Hangeul syllables can be entered by pressing keys using the left- and right-hand fingers in turn. In fact, the two-beolsik layout does not fully reflect the composition system of a Hangeul syllable, which, as mentioned, consists of an initial, a medial, and a final jamo. An alternative solution is the three-beolsik layout (shown on the right side of Fig. 11.4), which is the second most popular keyboard assignment.

The systematic design of Korean letters (Sampson, 1985; Lee & Ramsey, 2001) allows entry on mobile phones through a multitap method. One of the most popular methods is Chunjiin Hangeul. The left side of Fig. 11.5 shows the Chunjiin layout of a mobile phone keypad. The Chunjiin method enables entry by combining a consonant and a vowel. The upper three keys (1, 2, 3) represent the vertical and horizontal bars and a dot, which are used to produce a vowel through combination. For example, the key combination for the vowel ㅏ /a/ is "1–2" (a vertical bar and a dot) and for ㅜ /u/ it is "3–2" (a horizontal bar and a dot). Two consonants are assigned to each key from 4 to 9 and 0, grouped according to similar features, which are entered by a multitap method. For example, to enter the jamo ㅎ /h/ of Hangeul, the key 8 is entered twice. An example of the entry to produce the term Hangeul is shown beside the Chunjiin layout.

Another popular Hangeul entry system for mobile phones is the EZ Hangeul entry system, which is based on adding strokes to jamos. The right side of Fig. 11.5 shows the EZ Hangeul layout of a mobile keypad. The keypad has keys only for the simple shapes of jamos. Others are generated by adding strokes or repeating a single consonant. The * (asterisk) and the # (pound) keys are used, respectively, for stroke addition and consonant repetition. For example, the jamos ㄷ /d/ and ㅌ /t/ are entered by entering ㄴ /n/ and adding a stroke once and twice, respectively. An example entry to produce the term Hangeul is shown beside the EZ layout.

In fact, as Hangeul syllabic phonograms correspond well to ideograms and ideograms are sometimes used in Korean writing, Korean keyboards usually enable ideogram entry by providing phonogram-to-ideogram conversion for the typed-in characters. In this case, a predictive entry method is used just as in Japanese or Chinese. We next look at predictive entry methods based on phonetics.

11.4   PREDICTIVE ENTRY BASED ON PHONETICS

The earliest study of predictive entry methods based on phonetics was done in Japan in the 1960s (Kurihara & Kurosaki, 1967). The first Japanese word processor, JW-10, was commercialized in the 1970s by Mori and Yagihashi (1989). Pronunciation-based methods also became popular in China in the 1980s. One reason for this time lag was that the pronunciation of Chinese ideograms differs greatly according to dialect. Therefore, while entry by pinyin is intuitive for Mandarin speakers, people who are nonnative in Mandarin generally prefer a shape-based method (as explained in the following section). Due to this complication, entry by phonetics in Chinese is much more varied, with phonetic-based and shape-based methods and even combinations of these two types in use. Therefore, even though the pronunciation-based method is now one of the most popular methods among Chinese people, we use mainly Japanese examples in our explanation in this section.

The philosophy underlying predictive entry is to make use of ambiguity. In Chinese, Korean, and Japanese, one pronunciation corresponds to multiple ideograms. First, the user enters a sequence in phonograms or in Roman alphabetic transcription. Then the system looks for corresponding targets in a dictionary included within the software, and it sorts the candidates in a relevant order and displays them for the user. Last, the user chooses his preferred target from among the candidates. The technological aspects of ordering candidates are explained in more detail in Chap. 2. The representative transcription of Chinese is pinyin, that of Japanese is kana, and that of Korean is Hangeul syllabic phonograms.

When predictive entry is adopted, different language units can be considered for prediction, i.e., characters, words, or phrases. Historically, character-based methods were the first to appear, followed by word-based methods, and these were then developed into phrase-based entry. Especially in China and Korea, where a syllable corresponds to an ideogram, character-based methods were used in the early days. However, word-based or phrase-based methods are used more nowadays. There are two reasons for this.

First, the software that incorporates entry by a larger unit includes entry by a smaller unit anyway (i.e., a phrase-based method can also be used to enter characters by prediction). Second, the advantage of entry by a larger unit is greater speed, because most of the time required for predictive entry is for scanning and selecting candidates. With a phrase-based method, the user need select only once if the text entry system proposes a top-ranked candidate that matches the target. In contrast, a word-based method requires multiple selections. For the candidate ranking, though, the degree of ambiguity (i.e., the total number of candidates) is critical. The number of candidates for character-based entry is often very large. For example, the alphabet transcription "kai" in Japanese corresponds to hundreds of different ideograms. This ambiguity decreases drastically in word-based entry. For phrase-based entry, however, the number of candidates increases again, because all combinations of words qualify as candidates. Consequently, the choice of entry is between word-based and

>ぶんしょ ⇐ *bunsho*
　1.文書 2.分署 3.ぶんしょ
>1
文書>にゅうりょく ⇐ *nyuryoku*
　1.入力 2.ニュウリョク 3.にゅうりょく
文書>1
文書入力>の ⇐ *no*
　1.の 2.野 3.之 4.乃 5.ノ 6.埜
文書入力>1
文書入力の>けんきゅう ⇐ *kenkyu*
　1.研究 2.建久 3.けんきゅう 4.ケンキュウ
文書入力の>1
文書入力の研究

FIGURE
11.6

Word-based entry example in Japanese.

phrase-based. The former provides a small number of candidates, so ranking is fairly easy, but it requires multiple selections to produce a phrase; the latter provides a huge number of candidates and ranking requires powerful language modeling, but one-time selection is possible. We first look at word-based entry.

11.4.1   Word-Based Entry

The basics of word-based entry using a Japanese example are illustrated in Fig. 11.6. Here, the text "文書入力の研究" (studies of text entry) has been entered, and the kana transcription (with the Roman transcription in italic) is given as "ぶんしょ" (*bunsho*), "にゅうりょく" (*nyuryoku*), "の" (*no*), "けんきゅう" (*kenkyu*), chunked by words. The user enters each word transcription in the Roman alphabet or in kana and the entry software shows it in Japanese kana characters. The first line of the figure shows kana corresponding to *bunsho* after the prompt, >. The system software then shows candidates corresponding to this kana sequence. In this case, three candidates are shown. The user selects one of them (in this case, the first one "文書"), which appears as the entered text before the prompt > in the fourth row of the text. The rest of the words are entered similarly, word by word. Note that the entry *no* is very ambiguous, because this word unit also forms a character unit.

This form of entry was adopted in the early days of predictive entry by phonetics. The method was quickly developed into a phrase-based form (Mori & Yagihashi, 1989) because this raised the entry speed and the candidate-ranking technology matured. However, the spread of mobile phones in the 1990s led to a revision of word-based methods as the completion method was adopted. Completion is a method that enables the entry of text using only the prefix of each entry (see Chap. 5). Entry by completion thus decreases the number of keystrokes, which is important on hardware with which users have to make multiple strokes to produce one character. At the same time, though, this method increases the ambiguity of the user entry. Therefore, completion was revised in the 1990s after statistical language modeling using a corpus became common.

Currently, in Japan, most mobile phone entry systems use both word-based entry with completion and phrase-based entry (which we will explain in the following section), but the former is preferred because fewer keystrokes are needed. As noted in Section 11.2.2, kana phonograms include nine main consonants, which fits well with the mobile phone keypad. Figure 11.7 shows a standard keypad assignment of Japanese kana characters. Each consonant is assigned to a digit and kana are produced through the multitap method. For example, to obtain the kana corresponding to the sound "ke" (the first kana character in the example *kenkyu* on the right-hand side of the figure), the key for 2, which corresponds to the consonant "k", is tapped four times to indicate

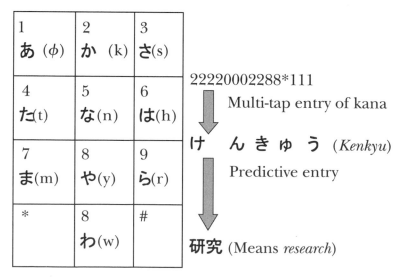

1 あ (φ)	2 か (k)	3 さ(s)
4 た(t)	5 な(n)	6 は(h)
7 ま(m)	8 や(y)	9 ら(r)
*	8 わ(w)	#

22220002288*111

⬇ Multi-tap entry of kana

け ん きゅ う (*Kenkyu*)

Predictive entry

⬇

研究 (Means *research*)

FIGURE 11.7   Japanese kana assignment on a phone keypad and an example of multitap entry.

the vowel "e". After the kana sequence for a whole word or a phrase is entered, the system converts it to an ideogram sequence by applying predictive entry techniques. A similar form of pinyin-based entry in Chinese has been commercialized, of which one example is provided by eZiText by ZI Corporation (http://www.zicorp.com/).

So far, kana characters are entered by a multitap method. However, as the entry method should incorporate predictive entry, the entry can be made by a one-key with disambiguation method (see Chap. 5) (Tanaka-Ishii *et al.*, 2000). For example, to enter *kenkyu*, each corresponding consonant digit can be entered for each phonogram (e.g., "2-0-2-8-1" instead of "2 2 2 2 0 0 0 2 2 8 8 8 * 1 1-1"), and then the system sorts and displays all corresponding words. Figure 11.8 shows such one-key with disambiguation entry with word completion made on the software called TMK10, in which the entry of "2-0" already gives the target as the top candidate. Note that this entry method is different from the T9 solution for Japanese. In Japanese, T9 proposes that entry be done in two stages: first, the user uses one-key with disambiguation and selects a result in the kana alphabet (for example the entry of "2-0-2-8-1" disambiguated to "けんきゅう"), then the result is converted into the final form containing ideograms ("けんきゅう" to "研究"). On the other hand, what we have shown in the example of TMK10 is one-stage entry of a final ideogram form obtained

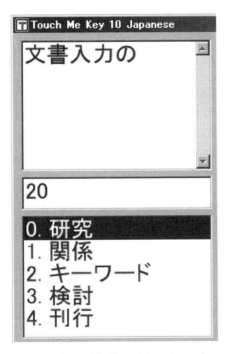

FIGURE

11.8

One-key with disambiguation using a phone keypad.

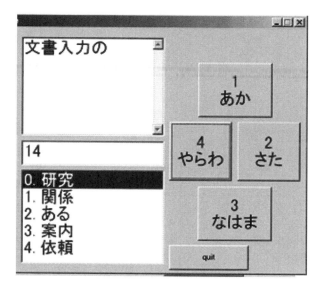

FIGURE
11.9

One-key with disambiguation using four keys.

from one-key with disambiguation (therefore, "2-0-2-8-1" to "研究"). Thus, this is a more generalized version of predictive entry.

This approach can be generalized and the number of keys needed to enter characters can become even fewer than the number of keys on a phone. Figure 11.9 shows entry of the same phrase as above using only four buttons (Tanaka-Ishii, 2002), with the layout on the right side. Each button has 15 to 20 kana characters assigned to it and words are entered by a one-key with disambiguation method. The word *kenkyu* is entered by one-key with disambiguation with completion by the first two digits of "1–4".

The degree of ambiguity is high in such an entry system. Still, a reasonable level of efficiency is achieved when using a good language model (see Chap. 2). According to our investigation (Tanaka-Ishii *et al.*, 2002), if the language model is adapted by using about 10,000 words taken from user documents, fewer keystrokes are needed to enter 1 word than are needed to enter it with a full keyboard.

11.4.2   Phrase-Based Entry

Phrase-based entry has become the most widely used method for inputting Japanese and Chinese to computers. Entries are made according to the phrase unit, and the text entry software analyzes the phonetically transcribed phrase and converts it. For the same example as above, the whole kana-transcribed phrase is entered and conversion of the entire phrase is done as one action (Fig. 11.10). The top candidate shown

>ぶんしょにゅうりょくのけんきゅう
　1. 文書入力の研究　2.分署入力の研究….

>1

文書入力の研究>

FIGURE   Phrase-based entry example in Japanese.

11.10

in this example is the correct target and is the one actually proposed by popular commercial software such as MS-IME and ATOK.

The technological foundation needed to enable this conversion is not at all trivial. First, the kana sequence is chunked into words, and multiple chunking possibilities should be considered. For all possible chunks, there are several candidates. For all such combinations of conversion candidates, the plausibility of conversion is calculated and the results are sorted according to the degree of plausibility. Since the 1980s, such conversion has been realized in Japan by using an HMM-like method based on the parts of speech. The bigrams of each part of speech were then realized as a connection matrix, and the value of the matrix indicating how plausibly a part of speech connects to another part of speech was hand-tuned. Such a result was reformulated into a proper HMM in the early 1990s (see Chap. 2) when the necessary corpora became more available (Nagata, 1998). Some of the recent Japanese commercial text entry software is based on this HMM phrase-based entry. Further improvements have been made by using word co-occurrence, context detection, and selection of a more plausible conversion.

The situation is much the same for Chinese pinyin-based entry. In China, too, most commercial software is based on statistical language models of which the representative is the HMM. Much work has recently been done in this area (Chen & Lee, 2000; Chen *et al.*, 2000; Gao &Lee, 2000).

Phrase-based methods have also been implemented on Japanese mobile phones, but this requires full entry of a kana sequence corresponding to each phrase. Phrase-based completion could decrease the number of keystrokes, but will greatly increase the ambiguity of candidates. So far, phrase-based completion has been realized only for phrases that are converted as one unit by registering the phrase as if it is a single word. Proper phrase-based entry by completion will require future study.

11.5   PREDICTIVE ENTRY BASED ON SHAPES

Another interesting way to enter text is based on character shapes. An ideogram is constructed from a combination of components. For example, "魚" means fish, while "鯖"

means mackerel (literally, blue fish) and "鯛" means porgy (literally, fish that migrates); both "鯖" and "鯛" include "魚" as a radical. Such constructive features of ideograms allow text entry based on shapes. As mentioned, the shape-based method has flourished in China because of the different phonetic systems. In contrast, the shape-based method is used in Japan and Korea to complement the phonetic-based method.

Shape-based methods are particularly useful when a user does not know how to read certain ideograms. Such a situation typically occurs when one uses a dictionary to look up characters whose reading is unknown. Conventionally, there are two ways to enter ideograms in ideogram dictionaries, and both can be considered a predictive entry method based on shapes:

- by the number of strokes and
- by the traditional radicals of ideograms.

For example, 11 strokes are normally used to write "魚", so this character is searched for by entering 11. Of course, hundreds of characters with 11 strokes will appear, and the user has to scan through this list to find the target (which can be done amazingly fast by native speakers).

With the radical method, since "鯛" includes the radical "魚", the user can select this radical from a set of radicals and use it as a filter to obtain only candidates that contain "魚" as a radical. In Japan, the JIS character standards include the set of radicals, but entry by radicals remains a complementary method to be used only when an ideogram's reading is unknown. In China, though, the radical method has become an efficient entry system called the Wubi method, invented by Yongmin Wang in 1983 (Wicentowski, 1996). In the Wubi method, a letter of the alphabet is assigned to each component of a character. The user can then enter a character as a combination of letters; i.e., the character is formed as a combination of letter-designated components.

Next, we introduce two other representative shape-based entry methods invented in China.

The four-corner method (Dylan, 1997) is based on a form of Chinese character encoding using four or five numerical digits per character. This form of encoding was invented by Yunwu Wang in the 1920s.

The four digits used to encode each character are selected according to the shape of the four corners of each character. Figure 11.11 shows an example of such coding for a character (which means "face"). The code for this character is 0128. The user has to memorize the code corresponding to each shape at each corner. The shape code is grouped into nine clusters (a Chinese poem can be recited to make the clusters easier to memorize). This method was one of the most popular methods for indexing dictionaries until pinyin was standardized in the 1950s. After the introduction of pinyin, this method has been used less frequently, but it remains arguably the oldest indexing method based on character shapes.

Another elegant form of shape-based entry is the five-stroke method (Wicentowski, 2001). Every stroke used to write characters is classified according to

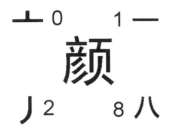

Encoding example for the four-corner method in Chinese.

the five prototypes: 1 for horizontal strokes such as 一 , 2 for vertical strokes such as |, 3 for left-falling strokes such as ノ, 4 for right-falling strokes such as 丶, 5 for curved strokes such as 乙. A character is then encoded using its first to fourth strokes and the last stroke. If a character contains fewer than five strokes, its code consists of all of its strokes in the proper order. For example, the first four digits of the code for "行" (to go) are "3-3-2-1" and the last stroke is encoded as "2", so the total code is "3-3-2-1-2". This coding method can represent $5^5 = 78,125$ characters, so the character is uniquely defined in most cases. In an ambiguous case, the corresponding characters are all shown. This method is widely used as a fast text-input method. Even on mobile phones, the eight-stroke method, derived from the five-stroke method, has been used commercially by eZiText by ZI Corporation (www.zicorp.com/). The keypad assignment of an eight-stroke prototype is shown in Fig. 11.12.

11.6   ENTRY ON OTHER DEVICES

Text entry concerns various devices. This section looks at entry in East Asian languages on devices other than keyboards and keypads.

Due to the large number of characters and our tradition in calligraphy, some non-East Asian readers might think that there must be a fitter modality for these languages; for example, through handwriting rather than using keypads or keyboards. However, this is not the case: entry by keyboard is the best fit method for East Asian languages, because the nature of the computer limits its pattern recognition ability. Having a large number of characters to be recognized makes handwriting recognition even more difficult than entry with keypads. Thus, entry on other devices tends to be an extension of entry on keypads and keyboards.

As computers are developed first for the U.S. market and every new device has its standard features designed for English, entry systems for languages other than English can be classified into following types.

Eight-stroke entry on a mobile phone in Chinese (by ZI Corporation).

1. Entry methods developed for alphabetic script adapted to the language

2. Entry methods developed originally for the language

3. Entry methods developed on a common framework independent of language

Keyboards and keypads, when it concerns hardware, belong in the first group. Predictive entry methods conceived and developed originally in East Asia belong to the second group. Speech recognition methods can be considered as belonging to the third group, because most similar methods can be applied to any language by changing only the acoustic and language models. For newer devices and methods, such as PDAs and text entry by eye gaze, the system is developed as combinations of such basic technologies. One common aspect is that most of them incorporate predictive entry (except for direct entry of ideograms by handwriting recognition, as explained below).

Entry on PDAs can be done through a soft keyboard, handwriting recognition, and a combination of both. For soft keyboards of the first group in the above list, there are various keyboards with layouts based on a standard full keyboard. In this case, a user can enter Japanese or Chinese text phonetically from alphabet transcription using predictive entry. Korean can be entered using a soft keyboard that looks like standard keyboards (Fig. 11.4). In addition, various entry methods designed for English on PDAs have been adapted to these three languages; these methods are all realized through entry based on phonetics with the result then being put through predictive entry to obtain the text containing ideograms.

Among the soft keyboards designed originally for a language (the second group), there are keypads designed based on the language framework. In Japanese, a soft keyboard that has a layout similar to that shown in Fig. 11.1 is popular. In Korean, there are soft keyboards conceptualizing Fig. 11.2 of which some examples have been produced as phone keypads as shown in Fig. 11.5. For Chinese, various soft keyboards support shape-based entry. Examples for Japanese and Chinese are shown in Fig. 11.13a.

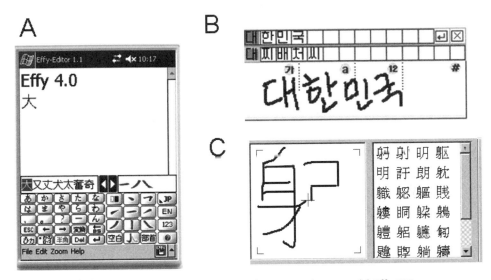

FIGURE

11.13
Entry of Chinese, Korean, and Japanese using pen and mouse. (a) Effy-CJK,
(b) DioPen, (c) IME-Pad.

With the Effy-CJK (http://www.timespace21.com/), English, Chinese, Korean, and
Japanese can all be entered. The left half of the soft keyboard shows Japanese entry
based on kana characters (see Section 11.2.2), and the right half shows shape-based
entry of ideograms that can be used for either Chinese entry or Japanese entry.

Two types of entry are used for technologies based on handwriting recognition:

- The user enters characters of a phonetic alphabet and uses predictive entry (in
  Korean and Japanese).

- The user enters ideograms directly (in Chinese and Japanese).

The former has the advantage of higher recognition precision because the number
of characters is small. The Korean version of continuous handwriting entry on
DioPen (www.ditek.co.kr/) is shown in Fig. 11.13[2]. The best predicted characters
from the handwriting are shown printed on the first line above the handwriting. The
second line shows other possible characters for a selected character in the first line.
In Japanese, too, similar entry methods are available from ATOK by JustSystems
(www.atok.com/).

The second type of handwriting system to enter ideograms directly is also popular for Chinese and Japanese. The core basics of handwriting systems are constructed

---

[2] The Korean written here reads *Daehanminkuk*, the official Korean name of the country.

on common frameworks independent of language type, but as noted, a large number of characters must be recognized for languages using ideograms, which affects the precision. To raise the recognition precision, the stroke orders of ideograms are considered in all handwriting recognition software. Thus, handwriting recognition in Japanese and Chinese can be considered as among the third group with some of the flavor of the second. Such direct handwriting entry is used by Japanese and Chinese, not only in PDAs, but also on PCs using a normal mouse, to enter characters whose reading is unknown. An example is the Microsoft IME-Pad (www.microsoft.com/), shown in Fig. 11.13c, where an ideogram is being written and the possible matching characters are shown on the right-hand side. Such software dynamically shows the possible characters even though the character entry is incomplete. Other applications of entry by handwriting recognition that have become popular recently are computer games such as those proposed by Nintendo (www.nintendo.co.jp/).

The situation of text entry by eye gaze is similar to that of the soft keyboard. In entry by eye gaze, a soft keyboard is shown on the screen and entry is done through use of an eye-gaze device. Questions regarding entry by gaze include whether to integrate a predictive method within the eye-gazing system and how this could be done. For more on the technological issues concerning eye-gaze entry, see Chap. 9.

11.7   IDEOGRAM ENTRY SYSTEM FOR NONNATIVES

All of the above entry methods were designed for native speakers familiar with the writing system of the language. However, people who are not native speakers often find it difficult to learn ideograms, partially because their ability to look up ideograms may be quite limited.

An overview of previous work on ideogram lookup for nonnatives can be found in Breen (2005). However, most methods, like the methods considered so far, are designed on the basis of traditional conventions. For example, the SKIP code (Halpern, 1999) is based on the traditional stroke counting method.

Before ending this chapter, we will look at some recent attempts to help nonnatives enter ideograms, one based on phonetics and the other based on shapes. The first is an interesting phonetic-based method used in entry systems that can accept an English word to input a Chinese word, such as the WanNengMa Input System (WanNenMa, 2005). For instance, if a user wants to input 办公室, he/she inputs the English word *office*. Thus, users with a knowledge of English can input words more efficiently. Surprisingly, in many cases this method has an additional advantage that the length of the input code of an English word is shorter than that of the corresponding pinyin. For the above example, *office* requires 6 letters, but *bangongshi* requires 10.

The second example of entry based on phonetics is the FOKS system (Bilac *et al.*, 2002) for Japanese. The user can enter his estimated reading of an ideogram and the system guesses the correct word. A system using this method can be implemented by

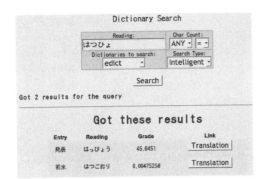 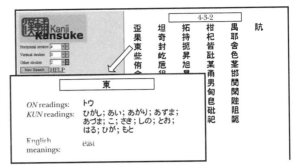

FIGURE   The FOKS and the Kansuke system: ideogram finders for nonnatives.

11.14

allowing greater ambiguity of the entry characters (so that a candidate can be found even for incorrect entries). The left side of Fig. 11.14 shows an example of an incorrect reading being entered and the estimated words. Even though this approach assumes that users have a certain basic knowledge of how to read ideograms, it helps them to enter ideograms by making an educated guess.

As for the shape-based method, we refer to the Kansuke (which literally means "ideogram helper") system (Tanaka-Ishii and Godon, 2006), built for both Chinese and Japanese ideograms. The idea here is to use three stroke prototypes, which form the basis of ideograms. The three prototypes are vertical, horizontal, and other (diagonal or bent) strokes. For example, for the character "東", the code is "4-3-2", meaning four horizontal strokes, three vertical strokes, and two other strokes (diagonals). An example of a search for the character using this Kansuke code is shown on the right side of Fig. 11.14. The user can select his target from the list shown on the right side of the screen by clicking, then the dictionary content taken from Breen (2005) explains the ideogram. The search can also be conducted based on components; for example, 漢 can be looked up using 氵 and 艹, both of which are also searched for via the Kansuke code (for example "0-0-3" to get 氵). The basic concept of the Kansuke system can be said to be within the tradition of the Chinese shape-based predictive method, but the system was totally redesigned to minimize the arbitrariness of the writing system and to enable the entry of ideograms even by complete beginners.

11.8   CONCLUSION

East Asian countries share a distinct culture of ideogram use. This difference from Western culture has led to the generation of unique writing systems and related entry technologies. The technologies based on prediction constitute one example of this, with their development dating back nearly 50 years. These technologies have been generalized in terms of other languages and are now being applied worldwide. As so often happens, variety in needs and practices has provided a source of new universal technologies.

REFERENCES

Bilac, S., Baldwin, T., & Tanaka, H. (2002). Bringing the dictionary to the user: the FOKS System. *Proceedings of the 19th International Conference on Computational Linguistics* (pp.84–91): *http://www.foks.info//index.html*. Morristown, NJ: Association for Computational Linguistics.

Breen, J. (2005). Jim Breen's WWWDic Site: *http://www.csse.monash.edu.au/jwb/cgi-bin/wwwjdic.cgi*

Chen, Z., & Lee, K. (2000). A new statistical approach to Chinese pinyin input. *Proceedings of the 38th Annual Meeting of the Association for Computational Linguistics* (pp. 241–247). Morristown, NJ: Association for Computational Linguistics.

Chen, Z., Li, M., Zhang, F., & Yang, R. (2000). Chinese pinyin input on mobile phone. In The 2nd International Symosium on Chinese Spoken Language Processing, October 13–15, 2000, Beijing, China.

Dylan, W. (1997). Four corner system. Accessed in 2006 at *http://www.sungwh.freeserve.co.uk/sapienti/fourcinp.htm*. Created on the 23rd November 1997 and last updated on 2nd August 2001.

Gao, J., & Lee, K.-F. (2000). Distribution-based pruning of backoff language models. Morristown, NJ: Association for Computational Linguistics.

Halpern, J. (1999). *Kanji learner's dictionary*. Tokyo: Kodansha International.

Kurihara, A., & Kurosaki, H. (1967). About a transformation method of kana into kanji text. *Technical Report of the University of Kyusyu, 39*, 659–664. [In Japanese]

Lee, I., & Ramsey, S. (2001). *The Korean language*. Albany: State University of New York Press.

Lee, U. (2002). *A research and analysis on the Standard Korean dictionary*. Seoul: The National Academy of the Korean Language.

Mori, K., & Yagihashi, T. (1989). *The birth of Japanese word processors*. Tokyo: Maruzen publishing. [In Japanese]

Nagata, M. (1998). *A study on Japanese text processing by statistical models*. Kyoto: University of Kyoto. [Ph.D. thesis; in Japanese]

Sampson, G. (1985). *Writing systems: A linguistic introduction*. Stanford, CA: Stanford University Press.

Tanaka-Ishii, K., & Godon, J. (2006). Kansuke: A kanji look-up system based on a few stroke prototypes. *International Conference on Computer Processing of Oriental Languages*: *http://www.ish.ci.i.u-tokyo.ac.jp/kansuke.html* (pp. 234–244). Berlin/Heidelberg: Springer.

Tanaka-Ishii, K., Inutsuka, Y., & Takeichi, M. (2000). Japanese input system with digits—Can Japanese be input only with consonants? *Human Language Technology Conference 2001* (pp. 211–218). Morristown, NJ: Association for Computational Linguistics.

Tanaka-Ishii, K., Inutsuka, Y., & Takeichi, M. (2002). Entering text with a four-button device. *International Conference on Computational Linguistics* (pp.988–994). Morristown, NJ: Association for Computational Linguistics.

WanNenMa (2005). Wannenma entry system: *http://www.hongen.com/pc/newer/ime/wnm/wnm01.htm*

Wicentowski, J. (1996) Wubixixing. Created in 1996, accessed in 2006 at *http://www.yale.edu/chinesemac/wubi/xing.html*

Wicentowski, J. (2001). Wubihua. Created in 1994, accessed in 2006 at *http://www.yale.edu/chinesemac/wubi/hua.html*

Yamada, H. (1980). A historical study of typewriters and typing methods: From the position of planning Japanese parallels. *Journal of Information Processing, 2.*

Yamada, H. (1983). Certain problems associated with the design of input keyboards for Japanese writing. In W. E. Cooper (Ed.), *Cognitive aspects of skilled typewriting* (pp.305–407).New York: Springer-Verlag.

12 | Text Entry in South and Southeast Asian Scripts

CHAPTER

Renu Gupta   University of Aizu, Aizu, Japan
Virach Sornlertlamvanich   NICT Asia Research Center, Pathumthani, Thailand

12.1   INTRODUCTION

About 2300 years ago, a script called Brahmi was developed and used in India (Salomon, 1996). Derivatives of this script spread through most of India and, by the 6th century, they had spread to Southeast Asia through trade and Buddhism. All scripts derived from Brahmi are today known as abugidas, and it is at this category of scripts—and, in particular, text entry in such—that this chapter is directed.

Although Brahmi is no longer in use, it is the source of most of the scripts used today in South Asia and Southeast Asia. Many of these languages belong to different language families; for example, Hindi is an Indo-European language, Thai comes from the Thai-Kadai language family, Tibetan belongs to the Sino-Tibetan group, and Khmer is an Austro-Asiatic language. Yet, the scripts used to write them are structurally similar because they are all derived from Brahmi. At the same time, these scripts differ from an alphabetic writing system, not merely in their symbols, but also in their organizing principles. Thus, they present a challenge for text entry through input devices that have been designed primarily for alphabetic writing systems.

If we were talking about only a few million users and a few scripts, it may not be worth investing resources in typing these scripts. However, India, with a population of over 1 billion, uses nine scripts from this writing system[1] for administration and education—Bengali (for Bangla and Assamese), Devanagari (for Hindi, Konkani, Marathi, Nepali, and Sanskrit), Gujarati, Gurmukhi (for Punjabi), Kannada, Malayalam, Oriya, Tamil, and Telugu. In addition, other scripts, such as Modi and Khaithi, are used within

---

[1]   In addition to nine abugidas, India also uses the Roman alphabet to write languages, such as Khasi, and the Perso-Arabic script (an abjad) for Kashmiri and Urdu. These scripts are not included in this discussion of Indian scripts.

a community. Further, many of the scripts currently used in Asia are structurally similar because they have been derived from Brahmi. Scripts currently in use include the scripts in Sri Lanka (Sinhala), Myanmar[2], Cambodia (Khmer), Laos (Lao), Thailand (Thai), and Tibet (Tibetan). Related scripts that now have restricted use include the scripts in Indonesia, the Philippines, and Japan. Indonesia has the following related scripts: Javanese, Sundanese, and Madurese on the island of Java; Balinese in Bali; Batak, Lampong, and Redjang in Sumatra; and Buginese and Makassarese in Sulawesi (Kuipers & McDermott, 1996). With the introduction of Bahasa as the national language of Indonesia, most of these scripts now have limited functions but, as the technology for writing them becomes available, interest in these scripts is growing[3]. Other Brahmi-derived scripts that are rarely used now are Cham in Vietnam and Cambodia, Baybayin to write Tagalog in the Philippines, and Siddham in Japan, which is restricted to writing Buddhist scriptures; here, again, there has been renewed interest in these scripts as evidenced both by sites such as *Modern Siddham*[4] and by attempts to create character sets in Unicode for these scripts.

Given this vast pool of users who use scripts with a similar organizing principle, appropriate technology for text input becomes important. In this chapter, we describe text entry devices and techniques used in two Asian countries: India in South Asia and Thailand in Southeast Asia.

12.2   CHARACTERISTICS OF AN ABUGIDA

As with alphabetic scripts, abugidas are written from left to right, but there is no differentiation between upper- and lowercase characters. In the Southeast Asian scripts, there is no explicit use of spaces or periods to determine word or sentence boundaries. In order to understand the problems of text entry, this section describes the structure of an abugida in two parts; there is an inventory of the symbols for one script (Devanagari) followed by a description of how characters are combined.

12.2.1   Script Inventory

Abugidas are organized in a series of matrices based on articulatory phonetics. There are three matrices, one each for the vowels, consonants, and sonorants/fricatives[5]. Table 12.1 shows this arrangement, using the symbols in Devanagari as an example.

---

[2]   The official language of the Union of Myanmar is Burmese. In this chapter we use the term *Myanmar,* which is the government-recognized name for the language.
[3]   See http://www.babadbali.com/aksarabali/presengl.htm.
[4]   See http://www.mandalar.com/DisplayJ/Bonji/index.html.
[5]   In everyday terms, sonorants are called glides and liquids, while fricatives are the sibilant sounds.

Vowels	Primary vowels	a अ	ā आ	i इ	ī ई	u उ	ū ऊ	ṛi ऋ
	Secondary vowels	e ए	ai ऐ	o ओ	au औ			

Consonants		Voiceless plosives		Voiced plosives		
		Unaspirated	Aspirated	Unaspirated	Aspirated	Nasals
	Velar	k क	kʰ ख	g ग	gʰ घ	ŋ ङ
	Palatal	tʃ च	tʃʰ छ	dʒ ज	dʒʰ झ	ɲ ञ
	Retroflex	ṭ ट	ṭʰ ठ	ḍ ड	ḍʰ ढ	ṇ ण
	Dental	t त	tʰ थ	d द	dʰ ध	n न
	Labial	p प	pʰ फ	b ब	bʰ भ	m म

Sonorants & Fricatives	y य	r र	l ल	v व
	sh श	ṣ ष	s स	h ह

TABLE 12.1 Phonological inventory of an abugida. In each cell, the transliteration is given in the top half, while the lower half provides the symbol in Devanagari.

The phonological inventory remains essentially the same across different scripts. Tamil and Redjang use fewer symbols because there are fewer phonemes in these languages, whereas Malayalam has added symbols for its larger phoneme base and Thai has included symbols to accommodate toncs.

As the script spread through India and Asia, the organizing principle remained intact but each country created its own set of symbols depending on the material used for writing. In north India, where a reed pen was used for writing, the scripts have a distinctive horizontal line, but in south India and Southeast Asia, where a stylus was used to write on palm leaves, the scripts had to be more rounded (Hosking & Meredith-Owens, 1966). So, different languages have mapped different symbols onto this inventory (Holle, 1999). Table 12.2 shows the variation across these Brahmi-derived scripts in the symbol used for the sound /k/.

Devanagari	Gujarati	Gurmukhi	Bengali	Oriya	Tibetan	Telugu	Kannada	Tamil	Malayalam	Sinhala	Burmese	Lao	Thai	Khmer	Javanese	Balinese	Tagalog	Batak	Buginese
क	૬	ਰ	ক	ଓ	༡	౫	ಕ	க	൶	ඔ	က	ຖ	ຖ	ស	ភ	৯	ᜎ	ᯉ	ᨀ

TABLE 12.2 Comparison of symbols across scripts (from Golshani, 2004).

12.2.2   Character Formation

From Table 12.1, an abugida appears to resemble an alphabet. However, the complexity arises from the fact that in an abugida each consonant has an inherent vowel, such as schwa. Hence, the shape of a character in a word is not fixed but is modified when combined with other characters. Using Devanagari as an example, we can see how this works with the symbol for /k/, namely क.

1. *Modification with vowels.* To indicate a vowel other than the inherent vowel, a diacritic is added to the character क. These vowel signs can occur in different positions relative to the consonant—before (कि), above (कै), after (की), or below (कृ). In certain symbols, such as र (for *r*), the vowel sign is positioned in the middle of the consonant symbol (रु). In scripts such as Bengali and Tamil, the vowel sign surrounds the consonant.

2. *Consonant cluster.* In a consonant cluster (such as *kl*), the inherent vowel in the symbol for *k* has to be "killed."
   A. One route is to use a diacritic (called a *virama*) below the consonant to be killed. For the cluster *kl* we would get क्ल but this creates unnecessarily long texts. Instead, the shape of the *k* grapheme is changed to give us क्ल.
   B. The cluster *kk* is written as a vertical ligature, क्क by stacking the symbols. Some of these ligatures are fairly complex, as in kt (क्त)or dv (द्व). These vertical ligatures are limited to the Indic scripts and are not found in most Southeast Asian scripts.
   C. The third method is seen in the cluster *ksh*, which could be written as क्ष but is conventionally written as a ligature—क्ष—that cannot be decomposed into the composite consonant symbols.

3. *Phonological order versus writing order.* The diacritics are not necessarily written or read in a linear sequence. For example, the sound /ki/ is written *ik*, with the vowel placed before the consonant symbol (कि). Similarly, in a consonant cluster, the *r* diacritic is placed above the following consonant symbol; in the cluster *rk* (र्क), the symbol for *r* is placed above the consonant *k*.

Modification with vowels	ki	कि
	ke	के
	ka	की
	ku	कृ
Consonant clusters	kl	क्ल
	kk	क्क
	ksh	क्ष
Writing order	ki	कि

TABLE   Modification of the base consonant क in Devanagari.

12.3

Table 12.3 summarizes the different shapes for the k consonant.

As we see, the shape of the symbol क (for k) changes; under different conditions, it can be written as क, कृ,, क्क, क्ष, or श्र). Although the number of combinations is not as large as in a logosyllabary, it is still significantly larger than in an alphabet. In Devanagari, for example, a character can be an independent vowel (11 characters), an independent consonant (33 characters), a consonant followed by a vowel (11 × 33), or two or more consonants followed by a vowel. This property means that for each combination, multiple shapes are required, and with tonal languages, such as Thai, this is increased by the addition of tone marks. In fact, printing presses design different blocks for each individual shape, but this is not possible in computers or mobile phones for which the keyboard/keypad has a limited number of keys for data entry; however, software can and should provide these multiple combinations for the user.

12.3   TEXT ENTRY ISSUES

When computers were introduced into a country, the necessary hardware and software was developed to enable users to enter text. This resulted in numerous solutions that were not compatible across platforms. To ensure consistency, government organizations tried to establish a common standard. In the case of hardware, all the countries chose to adapt the Qwerty keyboard to their scripts, because selecting an entirely new keyboard presented logistical problems. For software, compatibility is now possible because of Unicode.

Although these decisions help ensure a degree of compatibility, the downside is that they impose constraints; first, the hardware, namely, the keyboard or keypad, has a limited number of input keys and second, each script has been assigned a limited number of code points (128) in Unicode. These two limitations force choices on what characters should be included on the keyboard and in the Unicode character set for the script.

In this section we examine text entry issues in abugidas. The first part describes the Unicode character sets available for abugidas; we then introduce two notions central to text entry in abugidas—the orthographic syllable and the zero-width joiner. The final part lists five implementation issues in text entry.

12.3.1 Character Sets

Unicode is now being recognized as a viable standard by most Asian countries to resolve compatibility problems. Unicode (2003) recognizes the structural similarities among the abugidas of South and Southeast Asia but the encoding differs across countries.

The Unicode character sets for the Indian scripts are based on ISCII-1988 (Indian Standard Code for Information Interchange). In Unicode, the character sets for the Indian scripts are as follows: Devanagari (U+0900-U+097F), Bengali (U+0980-U+09FF), Gujarati (U+0A80-U+0AFF), Gurmukhi (U+0A00-U+0A7F), Kannada (U+0C80-U+0CFF), Malayalam (U+0D00-U+0D7F), Oriya (U+0B00-U+B7F), Tamil (U+0B80-U+0BFF), and Telugu (U+ 0C00-U+ 0C7F). For these scripts, the characters are organized in the same manner and are found in the same location. The Indian scripts are *virama*-based, which means that they employ a diacritic to kill the inherent vowel.

Scripts outside India have developed their own schemes that do not map onto ISCII. So, although Sinhala (U+0D80-U+0DFF), Myanmar (U+0100-U+109F), and Khmer (U+1780-U+17FF) are *virama*-based, they do not map onto ISCII. Thai (U+0E00-U+0E7F) and Lao (U+0E80-U+0EFF) differ in that they are not *virama*-based and they are based on the Thai Industrial Standard. The final script encoded in Unicode is Tibetan (U+0F00-U+0FBF), which has a different structure and use.

For each script, the character set includes the full forms of the vowels and consonants, diacritics, and special signs; for Indian scripts, it includes a small set of conjuncts where necessary and, for Southeast Asian scripts, there are tone marks.

12.3.2 Building Blocks

Since each script has been assigned only a limited number of codes in Unicode, the task of building a complex character has to be mediated by a shaping engine that combines several glyphs to produce a character. Handling this task involves the notion of the orthographic syllable and the use of zero-width characters.

1. *Orthographic syllable.* The basic unit for the shaping engine is an orthographic syllable that consists of a base consonant; other consonants can be attached to the base consonant as can vowel signs and tone marks. The order of input may not necessarily match the final shape. For example, *ki* is typed as *ki* but displayed as

ik. The rules for input and display vary across the different scripts because of differences in implementation; in each script, it is the task of the shaping engine to identify syllables in a stream of text and apply rules to define the shape of the entire syllable. Take the example of the following input in Devanagari:

प + ः+ र + fि → प्रि

Consonant *p* + virama+ consonant *r* + vowel *i* → syllable *pri*

The shaping engine for Devanagari employs rules that perform the following: (a) the diacritic for *r* is combined with *p* and placed as a diagonal stroke below, and (b) the vowel diacritic is displayed at the beginning of the syllable. Once an orthographic syllable is formed and displayed, it is treated as a "cell"; the cursor cannot be placed within the syllable.

2. *Zero-width characters.* These characters are not displayed on the screen but are used to specify whether two characters should be joined. In Unicode, two special characters—the zero-width joiner and the zero-width nonjoiner—are used to enable different forms of conjuncts, since in the Indian scripts there are alternative ways of representing some conjuncts:

क + ः + ष → क्ष

क + ः + ZWJ + ष → क्ष

क + ः + ZWNJ + ष → क्ष

12.3.3   Implementation Issues

Across countries that use abugidas, there are variations in implementation because of differences in both the scripts and the accepted standards for the technology in the various countries. Despite these differences, there are five main issues concerning text entry that are common across countries that use these scripts.

1. *Number of characters.* Abugidas use a larger number of base characters than an alphabet. However, since they do not distinguish upper- and lower-case, the solution devised is to use special keys, namely, Shift key, Ctrl key, and Alt key, to accommodate the larger number of characters. With the focus on accommodating the numerous characters, important symbols, such as the question mark, have been ignored. For example, in the Indian keyboards, the key usually assigned to the question mark is used for the symbol ञ. To type a question mark, one has to hold down AltGr + Shift and press the question mark key; either that or one can switch to English mode and type the question mark.

2. *Selection of characters.* Since the keyboard cannot accommodate all the complex combinations, the characters chosen for the keyboard need to be selected carefully. Clearly, the base characters shown in Table 12.1 should be displayed, but it is not obvious what else should be available for the user. For example, either complex ligatures could be assigned separate keys or their shape formation could be handled by the shaping engine. A second example from Indian scripts is vowels; the computer keyboard displays the forms for both the independent vowel and its diacritic, whereas mobile phones display only the independent vowels and leave the task of vowel form selection to the shaping rules. In Thai and Lao, the symbols are almost identical but the keyboards differ because the standards have been set by different countries.

3. *Keyboard layout.* On the Qwerty keyboard, the symbols were assigned to specific keys based on usability principles. Other concerns may drive the layout of the keyboard. The Indian keyboard design is driven by a need for compatibility across all nine Indian scripts, which is a linguistic solution. In mobile phones on which the display is even more restricted, key assignment becomes critical.

4. *Input sequence.* In an abugida, the writing order and the phonological order may not match. In tonal languages, such as Thai, the problem is exacerbated because the vowel diacritics and tones are stacked above the base consonant. In Khmer, instead of inputting characters one by one from left to right, the order of input is based on the spelling order, namely, consonant + conjunct consonant + vowel + sign, as shown in Fig. 12.1. Other concerns may drive the input order, as can be seen in Myanmar. One popular input method is based on the traditional typewriter input method shown in Fig. 12.2a; however, the common way to write this is the sequence shown in Fig. 12.2b, and this method is being promoted and recommended for the national standard.

FIGURE
12.1

Khmer input sequence based on the Unicode encoding scheme (Open Forum of Cambodia, 2004).

FIGURE
12.2

(a) Myanmar input sequence based on the traditional typewriter input method (from Htut, 2004). (b) Myanmar input sequence based on the order of writing, called Myanmar Primer (from Htut, 2004).

5. *Deletion.* Since the unit of analysis for the shaping engine is the orthographic syllable that is treated as a cell, there needs to be a mechanism that allows users to edit parts of a character. In India and Thailand, the Delete and Backspace keys are used to perform two different operations on a syllable.

These are only some of the general issues on text entry in abugidas. In the following sections we present two case studies, since we could not include all the scripts. India was chosen as representative of South Asian scripts, while Thailand represents issues in Southeast Asian scripts, such as tone inclusion. Although both these countries use abugidas, their encoding schemes differ. In addition, India has the option of entering text in the Roman script because English is an associate link language, whereas English is less widespread in Thailand.

12.4 TEXT ENTRY SYSTEMS IN INDIA

By the end of 2005 the number of Internet users in India jumped to more than 50 million (Internet World Statistics, 2006) and in April 2006 the number of mobile phone users stood at 96.9 million (Telecom Regulatory Authority of India, 2006). Despite these large numbers, the scripts used on these devices are not necessarily Indian scripts. Although Hindi is the fourth most spoken language in the world, there is a noticeable absence of Web pages written in Hindi. While this absence is partly due to the use of English by an elite class in India that has access to computers, it is also due to the lack of "vernacular software" (Hall, 1998). Small- and medium-sized merchants in India may want Indian language computers for their businesses, but in the absence of supply there is no demand (Keniston, 2001).

Software support for the local language market was provided by organizations, individuals, and vendors; an example is the iLeap software by C-DAC through the Government of India. Such software was highly creative, but incompatible across platforms (Keniston, 2001), despite efforts by the Government of India to establish standards for computing in 1986. Indians circumvented this problem by typing their messages either in English or in an Indian language—but in the only script available, which was the Roman script.

Businesses have recognized the need for local language software and directed efforts toward developing software for users to type in Indian languages on computers and mobile phones. With the adoption of Unicode, a standard has emerged but this is not supported by older browsers or operating systems.

12.4.1 Text Entry on Computers

To type text in an Indic script, there are two main options: input the text using English or input it directly through an Indian script.

Text Entry Through English

Programs such as *Baraha*[6] allow the user to type in the Roman script and convert the output into an Indian script. For example, to type the word *kal*, the user types K + A + L on an English keyboard and the word कल is displayed. This system is sometimes called transliteration or phonetic. Typing through the Roman script is extremely simple for users who already know English but it disadvantages users who are not familiar with the English alphabet and the location of the symbols on the English keyboard.

Text Entry Through an Indian Script

The second option for text entry is a keyboard that maps symbols for an Indian language on the keyboard. The most commonly used keyboard is *Inscript* (which stands for *Indian Script*), which was designed by the Department of Electronics and has been adapted by Microsoft. Since the organizing principle for all the Indian scripts is the same (see Section 12.2.1), the keyboard was designed so that it could be used for all nine Indian abugidas. For example, the symbol for *k* is located on the same key across all Indian scripts. Figure 12.3 shows the Inscript keyboard layout for Devanagari.

In the Inscript keyboard, the characters have been organized in the following manner:

1. Vowels and consonants are separated; vowels are placed on the left side of the keyboard while the consonants are on the right.

FIGURE 12.3   Inscript keyboard for Devanagari.

---

6   See http://www.baraha.com/.

2. Related sounds and characters are placed on the same key making them easier to find. For example, the same key is used for the characters *k* and *kh* (क and ख); *k* is accessed in the normal mode, whereas *kh* is written with the Shift key depressed. Similarly, the independent vowel for *a* (आ) and the vowel sign for *a* (ा) are assigned to the same key.

With the exception of these two principles, the logic underlying the placement of the characters is not obvious to users; they are not organized based on the sequence in the Indic scripts, so that the beginner spends a great deal of time hunting for the keys.

There have been attempts to modify the layout of these keyboards. The Devanagari keyboard developed at IIT Bombay (Joshi *et al.*, 2004) also separates the vowels and consonants, but the consonants are arranged in the phonological sequence (Table 12.1), namely, क, ख, ग, घ . . . (*k*, *k^h*, *g*, *g^h*, . . .). Since this is the order in which users learn the script, it reduces time spent hunting for keys — a point made by the designers based on their usability studies.

When typing directly in an Indian script, the user relies on the graphic shape of the symbol to input characters and does not have to go through an intermediate language or script, such as English. This keyboard also helps the multiscriptal user who wants to type a text in two or more different Indic scripts, since the keys are identical across Indian scripts. However, since the different Indic scripts have different numbers of characters, for certain scripts such as Tamil several keys are redundant, which slows down the typist.

Text Output

Due to the limited character set in Unicode and problems with rules in the shaping engine, the text that is entered is often not displayed correctly.

1. *Conjuncts.* When one types a word like *chitthi* (*letter*) in Devanagari, Baraha correctly displays चिट्ठी, but Unicode displays चिट्ठी because vertical conjuncts, such as ट्ठ, have not been encoded as Unicode characters (Technology Development for Indian Languages, 2002; Unicode, 2003). Fonts for many of these complex conjuncts are available in sophisticated packages such as Baraha and LaTeX (Acharya, 2001) but have been omitted from the Mangal font supported by Windows. At the same time, some programs permit the formation of obscure conjuncts. For example, when the consonant cluster *pt* (प्त) is typed in Devanagari, Microsoft Office outputs स because the program treats *pt* as a conjunct. To prevent the automatic conjunct formation, one has to use a zero-width joiner. A number of these issues for several Indian scripts, such as Kannada and Tamil, are still being sorted out (Baraha, 2006).

2. *Input method editor (IME).* For users of Indian scripts, an IME would allow them to select the appropriate character from a set. Initially, Microsoft did not consider Indic scripts complex enough to warrant the use of an IME (Kaplan & Wissink,

2003), but now a basic IME has been implemented in Windows. This displays a standard set of composite CV symbols — क, का, कि, की ... (*ka, kaa, ki, kii,* ...) — but does not offer alternatives such as complex ligatures.

There have been concerted efforts by various Indian institutions, such as IIT Madras, to resolve problems in the character sets and shaping rules. At the same time, alternative systems, such as LINUX-based solutions, are being promoted by the Government of India, and software, such as Baraha, that permits text entry through English is becoming more popular.

12.4.2   Mobile Phones

Text messaging or SMS on mobile phones is a popular mode of communication in India because of the low cost. Until the software for Indic scripts became available, Indians typed messages either in English or in Indian languages using the Roman script.

Although there is still no common standard among handset providers in India for the symbols assigned to each key, the logic for symbol assignation remains the same. Each key is used for one set of symbols and multiple taps on the key allow the user to select the correct symbol. The symbol sets are based on the script inventory of an abugida and, since users learn this sequence in school, it is easily recalled. Table 12.4 shows the layout on one mobile phone that permits text entry in both Hindi and English (Fig. 12.4). Referring back to Table 12.1, we see that the keys are based on the symbol sequence; the independent vowels are on keys 2 and 3, key 4 is used to access the velar consonants, key 5 gives the palatals, and so on.

ँ ः 1	अ-ऊ 2 abc	ए-औ 3 def
क-ङ 4 ghi	च-ञ 5 jkl	ट-ण 6 mno
त-न 7 pqrs	प-म 8 tuv	य-ह 9 wxyz
* +	—	# ॐ

TABLE 12.4   Assignment of Devanagari/English symbols on a mobile phone.

FIGURE

12.4

Devanagari/English mobile phone.

This keypad has even fewer buttons for text entry than the computer keyboard yet it is possible to type accurate text in Devanagari. The reason is that the vowel signs have been eliminated from the keypad but the *virama* has been retained; since the vowel sign depends on the context, the user merely inputs the *virama* sign plus an independent vowel and the shaping engine creates the correct character.

12.4.3 Predictive Input

Figure 12.5 is a screen shot of a demo for Hindi predictive software from Zi Corporation. The first line shows the user input, while the words at the bottom are candidate words for the user to select. In the text input line, the symbols remain discrete and have not been integrated into syllables. Given the likelihood of making a mistake while tapping keys and the difficulty of moving the cursor within the small display area, if the user has made a mistake he or she can easily locate the error in such a display.

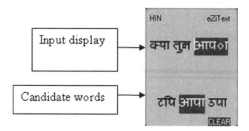

FIGURE
12.5

Text input in Devanagari on a mobile phone (from Zi Corporation; see
http://www.zicorp.com/ezinews/february2003/ezinews020603.htm#story2.1).

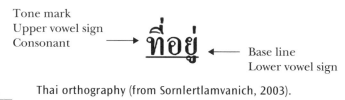

FIGURE
12.6

Thai orthography (from Sornlertlamvanich, 2003).

12.5   TEXT ENTRY SYSTEMS IN THAILAND

Unlike most of the Indian languages, Thai is a tonal language, which means that the
script has to indicate tones. In addition, in the Thai script there are no indications for
word and sentence boundaries, although there have been attempts to introduce
punctuation marks in Thai texts (Sornlertlamvanich & Charoenporn, 2001). Hence,
word and sentence segmentation remains a critical issue in text input.

The Thai script has 44 consonants, 21 vowel signs, and 4 tone marks. A Thai character consists of a consonant that possesses both an inherent vowel and an inherent tone;
the vowel and the tone can be modified by means of signs attached to the base consonant character. The vowel sign can be placed before, after, above, below, or on both sides
of the base consonant character; compound vowels are indicated by a combination of
vowel signs. A tone mark can be placed either above the base consonant character or, if
there is an upper vowel sign, above the vowel sign. Although there are four possible levels, namely, consonant, lower vowel, upper vowel, and tone mark, the combination can
at most be at three levels. This is because the upper and lower vowel signs cannot be
used together to modify a base consonant. The first cell in Fig. 12.6 shows the combination of consonant, upper vowel, and tone mark, while the third cell shows the combination of consonant, lower vowel, and tone mark.

12.5.1   Text Entry on Computers

In considering Thai text entry on computers, we examine the character sets, keyboard layouts, and rules for editing characters. Since Thai does not mark word and sentence boundaries, this section also describes how boundaries are estimated.

Character Sets

Several standards coexist for Thai data interchange. TIS-620 is the national 8-bit standard based on TIS-620 2533 that was defined by the Thai Industrial Standards Institute (1990). When ISO/IEC 8859-11 based on TIS-620 2533 was announced, the standards were widely accepted in the industrial sector. As a result, TIS-620, ISO-8859-11, and UTF-8 are accepted as standards for Thai language data exchange. However, a preliminary survey in the Web Language Engineering project[7] found that the most widely used character set in Web documents is none of the above, but Windows-874, which is the de facto Microsoft standard. Of the 85,000 Thai language Web pages examined in April 2006, 70% are Windows-874, 13% are TIS-620, 2% are UTF-8, and less than 0.02% are ISO-8859-11. Note that the Microsoft browser, Internet Explorer, can recognize all the character sets listed except for TIS-620.

Keyboard Layout

In 1995, the Thai Industrial Standards Institute specified that TIS-820 2538 would be the standard layout for Thai characters on computer keyboards (Thai Industrial Standards Institute, 1995). This is a modification of the TIS-620 2533 that was inherited from the Kesmanee model for Thai typewriters. Missing keys were added to the latest version of TIS-820 2538 to cover all the characters. However, the widespread version of keyboard layout is neither of these versions, but the version shown in Fig. 12.7.

Editing Rules

In general, a Thai text is written from left to right starting from a base character. If the base character is a consonant, it can be followed by an upper or lower vowel sign and modified by a tone mark, if any. Table 12.5 simulates the input sequence corresponding to the code points kept in storage.

Some intelligent input support modules, especially in high-end word processors, offer *input sequence normalization* that allows users to input the characters in their spelling sequence. The *input sequence normalization* provides the following error

---

[7] See http://www.tcllab.org/weblang.

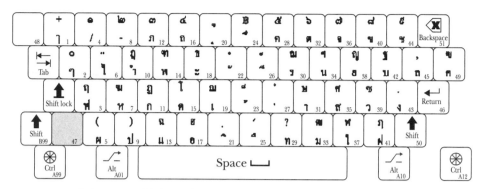

FIGURE

12.7
Layout of the most widely used Thai keyboard (de facto standard).

Thai text	Code point sequence						
ที่อยู่	ท	◌ี	◌่	อ	ย	◌ู	◌่
	U+0E17	U+0E35	U+0E48	U+0E2D	U+0E22	U+0E39	U+0E48

TABLE

12.5

Glyph position and its corresponding code point in storage.

Thai text	Input sequence			Normalized code point sequence		
ที่	ท	◌่	◌ี	ท	◌ี	◌่
	U+0E17	U+0E48	U+0E35	U+0E17	U+0E35	U+0E48

TABLE

12.6

Alternation of a vowel sign and a tone mark.

correction process to handle the input of diacritics and zero-width characters:

1. *Alternation.* A vowel sign always comes before a tone mark (Table 12.6).

2. *Replacement.* Characters that belong to the same group (i.e., group of upper and lower vowel signs and group of tone marks) can occupy only a single position in a syllable (Table 12.7).

Current text	Next input	Normalized text
ที่	ื	ที่
U+0E17 U+0E35 U+0E48	U+0E37	U+0E17 U+0E37 U+0E48

TABLE
12.7

Replacement of zero-width vowel sign of the same group.

3. *Duplication.* Multiple inputs of an existing zero-width character (i.e., upper and lower vowel signs and tone marks) in the current position are not allowed. Therefore, repeated input of the same character will be ignored.

The use of zero-width characters in Thai makes it necessary to provide sophisticated rules in the editing process. A composed character is handled as a "cell" and the cursor cannot be positioned within the character. The Delete key is used to remove the entire cell, not an individual sign in the composed character, whereas the Backspace key is used to delete signs on the consonant one by one. Insertion requires context information of at least two previous characters from the current cursor position to decide where to attach the input of a zero-width character. The input of the third character in Table 12.6, which causes *alternation* of vowel sign and tone mark, is an example of insertion.

Word Wrapping

The absence of word boundary markers in Thai text causes serious difficulties in automatic text processing. There are no accepted conventions for using spaces to indicate word, phrase, or sentence boundaries; instead, authors use spaces to reduce the ambiguity of a message. Therefore, a space can sometimes be a clue for *word wrapping* but we cannot always rely on it because the portion of the text may be too large for the allowed margin.

An appropriate word wrapping position is needed to render a text within the determined right margin. The priority order of the possible positions for wrapping is given below:

1. *Word boundary.* To indicate word boundaries, we need a powerful word segmentation module that can determine a word boundary on the fly and yield a highly accurate output. In practice, a portion of the text between two spaces (or the beginning or end of a paragraph) that includes the position in question is taken into account for word segmentation.

2. *After a symbol.* Modern Thai texts use symbols such as commas, semicolons, colons, and question marks along with conventional Thai symbols. In this case, the position next to the continuous Thai text and the ending symbol is considered as the unit to be wrapped.

3. *Syllable boundary.* There is no standard for hyphenation in Thai texts but newspaper articles have begun using hyphens for right alignment of paragraphs. For more precise wrapping, the text can be wrapped at the syllable boundary position with or without a hyphen. To perform hyphenation, rules of syllable construction that are less ambiguous than word segmentation need to be applied.

12.5.2   Text Entry on Mobile Phones

For mobile phones and other devices with a limited number of input keys, Thailand still does not have a national standard either for the keypad layout or for the input method. However, the large number of mobile phone owners has attracted phone manufacturers and operators to differentiate their products for the Thai market. The primary factor in capturing a market share is Thai text input and each party is trying to find the best solution for its products. At this moment, there is no move to standardize the layout of mobile phone keypads.

Table 12.8 shows the layouts used by some of the major mobile phone manufacturers in Thailand.

Most of the handsets adopt an extension of the T9 input method to display viable alternatives in Thai input mode as well as the original English input mode. However, the large number of characters in Thai makes it difficult for users to memorize the

	1	2	3	4	5	6	7	8	9	*	0	#
Type 1		ก-ง	จ-ญ	ฎ-ต	ถ-น	บ-ฟ	ภ-ภ	ว-ส	ห-ฮ	ะา̊ แไ	่	า̊ ๆ
Alcatel		ก-ง ะา	จ-ฌ ̆า̀	ญ-ฑ ๐๓	ฒ-ถ ๘๕	ท-ป ৴	ผ-ภ แ̂	ม-ล ฤภไ	ว-ห โ ̃ๆ		ฟอฮ	
Nokia	ก-ค	ฆ-ฉ	ช-ญ	ฎ-ณ	ด-ธ	น-ผ	พ-ย	ร-ษ	ส-ฮ	AV, LV	BV, UV	

TABLE 12.8 Comparison of three types of key assignment (from Phaholpinyo, 2006). Manufacturers of Type 1 are Samsung, Sony, Ericsson, Jfone, Distar, LG, Sagem, Sharp, and Panasonic. AV, after vowel; BV, before vowel; UV, upper vowel; LV, lower vowel.

1 [space]	2 ๐ ๏ ๐ ๏	3 ่ ็ ๊ ๋
4 ก ข ง จ	5 ด ต ถ ท	6 น บ ผ พ
7 เ ไ ใ โ	8 ม ย ร ล	9 ะ า ว ๆ
* อ ห	0 ั ็	# ก-1-a

TABLE   GOTTHAI key layout.

12.9

location of each character. As a result, new input methods have been proposed and three of these are described below.

GOTTHAI

Rojarayanon (2003) proposed the simple key layout shown in Table 12.9.

The characters are grouped according to their visual similarity. For example, ภ, ฎ, ฏ, ฦ are grouped under a representative character of ก. Also, upper characters are assigned to the upper row of the key layout, namely 2 and 3, while consonants in the middle layer are assigned to the middle rows of the key layout, namely, 4, 5, 6, 7, 8, and 9.

Input Method Using Two Key Strokes

Amonwiwattanakul (2001) proposed an input method that needs only two key strokes to input a Thai character. The Thai characters are divided into nine groups for assignment to a numeric input device as shown in Table 12.10. With the first click, the user selects the group; the second click is used to select the character within the group.

Smart-Q

Sornlertlamvanich (2001a,b) proposed an input method for Thai text using Roman transliteration. This gets around the problem of the large number of Thai characters as well as the variations in keypad layout. In order to implement "one click for one character," the method has to deal with two types of ambiguity. First, the appropriate sequence of characters in the Roman transliterated form has to be selected, for which the character n-gram model of the Roman transliterated form is taken into account. Second, the appropriate word based on its pronunciation has to be selected, for which the word n-gram model of the Thai text is taken into account. Due to the nonstandard Roman transliteration of Thai words, all possible spellings are permitted in order to yield the same or similar pronunciation of the original word. For example, "kan," "karn," "khan," and "kharn" can be interpreted as the same pronunciation. Figure 12.8 shows the possible words for the input sequence of "222." As a result, the word "แคบ" is selected with "แบก", "บาป", "บาก" , and "บรรพ" listed as the alternative candidates.

Number\Group	1	2	3	4	5	6	7	8	9
1	ก	ข	ค	ฆ	ง	฿	$		
2	จ	ฉ	ช	ซ	ฌ	ญ	ย		
3	ฎ	ฏ	ฐ	ฑ	ฒ	ณ	ฤ	ฦ	ำ
4	ด	ต	ถ	ท	ธ	น			
5	บ	ป	ผ	ฝ	พ	ฟ	ภ	ม	ว
6	อ	ศ	ษ	ส	ร	ล	ฬ	ฮ	ห
7	ะ	า	ิ	ี	ึ	ื	่	้	๊
8	เ	แ	โ	ไ	ใ	็			
9	ั	ุ	ู	+	๊	๋	ๆ	ฯ	ฯ

TABLE   Proposed key layout (Amonwiwattanakul, 2001).

12.10

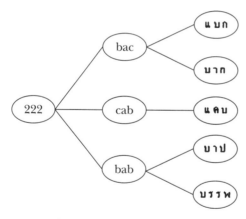

FIGURE   Possible words for the input sequence of "222."

12.8

12.6   CONCLUSION

The complex structure of abugidas presents problems when users try to enter text in devices that were originally designed for alphabetic writing systems, such as English. This chapter described the structure of an abugida and the general problems for text entry in computers and mobile phones. The case studies of India and Thailand illustrate the different solutions devised in two countries; although some of the variation arises from differences between the scripts, much of the variation arises from attempts to find immediate solutions to the technology as soon as it is introduced. In the Indian case, text entry in mobile phones has found innovative solutions that may lead to a revision of the standards for computers. This cross-fertilization between technologies as well as countries should eventually make text entry simpler for users.

12.7 FURTHER READING

For a linguistic description of the structure of all the abugidas, Daniels (1996) offers an accurate and readable account. For the Indian scripts, the Web site at IIT Madras (http://acharya.iitm.ac.in/multi_sys/) provides excellent tutorials on the scripts and text entry issues. This Web site, along with the Baraha Web site (http://www.baraha.com) also discusses problems with Unicode and text-processing issues.

For Southeast Asian scripts, Omniglot (http://www.omniglot.com/writing/) provides linguistic descriptions, while useful project reports are available from the Multilingual Information Technology Project (http://www.cicc.or.jp/english/hyoujyunka/top.html).

REFERENCES

Acharya (2001). *Fonts for Indian languages.* Madras: Systems Development Laboratory, IIT: *http://acharya.iitm.ac.in/ind_fonts.html*

Acharya (2003). Limitations of Unicode and ISCII. Madras: Systems Development Laboratory, IIT: *http://acharya.iitm.ac.in/multi_sys/uni_iscii.html*

Amonwiwattanakul, V. (2001). Thailand Petty Patent No. 375. Department of Intellectual Property, Ministry of Commerce of Thailand. [In Thai]

Baraha (2006). Indic Unicode issues in Windows XP: *http://www.baraha.com/documents.html*

Daniels, P. T. (1996). The study of writing systems. In P. T. Daniels & W. Bright (Eds.), *The world's writing systems* (pp.3–17). New York: Oxford University Press.

Golshani, E. (2004). Brahmi descended scripts: *http://www.geocities.com/Athens/Academy/9594/brahmi.html*

Hall, P. (1998). Vernacular software in South Asia: What happens now and what is needed. *International Working Conference of IFIP WG9.4 for Implementation and Evaluation of Information Systems in Developing Countries, March 1998, Bangkok.*

Holle, K. F. (1999). Table of old and new Indic alphabets: Contribution to the paleography of the Dutch Indies. *Written Language and Literacy, 2,* 167–246.

Hosking, R. F., & Meredith-Owens, G. M. (1966). *A handbook of Asian scripts.* London: British Museum.

Htut, Z. (2004). *Input methods and basic encoding in Myanmar language: http://www .myanmars.net/unicode/doc/20040507_zhtut.ppt*

Internet World Statistics (2006). *http://www.internetworldstats.com/asia.htm#in*

Joshi, A., Ganu, A., Chand, A., Parmar, V., & Mathur, G. (2004). Keylekh: A keyboard for text entry in Indian scripts. *Proceedings of the ACM Conference on Human Factors in Computing Systems – CHI 2004, Vienna.* Retrieved 22 May 2006.

Kaplan, M. S., & Wissink, C. (2003). Unicode and keyboards on Windows. *23rd Internationalization and Unicode Conference, March 2003, Prague.*

Keniston, K. (2001). Language, power, and software. In C. Ess (Ed.), *Culture, technology, communication: Towards an intercultural global village* (pp.283–306). Albany, NY: State University of New York Press.

Kuipers, J. C., & McDermott, R. (1996). Insular Southeast Asian scripts. In P. T. Daniels & W. Bright (Eds.), *The world's writing systems* (pp.474–484). New York: Oxford University Press.

Open Forum of Cambodia (2004). How to type Khmer Unicode [electronic version]: *http://www.khmeros.info/drupal/?q = en/download/docs*

Phaholpinyo, P. (2006). A survey of mobile phone type in Thailand and Thai input method on mobile phone. *NECTEC Technical Journal, 5(17).* [In Thai]

Potipiti, T., Sornlertlamvanich, V., & Thanadkran, K. (2001). Towards an intelligent multilingual keyboard system. Paper presented at the *Human Language Technology Conference (HLT 2001), 18–21 March 2001, San Diego.*

Rojarayanon, P. (2003). *GOTTHAI* (unpublished work).

Salomon, R. G. (1996). Brahmi and Kharoshthi. In P. T. Daniels & W. Bright (Eds.), *The world's writing systems* (pp.373–383). New York: Oxford University Press.

Sornlertlamvanich, V. (2001a). Thailand Patent Accession No. 067839. Department of Intellectual Property, Ministry of Commerce of Thailand. [In Thai]

Sornlertlamvanich, V. (2001b). Sansarn and Smart-Q: *http://www.tcllab.org/ virach/publication.html*

Sornlertlamvanich, V. (2003). Development of Thai encoding and the implementations. Paper presented at the *International Symposium on Indic Scripts: Past and Future, 17–19 December 2003, Tokyo.*

Sornlertlamvanich, V., & Charoenporn, T. (2001). Punctuation mark: The forgotten items in Thai writing system. In *Thai font* (pp.102–114). Bangkok: National Electronics and Computer Technology Center. [In Thai]

Technology Development for Indian Languages (2002). Revision of Unicode Standard-3.0 for Devanagari Script. *Journal of Language Technology: http://www.tdil.mit.gov.in/ newsIndexJan02.html*

Telecom Regulatory Authority of India (2006). Growth in telephony continues in April 2006 — 4.6 million subscribers added. Press Release No. 41/2006. New Delhi: Telecom Regulatory Authority of India.

Thai Industrial Standards Institute (1990). TIS 620-2533: Standard for Thai character codes for computers. Bangkok: TISI. [In Thai]

Thai Industrial Standards Institute (1995). TIS 820-2538: Layout of Thai character keys on computer keyboards. Bangkok: TISI. [In Thai]

Unicode (2003). *The Unicode standard 4.0.* Reading, MA: Addison–Wesley

13 | Text Entry in Hebrew and Arabic Scripts

CHAPTER

Tsuguya Sasaki   Bar-Ilan University, Ramat Gan, Israel
Kumiko Tanaka-Ishii   University of Tokyo, Tokyo, Japan

13.1   INTRODUCTION

"Ths nglsh sntnc s wrttn nl wth cnsnntl chrctrs" is the consonant sequence for the sentence "This English sentence is written only with consonantal characters." Hebrew and Arabic speakers read and write daily using such consonant-only sequences. Such a script is called *abjad* or *consonantary* by Daniels and Bright (1996) as explained in Chap. 10. This chapter concerns text entry in abjads.

Text consisting only of consonants might seem surprising to readers unfamiliar with Hebrew or Arabic. However, the contrast between consonants and vowels is universal in any natural language. Perhaps this was best stated by the famous French poet Mallarmé (1980)[1], who said that "vowels are like flesh, whereas consonants are like skeleton." Language technologies are affected by this essential difference between consonants and vowels. For example, in text-to-speech software, different voices are generated by changing only the vowel recordings and using the same consonant recording. Thus, as Mallarmé says, consonants are more static and universal, whereas vowels are more individual. Interestingly, it is known among anthropologists that chimpanzees cannot pronounce consonants (Savage-Rumbaugh & Lewin, 1996). Thus, consonants represent the essence of human voice and abjad is the script that most directly represents this nature underlying the human voice.

To produce text in this pure form of consonantal sequences, text entry is almost as simple as entering English, especially from the user's side. However, such scripts cause pedagogical and technical challenges: to vocalize text, people need to know how to complement the consonantal skeleton with other missing information. In Hebrew and Arabic there is a tradition of doing this through the use of different kinds of signs. Thus, the same text can be written in *vocalized* and *unvocalized* spellings

---

[1]   The original quote in French is "A toute la nature apparenté et se rapprochant ainsi de l'organisme dépositaire de la vie, le Mot présente, dans ses voyelles et ses diphtongues, comme une chaire; et, dans ses consonnes, comme une ossature délicate à disséquer."

with or without diacritics, respectively, which together form the writing culture of languages in Hebrew and Arabic. The production of a vocalized version from an unvocalized text is both a linguistic issue and a challenge for text entry software.

Another specific feature about Hebrew and Arabic scripts is the writing direction. In both scripts, the direction is from right to left. This writing direction causes complications, especially when mixed with numbers and left-to-right text. However, writing directions other than the horizontal left-to-right are used in several cases. For example, the traditional direction used for Japanese writing is to arrange characters from top to bottom and lines from right to left. Thus, writing from left to right is no more than an arbitrary writing direction. Although the traditional writing direction of Japanese is in limited use on computers, engineers of Hebrew and Arabic scripts have entirely solved this problem. The design of text entry related to directionality forms an important and interesting part of text entry software in abjads.

In this chapter, we briefly explain Hebrew and Arabic scripts. After that, we show how text is usually entered and rendered and then look at recent technologies applied on current devices.

13.2   ARABIC AND HEBREW SCRIPTS

An ambassador staying in Israel once characterized the peculiarity of Hebrew script succinctly: "Hebrew is a strange language—without the diacritics it is hard to read and with the diacritics it is hard to write." The ambassador's feeling is partly experienced by looking at Fig. 13.1, which shows the phrase "world peace" in Arabic and

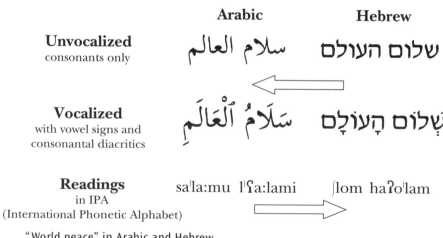

FIGURE   "World peace" in Arabic and Hebrew.

13.1

Hebrew. The first line shows "world peace" in unvocalized form, the common form of writing, which consists of only consonantal characters, whereas the second line shows the vocalized form, the complemented writing. These two lines should be read from right to left. Note that it is the unvocalized text that is used daily in ordinary texts, whether public or private, such as newspapers. The vocalized version is used for educational purposes and in cases in which the correct pronunciation of vowels is important, such as the printed versions of the Hebrew Bible and the Qur'an as well as in poetry.

In the third line of the figure, the pronunciation of the phrase is transcribed in IPA (International Phonetic Association, 2006). This line should be read from left to right. Roughly speaking, in Arabic, the phrase is pronounced "salaamu l'aalami," whereas in Hebrew it is pronounced "shlom ha'olam." The similarity of these two phrases in Arabic and Hebrew, especially in the consonant sounds, is a reminder that Arabic and Hebrew belong to the same language family: Semitic.

Let us return to the first line. Neither script makes a distinction between lower- and uppercase. There are two words, separated by white spaces, in both the Arabic and the Hebrew, the left ones corresponding to "world" and the right ones corresponding to "peace." In the word corresponding to "peace" in Hebrew, four characters that have the sound "s l v m" are seen from right to left. The Arabic case is more difficult because the script is cursive, so adjacent characters are ligated (connected). If this phrase is written character by character, the Arabic text would consist of م ل ا ع ل ا   م ا ل س. The word on the right-hand side has four characters having the sounds "s l ʔ m" (from right to left, with ʔ being a glottal stop). Thus, Arabic and Hebrew script have the same consonantary nature.

The Arabic word "world" includes the character ع, but this is not apparent in the first line of Fig. 13.1. In Arabic, some characters change their forms depending on their location in the word (these are called *allographs*, i.e., contextual forms). There are four allographs for each consonant: the isolated, initial, medial, and final forms. For example, ع (the isolated form) appears as ﻉ when placed at the beginning of a word (initial form), as ﻌ when placed in the middle of a word (medial form), and as ﻊ when placed at the end of a word (final form). Note that the notion of a script being cursive is different from whether the script includes allographs: Hebrew is not cursive, but the script has allographs for five characters, in this case with only two distinctions: regular and final.

A comparison of the first and second lines in the figure reveals how the vocalization is expressed in the form of *diacritics*, the nonspace combining marks. They are positioned over, under, or inside the characters they modify and are originally meant to ensure correct pronunciation. Diacritics roughly consist of two types:

◆ Vowel signs add a vowel to the consonant.

◆ Consonantal diacritics change the consonant sound.

For example, the ´ sign appearing in Arabic text shows that the vowel with the sound "a" follows the consonant. There is a consonantal diacritic in the upper right corner of the Hebrew word "peace" and another in the upper middle of the Arabic word "world" as ـﻪ . All other diacritics in this example indicate vowels.

Without such diacritics, the unvocalized word or text is ambiguous: for example, if the same system was used for English, "peace," "pace," and "pc" would be identical words, all represented as "pc." Such words having the same consonantal forms often share the same *root* and the same core meaning. An example of a word sharing the same root as "peace" in Arabic is سَالِم ("saalim" means *safe* or *integral*). The term إِسْلَام ("islaam" means *resignation* (to the will of God)) also shares the same root, although the unvocalized word form is slightly different, with a prefix being attached. In Hebrew, there is no word that shares exactly the same unvocalized form with "peace," but similar ones are שָׁלֵם ("shalem" means *complete*) and הִשְׁלִים ("hishlim" means *to complete*). Moreover, inflections often have exactly the same unvocalized spellings. In our example, "peace" is modified by "world" and thus has to be inflected in Arabic and Hebrew. The unvocalized word form for "peace" without any modification is exactly the same, but vocalized spellings have slightly different diacritics. Examples of "peace" without modification in Arabic and Hebrew are shown in Fig. 13.5, in the last line of the second column of each table. Thus, a reader of texts in abjad has to keep the next few words in sight to determine the sound and the meaning of the word currently being read; otherwise, the same word form will be understood in more than one way.

So far, we have explained the basics of Hebrew and Arabic scripts summarized as follows:

◆ The reading direction is from right to left.

◆ The common way of writing is in *unvocalized* form, which is *vocalized* with the aid of diacritics, consisting roughly of vowel signs and consonantal diacritics.

◆ Some characters change form (called allographs) depending on their location.

◆ In Arabic, writing is *cursive* and characters are *ligated* (connected).

In addition, the language learner should take note of certain exceptions. The first is that certain consonantal characters are used as an aid for indicating vowels. These characters are called *matres lectionis*: Hebrew has four and Arabic has three. Another important sign that is processed similar to consonantal characters is the Arabic *hamza* ء, which indicates a glottal stop in pronunciation. In addition to such common exceptions and rules, there are language-specific rules. For example, Hebrew uses *cantillation* marks as an additional type of diacritic[2]. Arabic has a calligraphic method called *tatweel* (or *kashida*)[3]. For a more detailed and formal explanation of abjads,

---

[2] Cantillation marks are used to indicate the accent marks and singing intonation of the Hebrew Bible.

[3] In English, white spaces are inserted in some places to adjust the text length to improve the appearance. In cursive languages, this is also done by elongating the characters.

see Daniels (1997), Bauer (1996), and Goerwitz (1996). Using the alphabet list given in these references is useful for further decryption of the "world peace" example.

To enter Hebrew or Arabic on computers, we need a way to process such kinds of script. In a broad sense, the ambassador's quote illustrates the problem of text entry in abjad. Unvocalized text is easily entered, simply character by character, but is hard to read. On the other hand, entering vocalized text requires knowledge regarding which diacritic should be attached on what occasions. With current language technology and a good interface, there is much potential for computer aid. Before discussing this further, we will briefly summarize the sociolinguistic aspects of Arabic and Hebrew scripts in the rest of this section.

All known abjads were originally created for Semitic languages, including Arabic and Hebrew, probably because of the prominent position consonants occupy in Semitic morphology. The four abjads still in use today—Arabic, Hebrew, Syriac, and Samaritan—developed from a common ancestor: the Proto-Canaanite abjad. Among these, the Syriac and Samaritan abjads are in limited use as languages.

Originally, the scripts were not equipped with diacritics. In the latter half of the first millennium CE, Hebrew, and then Arabic, grammarians followed their Syriac counterparts and created diacritics. As briefly described in the previous section, the two scripts share essential features although each language also has specific features, derived from the different cultures within which these languages are used. Their features, explained through the above example, are summarized in Table 13.1.

Being associated with Islam and Judaism, Arabic and Hebrew abjads, originally for Arabic and Hebrew, came to be also used for other languages spoken by Muslims and Jews, respectively. The Arabic abjad is also used in Persian and Urdu (both Indo-Iranian languages), with additional characters to reflect differences in their phonology compared to Arabic. The Hebrew abjad is also used in Yiddish (a Germanic language) and some other Jewish languages, often as an alphabet with certain consonantal

Script	Arabic	Hebrew
Cursive	Yes	No
Num. consonantal characters	28	22
Num. contextual forms per character	4 (isolated, initial, medial, final)	2 (regular, final)
Num. characters with contextual forms	28	5
Num. consonantal diacritics	2	3
Num. vowel signs	10	12
Num. mater lectionis (long vowels)	4	3
Cantillation marks	No	Yes
Tatweel	Yes	No
Digit description	Arabic-Indic	European
Punctuation marks	Arabic	European

TABLE   Differences between Arabic and Hebrew scripts.

13.1

characters converted to vowels. For more about the adaptations of Arabic and Hebrew scripts, see Kaye (1996) and Hary and Aronson (1996), respectively.

As Persian and Urdu scripts were derived from Arabic and Yiddish scripts were derived from Hebrew, the languages using abjad scripts are summarized in terms of Arabic and Hebrew. This chapter is structured accordingly, focusing on Arabic and Hebrew.

Both Arabic and Hebrew are classified morphologically as fusional languages; i.e., single word-forms are often composed of more than one morpheme and the boundary between morphemes is not always clear-cut. The so-called root–pattern formation—i.e., through roots, which generally consist of three consonants, and patterns, which are a kind of template consisting of vowels (and sometimes preformative/postformative consonants/vowels)—is the prototypical word-formation pattern in both languages (as well as other Semitic languages). The inflectional categories they share include person (first, second, and third), number (singular, dual, and plural), and gender (masculine and feminine).

Verb–subject–object is the default word order in Modern Standard Arabic[4], while subject–verb–object is the default order in Modern Hebrew. The temporal categories they have for verbs are tense (past, present, and future) and aspect (perfective and imperfective), respectively. The inflectional categories that exist only in Arabic include case (nominative, genitive, and accusative) and degree (comparative and superlative), which are expressed either periphrastically (i.e., syntactically) or by the word order in Hebrew. For a general overview of Arabic and Hebrew languages, see Kaye (1987) and Hetzron (1998), respectively.

13.3   STANDARD ENTRY

Text entry proceeds by the user producing a sequence of signals, which is followed by the appropriate software processing the signals so that they are properly rendered on the screen. In English, this process is trivial: a signal is mapped to a character code and the character image is shown on the screen. Texts in abjads, however, require several special procedures between the input and the output. These procedures are formulated based on the design of the character encoding and the standard way to enter characters using the standard full keyboard. Thus, in this section, we explain the standard way of entering scripts after explaining character encodings and the standard keyboard.

---

[4] Modern Standard Arabic and Modern Hebrew are distinguished from Classical Arabic and Biblical Hebrew, in which the Qur'an and the Hebrew Bible are written respectively.

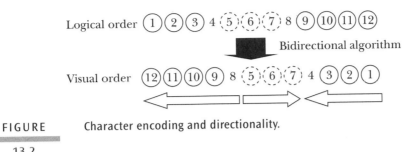

FIGURE

13.2

Character encoding and directionality.

13.3.1 Character Encodings

Abjad texts by default are written and read from right to left, but a complication occurs when the text is mixed with numbers and/or with other scripts. In the domain of encoding, such directionality is considered a feature of characters. Thus, the directionality of characters is embedded within the character code. Using the directionality information, the proper arrangement of characters is realized through what is called a *bidirectional algorithm* (Davis, 2005), a procedure to produce a proper visual image of text.

The input and output of a bidirectional algorithm is illustrated in Fig. 13.2. Suppose the user wants to produce a text consisting of 12 characters. Parts of the text are written from right to left (in the solid-line circles), but other parts of the text are written from left to right (in the dashed circles). The user will successively enter all of the text, character by character, in a linear sequence in the *logical order*. If the user is using text entry software based on character encoding with bidirectional support, the text with the correct *visual order*, as shown on the second line in the figure, should be produced by the application and rendered on the screen. Rearrangement of characters in such a way is done through the bidirectional algorithm. If character encoding without directionality support is adopted by the software application, the text will simply be produced as shown in the first input line.

All recent Arabic and Hebrew character encodings support directionality. The other issue regarding character encoding concerns how far consonantal characters and diacritics should be integrated. This decision has led to several different encodings.

The three major character codes used for Arabic script are listed in the first block of Table 13.2. ISO-8859-6 is an 8-bit character code covering ASCII and Arabic consonantal characters as well as diacritics, but it does not cover additional characters for Persian and Urdu. Windows-1256 is a proprietary 8-bit character code developed by Microsoft. It covers ASCII and Arabic consonantal characters as well as additional characters for Persian and Urdu. Unicode covers not only the Arabic consonantal characters, but also all the diacritics and additional characters for Persian and Urdu.

For Hebrew, too, the most widely used codes are listed in the second block of Table 13.2. ISO-8859-8-I is an 8-bit character code covering ASCII and Hebrew consonantal characters, but not diacritics. In fact, this encoding was originally derived

Arabic, Persian, Urdu character encodings

	Consonantal characters	Additional characters for Persian/Urdu	Diacritics
ISO-8856-6	Yes	No	Yes (except ´)
Windows-1256	Yes	Yes	No
Unicode	Yes	Yes	Yes

Hebrew character encodings

	Consonantal characters	Vowel signs	Consonantal diacritics	Cantillation marks
ISO-8859-8-I	Yes	No	No	No
Windows-1255	Yes	Yes	No	No
Unicode	Yes	Yes	Yes	Yes

TABLE 13.2   Popular character encodings.

from ISO-8859-8, which did not support directionality and thus became obsolete. Windows-1255 is a proprietary 8-bit character code created by Microsoft. It is identical to ISO-8859-8-I in the positions that are assigned to ASCII and Hebrew consonantal characters, but it covers diacritics except for cantillation marks in positions reserved for control characters in ISO-8859-8-I. Unicode covers not only Hebrew consonantal characters, but also all the diacritics, including cantillation marks. Unicode also supports the bidirectional algorithm. For a more detailed description of Unicode regarding abjads see Unicode Consortium (2003).

13.3.2   Standard Keyboards

The most common way to enter Arabic and Hebrew is by the Arabic and Hebrew versions of the standard full keyboard. Entry methods for these keyboard layouts essentially influence entry methods on recent mobile devices.

Average native speakers of Arabic usually produce texts in the unvocalized spelling, but the vocalized spelling can also be used, if one so wishes (and knows how to vocalize), without any additional tools. Thus, all Hebrew and Arabic consonantal characters and diacritics (except for Hebrew cantillation marks) are assigned to separate keys on standard full keyboards.

Even though there are systems to transcribe or transliterate[5] Arabic and Hebrew using ASCII characters, people rarely produce Arabic or Hebrew text by typing in

---

[5]   *Transliteration* with ASCII characters means representing all consonant and diacritics using ASCII characters. *Transcription* with ASCII characters means reproducing the sounds. There are many transliteration and transcription systems.

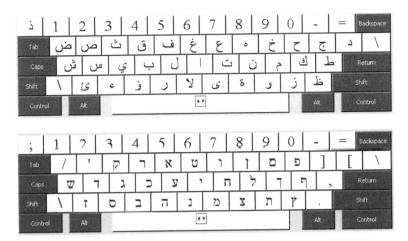

FIGURE   Popular Arabic and Hebrew keyboards.

13.3

these ASCII transliterations or transcriptions for several reasons. Neither the transcription nor the transliteration systems are standardized, so a text in Arabic or Hebrew can be transcribed or transliterated in multiple ways. Therefore, software applications that support entry by ASCII is very rare (although one example is given at the end of this chapter in Fig. 13.9).

Thus, all characters to be entered are assigned on the standard full keyboard. The keyboard layouts reflect the legacy of typewriters. There is no systematic phonetic similarity between Arabic/Hebrew and Roman characters on the same keys, nor does there seem to be any coordination between Hebrew and Arabic keyboard layouts.

The assignment policy differs for Arabic and Hebrew, however, due to differences in how many allographs are used and the character form variations of each script. Many allographs are used in Arabic because each of the 28 consonantal characters has four different forms (initial, medial, final, and isolated), so the total number of character forms including diacritics exceeds 100. Therefore, in Arabic, the user enters consonantal characters ambiguously, without entering information on which form the character takes. The form will be automatically disambiguated by the text entry software.

Under this principle, there are three standard keyboards for Arabic. Of these, Arabic 101 and 102 use almost the same layout, and the third one is the keyboard adapted to the French Azerty, which is used in North African countries. The first keyboard shown in Fig. 13.3 is the Arabic 101 keyboard. Some other diacritics not seen in this layout are assigned to keys and produced when the Shift key is pressed together with the respective keys.

On the other hand, Hebrew has only five consonantal characters with different forms, namely final forms, so the number of character forms is within the range of mapping on the standard full keyboard. Thus, character form variation is manually chosen by the user. Hebrew has only one standard keyboard, the second keyboard shown in Fig. 13.3. Some diacritics are assigned on the additional subpart of the keyboard in the upper right corner and are produced by pressing the Shift and Caps Lock keys at the same time. By pressing the Shift key, alphabetic characters can be produced using Hebrew keyboards.

13.3.3   Overall Process

Given the user input sequence generated by such a keyboard, the signals are processed and rendered on the screen in the proper visual form. The user input is *ambiguous,* in the sense that in Arabic the character form should be disambiguated, and *unstructured,* in the sense that multiple key presses should be combined. Text production is achieved through the following procedures:

1. The user provides character-by-character input in the logical order.
2. The characters are rearranged into the visual order through a bidirectional algorithm.
3. In Arabic, character forms are disambiguated.
4. Consonantal characters and diacritics are structured into *glyphs* (or *composed glyphs*). For Arabic, glyphs are ligated (connected).
5. The output text is rendered.

The transition of unvocalized text through this process is shown in Fig. 13.4. The first column shows the above procedure, the second column states what form the text is in

		Arabic	Hebrew
1. Input text	Logical order	س ا م ا ل س	סולש
2. After bidirectional algorithm	Visual order	م ا ل س	שלום
3. After character form disambiguation	Visual order	م ا ل ـس	
4. After structurization and ligation	Glyph list	م لا ـس	
5. When rendered	Output	سلام	שלום

FIGURE 13.4   Stages to produce unvocalized Arabic and Hebrew text.

after each process, and the third and fourth columns respectively show the transitions of Arabic and Hebrew. The example used here is the unvocalized text of "peace" shown in Section 13.2. Arabic text requires the application of all the processes, whereas Hebrew requires only two procedures. In the Arabic case for unvocalized text, procedure 4 requires only ligation, and the forming of glyphs is trivial.

To produce vocalized text, the user first enters a consonantal character followed by all diacritics attached to it and then repeats this two-stage process. In this case, procedure 4 becomes more complicated in that it includes parsing the input sequence into chunks to construct the composed glyphs. This is also the case for Hebrew.

The second, third, and fourth tasks between input and output are inherently fully automatic. A bidirectional algorithm is easily applied because the direction information is attached to each character. The disambiguation of character forms is uniquely done by considering the relative location of each character with respect to blank spaces. The input sequence is parsed into glyphs without ambiguity.

Most recent text editors and word processors customized for abjads incorporate this automatic procedure. Without it, users must edit text such as "srtcrhc ltnnsnc htw ln nttrw s cntns hslgh shT" (the reverse consonant sequence of "This English sentence is written only with consonantal characters"), which may appear when using noncustomized editors. Recommended editors for Hebrew are given in Sasaki (2006); they also support Arabic.

An entry example of "peace," this time in the vocalized form in both Arabic and Hebrew from the user's perspective, is shown in Fig. 13.5[6]. We see how the user

Arabic

Input	Output	Explanation
س	س	
◌َ	سَ	Vowel sign combined
ل	سَل	The preceding character changed to an appropriate contextual form
◌َ	سَلَ	Vowel sign combined
ا	سَلَا	The last two characters changed to an appropriate ligature
م	سَلَام	

Hebrew

Input	Output	Explanation
שׁ	שׁ	
◌	שׁ	Consonantal diacritic combined
◌	שָׁ	Vowel sign combined
ל	שָׁל	
ו	שָׁלו	
◌	שָׁלֹו	Vowel sign combined
ם	שָׁלֹום	

FIGURE
13.5

Entering vocalized "peace" in Arabic and Hebrew.

---

[6]   The diacritics on characters here are slightly different from those in Fig. 13.1. Figure 13.1 shows "peace" modified by "world," but this figure shows "peace" without any modification.

makes the entry character by character and text is automatically produced in the proper visual form.

In addition to this basic procedure, two minor issues concern the text procedure for abjads. First, the user will sometimes want to change decisions made automatically. Some cases of this are when the user wants to produce part of a text in reverse order, produce the medial form character in an isolated manner, or prohibit the ligation of characters. All such forms of manual text production are enabled via functional signals, which are also standardized at the level of character encoding (such as Unicode). For directionality, the RTL (right to left) or LTR marks codes are used. To prohibit ligation, and thus control the allographic appearance of character forms, the nonjoiner and joiner marks codes are used.

The second issue is the paragraph directionality. In English, all paragraphs are aligned at the left side of the sheet/screen with a left margin. In the case of abjad text, paragraphs are aligned at the right end by default, but this is not always the case when paragraphs of different scripts or mathematical notations are merged. By default, the paragraph direction is automatically determined by the first character with *strong directionality*, e.g., abjad characters or Latin characters[7]. The directionality of a paragraph continues by default to the next paragraph. However, as a paragraph can include characters of both directions, it is difficult to fully automate the paragraph direction. Thus, this feature is left for users to choose manually.

13.4   ENTRY ON MOBILE DEVICES

Unlike the case with PCs (see Section 13.3.2), a significant number of users, especially teenagers, simply write English or transcribe Arabic/Hebrew with ASCII characters (Palfreyman & Khalil, 2003). Arabic has a chat alphabet set, in which rough ASCII transcription of Arabic text is used for messaging. For example, "world peace" is represented by the ASCII text "salaamu ala3mi," with ع being indicated by the digit "3". Note that the vowels remain in such transcription.

If the users enter Hebrew and Arabic in their original scripts at all, the use of keypads with the multitap method is still the most common way of text messaging (SMS) on mobile phones in Hebrew and Arabic scripts. Then, a standard way of entering text is further applied to text entry on mobile devices. In this case, even when texts in abjad are entered, all are in the unvocalized form; i.e., no diacritics are supported except for hamza in Arabic (as explained below).

As for other scripts, characters are assigned to eight keys (from 2 to 9) on mobile devices. They are arranged in the Arabic or Hebrew alphabetical order, but assigned

---

[7]   There are also characters with weak directionality, such as punctuation marks.

1	2	3
	ب ت ة ث	ا ء
4	5	6
س ش ص ض	د ذ ر ز	ج ح خ
7	8	9
ن ه و ي	ف ق ك ل م	ط ظ ع غ

FIGURE 13.6   A popular mobile phone layout in Arabic.

1	2	3
	ד ה ו	א ב ג
4	5	6
מ נ	י כ ל	ז ח ט
7	8	9
ר ש ת	צ ק	ס ע פ

FIGURE 13.7   A popular mobile phone layout in Hebrew.

alphabetically from right to left in the order 3-2-6-5-4-9-8-7 instead of 2-3-4-5-6-7-8-9. Thus, what corresponds to "ABC" in English on the button for 2 is attached to the button for 3 and printed on the button as "CBA".

Two characters that are not part of the consonantal alphabet are included on the Arabic keypad: the diacritic hamza (the exceptional diacritic written like a consonantal character; see Section 13.2), assigned as the second character on button 3, and a special variant of the consonantal character used to indicate the feminine ending assigned as the third character on button 7. Figures 13.6 and 13.7 respectively show popular keypads in Arabic and Hebrew.

As in the standard entry, the allograph processing (processing of contextual forms) is also different for Arabic and Hebrew on mobile phones. In Arabic, appropriate character forms are automatically selected. In contrast, the five final forms of

Hebrew must be selected manually through more key presses, which are arranged after their corresponding regular form characters. Therefore, additional consonantal characters are assigned to keys 4, 5, 8, and 9.

Consequently, entry on a mobile phone can be considered an extension of the standard way of entry that is greatly simplified by restricting texts to unvocalized versions. As noted, entering text in an unvocalized form is not drastically different from entering English texts (except for the directionality and rendering issues). Thus, predictive methods are present for Arabic and Hebrew. One-key with disambiguation (see Chap. 5 for more of its definition) is enabled by using LetterWise by Eatoni (http://www.eatoni.com/); for example, "peace" in Arabic is produced by pressing "4-8-3-8," and the best candidate proposed is the Arabic "peace." Also, eZiText of ZI Corporation (http://www.zicorp.com/) for Hebrew and Arabic supports word completion in addition to one-key with disambiguation.

For entry on PDAs, as for any other script, either a soft keyboard or handwriting recognition is used for text entry. On PDAs too, the text appearing on the screen is still mostly limited to the unvocalized form. The layouts of various soft keyboards follow those of standard keyboards in both Arabic and Hebrew. Further text-editing functions, especially to support quicker entry with fewer actions based on predictive methods, are now also available on PDAs. A screen shot of word completion in Hebrew on a PDA in Fig. 13.8 is taken from the Hebrew Language Support of a product from the Paragon Software Group (http://www.paragon-gmbh.com/); on the screen, words such as "collaboration," "method," and "incorporation" are shown as candidates to be

FIGURE   Hebrew word completion example on a PDA (Hebrew Language Support by Paragon
                Software).
13.8

selected[8]. Some handwriting technologies are also available on PDAs, such as those from ZI Corporation's Decuma (http://www.zicorp.com/), but such technologies still seem to be in the early stages of refinement.

In short, text on mobile devices is limited to unvocalized text because of the screen size (even with a high-resolution display). To compensate, compared with PC entry methods, more ambitious and intelligent text entry methods based on prediction are available.

13.5   TOWARD COMPUTER-AIDED ENTRY

The predictive methods so far available for abjads are limited to technologies developed for English that are integrated into abjads at the level of unvocalized text. We believe, however, that text entry in abjads can be aided by computer prediction, especially for vocalized text.

There is a great need to find ways of producing the diacritics automatically or semi-automatically, and this need is related to a literacy problem. Many Arabs and Israelis live outside the countries of origin. Younger generations do not always have enough opportunities to achieve proficiency in the languages of their parents. For such people and those who study Arabic or Hebrew as a foreign language, vocalized texts are needed to read Arabic or Hebrew text. The potential of computer support of vocalized text production is thus even broader. As noted by the ambassador we earlier quoted, producing vocalized text is an extremely complicated task, even for natives. The writer needs specialized knowledge of which diacritics to attach to which characters on what occasions. This situation is emphasized in the Hebrew language: vocalizing text is a profession (Sasaki, 2005).

The difficulty of producing vocalized text has not been greatly alleviated by computers. Diacritization consists of a huge number of rules as to which diacritic is put on which consonantal character under what context. With current popular text editors, however, any combination of a consonantal character and a diacritic is possible, producing nonexistent composed glyphs. A possible extension of current abjad text entry will be to integrate such rules. This will be even more useful if achieved interactively through predictive methods of word completion or even through one-key with disambiguation, in which all possible cognates will be automatically shown as selection candidates.

Related studies have already been reported in both the natural language processing (NLP) and the user interface domains. First, in the NLP domain concerning Semitic languages, there have been many studies on automatic diacritization and transliteration. As transliteration[5] is the alphabetically complete representation of vocalized text,

---

[8]   The translation of the text displayed on the screen is "The fact which is known is that the medieval studies of Hebrew language were founded on and incorporated with studies on Arabic language."

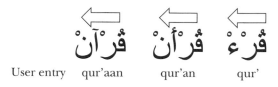

User entry   qur'aan   qur'an   qur'

' indicates entry of hamza

FIGURE   Entering "Qur'an" in Arabic and automatic prediction of the hamza diacritic.

13.9

automatic transliteration from unvocalized text requires simultaneous diacritization. In a recent study, Nelken and Shieber (2005) applied finite state transducers based on trigrams and obtained close to 90% precision (per diacritic). Thus, even though fully automatic processes are still limited, language technologies to aid users through automatic diacritization already exist.

A product in this area has been commercialized by Basis Technology (http://www.basistech.com/). Their Arabic Editor (Basis Technology, 2006) allows Arabic entry from ASCII transcription. Diacritization is done based on the transcription[5]. Some of the diacritization production is even automated. For example, Fig. 13.9 shows how the correct form of hamza ﻉ is properly produced depending on the context. The example used here is the Arabic term "Qur'an," meaning the central religious text of Islam, which contains hamza. This hamza is notoriously difficult for beginners, because it changes forms and places depending on the context, and the rules related to hamza production are complicated. In the rightmost and middle parts of Fig. 13.9, hamza appears at different positions, whereas in the third part the form of hamza has changed into ~. Such hamza usage rules are embedded in this editor so that the user does not need expertise in the correct use of hamza.

13.6   CONCLUDING REMARKS

In an English writing system, text is often abbreviated into consonant-only sequences such as "bldg." Shieber and Baker proposed predictive entry software, called "abbreviated input"(Shieber & Baker, 2003), with which abbreviated words or phrase entry such as "bldg" is expanded into "building" or "bulldog." Thus, with abbreviated input, a candidate proposed for "Ths nglsh sntnc s wrttn nl wth cnsnntl chrctrs" should be expanded into "This English sentence is written only with consonantal characters." Even though the input for their system can include vowels as well as consonants, the "abbreviated input" can be considered a generalized version of predictive method suitable for consonantary. From the richness of thousands of years of history and culture, many universal ideas can be distilled. We hope this chapter inspires readers to search for such ideas from within abjads.

13.7 ACKNOWLEDGMENTS

Parts of this chapter reflect the kind and insightful comments of Mr. Jack Halpern (CEO of The CJK Dictionary Institute, Inc., Japan), Professor Kamel Smaïli (LORIA, France), and Mr. Jalal Maleki (Linköping University, Sweden). We are grateful for their help.

REFERENCES

Basis Technology (2006). Arabic editor: *http://www.basistech.com/arabic-editor/*

Bauer, T. (1996). Arabic writing. In P. Daniels & W. Bright (Eds.), *The World's writing systems* (pp.559–568). London: Oxford University Press.

Daniels, P. T. (1997). Scripts of Semitic languages. In R. Hetzron (Ed.), *The Semitic languages* (pp.16–45). London: Routledge.

Daniels, P. T., & Bright, W. (1996). *The World's writing systems*. London: Oxford University Press.

Davis, M. (2005). Unicode standard annex 9: The bidirectional algorithm: *http://www.unicode.org/reports/tr9/*

Goerwitz, R. L. (1996). The Jewish scripts. In P. Daniels & W. Bright (Ed.), *The World's writing systems* (pp.487–498). London: Oxford University Press.

Hary, B., & Aronson, H. (1996). Adaptations of Hebrew script. In P. Daniels & W. Bright (Eds.), *The World's writing systems* (pp.727–742). London: Oxford University Press.

Hetzron, R. (1998). Hebrew. In B. Comrie (Ed.), *The World's major languages* (pp.686–704). London: Oxford University Press.

International Phonetic Association (2006). Reproduction of the international phonetic alphabet (revised to 2005): *http://www2.arts.gla.ac.uk/IPA/ipachart.html*

Kaye, A. S. (1987). Arabic. In B. Comrie (Ed.), *The World's major languages* (pp.664–685). London: Oxford University Press.

Kaye, A. (1996). Adaptations of Arabic script. In P. Daniels & W. Bright (Eds.), *The World's writing systems* (pp.743–762). London: Oxford University Press.

Mallarmé, S. (1980). *Oeuvres complétes* (p.901). Paris: Gallimard.

Nelken, R., & Shieber, S. (2005). Arabic diacritization using weighted finite-state transducers. *ACL Workshop on Computational Approaches to Semitic Languages, University of Michigan, Ann Arbor, USA* (pp.79–86).

Palfreyman, D., & Khalil, M. (2003). A funky language for teenzz to use: Representing Gulf Arabic in instant messaging. *Journal of Computer-Mediated Communication, 9*. Online at *http://jcmc.indiana.edu/*

Sasaki, T. (2005). Literacy in Israel. *Kotoba to Shakai (Language and Society), 9,* 12–28. [In Japanese]

Sasaki, T. (2006). Text editing in Hebrew and Jewish languages: *http://www.ts-cyberia.net/editing h-j.html*

Savage-Rumbaugh, S., & Lewin, R. (1996). *The ape at the brink of the human mind.* New York: Wiley.

Shieber, S., & Baker, E. (2003). Abbreviated text input. *International Conference on Intelligent User Interfaces* (pp.293–296). New York: ACM Press.

Unicode Consortium (2003). The Unicode Standard, version 4.0, Chap. 8, Middle Eastern scripts: *http://www.unicode.org/versions/Unicode4.0.0/.* Reading, MA: Addison–Wesley.

4 | Accessibility, Universality

14 | Text Input for the Elderly and the Young

CHAPTER

Janet C. Read   University of Central Lancashire, Preston, Lancashire, UK

14.1   INTRODUCTION

This chapter considers text input from the perspective of two user groups, the elderly and the young. Brouwer-Janse *et al.* (1997) describe the two user groups of the elderly and the young as "outstanding," a rather unusual word, perhaps, but nonetheless this draws attention to the fact that both groups display generational differences that impact on interface design (Read *et al.*, 2004b). In considering these two groups in a single chapter, the focus is on justifying designing for them, highlighting the differences that need to be designed for, and outlining any specialist technologies.

In recent times, many have stressed the need to design devices and systems for the young and the old; some of these, like Newell (1993) and Shneiderman (2003) preach the maxim of universal design, the view that systems should be designed in such a way that all can use them. Others, like Druin and Inkpen (2001) and Gregor *et al.* (2002), expound the needs of particular populations, stressing how systems should be customized to suit one of the user groups.

Notwithstanding the universal belief of usability for all, there are good reasons to consider how to design for these outlying groups. With respect to the elderly, one motivation is that we ourselves will one day be elderly; another is that as a consumer group, the elderly have considerable buying power in the technology market. Our desire to design for children is partially grounded on a belief that children, as guardians of the future, deserve usable technology now, but is also again motivated by market considerations, with children and their parents as high-volume purchasers of technology. The two user groups are also "larger", especially the elderly group, than they were in earlier times, as the demographics of populations change over time. Modern Western society is sometimes referred to as a "rectangular" society, this being one with roughly equal numbers of individuals in each age decade; thus, there are currently around as many 0- to 9-year-olds as there are 70- to 79-year-olds. A century ago there were fewer older people.

Just as demographics have changed, so have the technologies with which people work and interact. Physical work, and manual work with large mechanical tools, has been replaced with more sedentary work, and the computer, once a machine for the specialist, has pervaded every part of society. This pervasive nature of the computer, and of its associated technology, has not missed the elderly and the young. Computers are found in schools and homes, in entertainment spaces and communication spaces, in playgrounds and hospitals. The computers are already in these spaces; the challenge is for the young and the elderly to be able to access the technology.

Where computer technology is used for communication, for storage of thoughts and ideas, and for manipulation of written language, text input becomes an important feature of the user experience. The elderly or young computer user needs to be able to find a method to carry out effective text input in order to access the technology. The problem is not limited to traditional computers; mobile phones, small devices, and information terminals all require text input and several different methods are needed.

This chapter therefore considers text input for the elderly and the young. It begins with a discussion of age and experience and then breaks into two sections, the first considering the elderly, the second considering the young. Each of these sections is presented in three parts: a summary of the research studies on text input with the user group, a consideration of some of the special design solutions, and then a presentation of guidelines for text input with the target group. The chapter concludes with a case study that draws together some of the themes of the chapter and considers some of the issues in designing text input evaluation studies.

14.2   OVERVIEW OF AGE EFFECTS

With age comes change; children grow into adults, adults grow old. Aging is often considered to be only about the bodily function of individuals, but this very limited view does not take into account the social environment and the effects of experience. In the following sections, some of the different aspects of aging are considered.

14.2.1   Muscle Function

When viewed in a biological way, the human body spends the first few years of its life in rapid growth before settling to a point, around the early 20s, at which it peaks in strength and general motor ability. From the age of about 30, most of the body systems start to show a regular decline of around 0.8 to 1% per year (Hayflick, 1977). This physical decline is reasonably slow but includes the functioning of the cardiovascular system, which, at age 75, is often only 70% of what it was at age 30; this reduction also affects the functioning of the brain, which in turn affects reaction times and muscle strength.

The classical work on fine movements (important in many text input activities) and age is the work by Miles (1931), which measured reaction time and motility of 863 men, women, and children ages from 6 to 95. In particular, as part of the study,

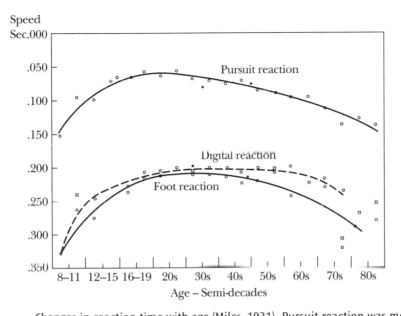

FIGURE

14.1
Changes in reaction time with age (Miles, 1931). Pursuit reaction was measured by stopping the moving index of an electric clock; digital reaction required the participant to lift his or her forefinger as soon as possible after a buzzer sounded.

Miles (1931) measured reaction times using finger movements and showed that as far as the digital reaction time (movement of their digits) was concerned, degradation only really began in the 80s, whereas for pursuit reaction, the times began reducing in the 30s. These results can be seen in Fig. 14.1.

The figures for digital reaction suggest that reaction times are not a factor in text input except with quite old users. The study also demonstrates that the reaction times of children are quite a lot slower than for adults. These findings have implications for the design of multitap methods on reduced keyboards if these devices are intended for young children.

14.2.2   Vision

The vision of adults and children differs significantly. With respect to focusing, around 25% of children are near-sighted (Sperduto *et al.*, 1983), whereas almost all people over the age of 50 need help with close distance focusing. Elderly people, however, are more likely than children to have their vision corrected by lenses, but against that, they often have difficulties with low contrast and with reading in low light. Rather than difficulties with focus and definition, the problems for children in text input tasks are more often related to their lack of understanding of visual cues; that is, they often are unsure of what the characters on a keyboard represent.

The field of vision is different for children and the elderly, children have a narrow field as a result of their close focusing, but for older people, the size of the visual field diminishes due to changes within the eye, with the result that older people often have to move their heads to see areas that younger people can access by eye movements alone (Jaffe *et al.*, 1986).

During text input, nonstandard vision (sightedness, field of vision or acuity) especially affects the experience of users when keyboard methods are being used. This is more of a problem for an unfamiliar keyboard. Thus, in a novel soft keyboard configuration designed with low contrast and small character labels, it is expected that elderly participants would perform less well than young adults. For children, a large soft keyboard taking up a large screen might present difficulties as the edges of the screen may be outside the child's vision.

14.2.3   Social Factors

There are social factors that impact performance in text input tasks; these include the discretion with which a task is carried out, the needs of the individual, and the desire to please. Children begin with quite neutral social constraints, but as they enter school, for instance, they are pressured to produce "good work" and anxieties creep into their work. Teenage children are more likely to rebel against social norms; adopting their own languages (as used in text speak[1]) is one such rebellion and this group seeks acceptance only from its peer group. Once in the competitive work place, adults begin to discriminate between what they can do and what they are willing to do. These choices may be based on risk assessments created from their family situations and their work situations. In general they are likely to increase carefulness, efficiency, and performance. As individuals age, they move out of the workplace but then may need to overcome a lack of self-belief about learning and performance that is encouraged in the popular press. The older person is less likely to take risks with new activities, not because others will see him or her fail, but for the fear of self-disappointment.

Text input to peers in e-mail applications demonstrates these points quite well. Children strive for correct spelling, while teenagers abbreviate their writing with text speak and will be less concerned about spelling and grammar, and older people will write tidy e-mails taking care with grammar. This pattern may change as the current generation of young people becomes older. Despite learning conventions of "correct"

---

[1] Text speak is the name given to the abbreviated language that is commonly used in texting and e-mail. Instead of writing all the letters in a word, abbreviations are used. For example CU is used for "see you" and transl8it would be used for "translate it." Incidentally, http://www.transl8it.com is a Web site that converts text speak into regular language. Text speak is a consequence of e-mail and SMS but the idea of abbreviating words into letter combinations is not new. An 1801 poem was found to have CU for "see you."

writing in the workplace, the older people of 2050 may well also use abbreviated language, especially in informal communications.

14.2.4 Experience and Learning

Related to the discussion on visual cues in Section 14.2.2, task experience is a factor that thankfully partially compensates for biological or organic deterioration. As individuals age, providing the memory function is not impaired, they become better equipped to deal with new situations as they have greater knowledge, more techniques, and a well-constructed platform from which to construct new solutions. In particular, the experienced person makes better anticipatory judgments.

The relationships between bodily changes and experience on performance can be illustrated as in Fig. 14.2. This figure demonstrates how the organic body performance rises and peaks before a steady decline, while experience rises throughout life (Kimmel, 1990; Hayflick, 1977).

The figure illustrates how performance in a particular task, for our case text input, will depend on the extent to which that task relies on prior knowledge or on organic capacities. Thus, one might expect that text input by speech recognition will be "easier" for the inexperienced than Qwerty keyboard text input, as Qwerty keyboard text input requires prior knowledge about the keyboard, while speaking is almost an organic function. Another feature of experience that impacts on performance is the anticipatory behavior that comes with experience. In a keyboard-based text input task it is common to see experienced users moving their fingers in the direction of the next key even before the previous key has been tapped.

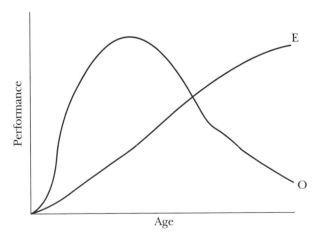

FIGURE

14.2

Curves demonstrating how performance, based on organic changes (O) and experience (E), differs with respect to age.

In some instances, the experience that is crucial to the task is not begun at the same time as the bodily aging. An example is the use of text input by elderly people; these individuals may have learned to enter text input quite late in life and so there is a debate about how well the graph matches specific text input activities.

14.3   TEXT INPUT FOR THE ELDERLY

Having outlined some of the physical concerns related to aging, this next section focuses on elderly users and is presented in three parts. The first part looks at studies of elderly people engaging in text input and summarizes findings with respect to the different input methods, these being full-sized keyboards, mobile tablet-based devices, recognition methods, and reduced keyboards. This is followed with a brief look at some of the technology solutions that are proposed for elderly users, and then the section is closed with some guidelines for the design of text input systems for the elderly.

14.3.1   Research Studies

Studies that look at how elderly people perform on full-sized keyboards are relatively common. Several studies compare older and younger users to see how performance differs on text input tasks. Murata *et al.* (2002) considered three different age groups, 20–29, 50–59, and 60–69, and, using 20 subjects in each age group, recorded fatigue, data entry rate, and effectiveness (counting error rates and percentage errors). This study established that the younger participants were around twice as fast as the older ones. An earlier study by Salthouse (1984) confirmed that although older adults are generally slower than their younger counterparts, their accuracy in text input is generally quite similar, especially once a period of practice has elapsed. Given that vision is likely to have been corrected and that reaction times are unlikely to be variable, it is highly possible that most of these differences are caused by the unfamiliarity of the elderly users with the keyboard layout. Whether this trend will remain the same as a new generation of elderly users that have had extensive keyboard use comes along is an interesting point of debate.

Soft keyboards sometimes suffer in text input comparisons, partially as a result of their sometimes unfamiliar layouts and also due to the lack of kinesthetic feedback from the keys. In addition, as they are often used with single pointers rather than both hands, they cannot take advantage of the movement learning from regular Qwerty keyboard use. Comparing text input by keyboard with text input using a stylus and soft keyboard was the focus of a study by Wright *et al.* (2000). In this work, 18 older adults with a mean age of 62 entered 11 text phrases using stylus and physical keyboard. The participants all took longer with the pen and, with the exception of one participant; they all preferred the physical keyboard. This backs up the notion that experience is the key for elderly users in text input. This study was followed up with a more prolonged study that demonstrated that, with practice, the speed of entry did not significantly improve even though accuracy showed some improvement. The Wright *et al.* (2000) study also looked at the errors made by the participants, finding miskeying to be the most prevalent, followed by pressure-related errors (found the location but failed to press hard enough) and then spelling errors.

Recognition-based text input has not been well studied with elderly users. Ogozalek and van Praag (1986) compared speech with keyboard use among two different age groups, 18–40 and 65–79. This study required the 24 participants (12 in each age range) to carry out a composition exercise using a listening keyboard (voice simulation using a Wizard of Oz method (Gould *et al.*, 1983)) and using a traditional physical keyboard. In the Wizard of Oz studies, there is a simulation of an interface, in this instance, the participants "spoke" to the computer and saw their spoken words appear on the screen but, in fact, rather than there being any real recognition taking place, a human "wizard" was listening to the participant and entering the words at another computer, unknown to the participant. The advantage of Wizard of Oz for this sort of work is that it allows the researcher to gather opinions about the usefulness of technologies that are difficult to implement and allows the gathering of some performance metrics.

All the participants in this study had prior experience using keyboards. In this study there was no difference in the time taken, which averaged 10 WPM (and adds further weight to the hypothesis that experience with the keyboard is central to rate of entry), and both groups preferred the voice input. Given that this study used Wizard of Oz, the findings need to be taken in the light of the limitations, that is to say, the participants did not encounter the inevitable erroneous outputs from the recognition engine.

With respect to text input on reduced keyboards (as found on mobile phones) there is also very little research to consider, as the current elderly population has not generally embraced SMS technology (Short Message Service technology that allows for texting) (Quadrello *et al.*, 2005). From the few studies that have looked into this, the problems for text input for SMS remain the problems inherent in mobile devices, these being the cumbersome methods (like multitap); the rubbery, small buttons; and the small size of the screens (Kurniawan *et al.*, 2006; Omori *et al.*, 2002).

14.3.2   Text Input Technologies

Many of the special technologies that are used by the elderly were initially designed for the disabled. To assist in visual clarity, especially under low light conditions, larger print is helpful. KeyTools has a large-print keyboard (see Fig. 14.3) that can be purchased in two colors, and the black writing on white keys variation offers a good level of contrast.

Mobile phone manufacturers are finally starting to take notice of elderly users and their requirements. The Japanese firm TU-KA has designed an easy to use phone for elderly people that is promoted as "needing no manual." Unfortunately, the phone (shown in Fig. 14.4), while simple, offers no text input facility, which rather narrows its appeal.

FIGURE   A large-print keyboard from KeyTools (http://www.keytools.com).

14.3

FIGURE   The no-nonsense mobile from TU-HA (www.wireless.3yen.com).

14.4

FIGURE
14.5

The LG NS1000 mobile phone. This phone offers texting and F2F calls. The larger buttons and clear designs are intended to assist the elderly.

A phone that can support text input is the LG NS1000 (see Fig. 14.5). Primarily intended for use by people in their own homes, this phone has bigger than usual keys with very bold numbers on the keys.

The drawback of the NS1000 is that the screen is small and the letters on the keys (which are essential for texting) are difficult to read.

14.3.3   Guidelines for Elderly Text Input

From the literature and the research studies, several guidelines emerge:

+ First-time users of input devices will tend to be slower than most young adults and so time-out (the time taken before the phone assumes the user has moved on) and other functions will need to adapt for this.

+ Older users have difficulties with contrast and so keys should be designed for minimum glare and with clear, but not oversized, characters on them (see also ETSI, 1997).

+ Mobile phones that are intended for texting should have clear alphabet symbols.

As well as the specialist literature on text input for elderly users there is a wealth of literature on general interaction that offers further guidelines for design.

14.4   TEXT INPUT FOR CHILDREN

This section is presented in the same three parts as the previous section. The first section looks at studies of children engaging in text input and summarizes findings with respect to the different input methods, these being full-sized keyboard, reduced keyboards, mobile tablet-based devices, and recognition methods. The next part looks briefly at some of the technology solutions that are proposed for children and the section closes with some guidelines for the design of text input systems for children.

14.4.1   Research Studies

Opinion is strongly divided as to the usefulness of keyboard-based text input for young children, with two opposing views, one suggesting that children should learn keyboarding at an early age (Beck & Fetherston, 2003). The opposing view is that children need to write words with pens to assist in spelling development (Cunningham & Stanovich, 1990). In many languages, spelling is a major problem for children and indeed, in carrying out text input evaluations with children, spelling errors by the children during text-copy tasks can be a problem for the validity of the results (Read *et al.*, 2001).

When using full-sized keyboards for text input, young children, unless formally instructed, tend to use a single finger (the index or middle) of their dominant hand (Beck & Fetherston, 2003). In particular, if they are engaged in text-copy exercises, the other hand is often occupied with tracking reading position on the intended text. As children get older, they start to use two-handed two-finger typing before starting to use the other fingers. There is a new generation of typists that are fast at "hunt and peck" and who have never had keyboarding instruction; a study by Read and Horton (2006) showed that teenagers use two- or four-finger typing and consequently make many errors in their text input.

With regard to reduced keyboards, as found on mobile phones, research concentrates on older children and teenagers. Grinter and Eldridge (2001) studied text input with teenagers and found that the preferred mode was multitap, as this allowed experienced text users to text without looking at the screen or keypad. Teenagers are known to use many abbreviations in their text messages; in a later study, the same authors (Grinter & Eldridge, 2003) established that in 477 messages sent by teenagers, there were 166 unique short forms (text speak), which were predominantly made by dropping single letters, using letters to make the sound of words, and using standard abbreviations. This behavior has impacts on the design of text input systems as these abbreviations are known to permeate into other text-based activities of this age group and, therefore, predictive systems may need adjustments or at least incorporate some leniency.

Using soft keyboards on small devices can be problematic for small children as, due to the way they hold the pointing device, their hands may interfere with the touch screen (Read and Horton, 2004); but older children find these devices easy to use. Where text input requires the use of pointing activities research suggests that the pointing ability of children is less accurate the younger they are (Kerr, 1975; Sugden, 1980; Hourcade, 2003). In a study by Danesh *et al.* (2001) it was determined that children preferred to use Graffiti rather than the soft keyboard in a PDA application but the authors noted that this could be due to the application, which was designed in such a way that the soft keyboard covered the area of interest.

Recognition-based systems are seen as good alternatives for children. Read *et al.* (2005) used handwriting recognition with young children for text input and determined that it was usable, and O'Hare and McTear (1999) used speech recognition in a secondary school setting. The great difficulty for handwriting recognition is the lexicon, which relies on the children being able to spell the words they are writing; the great challenge for speech is to design a recognizer that can be used without training.

14.4.2   Text Input Technologies

Initially created for the school market, the BigKeys product range comprises keyboards with keys that are bigger than those found on standard keyboards. The assumption, in giving big keys to children, is that next-to errors (in which the fingers catch the adjacent key) are reduced and the letter or image on the key can be made more prominent. The BigKeys keyboards are configured so there is no run on, that is, a prolonged key press does not result in multiple characters. There are two models of keyboards; the BigKeys LX, which is shown in Fig. 14.6, is the more sophisticated, with 60 keys and all the functions of a standard keyboard.

"Layout shifting" (using a single switch to toggle between Qwerty and alphabetic layouts) is utilized to effect in the BELS (BigKeys Early Learning System), which is a more recent add-on to the keyboard. This system uses gloves (or sleeves that overlay the keys on the BigKeys Plus keyboard) and visual stickers to assist children in letter recognition. A gloved keyboard with stickers is shown in Fig. 14.7.

FIGURE
14.6

The BigKeys keyboard designed with a Qwerty lower key set and available in color.

FIGURE
14.7

The BELS system for letter recognition showing a BigKeys keyboard with a glove with pictorial keys.

The nice feature of this system is that with a simple interchange of a glove, the keyboard can be picture based, lowercase, or uppercase and also, by switching the keyboard, can be alphabetic or Qwerty to suit. This flexibility lets the product adapt to the needs of the child rather than the other way around.

As well as specially designed full-sized keyboards for children there are several devices that have been intentionally created for children and which, by virtue of their designs, alter or affect the text input process. One device that has an enthusiastic following is the AlphaSmart. The AlphaSmart (pictured in Fig. 14.8) is a cut-price word-processing machine that has a full Qwerty keyboard but which has only a small display, making it ideal as a low-cost solution for a typing tool while offering a basic word-processing facility.

FIGURE

14.8

The Alpha Smart Dana, a low-cost text input device
(http://www.keytools.com/pdf/alpha_dana.pdf).

The major advantage of this device is that, due to it being available for purchase for around 30% of the cost of a laptop PC, whole classrooms can be equipped with the devices and children can become competent keyboard users.

The manufacturer LeapFrog has introduced children to several new concepts. Their IQuest palm device (see Fig. 14.9) can be used to synchronize with text books and it takes advantage of the small size of children's fingers to include a full Qwerty keyboard in a very small space.

A more innovative text input device is the LeapFrog FlyPen that is a digital pen using digital paper and recognition software to allow children to write their text and then have it spoken back to them by the pen (Fig. 14.10).

This pen uses character-wise letter recognition, which makes it potentially more useful for children than word-based systems. The downside is that the associated speech output can be confusing to the child as the word spoken may bear little resemblance to the word the child intended to write.

FIGURE   The IQuest PDA for children (http://www.leapfrog.com).

14.9

FIGURE   The LeapFrog FlyPen (http://www.leapfrog.com).

14.10

14.4.3   Guidelines for Children's Text Input

From the literature and the research studies, several guidelines emerge:

✦ Input devices for young children need the text labels to coincide with the representations that they are introduced to at school.

✦ In text input tasks, predictive behavior is probably a poor option but, if implemented, needs to take account of the variable spelling abilities of young children.

✦ Text input devices that use dictionaries need to be adaptable for new abbreviated text forms as used by teenagers.

As well as the specialist literature on text input for children there is a wealth of literature on general interaction that offers further guidelines for design.

14.5   CASE STUDY—EVALUATING TEXT INPUT WITH CHILDREN

In a study of children doing text input with digital ink, it was possible to see some of the underlying issues of evaluating text input for children. Described in Read *et al.* (2004a and 2005), several studies have been undertaken to see how children use digital ink technologies during text input activities. Using several different instances of use, and with a pool of children between 6 and 8 years of age, both copied-phrase set experiments and free writing (composition activities) were studied. When studies with digital ink are carried out, there is captured an image of the writing, as created by the child, and then, later on, this same writing can be recognized and converted into text. These multiple representations of text, and the dynamic nature of digital ink (it can be replayed to ascertain the order in which strokes were written), allow for some interesting observations to be made. The more interesting findings from this work are investigated in the following sections.

The first interesting aspect is seen in the copying process. It is assumed that copied text input allows for more robust evaluation as it takes away the thinking time and, one might assume, the issue of spelling. When children copied phrases in these studies they often missed words, interchanged similar words like "a" and "the," and misspelled words like "too" and "to" (Read & Horton, 2006). They have also been noted to add capitalization and full stops (periods). These last two behaviors are rooted in the social world of the child and are most prominent at those stages when they are focusing on these "niceties" of literature in their school curriculum.

Once the phrase is copied, these social behaviors can be seen in some of the correcting mechanisms that children do. When children copied phrases using digital ink, an interesting behavior that was noticed was their tendency to go back to writing to correct short ascenders and short descenders. This is a direct result of the child wanting the work to "look nice," and, while wholly understandable, this has serious consequences for any subsequent recognition process. The effect of the added stroke is not in itself a problem, this is the very same situation that is encountered when a user crosses a "t", but, the addition of a taller stick to a "d" is not accounted for in the recognition algorithm so it will produce an error.

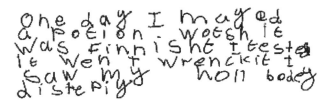

FIGURE   Free writing from a child age 8, demonstrating phonic writing.

14.11

Evident in copied text, but more evident in composed text, the spelling of children causes problems in recognition-based and prediction-based text input. In recognition-based input, if the recognition is carried out word by word, poor spellings result in significant problems. Figure 14.11 shows some free writing that was input by a child age 8.

When this writing was pushed through a recognizer that was working at a word level, the resulting text was the following:

```
One hay I may tell a potion wets, it
was Finnis ht tested it Went wryneck
— I saw m holy they distensile
```

When this text was presented back to the child, the child had no idea that it was in any way related to that which he had written. Indeed, had the original handwritten text been lost, it would have been difficult for the child or the researcher to ascertain what was intended. If this child had carried out this text input at a keyboard, the writing would have probably have read like this:

```
One day I mayed a potion. Wotsh it was
Finnisht I tested it wen I wrenck it I
saw my holl bodey distepiy.
```

It can be seen that once again the spelling is problematic and there would be many red lines! Of the 23 words written in this instance, 8 will flag up as misspelled in Word, and the offered alternatives, with the exceptions of "wen" and "bodey," do not include the word the child intended to write.

These examples show that the impact of any spell-checking software on composed text input by children cannot be ignored. Unless the researcher or the investigator is tracking what the child does, the original text will often be lost as the child right-clicks on the red lines and chooses a "real" word. This real word may bear no resemblance to the word that the child originally intended and so the intended text is then lost. Even in copied text activities, the appearance of a red line will trigger correction behavior in the child.

This study has highlighted some key aspects in carrying out evaluation studies with children. The following guidelines are derived from this work:

+ For copied text input, select phrases that minimize spelling errors.

+ Where possible, have the children repeat back what they have written to ensure that the intention is captured.

+ Either turn off spell-checking systems or ensure all levels of text input are captured.

There is much work still to be done to discover the best ways of evaluating text input by children, and similarly, work is needed to find appropriate evaluation methods for use with the elderly.

14.6   FURTHER READING

There is a considerable shortage of books on text input and even fewer on text input for the outliers. Interested readers may need to dig deep to find appropriate texts. General texts on child development and aging can be read to get a bigger picture of some of the age-related issues. A particularly accessible book on child development is the one by Kail (2002), and for a discussion of designing for children, the general purpose book by Druin (1999) offers some interesting case studies but very little about text input. The summary by Hourcade (2006) in the *Handbook of Human Factors* is illuminating and this book also contains a section by Nichols *et al.* (2006) on design for aging. For a good overview of how the body changes during the aging process, the classic text by Kimmel (1990) is a good starting point. For guidelines for the young, the work done by Clarke (2005) for the ETSI organization contains some useful data.

REFERENCES

Beck, N., & Fetherston, T. (2003). The effects of incorporating a word processor into a year three writing program. *Information Technology in Childhood Education Annual, 1,* 139–161.

Brouwer-Janse, M. D., Suri, J. F., Yawitz, M., de Vries, G., Fozard, J. L., & Coleman, R. (1997). User interfaces for young and old. *Interactions, 2,* 34–46.

Clarke, A. (2005). *Guidelines for the design and deployment of ICT products and services used by children (ETSI EG 202 423)*. Sophia Antipolis, France: European Telecommunications Standards Institute.

Cunningham, A. E., & Stanovich, K. E. (1990). Early spelling acquisition: Writing beats the computer. *Journal of Educational Psychology, 82,* 159–162.

Danesh, A., Inkpen, K., Lau, F., Shu, K., & Booth, K. (2001). Geney: Designing a collaborative activity for the Palm handheld computer, *Proceedings of the ACM Conference on Human Factors in Computer Systems—CHI 2001* (pp.388–395). New York: ACM Press.

Druin, A. (Ed.) (1999). *The design of children's technology.* San Francisco: Morgan Kaufmann.

Druin, A., & Inkpen, K. (2001). When are personal technologies for children? *Personal and Ubiquitous Computing, 5,* 191–194.

ETSI (1997). Characteristics of telephone keypads and keyboards: Requirements of elderly and disabled people (ETR 346). Sophia Antipolis, France: European Telecommunications Standards Institute.

Gould, J. D., Conti, J., & Hovanyecz, T. (1983). Composing letters with a simulated listening typewriter. *Communications of the ACM, 26,* 295–308.

Gregor, P., Newell, A. F., & Zajicek, M. (2002). Designing for dynamic diversity—interfaces for older people. *Proceedings of ASSETS 2002* (pp.151–156). New York: ACM Press.

Grinter, R. E., & Eldridge, M. A. (2001). "y do tngrs luv 2 txt msg?" in W. Prinz, M. Jarke, Y. Rogers, K. Schmidt and V. Wulf (eds.): *Proceedings of the Seventh European Conference on Computer Supported Cooperative Work (ECSCW '01), Bonn, Germany* (pp.219–238). Dordrecht, Netherlands: Kluwer Academic Publishers.

Grinter, R. E., & Eldridge, M. A. (2003). Wan2tlk?: Everyday text messaging. *Proceedings of the ACM Conference on Human Factors in Computer Systems—CHI 2003* (pp.441–448). New York: ACM Press.

Hayflick, L. (1977). The cellular basis for biological aging. In C. E. Finch & L. Hayflick (Eds.), *Handbook of the biology of aging.* New York: Academic Press.

Hourcade, J. P. (2003). *User interface technologies and guidelines to support children's creativity, collaboration and learning.* College Park: University of Maryland. [Ph.D. thesis]

Hourcade, J. P. (2006). Design for children. In G. Salvendy (Ed.), *Handbook of human factors and ergonomics* (pp.1446–1459). Hoboken, NJ: Wiley.

Jaffe, G. J., Alvarado, J. A., & Juster, R. P. (1986). Age-related changes of the normal visual field. *Archives of Ophthalmology, 194,* 1021–1025.

Kail, R. V. (2002). *Children.* Upper Saddle River, NJ: Prentice Hall.

Kerr, R. (1975). Movement control and maturation in elementary-grade children. *Perceptual and Motor Skills, 41,* 151–154.

Kimmel, D. C. (1990). *Adulthood and aging.* New York: Wiley.

Kurniawan, S., Mahmud, M., & Nugroho, Y. (2006). A study of the use of mobile phones by older persons. *Proceedings of the ACM Conference on Human Factors in Computer Systems—CHI 2006* (pp.989–994). New York: ACM Press.

Miles, W. P. (1931). Measures of certain human abilities throughout the life span. *Proceedings of the National Academy of Sciences USA, 17,* 627–633.

Murata, A., Nakamura, H., & Okada, Y. (2002). Comparison of efficiency in key entry among young, middle and elderly age groups–Effects of aging and character size on work efficiency in an entry task. *Proceedings of the IEEE International Conference on Systems, Man and Cybernetics 2002* (pp.96–101). New York: IEEE Press.

Newell, A. F. (1993). Interfaces for the ordinary and beyond. *IEEE Software, 10,* 76–78.

Nichols, T. A., Rogers, W. A., & Fisk, A. D. (2006). Design for aging. In G. Salvendy (Ed.), *Handbook of human factors and ergonomics* (pp.1418–1446). Hoboken, NJ: Wiley.

O'Hare, E. A., & McTear, M. F. (1999). Speech recognition in the secondary school classroom: An exploratory study. *Computers and Education, 33,* 27–45.

Ogozalek, V. Z., & van Praag, J. (1986). Comparison of elderly and younger users of keyboard and voice input computer-based composition tasks. *Proceedings of the ACM Conference on Human Factors in Computer Systems—CHI '86* (pp.205–211). New York: ACM Press.

Omori, M., Watanabe, T., Takai, J., Takada, H., & Miyao, M. (2002). Visibility and characteristics of the mobile phones for elderly people. *Behaviour and Information Technology, 21,* 313–316.

Quadrello, T., Hurme, H., Maenzinger, J., Smith, P. K., Viesson, M., Vida, S., & Westerback, S. (2005). Grandparents use of new communication technologies in a European perspective. *European Journal of Ageing, 2,* 200–207.

Read, J. C., & Horton, M. (2004). The usability of digital tools in the primary classroom. *Proceedings of EdMedia2004* (pp.4386–4391). New York: Association for the Advancement of Computing in Education.

Read, J. C., & Horton, M. (2006). When teenagers tType. *Proceedings of the BCS HCI Conference—HCI2006.* London: British Computer Society.

Read, J. C., MacFarlane, S. J., & Casey, C. (2001). Measuring the usability of text input methods for children. *Proceedings of the BCS HCI Conference—HCI 2001—People and Computers Series XV* (pp.559–572). London: Springer-Verlag.

Read, J. C., MacFarlane, S. J., & Horton, M. (2004a). The usability of handwriting recognition for writing in the primary classroom. *Proceedings of the BCS HCI Conference—HCI 2004—People and Computers Series XVIII* (pp.135–150). London: Springer-Verlag.

Read, J. C., Mazzone, E., & Horton, M. (2005). Recognition errors and recognizing errors—Children writing on the tablet PC. In *Lecture notes in computer science* (pp.1096–1099). Berlin: Springer-Verlag.

Read, J. C., Newell, A., Zajicek, M., Petrie, H., & Edwards, A. (2004b). Extreme HCI?—Challenges and opportunities. *Proceedings of the BCS HCI Conference—HCI 2004* (pp.213–214). London: British Computer Society.

Salthouse, T. A. (1984). Effects of age and skill in typing. *Journal of Experimental Psychology General, 113,* 345–371.

Shneiderman, B. (2003). Promoting universal usability with multi-layer interface design. *Proceedings of the Conference on Universal Usability—CUU '03, 10–11 November 2003, Vancouver, BC, Canada* (pp.1–8).

Sperduto, R. D., Seigel, D., Roberts, J., & Rowland, M. (1983). Prevalence of myopia in the United States. *Archives of Ophthalmology, 101,* 405–407.

Sugden, D. A. (1980). Movement speed in children. *Journal of Motor Behavior, 12,* 125–132.

Wright, P., Bartram, C., Rogers, N., Emslie, H., Evans, J., Wilson, B., & Belt, S. (2000). Text entry on handheld computers by older users. *Ergonomics, 43,* 702–716.

15 Text Entry When Movement is Impaired

Shari Trewin   IBM T. J. Watson Research Center, Yorktown Heights, NY USA
John Arnott   University of Dundee, Dundee, Scotland, UK

15.1   INTRODUCTION

In a study commissioned by Microsoft, Forrester Research (2003) found that one in four working-age adults has some dexterity difficulty or impairment. Physical impairments can make traditional text entry mechanisms difficult or impossible to use (Jacko & Vitense, 2001; Sears & Young, 2003). For example, Parkinson's disease can cause bradykinesia (slowness of movement), making it difficult for an individual to lift his or her finger off a key quickly. Multiple sclerosis can cause numbness in the fingers, so that it is difficult for an individual to tell whether his or her finger is positioned correctly on the keyboard and whether the key has been pressed hard enough. Both of these conditions can cause tremor, which may cause unwanted extra key presses. A person with a high spinal cord injury may not have sufficient movement to be able to press keys on a keyboard at all. Overuse of keyboards can lead to cumulative trauma disorders (Kroemer, 2001), for which an alternative to keyboard text entry is needed to avoid further damage.

Environmental factors can also impair a user's movement, affecting the ability to enter text with a keyboard. Standard keyboards are not appropriate for highly mobile situations, in which the user is carrying the device and may not have a desk available to work on. Anyone working in a moving vehicle must contend with bumps, jerks, and environmental vibration. Some work environments require users to wear protective clothing that also impedes accurate fine physical movements and are hostile to standard technology, for example, a diver inspecting an underwater structure and recording the results or a nurse entering a patient's information while using his or her hands to perform the examination.

This chapter describes text entry mechanisms typically used by individuals with motor impairments or individuals in environments that make standard text entry mechanisms impractical. It begins by examining keyboards and techniques for speed-ing up keyboard typing and reducing typing errors. It moves on to examine alternatives to standard keyboards: specialized keyboard hardware; speech input; and on-screen keyboards and the different ways in which they can be controlled. Techniques for sup-porting people who use text entry as their sole means of communication are described. Finally, a case study of character disambiguation illustrates how an assistive technique designed for people with disabilities can migrate to a major mass-market application.

15.2   USING KEYBOARDS

Typing with early typewriters was much slower and more tiring than handwriting. One of the things that spurred further development was their potential for use by people who could not write by hand (Cooper, 1983). Modern keyboards enable many people to write, and people often prefer to use standard keyboards whenever possi-ble (Edwards, 1995). This is partly because they are always available on computers at home, work, college, or other public places. They are usually faster than more spe-cialized devices, and using them does not identify the user as different or disabled.

Sometimes minor adjustments can make a standard keyboard more usable. For some people, positioning is very important. Having the keyboard at an appropriate height and tilt angle can have a dramatic effect on typing accuracy. For those who find it tiring to hold their arms above the keyboard, arm supports can be fitted to tables. Wrist rests can also provide a steadying surface for keyboard use and help to reduce the risk of wrist injury. Some users wear finger or hand splints, while others use a prodder or head stick to activate keys.

Text entry rates vary enormously and can be as little as a couple of words per minute. Errors may be frequent, caused by inaccurate or unintended motion or by environmental vibration (e.g., using a laptop keyboard on a train).

15.3   ASSISTIVE INPUT TECHNIQUES

There are many software technologies that have been developed with the aim of mak-ing text entry easier, faster, or more accurate. Some of those most commonly used are adjustments to the keyboard response, abbreviation expansion, and word prediction.

15.3.1   Keyboard Response

The way the keyboard reacts to a given input can be changed. For example, the delay before a key starts to repeat can be altered. This is useful for individuals who find it difficult to initiate controlled movements and tend to press keys for longer. Another option sets the computer to ignore repeated key presses within a set time that is less than a particular threshold value. This filters the input for cases in which the user presses a key more than once, perhaps due to tremor. Another powerful option is "Sticky Keys." This registers the pressing of keys such as Shift and Control and holds them active until another key is pressed. This removes the need for the user to operate several keys simultaneously to activate keyboard shortcuts, making them easier for one-handed typists. Simple alterations like these to keyboard response can be very effective in improving ease of use (Brown, 1992; Nisbet & Poon, 1998; Trewin & Pain, 1998).

15.3.2   Abbreviation Expansion

Popular word processing programs often include abbreviation expansion capabilities. Abbreviations for commonly used text can be defined, allowing a long sequence such as an address to be entered with just a few keystrokes. With a little investment of setup time, those who are able to remember the abbreviations they have defined can find this a useful technique. Abbreviation expansion schemes have also been developed specifically for people with disabilities (Moulton *et al.*, 1999; Vanderheiden, 1984).

Automatic abbreviation expansion at phrase/sentence level has also been investigated: the Compansion (Demasco & McCoy, 1992; McCoy *et al.*, 1998) system was designed to process and expand spontaneous language constructions, using Natural Language Processing to convert groups of uninflected content words automatically into full phrases or sentences. For example, the output sentence "John breaks the window with the hammer" might derive from the user input text "John break window hammer" using such an approach.

With the rise of text messaging on mobile devices such as mobile (cell) phones, abbreviations are increasingly commonplace in text communications. Automatic expansion of many abbreviations may not be necessary, however, depending on the context in which the text is being used. Frequent users of text messaging can learn to recognize a large number of abbreviations without assistance.

15.3.3   Word Prediction

Word prediction is an assistive input technique that is used by people with and without disabilities on desktop systems, handheld devices, and augmentative communication systems.

As a user begins to type a word, the prediction system offers suggestions for what the word might be. If the desired word is suggested, the user can choose it with a single command. For example, in Fig. 15.1, a menu of words is presented based on the initial characters ("ma") of the partially completed word in the line of user-entered

```
I am working on ma .........

        1. magnet
        2. maple
        3. marking
        4. mathematics
        5. matrix
```

FIGURE   An example of word prediction, with a list of five predicted words.

15.1

text; the user can select one of the words, e.g., "mathematics," with a single selection action, thus reducing the overall number of selection actions required to type the word. In practice, word prediction systems have been observed to reduce the number of keystrokes required by up to 60% (Newell *et al.*, 1995). Word prediction can speed up text entry for very slow typists, particularly switch users. Those who type at a rate of greater than around 15 words a minute may find that the time spent searching the lists of suggestions for the right word is greater than the time saved (Millar & Nisbet, 1993). Nevertheless, faster users may still find word prediction helpful in reducing fatigue, reducing errors, or improving spelling (Millar & Nisbet, 1993).

15.4   ALTERNATIVES TO STANDARD KEYBOARDS

15.4.1   Specialized Keyboard Hardware

There are many specialized keyboards that users can try if a standard keyboard is inappropriate for their situation (Alliance for Technology Access, 2004). Ergonomic keyboards are designed to reduce the chances of injury. As illustrated by the Maltron two-handed ergonomic keyboard shown in Fig. 15.2, ergonomic keyboards typically retain the basic Qwerty key layout but change the shape of the keyboard. These changes allow the typist's hands and arms to be held in a more natural, neutral position. The Microsoft Natural Keyboard and Kinesis Ergonomic Keyboard are popular ergonomic keyboard models.

Keyboards with enlarged keys for easier targeting, or small keys requiring little range of motion (e.g., the BlackBerry PDA device), are available. As described in Chap. 6, gestures made with a pen are another option for individuals with good control of one hand but limited space to work in. The EdgeWrite pen-based text entry method for handheld devices (Wobbrock *et al.*, 2003) uses a square hole imposed over the text entry area. The user draws along the edges and diagonals of the square,

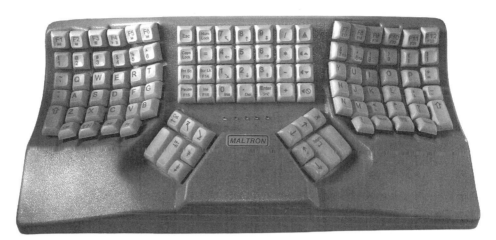

FIGURE

15.2

A Maltron ergonomic two-handed L90 US PC Qwerty keyboard, available from www.maltron.com. Used by permission of PCD Maltron Ltd.

and characters are generated according to the sequence of corners that are hit. Accuracy of the path taken is unimportant. This method was shown to be more accurate than the Graffiti text entry system for users both with and without physical impairments (Wobbrock *et al.*, 2003). In this study, some of the participants with physical impairments were unable to use Graffiti at all, but entered text successfully using EdgeWrite.

Membrane keyboards replace traditional keys with a reprogrammable touch-sensitive surface, so that a specialized keyboard can be designed to suit the individual's needs, and the user can swap between different layouts as needed. One-handed chord keyboards such as the Twiddler (Lyons *et al.*, 2004) have fewer keys than a standard keyboard, and the keys are pressed in combinations in the same way as a woodwind instrument is played. With training, chording can be a very fast text entry mechanism, with one experienced user reaching an average speed of 60 words per minute (Lyons *et al.*, 2004) on a one-handed keyboard. Mobile telephones use a similar reduced keyboard for text entry, but each physical key is mapped to several characters. The characters are disambiguated using multiple key presses, as in the multitap typing system, or by disambiguation algorithms, as described in Section 15.6. Word rates up to and including real speech rates can be achieved on two-handed chord keyboards (as in verbatim court reporting), but high manual dexterity is required for this.

For some individuals, typing accuracy can be improved by using a keyguard. Keyguards are simply attachments that fit over the standard keyboard with holes punched through above each of the keys. They provide a solid surface for resting hands and fingers on and reduce the likelihood of accidental key presses. Some users find that keyguards improve both speed and accuracy of their typing. Others find that they slow down their typing (McCormack, 1990), and they can make it difficult to see the letters on the keys (Cook & Hussey, 1995).

15.4.2   Speech Input

Speech input, introduced in Chap. 8, is an obvious text entry method to use when the user cannot press keys on a keyboard but has clear, unimpaired speech. Studies suggest that people with disabilities who use speech for text entry have text entry rates and error rates similar to those of people with no disabilities. For example, Sears *et al.* (2001) compared speech-based text entry for a group of users with high-level spinal cord injuries and a group with no disabilities and found that both groups produced text at a rate of approximately 13 words per minute. Both groups spent over 2 minutes on correction activities for every minute spent on dictation. In a second study of experienced speech users with disabilities, Koester (2004) reported an average text entry rate of 16.9 words per minute, with 56% of task time spent fixing recognition errors.

Speech users tend to be individuals who cannot enter text comfortably or easily using a keyboard. Improvements in text entry speed are typically seen only for those whose typing rate is less than 15 words per minute. However, the significant reduction in physical effort leads to less pain and fatigue and allows users to enter more text per session. Speech users with disabilities were more tolerant of the technology, reporting significantly higher levels of satisfaction with the speech technology than those without disabilities (Koester, 2004; Sears *et al.,* 2001). They also used quite different error correction strategies, with more focus on immediate correction versus navigating back to correct errors later.

15.4.3   On-Screen Keyboards

Some people can use a pointing device more easily than they can press keys on a physical keyboard. An on-screen keyboard, illustrated in Fig. 15.3, allows a user to enter text by pointing at and selecting keys on the screen. An on-screen keyboard can

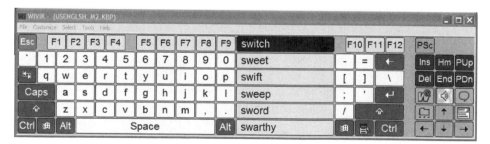

FIGURE

15.3

The WiViK on-screen keyboard showing word prediction options given when the user has typed the characters "sw". Used by permission of Bloorview MacMillan Children's Centre.

be controlled in many different ways. In addition to pointing with a mouse, trackball, or similar device, users can point at keys using head or eye movements as described in Chap. 9. Selection of keys might be done by clicking a mouse button, pressing a switch, or simply dwelling on the key for a specified length of time.

With an on-screen keyboard, text can be entered with as little as a single binary input signal, by using scanning. This usually operates by highlighting rows of the keyboard in turn. The highlighting dwells over each row for a predetermined time and then moves to the next row, dwells there, and so on, until the user selects a row. The keys on this row are then highlighted in turn until a particular key is selected.

Brewster *et al.* (1996) report that for some users, each item must be highlighted for as much as 5 seconds. There has been much research on efficient scanning mechanisms, virtual keyboard layouts, and other ways of accelerating scanning input rates (e.g., Brewster *et al.*, 1996; Simpson & Koester, 1999).

Users with severe physical impairments typically make scanning selections by pressing a physical switch that can be activated by hand, foot, head, or any distinct controlled movement. There are also mouth switches, operated by tongue position or by sudden inhalation or exhalation (sip–puff switches), and vision-based switches, operated by making a specific motion in front of a camera (e.g., the Riverdeep TouchFree Switch). If a user is capable of generating several of these motions independently then it is possible to increase the number of switches to accommodate this and increase the information transfer bandwidth. For example, an individual might use one switch to move the scan to the next item, a second to make selections, and a third to undo the previous selection.

One of the more innovative developments in on-screen text entry interfaces is the Dasher system (Ward & Mackay, 2002), a navigation-based interface driven by continuous pointing gestures, illustrated in Fig. 15.4. It can be operated with various input devices such as eye-trackers, joysticks, and touch-screens appropriate for users with special needs. It is reported that an experienced user of the eye-tracking version of Dasher was able to write text as fast as normal handwriting, at 25 words per minute, and with a mouse, experienced users can write at 39 words per minute (Ward & Mackay, 2002).

Probably the most exciting developments in computer input in recent years have been in the field of brain–computer interfaces. For reviews of research progress see Moore (2003) and Wolpaw *et al.* (2002). A brain–computer interface is a system in which electrical brain activity, typically EEG signals, is measured and interpreted by a computer in order to provide computer-based control without reliance on muscle movement. Contrary to popular opinion, such interfaces do not "read" a person's thoughts. Instead, the person learns to control an aspect of their brain signals that can be detected and measured.

Such interfaces represent what may be the only possible source of communication for people with severe physical impairments such as locked-in syndrome. Brain–computer interfaces have been shown to enable severely impaired individuals to enter text (Hinterberger *et al.*, 2003; Moore, 2003; Wolpaw *et al.*, 2002). Clinical trials

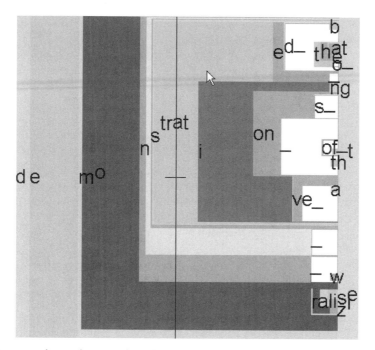

FIGURE   The Dasher user interface. On a screen, Dasher uses colored boxes that the user
              navigates through in order to enter text. Used by permission of The Dasher Project.
15.4

are under way for at least one commercial system, the BrainGate by Cyberkinetics, Inc. (http://www.cyberkineticsinc.com). A related computer control system already on the market, Cyberlink Brainfingers by Brain Actuated Technologies, Inc. (http://www.brain-fingers.com), is a hybrid brain and body signal transducer consisting of a headband that measures brain and muscle activity in the forehead. People with severe motor impairments have successfully used it to enter text via on-screen keyboards.

15.5   AAC TEXT INPUT

Augmentative and alternative communication (AAC) systems are designed to help people with communication impairments (e.g., nonspeaking people) to interact with others. (With synthetic speech as an output mode, for example, "spoken" interaction becomes possible for people who otherwise cannot speak.) Efficient text entry into AAC systems is very important in order to help such people compose text and produce original statements as easily and quickly as possible in conversational situations. While conversation can proceed at rates ranging from 150 to 250 WPM for speaking people with no communication impairments, those who need to use AAC are usually limited to much lower rates (fewer than 8 WPM in some cases) (Beukelman & Mirenda, 2005). Physical disability often accompanies speech impairment, so special input methods (both hardware and software) have been developed to assist text entry. Some of these invoke extra cognitive effort for the user, however, necessitating a trade-off between cognitive load and physical difficulty in entering or encoding information into an AAC system. Assistive techniques can use text encoding and methods such as abbreviation, prediction, and disambiguation, typically exploiting the redundancy in natural language. These methods alone cannot give the large increase in word rate required to approach natural conversational rates, however. Further increase in rate is needed, so storage and retrieval of larger text passages, including phrases, sentences, and paragraphs, are required within an AAC system (Alm & Arnott, 1998). Efficient text retrieval thus becomes a key requirement for an AAC system to make appropriate text items accessible and available for use in conversation. Prediction methods and appropriate structuring of the textual information, as well as good user-interface design, are needed to help the system achieve this.

Conversation can be relatively predictable in the paths and structures that it adopts; conversation modeling and pragmatics have therefore been applied to try to exploit this (Alm & Arnott, 1998; McCoy *et al.*, 2003; Todman, 1999, 2000, 2003; Todman & Alm 1997). Phatic communion strategies can be used to facilitate social interaction, for example, using items such as greetings, farewells, small talk, and back-channel and filler remarks (Alm *et al.*, 1992). Phrases, sentences, scripts, schemata, and frames (Carpenter *et al.*, 1997; Dye *et al.*, 1998; Harper *et al.*, 1998; Higginbotham *et al.*, 1999) can also be stored within AAC systems for use in conversational or transactional settings. Research has also been conducted into storytelling in AAC, using stored stories (Waller *et al.*, 2001) and personal narratives (Hine & Arnott, 2002a,b; Hine *et al.*, 2003). The design of the user interface and the text retrieval method are paramount in determining how easy such a system is to use and how quickly and efficiently items can be retrieved from the system for use in conversation.

A nonspeaking person was seen to achieve a conversational rate of 64 WPM with well-rated quality of conversation using an AAC system (TALK) based on conversational pragmatics, and higher rates, of about 80 WPM, occurred when greater use was made of extended personal narrative (Todman, 1999, 2000). While these rates are not as high as natural speaking rates, they indicate that a substantial improvement is possible through the use of text storage and retrieval in AAC. Text input facilities are still needed, of course, for the creation of novel and spontaneous statements during conversation and for general writing tasks such as essay composition and the writing of stories, letters, and messages, including e-mail. Efficient text input thus continues to be very important in an AAC context and there is a continuing need for improved input methods for use within a framework of efficient user interfaces that do not impose excessive cognitive demands upon their users. Further research and development on text input could therefore have very positive outcomes for people who use AAC systems to help them to communicate with others.

15.6 CASE STUDY: DISAMBIGUATION

The early development of assistive text input techniques such as disambiguation and prediction occurred particularly in the area of special needs and AAC, in which there was a clear role for them to play in facilitating text input for people with disabilities. The migration of these techniques to mass-market applications followed the widespread adoption of text input to mobile devices such as mobile (cell) phones and PDAs. Mobile devices present restrictive or "disabling" interfaces to their users because of the limited space available for the display screen and keypads. Phone keypads usually contain only 10 digit keys and a small number of additional control keys, for example, which means that multiple alphabetic characters are assigned to each digit key for purposes of text input (in a manner similar to that in Fig. 15.5), and multiple key presses are required to select individual characters (e.g., using a basic multitap coding scheme).

Research in the 1980s highlighted the possibility of typing text on a reduced set of keys or switches (i.e., fewer than 26) with an efficiency approaching one key press per selected character (Arnott & Javed, 1990; Foulds *et al.*, 1987; Kamphuis & Soede, 1989; Kreifeldt *et al.*, 1989; Levine & Goodenough-Trepagnier, 1990; Levine *et al.*, 1987; Minneman, 1985; Witten, 1982). Each key on a reduced key set represents more than one alphabetic character. Automatic disambiguation processes were proposed and developed to predict which of the characters on a key was the one required when that key was activated. With a 12-key reduced key set, for example, the prediction is usually correct and the net result (including some additional key presses to correct any errors) is a keying efficiency slightly greater than one key press per character. Alternative coding schemes that did not use automatic disambiguation required multiple (typically at

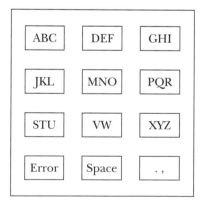

FIGURE

15.5
An example of a 12-key ambiguous (reduced) selection layout for typing text; autodisambiguation is used to help resolve the ambiguity caused by the multicharacter keys (as on mobile/cell phones). Different layouts and character–key assignments can be assembled (Arnott & Javed, 1992; Harbusch & Kühn, 2003; Lesher *et al.*, 1998); such reduced layouts are designed for people whose disabilities mean that a small number of large keys is easier to access and use than a large number of small keys.

least two) key presses per alphabetic character (Foulds *et al.*, 1987; Minneman, 1985; Witten, 1982). Research continued into the 1990s with further emphasis on improving keying efficiency and key (or switch or sensor) layouts, particularly for people with disabilities (Arnott & Javed, 1992; King *et al.*, 1995; Lesher *et al.*, 1998; Oommen *et al.*, 1992).

Mobile public (cell-phone) telephony had commenced in the 1980s, and the SMS (Short Message Service) introduced in GSM mobile networks began to grow in popularity and use during the 1990s. Developers of JustType (King *et al.*, 1995) established the Tegic Communications company in 1995 to continue development of the JustType concept in the context of text interfaces for people with disabilities. Tegic Communications went on to develop a version called T9 for use in text input on mobile devices, and this has subsequently been adopted by many manufacturers of mobile devices to assist users to enter text on 12-key telephone keypads for SMS messaging. The disambiguation technique, developed in the field of assistive technology for special interfaces for people with disabilities, thus moved into a much wider marketplace in the form of mobile text messaging for use by the general population and is now used daily by vast numbers of people.

Users of text messaging on mobile devices use abbreviation extensively. Assistive text input techniques such as disambiguation and template phrases have also been incorporated into mobile devices to help users to enter text on reduced keypads. Assistive input techniques have thus found mainstream application in this market. It may be that other AAC techniques will make this transition; template phrases already represent an element of message pragmatics within text messaging facilities, for example.

15.7   FURTHER READING

A number of papers describe the effects of physical impairment on text entry using standard keyboards (Jacko & Vitense, 2001; Sears & Young, 2003, Trewin & Pain, 1999). Kroemer (2001) provides an extensive annotated bibliography of literature on keyboards and keying from 1878 to 1999 that includes many papers examining the relationship between various parameters of keyboard design, for example, key size and slope, typing comfort, and potential for overuse injuries. Online, the typing injury FAQ (http://www.tifaq.org/) provides up-to-date information about typing injuries, ergonomics, alternative keyboards, and other text entry mechanisms.

When standard keyboards are unavailable or inappropriate, assistive technology can enable text entry. The Alliance for Technology Access (2004) and Cook and Hussey (1995) give overviews of some of the alternative and supplementary technologies available and describe the process of selecting appropriate assistive software and devices.

Von Tetzchner and Martinsen (2000) give an introduction to AAC, including communication aids, motor impairment, developmental language disorders, learning disability, and autism. They also address aspects such as assessment, teaching, signing, vocabulary development, and conversational skills. Beukelman and Mirenda (2005) provide an introductory text intended to give students and professionals further insight into the field of AAC and the communication needs of people with communication impairments. The book emphasizes the interdisciplinary nature of AAC and is arranged in three major sections, covering (i) an introduction to AAC processes, (ii) AAC for people with developmental disabilities, and (iii) AAC for people who have acquired disabilities during their lifetime.

REFERENCES

Alliance for Technology Access (2004). *Computer resources for people with disabilities: A guide to assistive technologies, tools and resources for people of all ages (4th ed.)*. Alameda, CA: Hunter House.

Alm, N., & Arnott, J. L. (1998). Computer-assisted conversation for non-vocal people using pre-stored texts. *IEEE Transactions on Systems, Man and Cybernetics Part C, 28*, 318–328.

Alm, N., Arnott, J. L., & Newell, A. (1992). Prediction and conversational momentum in an augmentative communication system. *Communications of the ACM, 35*, 46–57.

Arnott, J. L., & Javed, M. Y. (1990). Small text corpora in character disambiguation for reduced typing keyboards. *Proceedings of the Thirteenth Annual RESNA Conference* (pp.181–182). Washington, DC: Resna Press.

Arnott, J. L., & Javed, M. Y. (1992). Probabilistic character disambiguation for reduced keyboards using small text samples. *Augmentative and Alternative Communication, 8*, 215–223.

Beukelman, D. R., & Mirenda, P. (2005). *Augmentative and alternative communication: Supporting children & adults with complex communication needs (3rd ed.)*. Baltimore: Paul H. Brookes Publishing.

Brewster, S., Raty, V., & Kortekangas, A. (1996). Enhancing scanning input with non-speech sounds. *Proceedings of the Second Annual ACM Conference on Assistive Technologies— ASSETS '96* (pp.10–14). New York: ACM Press.

Brown, C. (1992). Assistive technology computers and people with disabilities. *Communications of the ACM, 35*, 36–45.

Carpenter, T., McCoy, K, & Pennington, C. (1997). Schema-based organization of re-usable text in AAC: user-interface considerations. *Proceedings of the RESNA '97 Annual Conference* (pp.57–59). Washington, DC: Resna Press.

Cook., S., & Hussey, A. (1995). *Assistive technologies: Principles and practice*. St. Louis: Mosby-Year Book.

Cooper, W. (1983). *Cognitive aspects of skilled typewriting*. New York: Springer-Verlag.

Demasco, P., & McCoy, K. F. (1992). Generating text from compressed input: an intelligent interface for people with severe motor impairments. *Communications of the ACM, 35*, 68–79.

Dye, R., Alm, N., Arnott, J. L., Harper, G., & Morrison, A. (1998). A script-based AAC system for transactional interaction. *Natural Language Engineering, 4,* 57–71.

Edwards, A. D. N. (1995). *Extra-ordinary human–computer interaction: Interfaces for users with disabilities.* Cambridge, UK: Cambridge University Press.

Forrester Research, Inc. (2003). *The wide range of abilities and its impact on computer technology.* Cambridge, MA: Forrester Research.

Foulds, R., Soede, M., & van Balkom, H. (1987). Statistical disambiguation of multi-character keys applied to reduce motor requirements for augmentative and alternative communication. *Augmentative and Alternative Communication, 3,* 109–195.

Harbusch, K., & Kühn, M. (2003). An evaluation study of two-button scanning with ambiguous keyboards. *Proceedings of the 7th European Conference for the Advancement of Assistive Technology—AAATE 2003* (pp.954–958). Taastrup, Denmark: Association for the Advancement of Assistive Technology in Europe.

Harper, G., Dye, R., Alm, N., Arnott, J. L., & Murray, I. R. (1998). A script-based speech aid for non-speaking people. *Proceedings of the Institute of Acoustics, 20,* 289–295.

Higginbotham, D. J., Wilkins, D. P., & Lesher, G. W. (1999). Frametalker: A communication frame and utterance-based augmentative communication device. *Proceedings of the RESNA '99 Annual Conference* (pp.40–42). Washington, DC: Resna Press.

Hine, N., & Arnott, J. L. (2002a). A multimedia story-telling system for non-speaking people. *Proceedings of the 10th International Conference on Augmentative & Alternative Communication—ISAAC 2002, 21–23 November 2002, Vancouver, BC, Canada* (pp.87–88).

Hine, N., & Arnott, J. L. (2002b). A multimedia social interaction service for inclusive community living: Initial user trials. *Universal Access in the Information Society, 2,* 8–17.

Hine, N., Arnott, J. L., & Smith, D. (2003). Design issues encountered in the development of a mobile multi-media augmentative communication service. *Universal Access in the Information Society, 2,* 255–264.

Hinterberger, T., Kubler, A., Kaiser, J., Neumann, N., & Birbaumer, N. (2003). A brain–computer interface (BCI) for the locked-in: comparison of different EEG classifications for the thought translation device. *Clinical Neurophysiology, 114,* 416–425.

Jacko, J., & Vitense, H. (2001). A review and reappraisal of information technologies within a conceptual framework for individuals with disabilities. *Universal Access in the Information Society, 1,* 56–76.

Kamphuis, H. A., & Soede, M. (1989). KATDAS: A small number of keys direct access system. *Proceedings of the 12th Annual RESNA Conference* (pp.278–279). Washington, DC: Resna Press.

King, M. T., Kushler, C. A., & Grover, D. A. (1995). JustType—Efficient communication with eight keys. *Proceedings of the RESNA '95 Annual Conference* (pp.94–96). Washington, DC: Resna Press.

Koester, H. H. (2004). Usage, performance and satisfaction outcomes for experienced users of automatic speech recognition. *Journal of Rehabilitation Research and Development 41,* 739–754.

Kreifeldt, J. G., Levine, S. L., & Iyengar, C. (1989). Reduced keyboard designs using disambiguation. *Proceedings of the Human Factors Society 33rd Annual Meeting* (pp.441–444). Santa Monica, CA: HFES.

Kroemer, K. (2001). Keyboards and keying: An annotated bibliography of the literature from 1878 to 1999. *Universal Access in the Information Society, 1,* 99–160.

Lesher, G. W., Moulton, B. J., & Higginbotham, D. J. (1998). Optimal character arrangements for ambiguous keyboards. *IEEE Transactions on Rehabilitation Engineering, 6,* 415–423.

Levine, S. H., & Goodenough-Trepagnier, C. (1990). Customised text entry devices for motor-impaired users. *Applied Ergonomics, 21,* 55–62.

Levine, S. H., Goodenough-Trepagnier, C., Getschow, C. O., & Minneman, S. L. (1987). Multi-character key text entry using computer disambiguation. *Proceedings of the 10th Annual Conference on Rehabilitation Technology* (pp.177–179). Washington, DC: Resna Press.

Lyons, K., Starner, T., Plaisted, D., Fusia, J., Lyons, A., Drew, A., & Looney, E. (2004). Twiddler typing: One handed chording text entry for mobile phones. *Proceedings of the SIGCHI Conference on Human Factors in Computing Systems* (pp.671–678). New York: ACM Press.

McCormack, D. (1990). The effects of keyguard use and pelvic positioning on typing speed and accuracy in a boy with cerebral palsy. *American Journal of Occupational Therapy, 44,* 312–315.

McCoy, K. F., Hoag, L. A., & Bedrosian, J. L. (2003). Pragmatic theory and utterance-based systems: Application of the co-operative principle. *Proceedings of the 7th ISAAC Research Symposium* (pp.76–79). Toronto: ISAAC.

McCoy, K. F., Pennington, C. A., & Badman, A. L. (1998). Compansion: From research prototype to practical integration. *Natural Language Engineering, 4,* 73–95.

Millar, S., & Nisbet, P. (1993). *Accelerated writing for people with disabilities.* Edinburgh: University of Edinburgh, ISBN 1 898042 01 2.

Minneman, S. L. (1985). A simplified touch-tone telecommunications aid for deaf and hearing impaired individuals. *Proceedings of the 8th Annual Conference on Rehabilitation Technology* (pp.209–211). Washington, DC: Resna Press.

Moore, M. (2003). Frontiers of human–computer interaction: Direct-brain interfaces. In *Frontiers of engineering: Reports on leading-edge engineering from the 2002 NAE Symposium on Frontiers of Engineering* (pp.47–52). Washington, DC: National Academy of Sciences.

Moulton, B. J., Lesher, G. W., & Higginbotham, D. J. (1999). A system for automatic abbreviation expansion. *Proceedings of the RESNA Annual Conference* (pp.55–57). Washington, DC: Resna Press.

Newell, A., Arnott, J., Cairns, A., Ricketts, I., & Gregor, P. (1995). Intelligent systems for speech and language impaired people: A portfolio of research. In A. D. N. Edwards (Ed.), *Extra-ordinary human–computer interaction: Interfaces for users with disabilities* (pp.83–101). Cambridge, UK: Cambridge University Press.

Nisbet, P., & Poon, P. (1998). *Special access technology*. Edinburgh: University of Edinburgh, ISBN 1 898042 11 X.

Oommen, B. J., Valiveti, R. S., & Zgierski, J. R. (1992). Correction to 'An adaptive learning solution to the keyboard optimization problem.' *IEEE Transactions on Systems, Man and Cybernetics, 22,* 1233–1243.

Sears, A., Karat, C.-M., Oseitutu, K., Karimullah, A., & Feng, J. (2001). Productivity, satisfaction, and interaction strategies of individuals with spinal cord injuries and traditional users interacting with speech recognition software. *International Journal of Universal Access in the Information Society, 1,* 14–15.

Sears, A., & Young, M. (2003). Physical disabilities and computing technology: An analysis of impairments. In J. Jacko & A. Sears (Eds.), *The human–computer interaction handbook: Fundamentals, evolving technologies and emerging applications* (pp.482–503). Hillsdale, NJ: Lawrence Erlbaum.

Shaw, R., Loomis, A., & Crisman, E. (1995). Input and integration: Enabling technologies for disabled users. In A. D. N. Edwards (Ed.), *Extra-ordinary human–computer interaction: Interfaces for users with disabilities* (pp.263–278). Cambridge, UK: Cambridge University Press.

Simpson, R., & Koester, H. H. (1999). Adaptive one-switch row-column scanning. *IEEE Transactions on Rehabilitation Engineering, 7,* 464–473.

Todman, J. (1999). The use of stored text for socially effective conversation. *Proceedings of the RESNA Annual Conference* (pp.16–18). Washington, DC: Resna Press.

Todman, J. (2000). Rate and quality of conversations using a text-storage AAC system: Single-case training study. *Augmentative and Alternative Communication, 16,* 164–179, 2000.

Todman, J. (2003). Pragmatic aspects of communication. *Proceedings of the 7th ISAAC Research Symposium* (pp.68–75). Toronto: ISAAC.

Todman, J., & Alm, N. (1997). Pragmatics and AAC approaches to conversational goals. *Proceedings of the ACL/EACL Workshop on Natural Language Processing for Communication Aids* (pp.1–8). Madrid: Association for Computational Linguistics.

Trewin, S., & Pain, H. (1998). A study of two keyboard aids to accessibility. In H. L. Johnson, L. Nigay, & C. Roast (Eds.), *People and computers XIII: Proceedings of HCI 98* (pp.83–97). Berlin: Springer-Verlag.

Trewin, S., & Pain, H. (1999). Keyboard and mouse errors due to motor disabilities. *International Journal of Human–Computer Studies, 50,* 109–144.

Vanderheiden, G. (1984). A high-efficiency flexible keyboard input acceleration technique: Speedkey. *Proceedings of the 2nd International Conference on Rehabilitation Engineering* (pp.353–354). Washington, DC: Resna Press.

von Tetzchner, S., & Martinsen, H. (2000). *Introduction to augmentative and alternative communication (2nd ed.)*. London: Whurr Publishers.

Waller, A., O'Mara, D., Tait, L., Booth, L., Brophy-Arnott, M. B., & Hood, H. E. (2001). Using written stories to support the use of narrative in conversational interactions: case study. *Augmentative and Alternative Communication, 17,* 221–232.

Ward, D. J., & Mackay, D. J. (2002). Fast hands-free writing by gaze direction. *Nature, 418,* 838.

Witten, I. H. (1982). *Principles of computer speech* (pp.247–249). London: Academic Press.

Wobbrock, J., Myers, B., & Kembel, J. (2003). EdgeWrite: a stylus-based text entry method designed for high accuracy and stability of motion. *Proceedings of the 16th Annual ACM Symposium on User Interface Software and Technology* (pp.61–70). New York: ACM Press.

Wolpaw, J. R., Birbaumer, N., McFarland, D., Pfurtscheller, G., & Vaughan, T. (2002). Brain–computer interfaces for communication and control. *Clinical Neurophysiology, 113,* 767–791.

16 Text Entry for People with Visual Impairments

Chieko Asakawa
Hironobu Takagi   Tokyo Research Laboratory, IBM Research, Tokyo, Japan

16.1   INTRODUCTION

According to the World Health Organization, in 2002 more than 161 million people were visually impaired, and 37 million of them were blind[1]. (World Health Organization, 2004). These numbers are much larger than most people think. This impairment is characterized by its limitations on obtaining information from a human being's widest cognitive channel, sight. Most people obtain at least 80% of their information through the sense of sight. It is obviously a severe problem for the visually impaired to be unable to write or read printed documents on their own, and this makes it hard for them to live actively in society.

Computers have been drastically changing this situation, enabling these individuals to access digital documents directly without sighted assistance. In contrast to problems with printed mail, it is easy to read e-mail via speech synthesis or Braille output. They may barely be able to fill in paper forms, but it is possible to complete Web-based electronic forms. Text entry is crucial to allow them not only to interact with the computer itself, but also to reach society and the world's knowledge through the Internet.

One of the most prominent recent trends is for visual interfaces to evolve toward being more visually intuitive. Unfortunately, this basically positive trend also has a negative aspect. Such highly visual interfaces make it more difficult for screen readers[2] to provide effective speech feedback for text input (Boyd *et al.,* 1991; Buxton *et al.,* 1986; Scadden, 1984; Theofanos & Redish, 2003). For example, some applications can be controlled only using mouse operations, but mouse operations are very difficult for the visually disabled.

---

[1] In this chapter, "visually impaired" means anyone who has a visual impairment and includes total blindness. The word "blind" refers only to people who are totally blind.

[2] A screen reader is a resident application that works with an operating system, such as Windows or Linux, to assist visually impaired users in inputting text via a keyboard and in obtaining information via the screen.

In this chapter, we will first review the history of input innovations focusing on the Latin alphabet. We will then consider the difficulties of supporting text entry for ideographic characters, since people in cultures with such graphic characters still have fundamental difficulties in handling those characters. Then we will introduce future challenges, such as the challenges of various types of selection-based text input interfaces. Finally, we will discuss some guidelines for the developers of text entry interfaces that can make them more accessible for visually impaired users.

16.2 TEXT ENTRY FOR LATIN ALPHABETS

16.2.1 Keyboard and Braille Input

Text entry for visually impaired people can be divided into two methods, one for standard keyboard entry used by the majority of users, and one for six-dot Braille entry. Braille input is still very important, though its use is declining. In this chapter, we will review the history of these two types of entries.

There are several character sets that are grouped under the label of Latin alphabets, but they generally have fewer than 30 basic characters. This characteristic allows us to lay out a keyboard with individual keys for each character. It means that each physical key is associated with one specific character. This fundamental design of the keyboard allows visually impaired users to use their sense of touch to input text without seeing the keyboard. One of the motivations for inventing the original typewriters was to allow visually impaired people to write documents. One of earliest developers, Pellegrino Turri, originally developed his typewriter for a blind friend in 1808. Many similar machines were built for visually impaired people (Adler, 1973). Currently, the touch-typing method (actually called "blind touch" in Japanese), a method to input text without looking at the keyboard, is the most popular text method for rapid text input. The most popular layout for touch-typing is known as the Qwerty keyboard, named for the placement of those letters in that order on the keyboard.

Before computers appeared, Braille was the only medium for the visually impaired to read text. One Braille cell consists of six dots that can represent 1 of 62 different characters. To input Braille, at first a Braille input board was used. In that approach, the author needed to write each character dot by dot, which required making up to six dimples for each Braille cell. Later, Braille typewriters with six keys became popular, which could emboss an entire cell in one step by activating six pins to create the dimples[3]. This method is the easiest text entry method for Braille readers, since the Braille dot patterns are mapped directly to key actions. In addition, this is a very simple layout compared to a standard keyboard, so some experienced Braille typists find

---

[3] See Perkins School for the Blind (http://www.perkins.org/).

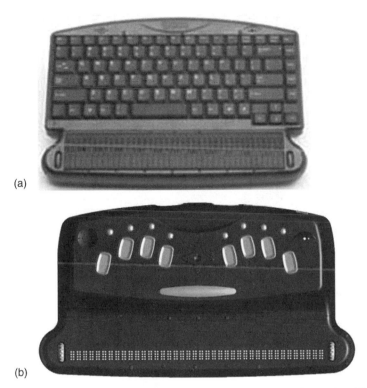

(a)

(b)

FIGURE

16.1

PDAs with different keyboards (available from Freedom Scientific at www.freedomscientific.com). (a) PDA with standard keyboard (Freedom Scientific PAC Mate™ QX440). (b) PDA with Braille keyboard (Freedom Scientific PAC Mate™ BX440).

it difficult to switch. Visually impaired users can select either of these input methods depending on their situations.

There are also various kinds of PDAs and note-taking devices for the visually impaired available in the market. Figure 16.1a shows one with a standard keyboard, and Fig. 16.1b shows one that has a six-dot Braille keyboard. The pictured PDAs also include Braille pin grids for output. Such a pin grid is an alternative to punching the Braille characters onto paper.

16.2.2   Inventions to Access Computer Screens

Computers offered new media and digital documents for visually impaired people. These individuals are now able to read and write digital documents using computers. To input text using either input method, it is essential for the visually impaired to get feedback on what they have input, which was not possible with regular typewriters.

The Optacon (Linvill & Bliss, 1966), a device developed in the 1960s, made that possible. It captured characters with a small camera and represented them directly as a kind of enlarged touchable representation using a vibrating matrix of pins. The resolution of the Optacon was low and the device required substantial training before users were able to read printed documents with it. In addition to reading printed documents, it could be used to read characters on a computer screen, and it was used by the first blind computer professionals in the 1980s.

In the mid-1980s, speech output capabilities that could read the characters on the screen first appeared, and this method has become the de facto standard for most visually impaired computer users (Boyd *et al.*, 1990; Edwards *et al.*, 1995; Mynatt & Weber, 1994; Thatcher, 1994). Braille output also became possible with Braille pin displays that were connected to computers as peripheral devices[4]. Visually impaired users could then determine what text they had input by using speech or Braille output functions.

Screen readers that support such speech and Braille output have been developed all over the world. Visually impaired users can access computers after installing one of these applications. JAWS® (Freedom Scientific), the most popular screen reader in the world, provides various kinds of feedback corresponding to the text entered. For example, the user gets feedback every time a key is pressed. This is character-by-character feedback. This feedback is sometimes too noisy for more advanced users and such users can set the program to provide feedback only when the space key is pressed. This is word-by-word feedback. Another important kind of feedback is related to capital letters by using different tones.

16.3   TEXT ENTRY FOR IDEOGRAPHIC CHARACTERS

This section considers some of the input problems beyond Latin characters. As mentioned earlier, basically fewer than 30 characters are needed in countries that use Latin alphabets, and those characters can be entered directly using a keyboard or Braille input device. However, thousands of characters are needed in countries that use ideographic characters, such as Japan and China. In Japan, 1945 ideographic characters (called kanji) are officially approved for everyday use, China recognizes 3755 characters, Hong Kong uses a set of 4759 characters, and Taiwan allows for 4808 characters (see Chaps. 2 and 11). The need to read and write these characters causes severe problems for visually impaired people in these countries.

It is obvious that each ideographic character cannot be entered directly via a regular keyboard. Historically, there actually were some special typewriter keyboards with thousands of keys, but they required extensive training and were never in common

---

[4]   See Web page of the National Federation of the Blind (http://www.nfb.org/).

usage. Therefore, special methods are widely used with standard keyboards for the input of ideographic characters. Most of these methods consist of two basic steps, the input of phonetic characters and a conversion into ideographic characters. In China, pinyin is the phonetic character set used for entering ideographic characters (Chinese characters). Mainland China and Taiwan have different pinyin. In Japan, hiragana is the official phonetic character set, and a sequence of letters is assigned to generate each hiragana. This process does not cause ambiguity in either of these languages, so it can be done by visually impaired people without difficulty. The next step is conversion from phonetic characters to ideographic characters. This conversion process often yields ambiguity, therefore some type of selection interface is integrated into the character entry method. Making this selection interface accessible is a technical challenge, because the ideographic characters are essentially visual.

Using Japanese input as an example, after the user enters the hiragana representation of the pronunciation, a list appears with the possible kanji (Japanese ideographic character) candidates that match that hiragana string. Normally there are several candidate kanji for each hiragana string. Sighted people can select the appropriate kanji from such a list by using their eyes, but people with visual impairments cannot see the list of ideographs.

The most common method used to allow visually impaired users to select the appropriate candidate is to provide a meaning for each kanji character. However, a single kanji character usually has several possible meanings that the screen-reading software must provide. Also, proper input depends on the user's kanji literacy skills to determine the correct candidates based on the meanings. Figure 16.2 shows an example of a kanji candidate list and the corresponding explanations (translated into English) for the first three characters. Figure 16.2 is a relatively simple example, because it is a single character conversion (though even here there are some complex options among the nine choices). The katakana "hashi" has three primary candidates, and each of them can be explained simply in a short phrase, such as "edge of a building," "a bridge for crossing a river," and "chopsticks for eating." Remember that the kanji characters for "edge," "bridge," and "chopsticks" are all pronounced with the same phonetic reading, so all of them are written with the same hiragana.

Table 16.1 is an example of a more complex compound word that consists of two kanji characters. Sometimes the proper kanji is an idiomatic usage whose meaning as a pair of characters is not directly or obviously related to the meanings of the components. In this example, including personal and place names, there are about 45 candidates for the hiragana "seisan," of which 7 idiomatic examples are shown in the table.

In this particular case, it is hard for a user to select the right kanji pair for "accounting" or "reset total" based only on these explanations. It is not easy to distinguish between the component kanji that are translated as "pure mind" and "spirit." There are some assistive technologies that tell users the meaning of an idiom by referring to a dictionary during text entry, but they cannot completely cover all text entry situations because they depend on limited dictionaries. Often a user needs to select a kanji character with a best guess even when their assistive technology includes such a dictionary system.

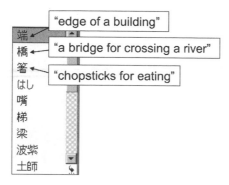

"edge of a building"

"a bridge for crossing a river"

"chopsticks for eating"

FIGURE   An example of kanji candidates for the phonetic word "hashi."

16.2

Kanji characters	Explanation for "SEI"	Explanation for "SAN"	Meaning of idiom
生産	"SEI" of live	"SAN" of raising	manufacturing
清算	"SEI" of pure mind	"SAN" of math	accounting
精算	"SEI" of spirit	"SAN" of math	reset total
青酸	"SEI" of blue	"SAN" of acerbic	hydrocyanic
成算	"SEI" of make	"SAN" of math	be confident of success
正餐	"SEI" of right	"SAN" of dinner	dinner
凄惨	"SEI" of dread	"SAN" of misery	dreadful

TABLE   Candidates for the kanji characters for "seisan" and (translated) explanations as
             provided by a screen reader.
16.1

Currently, active research and development work are continuing for other scripts, such as Indian and Arabic scripts (Lahiri *et al.*, 2005). If you have an interest, please check for the latest status at academic conferences and in research reports. (See Related Organizations and Research Groups.)

In summary, there are two essential requirements to support nonvisual ideographic text entry. First, each kanji character must be explained at text entry time. Second, the explanations need to be as explicit as possible to support accurate character selection. Even if these requirements are met, it still remains as a fundamental issue that ideographic characters cannot be intuitively represented nonvisually to support quick and efficient text entry.

16.4   SELECTION-BASED TEXT ENTRY INTERFACES

Non-visually impaired users are surprised at the high-speed voices visually impaired users listen to. The speaking speed for normal conversation is about 150 WPM (words per minute), but experienced visually impaired users can understand (and usually set their software for) much higher speeds, from 400 to 500 WPM (Asakawa *et al.*, 2003). However, even when using a high-speed voice, the bandwidth for obtaining information is far below the bandwidth of vision. As already described, the two primary media used for nonvisual access are voice output and Braille. Both of these media require much longer times for obtaining information compared to vision. Adjusting the bandwidth gap between visual and nonvisual media is the most important factor that improves (or degrades) the usability of an information source for the visually impaired (Takagi *et al.*, 2002).

This bandwidth issue directly impacts the usability of selection-based input techniques (Byrne *et al.*, 1999; Kieras & Meyer, 1997). Selection-based input is one of the techniques expected to improve user performance and to reduce the error ratio. In this book, various types of selection-based interfaces are discussed. In terms of difficulty for visually impaired users, we can divide them into two categories, static selection interfaces and dynamic selection interfaces. The dynamic interfaces are increasingly used for various types of text entry and they cause various kinds of problems for visually impaired users.

A static selection interface, such as a pull-down menu or a list box, is not in itself the problem. These are widely used in various graphical user interfaces, so nonvisual usage scenarios are already mature and well known among visually impaired users. An example of performance-improving options for the visually impaired is the availability of various ways to do menu selection, as with the Edit menu of word processing software. Such menus usually offer at least three ways to select a command from the menu without using a pointing device such as a mouse. First, the commands can be selected by moving the cursor up and down with the cursor keys. Second, statically assigned shortcut keys can be used when the menu is opened, such as a "C" for the copy command or "P" for the paste command. Third, there are statically assigned shortcut key combinations to invoke common commands, such as Ctrl + C for the copy command and Ctrl + V for the paste command, even without opening the Edit menu. Such shortcut keys and key combinations are shown in the menus, so users can naturally learn these keys and improve their performance in tasks.

However, these shortcut key approaches cannot be applied to dynamically changing selection interfaces. The basic idea is to change the selection candidates according to the entry context (e.g., previous words and characters). This means the static key-assignment approach cannot really be applied to these interfaces. Figure 16.3 shows an example of the experimental Google Suggest™ interface. This interface shows a list of popular search keywords below the input box as the text is input. When a user inputs "a", it lists 10 keywords, such as "amazon" and "ask jeeves." With the addition of a "c", the list dynamically changes and presents keywords starting with "ac", such as

FIGURE
16.3

Examples of a visually oriented design for a selection interface. Google Suggest™ provides a dynamically changing selection list that responds to each typed key (http://www.google.com/webhp?complete = 1&hl = en). (a) When the user inputs "a", the words starting with "a" are listed. (b) When the user adds a "c", the words starting with "ac" are listed.

"acrobat reader" and "academy awards." Sighted users do not need to move their focus from the candidate list, since the list is dynamically changing according to their input. As soon as they notice the desired keyword or phrase in the list, they can move the cursor to that item and press Enter to perform the search.

This interface fully utilizes visual cognition and improves the performance while also providing additional information about the popularity of the searches. The improvement over a typical (without selection) input box and this input box with selection depends on the wide cognitive bandwidth of the sense of vision. Users without visual impairments can immediately scan the list "at a glance." It is obvious that the design should be refined to fully achieve the original goal of the system, but basically this type of selection interface is promising for improving usability.

In contrast, the alternative (accessible) methods to scan such a list to obtain sufficient information are clearly slower than the methods used by people without visual impairments. As already noted, speech and Braille are serial information channels, so users need to listen (or read in Braille) one entry (candidate) after another using the cursor keys. This sluggish cursor key movement for the visually impaired corresponds to rapid eye movements for the users without visual impairments. That is why this type of selection-based interface does not improve performance for visually impaired. This issue has potential to widen the productivity gap between sighted and visually impaired. More research activities are necessary to solve it, and we hope it will be pursued.

16.5   DESIGN GUIDELINES

This book covers various types of new text entry techniques. It is obvious that we cannot stop the evolution of input techniques, even if some of them are less accessible for visually impaired users. For example, most pen-based interfaces cannot be used by visually impaired users, but these techniques have great potential to improve mobile computing. At the same time, everyone hopes future information technology will become more accessible for all users as an important social infrastructure. For now, we think that a best-effort strategy will help, so the basic strategy should be "make it accessible, whenever possible." In the near future, we should establish more general and robust principles to ensure the accessibility of text entry systems. In this section, we would like to introduce some design guidelines for making text entry systems accessible (focusing on visual accessibility concerns) and also introduce some key points to guide our explorations.

Guideline 1: Provide nonvisual entry operations by supporting nonvisual input devices with fixed roles, such as cursor keys or keyboards.
It almost goes without saying, but the most important basic prerequisite is device-level accessibility. If a device provides only a pointing interface such as a pen or a mouse, the device cannot be made accessible. The key-based interfaces, such as those using cursor keys and Qwerty keyboards, are commonly used accessible devices. MacKenzie and Soukoreff (2002) classified key-based text entry devices by the level of ambiguity. His scale goes from hypothetical single-key keyboards to imaginary alphabetic keyboards with distinct keys for capital and lowercase letters. We believe all kinds of keyboards can be used accessibly. The minimum number of keys for practical text entry

seems to be three keys, two for scrolling and one for selection. Therefore, all devices should have at least three keys for text entry.

The Twiddler is a one-handed keyboard with 12 keys, and nonvisual chording input is possible (Lyons *et al.*, 2004). Lee proposed a hand–glove-based entry device for a mobile environment and for the visually impaired (Lee *et al.*, 2003). Each part of a finger is similar to a button for this device. Multiple buttons can be selected at one time, so six-key Braille entry (see Section 16.2.1) is also possible. This device can be regarded as an enhancement of the keyboard.

Then entry methods should be provided using these accessible devices. If the interface is optimized for inaccessible devices, such as pie-menu-based predictive interfaces for pen computers, there should be alternative entry methods to make the interface operable by accessible devices. A good example of accessibility enablement is the POBox (Masui, 1998). The POBox was originally developed as a predictive input technique for pen-based interfaces. However, the prediction engine itself is independent of the devices, so the technique was ported to various types of devices[5]. Among them, the mobile phone version can be made accessible, since it requires only a number pad and the cursor keys on a phone.

It is not appropriate to reject all entry interfaces with inaccessible devices, since there are possibilities of inventing new categories of text entry methods. For example, the EdgeWrite (Wobbrock *et al.*, 2004a,b), a unistroke text entry method for hand-held devices, is such an exceptional breakthrough device. The unique characteristic of this method is that it is possible to use it as long as the user can sense the four corners of the input device. For example, a joystick can be used for text entry and it does not require vision to detect the four corners. Therefore this technique can be used by visually impaired users. Of course, it is necessary to investigate the performance, but we can definitely say that new possibilities still exist. We encourage researchers in this area to consider studying use by the visually impaired in the early stages of research and development.

Even if a keyboard is provided for a device, it will not be accessible if the role of each key is continually changing. An example of such inaccessibility is a button matrix with small LCD displays on top of each key[6]. Each key can be changed programmatically, so it is possible to change the role of each key according to the user's key input. In this case, attention should be paid to the consistency of the assigned functions for each key.

The voice input techniques are basically accessible for the visually impaired, but they need correction interfaces. It is essential to provide a correction interface for voice-recognition-based systems, since their accuracy is limited according to the current technologies. Current correction interfaces are sometimes very difficult for the visually impaired to use, since the user needs to select a correct word from a list of words that sound very similar. Therefore, it is necessary to provide additional

---

[5]   Implementations of POBox: http://pitecan.com/OpenPOBox/implementations/index.html.
[6]   The Optimus keyboard: http://www.artlebedev.com/portfolio/optimus/.

information for each candidate. Also, the selection interface should be accessible. Making voice recognition systems usable for the visually impaired is an urgent research area.

Guideline 2: If a target platform is extensible, provide a programming interface for screen reading. If the target platform is not extensible, provide a TTS capability within the device.

If the target platform of an entry system is extensible, such as a PC, an API (application programming interface) for screen readers should be available. Each operating system has its own API for accessibility, such as the MSAA (Microsoft Active Accessibility) API for the Windows platform and the GNOME Accessibility API for the Linux/GNOME desktop platform. Screen readers can use these APIs for accessibility to get information from applications, so these APIs can be used by each application. In the case of Windows XP, the Input Method Editor and Text Service Framework support accessible multilingual text entry[7]. These APIs for accessibility are changing, so developers have to track the current status of the APIs for the platforms they work on.

If the target platform is extensible but does not provide any API for accessibility, screen-reading software may be able to provide help. Such screen-reading software will need to be tested for text entry for the target application. The basic checks are quite simple, checking whether text can be input without looking at the screen and without using pointing devices. If the screen reader cannot verbalize sufficient information, then the application should be modified to be more compatible with the screen reader. In many cases, screen reader venders publish guidelines explaining how to make applications compatible with their screen readers. The documentation should be sufficient to modify application systems.

If the target platform is not extensible, it should include its own TTS (text to speech) capabilities. This "self-talking" technique makes applications accessible by sending the required information to a TTS engine to describe the user's operations without using any screen reader. The target device must have a suitable TTS engine, but such TTS engines are not extensible components and are available as software or hardware. They should be integrated into the device as part of the specifications of the device.

Guideline 3: Conduct usability testing sessions with visually impaired users.

Sighted developers usually have little or no exposure to voice interfaces, so it is difficult for them to evaluate the usability of voice interfaces. Therefore, it is important to conduct some usability testing sessions with visually impaired users, preferably both novices and experts (Theofanos & Redish, 2003). The metrics to measure should be the same as for the usual usability testing, such as performance for text input, cognitive workload, learning curves, accuracy of entered text, and so on. It is often difficult

---

[7]   Input Method Editor and Text Services Framework Accessibility: http://msdn.microsoft.com/library/default.asp?url=/library/en-us/dnacc/html/atg_tsf.asp.

to find appropriately skilled visually impaired subjects for usability experiments, because the visually impaired population is small, but even limited tests with a few users can be very revealing of problems. Such tests will show many ways to improve the accessibility and usability of text entry systems.

16.6   CONCLUSION

In this chapter, we first reviewed the history of nonvisual text entry systems in countries that use Latin alphabets. Then we described the current methods for entering ideographic characters. The most commonly used method involves explaining the meaning of each candidate character, but there is room to improve the usability. We also introduced some of the problems of selection-based text entry interfaces. These interfaces have capabilities to improve performance by showing candidates for the user's next input. The performance of the selection process usually depends on the high-bandwidth sense of sight, so it is difficult to improve their performance for visually impaired users. Finally, we introduced three guideline items to make entry systems more accessible. These are basic and simple guidelines, but important to improve future text entry systems.

Text entry has an important role for people with visual impairments, since it is difficult for them to communicate with other people using text without the assistance of computers. Developers should work to build an IT infrastructure that is beneficial for all of the people living in our society. There are possibilities to invent new levels of usable and high-performance text entry systems for various groups of users. We hope this article will be a starting point to think about the difficulties of text entry for people with visual disabilities. We also hope this will be a trigger to inventing new interfaces.

RELATED ORGANIZATIONS AND RESEARCH GROUPS

Perkins School for the Blind: *http://www.perkins.org/*

National Federation of the Blind: *http://www.nfb.org/*

American Foundation for the Blind: *http://www.afb.org/*

American Council for the Blind: *http://www.acb.org/*

ACM Special Interest Group on Accessible Computing: *http://www.acm.org/sigaccess/*

The World Wide Web Consortium, Web Accessibility Initiative: *https://www.w3.org/wai/*

TRACE R&D Center: *http://trace.wisc.edu/*

MAJOR PRODUCTS

Screen reader; JAWS®, Freedom Scientific: *http://www.freedomscientific.com/*

Screen reader; Window-Eyes, GW Micro: *http://www.gwmicro.com/*

Voice Web browser; IBM Home Page Reader, IBM Corp.: *http://www.ibm.com/able/*

Screen magnifier; ZoomText®, Ai Squared: *http://www.aisquared.com/*

Screen magnifier; MAGic®, FreedomScientific: *http://www.freedomscientific.com/*

Braille PDA; PAC Mate™, Freedom Scientific: *http://www.freedomscientific.com/*

Braille PDA; BrailleNote, HumanWare: *http://www.humanware.com/*

Braille pin display; ALVA, Optelec Tieman Group: *http://www.optelec.nl/*

REFERENCES

Adler, M. (1973). *The writing machine.* London: Allen & Unwin.

Asakawa, C., Takagi, H., Ino, S., & Ifukube, T. (2003). Maximum listening speeds for the blind. *Proceedings of the 9th International Conference on Auditory Display (ICAD 2003), 6–9 July 2003, Boston* (pp.276–279).

Boyd, L. H., Boyd, W. L., & Vanderheiden, G. C. (1990). The graphical user interface: Crisis, danger and opportunity. *Journal of Visual Impairment and Blindness,* December 1990, 496–502.

Boyd, L. H., Boyd, W. L., & Vanderheiden, G. C. (1991). Graphics-based computers and the blind: Riding the tides of change. *Proceedings of the 6th Annual Conference Technology and Persons with Disabilities (CSUN), Los Angeles.*

Buxton, W., Foulds, R., Rosen, M., Scadden, L., & Shein, F. (1986). Human interface design and the handicapped user. *Proceedings of the SIGCHI Conference on Human Factors in Computing Systems (CHI '86), 13–17 April 1986, Boston* (pp.291–297). New York: ACM Press.

Byrne, M. D., Anderson, J. R., Douglass, S., & Matessa, M. (1999). Eye tracking the visual search of click-down menus. *Proceedings of the SIGCHI Conference on Human Factors in Computing Systems (CHI '99), 15–20 May 1999, Pittsburgh* (pp.402–409). New York: ACM Press.

Edwards, W. K., Mynatt, E. D., & Stockton, K. (1995). Access to graphical interfaces for blind users. *Interactions, 2,* 54–67. New York: ACM Press.

Kieras, D. E., & Meyer, D. E. (1997). An overview of the EPIC architecture for cognition and performance with application to human–computer interaction. *Human–Computer Interaction, 12,* 391–438. Hillsdale, NJ: Lawrence Erlbaum Associates.

Lahiri, A., Chattopadhyay, S. J., and Basu, A. (2005). Sparsha: a comprehensive Indian language toolset for the blind. *Proceedings of the 7th International ACM SIGACCESS Conference on Computers and Accessibility (ASSETS '05), 9–12 October 2005, Baltimore* (pp.114–120). New York: ACM Press.

Lee, S., Hong, S. H., & Jeon, J. W. (2003). Designing a universal keyboard using chording gloves. *Proceedings of the 2003 Conference on Universal Usability (CUU '03), 10–11 November 2003, Vancouver, British Columbia, Canada* (pp.142–147). New York: ACM Press.

Linvill, J. G., & Bliss, J. C. (1966). A direct translation reading aid for the blind. *Proceedings of the IEEE, 54,* 40–51.

Lyons, K., Starner, T., Plaisted, D., Fusia, J., Lyons, A., Drew, A., & Looney, E. W. (2004). Twiddler typing: One-handed chording text entry for mobile phones. *Proceedings of the SIGCHI Conference on Human Factors in Computing Systems (CHI '04), 24–29 April 2004, Vienna, Austria* (pp.671–678). New York: ACM Press.

MacKenzie, I. S., & Soukoreff, R. W. (2002). Text entry for mobile computing: Models and methods, theory and practice. *Human–Computer Interaction, 17,* 147–198.

Masui, T. (1998). An efficient text input method for pen-based computers. *Proceedings of the SIGCHI Conference on Human Factors in Computing Systems (CHI '98), 18–23 April 1998, Los Angeles* (pp.328–335). New York: ACM Press.

Mynatt, E. D., & Weber, G. (1994). Nonvisual presentation of graphical user interfaces: contrasting two approaches. *Proceedings of the SIGCHI Conference on Human Factors in Computing Systems (CHI '94), 24–28 April 1994, Boston* (pp.166–172). New York: ACM Press.

Raman, T. V. (1996). Emacspeak—A speech interface. *Proceedings of the SIGCHI Conference on Human Factors in Computing Systems (CHI '96), 13–18 April 1996, Vancouver, British Columbia, Canada* (pp.66–71). New York: ACM Press.

Scadden, L. A. (1984). Blindness in the information age: Equality or irony? *Journal of Visual Impairment and Blindness, 78,* 394–400.

Takagi, H., Asakawa, C., Fukuda, K., & Maeda, J. (2004). Accessibility designer: Visualizing usability for the blind. *Proceedings of the 6th International ACM SIGACCESS Conference on Computers and Accessibility (ASSETS '04), 18–20 October 2004, Atlanta* (pp.177–184). New York: ACM Press.

Thatcher, J. (1994). Screen reader/2: Access to OS/2 and the graphical user interface. *Proceedings of the First Annual ACM Conference on Assistive Technologies (ASSETS '94), 31 October–1 November 1994, Marina Del Rey, CA* (pp.39–46). New York: ACM Press.

Theofanos, M. F., & Redish, J. G. (2003). Bridging the gap between accessibility and usability. *interactions, 10,* 36–51. New York: ACM Press.

Wobbrock, J. O., Myers, B. A., & Aung, H. H. (2004a). Writing with a joystick: A comparison of date stamp, selection keyboard, and EdgeWrite. *Proceedings of the 2004 Conference on Graphics Interface, 17–19 May 2004, London, ON, Canada, Vol. 62* (pp.1–8). Waterloo, ON: School of Computer Science, University of Waterloo.

Wobbrock, J. O., Myers, B. A., Aung, H. H., & LoPresti, E. F. (2004b). Text entry from power wheelchairs: EdgeWrite for joysticks and touchpads. *Proceedings of the 6th International ACM SIGACCESS Conference on Computers and* Accessibility *(ASSETS '04), 18–20 October 2004, Atlanta.* New York: ACM Press.

World Health Organization (2004). Fact Sheet 282: Magnitude and causes of visual impairment: *http://www.who.int/mediacentre/factsheets/fs282/en/*

Index

About the Authors

I. Scott MacKenzie is an Associate Professor of Computer Science and Engineering at York University in Toronto, Canada. His research is in human-computer interaction with an emphasis on human performance measurement and modeling, interaction devices and techniques, alphanumeric entry, and mobile computing. Home page: http://www.yorku.ca/mack/.

Kumiko Tanaka-Ishii is an associate professor in the Department of Creative Informatics, Graduate School of Information Science and Technology, the University of Tokyo, Japan. Her research interests are in the area of language processing, particularly language interfaces, natural language processing, computational linguistics, and computational semiotics.

Dr. Jacob O. Wobbrock is an Assistant Professor in the Information School and an Adjunct Assistant Professor in Computer Science & Engineering at the University of Washington. His research interests include input and interaction techniques, computer access, and mobile computing within the field of human-computer interaction (HCI). Dr. Wobbrock received his Ph.D. from the Human-Computer Interaction Institute in the School of Computer Science at Carnegie Mellon University. In addition, he holds B.S. and M.S. degrees in Symbolic Systems and Computer Science, respectively, from Stanford University. Along with Dr. Brad A. Myers, he is the inventor of the EdgeWrite text entry method.

Sadaoki Furui received his B.S., M.S., and Ph.D. degrees in mathematical engineering and instrumentation physics from Tokyo University, Tokyo, Japan in 1968, 1970, and 1978, respectively. He has been working in a wide range of research on speech analysis, speech recognition, speaker recognition, speech synthesis, and multimodal human-computer interaction. In 1970, he joined Nippon Telegraph and Telephone Research Laboratories, Japan. In 1997, he joined the Computer Science Department of Tokyo Institute of Technology as a Professor.

Tsuguya Sasaki holds a PhD from the Department of the Hebrew Language, The Hebrew University of Jerusalem, and is lecturer at the Department of Hebrew and Semitic Languages, Bar-Ilan University. His research interests include grammar, lexicon and sociolinguistics of Modern Hebrew, and Hebrew-Yiddish contact linguistics.

Dr. Sung-Hyuk Cha has a Ph.D. in Computer Science from the State University of New York at Buffalo. During his PhD years, he was affiliated with the Center of

Excellence for Document Analysis and Recognition (CEDAR) working on Pattern Recognition and Document Analysis. He has been an Assistant Professor at Pace University since 2001. He has over 100 publications and his interests include computer vision, data mining, and pattern recognition.

Dr. Charles Tappert has a Ph.D. in Electrical Engineering from Cornell University. He worked on speech and handwriting recognition at IBM for 26 years, taught at the U.S. Military Academy at West Point for seven years, and has been a professor of computer science at Pace University since 2000. He has over 100 publications and his research interests include pattern recognition, pen computing and voice applications, human-computer interaction, and artificial intelligence.

Shumin Zhai is a Research Staff Member at the IBM Almaden Research Center. Named a "Distinguished Scientist" by ACM in 2006, his work has produced about 100 technical papers, received numerous patents, contributed to three IBM Research Division Accomplishments, and been broadly reported in the news media. He is on the editorial boards of *Human-Computer Interaction, ACM Transactions on Computer-Human Interaction,* and other journals. He has been a visiting professor and has lectured at various universities in the U.S., Europe and China. He earned his Ph.D. degree at the University of Toronto.

Dr. Shari Trewin studied text entry and computer control by people with physical impairments at the University of Edinburgh, Scotland, earning her PhD in 1998. She is currently at the IBM T.J Watson Research Center, New York, where she focuses on the design of tools to enhance the accessibility of technology for people with disabilities. She was part of the team that created the award winning IBM Web Adaptation Technology, and she has co-edited 5 American National Standards in the area of abstract user interfaces.

Per Ola Kristensson is a Ph.D. candidate in Computer Science at Linköpings universitet, Sweden. He has been researching ShapeWriter since 2002, and worked as a graduate intern at IBM Almaden Research Center from 2003 to 2005.

Jin-Dong Kim is Project Lecturer of University of Tokyo and Senior Research Associate of University of Manchester. He received his M.S. and Ph.D. in 1996 and 2000 respectively from Korea University, where he worked as a researching member of Natural Language Processing Laboratory. Currently, he is working as Research Associate for Tsujii Laboratory at University of Tokyo and National Centre for Text Mining at University of Manchester with the researching topic of text mining from biomedical literature. His research interest includes natural language processing, text mining and knowledge representation.

Dr. Janet Read is an academic in the UK, where she teaches human computer interaction, leads the innovative ChiCI group and supervises research students. She is internationally known for her work on child computer interaction but is also known for her work on handwriting recognition and pen based systems.

Dr. Ming Zhou got his Ph.D. from Harbin Institute of Technology in 1991. He has been the manager of Natural Language group, Microsoft Research Asia since 2001. Prior to Microsoft, he was an associate professor at Tsinghua University. He is the inventor of the famous Chinese-Japanese machine translation product "J-Beijing" in Japan. He designed the first Chinese-English machine translation system in 1988 and the first Chinese Speller in 1995. He has served as area chair at various prestigious NLP conferences including ACL2000, ACL 2003, Coling-ACL 2006, IJCAI 2007, EMNLP 2005, HLT/NAACL 2006 and as PC co-chair of AIRS 2004.

Virach Sornlertlamvanich received the D.Eng. degree from Tokyo Institute of Technology in 1998. He worked with NEC Corporation as a sub-project leader for Thai language processing in the Multi-lingual Machine Translation Project. He later founded the Linguistics and Knowledge Science Laboratory (LINKS) to conduct the research on Natural Language Processing (NLP) in the National Electronics and Computer Technology Center (NECTEC) of Thailand in 1992. He initiated a wide range of applied NLP projects, such as ParSit, LEXiTRON, and Sansarn. He was awarded by the National Research Council of Thailand as the Most Outstanding Researcher of the Year 2003. He is currently the co-director of Thai Computational Linguistics Laboratory (TCL), NICT Asia Research Center, and a project leader in NECTEC, Thailand.

Kari-Jouko Räihä is Professor of Computer Science at the University of Tampere, Finland, where he leads the Unit for Computer-Human Interaction (TAUCHI). He has done research on various topics in HCI, including direct manipulation interfaces, spoken dialogue systems, and information displays. His main interest is gaze-based interaction. He is the coordinator of COGAIN, an EC-funded Network of Excellence on Communication by Gaze Interaction.

Renu Gupta is an Assistant Professor at the University of Aizu in Japan. She received her Ph.D in Education and Linguistics from Stanford University. Her research interests include writing systems and educational technology. Her papers have been published in British Journal of Educational Technology and English for Specific Purposes.

John Arnott is Professor of Communication Systems in the School of Computing at the University of Dundee, Scotland, UK. His research areas have included chord keyboards in speech interfaces, speech synthesis, text prediction and disambiguation to assist text input for people with disabilities, augmentative and alternative communication interfaces for people with impaired communication and assistive technology to promote independence and quality of life for older people and people with disabilities. He has a Ph.D. in computing and augmentative communication and is a Fellow of the British Computer Society.

Päivi Majaranta (M.Sc.) is the scientific coordinator of the five-year European Network of Excellence on Communication by Gaze Interaction (COGAIN, 2004-2009). Her research interests are computer-aided communication and especially eye-aware and eye-operated computer interfaces. Currently, she is doing her Ph.D. research on gaze-based text entry.

Miika Silfverberg is a cognitive psychologist who works as a Principal Scientist in the Multimedia Technologies Laboratory of Nokia Research Center. He specializes in user experience of new input devices and text entry systems. He has experience in both basic interaction research and in practical product development for mobile phones.

Hironobu Takagi completed a Ph.D. in 2000 in the Department of Science, University of Tokyo and joined the IBM Tokyo Research Laboratory. Since then, he has conducted research and development on nonvisual computer interfaces. Dr. Takagi is a member of the Association for Computing Machinery (ACM), IPSJ, and JSSST.

Chieko Asakawa joined the Tokyo Research Laboratory in 1985. She has conducted research and development on various nonvisual computer interfaces for the blind, including the Home Page Reader. Dr. Asakawa received recognition from the Japanese Ministry of Health and Welfare in 1999 and was inducted into the Women in Technology International Hall of Fame in 2003. She received a Ph.D. from the Department of Advanced Interdisciplinary Studies in the Graduate School of Engineering at the University of Tokyo in 2004. Dr. Asakawa is a member of the IBM Academy of Technology, ACM, IEICE, and IPSJ.